FROM KUTCH TO TASHKENT

From Kutch to Tashkent

The Indo-Pakistan War of 1965

FAROOQ BAJWA

PENTAGON PRESS

From Kutch to Tashkent: The Indo-Pakistan War of 1965

ISBN 978-81-8274-76•-•• •

First Indian Edition: 2014

Original English Edition published by C. Hurst & Co. Ltd., 41 Great Russell Street, London, WC1B 3PL. Indian Edition published in arrangement by Pentagon Press.

Published by
PENTAGON PRESS
206, Peacock Lane,
Shahpur Jat
New Delhi-110049
Ph.: +91-11-64706243,26491568
Telefax:+91-11-26490600
Email: rajan@pentagon-press.com
Website: www.pentagon-press.com

Printed at Avantika Printers Private Limited

CONTENTS

GENESIS OF THE KASHMIR DISPUTE

Birth of two nations

Independence for the state of Pakistan on 14 August 1947 is a date forever marked by the tragedy and triumph of that day. It marks the birth of a homeland for the Muslims of the subcontinent which was now one of the largest Muslim countries in the world, but also a tragedy of death, dispossession and flight.Many millions of Muslims from what was now India made their way to the newly-founded Dominion of Pakistan, and in the opposite direction almost as many Sikhs and Hindus left their homes to move to the Union of India.

The British had begun to build an empire in the Indian subcontinent from the eighteenth century and by 1858 they directly or indirectly controlled the whole subcontinent from the Khyber Pass to Burma. From the end of the First World War in 1918, however, the pressure on the British government to grant some real degree of autonomy, if not outright independence, to India was growing stronger. Eventually the cripplingly heavy financial and military cost paid by Britain during the Second World War, coupled with large-scale civil disobedience in the subcontinent, made British departure from India a certainty. The only questions left to answer by 1945 were the exact date of the departure and how many successor states to the British Raj would be left behind. In retrospect the worst fears of many, that the subcontinent would split into dozens of states, were to prove unfounded, and two states emerged from the British Raj; India and Pakistan. The eventual agreement was a division of the subcontinent primarily along religious lines with the state of Pakistan having a large Muslim majority and the state of India a large Hindu one.

Mohammed Ali Jinnah became the first Governor-General of the new state of Pakistan, and the geography of the new state was unique, with its western and eastern provinces separated by almost a thousand miles of Indian territory. Two of the largest provinces of the subcontinent, Bengal and Punjab, were also divided between Muslim and non-Muslim areas, with West Punjab and East Bengal going to the state of Pakistan. The scale and speed of the partition are still hard to conceive but it seemed that after two hundred years of Indian involvement, the British rulers were now in a hurry to leave.

In the hasty transfer of power by the British, there were many difficult issues to resolve. Amongst the thorniest was the problem of what to do with the British Indian Army, which by 1945 was one of the largest armies in the world in its own right. At one stage during the Second World War its numbers rose to 2.5 million men, comprising both Muslim and non-Muslim units and soldiers. Under the terms of Partition, British Indian Army officers were asked to choose which of the armies of the two new states they wished to join, and an approximate one-third/two-third division of the army and its supplies was eventually made between Pakistan and India. The first commanders-in-chief of the new armies for both India and Pakistan in 1947 were British, which was to have an important bearing on the later dispute over the state of Jammu and Kashmir.

Another of the major issues to be resolved was that of the princely states. In 1947 there were around 560 princely states within the British Raj—principalities under the control of local rulers but whose foreign policy, defence and communications were controlled by the British. Some of these princely states were huge in size and population while others were tiny, but in the short time available the issue of what to do with the princes and their territories was still not fully resolved even in August 1947. The last Viceroy, Lord Mountbatten, decided that the princes would be allowed to opt for either the state of India or Pakistan; independence was not to be an option. By the end of 1947 all had chosen to be absorbed into either India or Pakistan, with two exceptions; Hyderabad and Kashmir. These were amongst the largest of these princely states and almost polar opposites; Hyderabad was ruled by a Muslim prince but with a large Hindu majority and surrounded by Indian territory, while Kashmir was ruled by a Hindu Raja but with an overwhelming Muslim population and most of its means of communication running almost exclusively through Pakistan.

The fate of Jammu and Kashmir was to prove the one issue which poisoned relations between India and Pakistan from their independence and still remains one of the great unresolved disputes of international politics. It was over the future of Kashmir that war broke out in 1965, and it has threatened to cause further hostilities on a number of other occasions.

The State of Jammu and Kashmir

During the period of British expansion in the subcontinent, most of the existing local ruling families lost both territory and status; the exception was Jammu, a small hilly state in the foothills of the Himalayas, north of the Punjab and bordering Kashmir. During the mid-nineteenth century the state was ruled by a Hindu Dogra dynasty which had expanded its territory with both Sikh and British encouragement from the early nineteenth century. However, the prize catch came in 1846, when the then

3

Raja of Jammu was permitted to purchase the Vale of Kashmir following the British conquest of Punjab. The Sikh rulers of Punjab who had ruled Kashmir during the early nineteenth century had been obliged to cede Kashmir to the British East India Company in 1846. Fortunately for the rulers of Jammu (but less so for the people of Kashmir) the British Governor at the time was reluctant to assume responsibility for such a remote area. It was therefore decided that the British would effectively sell Kashmir on a long lease to the rulers of Jammu for the sum of around £500,000.

Over time the rajas of what was now the state of Jammu and Kashmir were encouraged to further expand their state by taking over Muslim districts bordering Punjab such as Bhimber as late as the twentieth century, and also to push north towards central Asia. By 1900 the Hindu rajas of Jammu were therefore ruling a mini-empire of their own, most of whose inhabitants had little in common with their rulers; Ladakh had a mainly Buddhist population; Sunni Muslims were prevalent in the Valley of Kashmir, Poonch and Bhimber; Shia Muslims were predominant in Baltistan and Gilgit; and a sizeable Ismaili Muslim population lived in the Hunza valley. As a result of this expansion, by 1947 the State of Jammu and Kashmir was in a very important strategic position as it shared a border not only with both the new states of India and Pakistan but also with Afghanistan, China and Tibet. Had the British followed the logic of Partition as in the case of Bengal and Punjab, it is entirely conceivable that a workable border could have been drawn with the Muslim west of the state going to Pakistan and the Buddhist and Hindu eastern part to India (Alastair Lamb, *Incomplete Partition*, Oxford University Press, 1991, 17–19).

Once the decision to partition the Indian Raj was officially announced in June 1947, the then (and last) British Viceroy, Lord Mountbatten leaned on princely rulers to accept the inevitable takeover by, and accession to, one of the two successor states. This 'advice' was usually followed but in a few notable cases, the rulers prevaricated for as long as possible. The then Maharaja of Jammu and Kashmir, Hari Singh, delayed a decision and had not committed himself to either state by 15 August 1947, the date when both India and Pakistan achieved independence. His delaying tactics were primarily motivated by a desire to remain independent from both the new states after the British departure, and his cause was helped by the fact that it was not until after the two states had achieved independence (Pakistan on 14 August and India on 15 August) that the citizens of the two states learned their exact borders on 17 August. In order to draw up the boundaries of the large provinces of Punjab and Bengal, Mountbatten had appointed a British barrister, Sir Cyril Radcliffe, to chair the newly formed Boundary Commission, effectively determining the borders of India and Pakistan in those provinces. Although it was not apparent at the time, the boundary award announced on 17 August 1947 by Radcliffe contained some critical decisions with wide-reaching implications for the future of Kashmir. The district of Gurdaspur, a Muslim majority district in the northern part of Punjab and also bordering Kashmir, was awarded to India by Radcliffe against all prevailing logic and was the first indication, as far as Pakistan was concerned, that the British were now decisively tilting towards India in the post-independence world. There is mounting evidence of Mountbatten's influence in making this decision—a seemingly illogical one as Gurdaspur should, by all the terms of reference given to Radcliffe, have been awarded to Pakistan. That, however, would have meant that India no longer shared an effective land border with Kashmir, as it was only with the award of Gurdaspur that India could realistically have an all-weather land route to the Valley of Kashmir. The route across the only other land border was through the Kangra hills at the foothills of the Himalayas, which was impassable during the winter months. The rationale for this decision was never provided by Radcliffe, who left India even before the announcement of his border award and burned all his papers, leaving historians to speculate about some of his decisions, not least the award of Gurdaspur to India.

If Radcliffe was leant on by Mountbatten, as seems likely, then the possible reasoning needs to be examined. First, it was well known that Mountbatten had hoped to become the Governor-General of both India and Pakistan in August 1947, an idea rejected by Jinnah who became the first Governor-General of Pakistan, leaving Mountbatten as the Governor-General of India. Many contemporary accounts speak of Mountbatten viewing this as a snub by Jinnah. Secondly, there were reports of a relationship between India's Prime Minister Nehru and Edwina Mountbatten (Mountbatten's wife)—a rumour at the time, but now a fact that is rarely disputed. Thirdly, and perhaps most seriously, following the end of the Second World War Kashmir was now strategically very important as it was close to the Soviet Union and China, it was now seen as a huge asset by the British. India was almost certainly seen by the British as more capable than Pakistan of opposing any future communist incursions in the area.

As mentioned earlier, what became apparent during the British departure was that Hari Singh wanted to achieve his own independence in 1947 and did not want to accede to either India or Pakistan. This was a relatively common desire amongst many of the rulers but Kashmir was large enough and (the Maharaja hoped) geographically vital enough for him to try to play India and Pakistan off against each other in the hope that he might be guaranteed a continuing and important role as head of state. This was an option on which the British, India and Pakistan were united in their opposition, but one that the Maharaja secretly nurtured for as long as possible. Within the State of Kashmir there had been limited political activity prior to 1947, but a number of prominent political figures had emerged in the state immediately prior to the British transfer of power. Amongst the better known were Sheikh Abdullah of the National Conference (broadly secular and nationalist), who was one of major voices in Kashmiri politics, and Ghulam Abbas who led the Muslim Conference (broadly religious and pro-Pakistan). The latter was ignored by Nehru and Mountbatten despite a legitimate claim to a significant portion of Kashmiri opinion as he was closer to the Muslim League of Jinnah.

The horror of the communal violence which marked the end of the British Raj did not escape Kashmir in 1947, and there it involved the added horror of the local soldiers of Jammu and Kashmir being actively ordered to participate in trying to drive as many Muslims out of the state as possible. Complete ethnic cleansing was going to prove impossible as the huge Muslim population of Kashmir meant that it would always remain largely Muslim, but it has been estimated that between August and September 1947 around 500,000 Muslims were driven from Jammu, with as many as 200,000 killed or later unaccounted for (Lamb, 123). Tales of massacres of Kashmiri Muslims quickly spread to Poonch, where there were estimated to be around 60,000 Muslim veterans of the British Indian Army. A full-scale rebellion in Poonch against the Maharaja's rule broke out in September 1947 with a formal command structure and with limited help from the new and still British-controlled Pakistan Army. At this stage, however, neither India's army nor Pakistan's was involved to any great degree, and given the sheer scale and horror of the killings taking place all over the states of India and Pakistan, Kashmir's communal massacres did not receive much publicity.

Fighting in Kashmir

Owing to the struggle for survival and the multitude of serious problems from 14 August 1947, the state of Pakistan did not make Kashmir an immediate priority as Nehru did, but whether this would have made any real difference is debatable given the relative strength of the states in August 1947. Towards the end of September 1947, however, it became obvious to Jinnah that Hari Singh was merely buying time and did not wish to accede to Pakistan, despite what appeared to Jinnah to be the only logical choice given the large Muslim majority population of the state and its far more developed communication, economic and cultural links with West Pakistan.

In October 1947 the full scale rebellion referred to above broke out in Poonch, and with assistance brought by some individual Pakistani army officers and Pakhtun tribesmen the Maharaja's forces were facing defeat at the hands of the Poonchi forces. On the night of 21/22 October the Poonchis, aided by a small party of Pakhtun tribesmen, managed to overcome the Dogra regiment at the Jhelum bridge at Domel, leaving the road to Srinagar, just 100 miles away, open. The problem for the Poonch fighters and their Pakhtun helpers was that they possessed no armoured cars or aircraft to reach Srinagar quickly, and although many of them had military experience they were an informal fighting force.

The situation was now critical for Hari Singh, who now belatedly realised that he could not handle this situation himself and therefore, on 24 October, sent the deputy prime minister of Kashmir to Delhi to officially ask the government of India for military assistance. The Maharaja himself left Srinagar for Jammu, fearing that his capital city would soon be taken by the Muslim rebels. There is speculation that in the request for military help by Hari Singh there was also a qualified offer of accession to India in return, but there is no definitive proof of this. The fact that he chose to request assistance from India and not Pakistan, however, demonstrated that the Hindu ruler preferred to deal with India. By 24 October, the Poonch fighters had declared a state of Azad Kashmir (Free Kashmir) and were within 30 miles of Srinagar.

On 25 October Nehru sent a telegram to the British Prime Minister, Clement Attlee, which stated:

We have received urgent appeal for assistance from the Kashmir government. We would be disposed to give favourable consideration to such a request...(The) security of Kashmir, which must depend on internal tranquillity...is vital to security of India...I should like to make it clear that question of aiding Kashmir in this emergency is not designed in any way to influence the State to accede to India...question of accession in any disputed territory...must be decided in accordance with wishes of people.

Attlee replied two days later to urge Nehru not to intervene militarily as 'it would only aggravate the problem', but by then India had already done so, indicating that Nehru's message was merely to inform Attlee rather than take or heed any advice (S. Wolpert, *Nehru: A Tryst with Destiny*, New York: Oxford University Press, 1996, 415).

On 26 October a massive airlift of Indian soldiers and military equipment began from Delhi to Srinagar, with two Indian Army infantry battalions landing in Srinagar airport by the end of that day. Given the sheer scale of the airlift operation it is inconceivable that this airlift had not been ready for days if not weeks, which means that Nehru and his government must have planned for such an eventuality. The only question (now academic and legal) is whether the ruler of Kashmir had even signed the Accession document when Indian troops landed at Srinagar airport on 26 October.

On 26 or 27 October (the exact date is unclear) the Maharaja of Jammu and Kashmir signed an Instrument of Accession to India. Despite the ongoing airlift, Mountbatten had, it seems, urged Nehru not to send any troops to Kashmir without the accession being signed, and it was his job now as Governor-General to accept or refuse to sign the Accession Treaty with Kashmir. There was never any doubt that Mountbatten would

9

have to sign, but given the distaste with which the whole Kashmir manoeuvre was being viewed by the British government (a later British High Commissioner to India would describe India's takeover of Kashmir as 'squalid'), Mountbatten made the acceptance a qualified one on 27 October by stating in his letter of acceptance that:

consistently with their policy that in the case of any State where the issue of accession has been the subject of dispute, the question of accession should be decided in accordance with the wishes of the people of the state, it is my Government's wish that as soon as law and order have been restored in Kashmir and her soil cleared of the invader the question of the State's accession should be settled by a reference to the people (Lamb, 137).

The use of the phrase 'reference to the people' was the second mention of some need to legitimise the Maharaja's decision by some form of public affirmation, and it quickly translated itself into talk of a plebiscite in the state. Nehru elaborated on this idea on 2 November 1947 by stating on All India Radio that the pledge to have the matter of accession decided by the people of Kashmir was one 'we have given and...we will not and cannot back out of' (Government of India, *White Paper on Kashmir*, 1948, Part IV quoted in Lamb, 138). There has been an understandable debate as to whether Nehru was ever sincere in making this pledge in 1947, but it is quite possible that he was. The reason why some historians have felt an early referendum may well have favoured India was that in 1947, the electoral roll of Kashmir had only 7 per cent of the population registered to vote and was heavily weighted in favour of the small Hindu minority. If a referendum had been carried out without the principle of universal suffrage being respected and the electoral rolls remaining as they were, it is entirely possible that India might have achieved a favourable outcome in November 1947.

Pakistan's options

Faced with the news that not only had Hari Singh acceded to India but that Indian troops had landed in Srinagar in time to prevent the Poonchis and other rebels from taking the city, the leadership in Pakistan had to accept the bitter reality that an important bordering state with a large Muslim population was going to fall completely under Indian control unless something was done. Indian control over the State of Jammu and Kashmir had very serious implications for Pakistan on a number of counts. Firstly, the mighty rivers Jhelum and Chenab flow from Kashmir into West Pakistan and were essential for the agricultural life of the country. Secondly, if the whole state of Jammu and Kashmir was to be part of the state of India, not only would Pakistan potentially be under threat from its northern border, but it would also have no land border with China and Central Asia. Thirdly, the whole logic of independence was under threat as Pakistan was created as a homeland for the Muslims of the subcontinent. If Kashmir was to be annexed (from a Pakistani perspective) it would mean that the Indian leadership had never accepted Partition as a permanent reality and was always going to be looking out for an opportunity to undo it.

The combination of these factors meant that within two months of independence, the new state of Pakistan, already reeling with a multitude of serious problems, was now facing what it considered a deadly threat to its very survival. From the moment that Indian troops landed in Srinagar, there was simply never a chance that any Pakistani leader could ignore the Kashmir issue until it was resolved in a manner acceptable to Pakistan. It was not simply an issue for the political and military in Pakistan; given the close proximity of Punjab and the North West Frontier Province to the state of Jammu and Kashmir, there were close family and personal ties for millions of Pakistanis and

11

Kashmiris; this helped ensure that the 'liberation' of Kashmir would become and remain a popular rallying cry in Pakistan.

However, as the Pakistan Army was not even fully formed and not in any state for war, Pakistan had now to face the harsh reality of its inferior military position. Despite the poor odds, on 27 October Jinnah, the Governor-General of Pakistan, ordered his army units to enter Kashmir to counter what Pakistan viewed as an Indian military invasion and annexation of a neighbouring state. Field Marshal Sir Claude Auchinleck, the Supreme Commander in the subcontinent with notional command over both the armies of India and Pakistan, flew into Lahore to inform Jinnah on 28 October that if Jinnah insisted on moving Pakistani troops into Kashmir, he would have to order all British officers in the Pakistan Army to resign, including the acting Commander in Chief of the Pakistan Army, General Sir Douglas Gracey. With India having airlifted troops into Srinagar and with British officers in charge of both India's and Pakistan's armies, the military involvement of Pakistani troops would have effectively meant British officers being involved in fighting against each other, something neither Mountbatten nor Auchinleck would permit. Jinnah simply had no choice but to rescind the order; as one historian put it, Jinnah 'was forced to back off, finally seeing how high a price Mountbatten could make him pay for not having agreed to [his] fondest desire to serve as governor-general of both dominions' (Wolpert, *Nehru*, 419).

With Indian troops now having secured Srinagar and the ruler having signed the Accession document with India, India now officially laid claim to the whole state of Jammu and Kashmir as a part of India. Pakistan was outraged by the unfairness of what it saw as British and Indian collusion to prevent the people of Kashmir exercising their right to join Pakistan, and immediately and publicly challenged the validity and legitimacy of the accession; although the immediate threat of war between the new states had lessened with Jinnah's retraction of the order for Pakistani military units to move into Kashmir, tension remained high. Jinnah knew that Pakistan had to do all it could with a limited hand and resolved to do so. Mountbatten flew to Lahore on 1 November to meet Jinnah and try to resolve the Kashmir situation without a full-scale war breaking out between the two newly independent states. It became clear during these talks that Jinnah did not trust the Indians and Mountbatten to carry out a fair referendum, for the reasons outlined above, and Jinnah did not share Nehru's view of Sheikh Abdullah as being the undisputed voice of the Kashmiri people. The first prime minister of Pakistan, Liaquat Ali Khan, described Sheikh Abdullah as a 'Quisling' in correspondence with Nehru and refused to recognise him as the authentic voice of Kashmiri Muslims. Jinnah's proposal to resolve the matter with an immediate ceasefire and withdrawal of all forces from Kashmir, was something that Mountbatten knew Nehru was not even going to contemplate. As Mountbatten left Lahore, his mission a failure, Jinnah informed him that 'he had lost interest in what the world thought of him (Jinnah) since the British Commonwealth had let him down when he asked them to come to the rescue of Pakistan' (Wolpert, *Nehru*, 420).

For Pakistan, some bitter vindication of one of their charges, that India would fail to protect the Muslims of Jammu and Kashmir, came on the night of 5/6 November when 5,000 Muslims were forced from their homes in the city of Jammu by Kashmir State troops. They were led in convoys straight into a trap, and the entire convoy was massacred. Although Nehru declared himself horrified to learn of the incident and described the Hindu organisation responsible for the massacre as 'injurious and dangerous', the fact remained that this happened in an area now controlled by the Indian Army and no punishment was ever forthcoming for the perpetrators of the crime (Wolpert, *Nehru*, 422).

Despite the official withdrawal of the order for Pakistani troops to enter Kashmir, unofficial encouragement was given to Pakistani soldiers to cross the state line and fighting between the Indian Army and irregular Muslim forces continued throughout the winter of 1947/48. Given its much larger numbers and resources, the Indian Army was unsurprisingly able not only to contain but to push back the Muslim fighters inside Jammu and Kashmir. By May 1948 it looked likely that Indian troops could take the whole state, which would have been viewed by Pakistan as a strategic disaster. General Gracey, the British commander of the Pakistan Army, reversed the previous decision not to commit Pakistani army units to the fighting, and regular troops of the new Pakistan Army were now able to enter the war officially for the first time. This move could not have been done without political clearance from London, but it came just in time to enable Pakistan to establish a line inside Kashmir through Poonch and Mirpur and push the Indian forces back towards Srinagar.

By the middle of 1948, Pakistan was in control of Gilgit, Baltistan, a narrow part of Kashmir, Poonch and Mirpur. India held Ladakh, Jammu, a portion of Poonch and the bulk of the Kashmir province, including Srinagar. Fierce fighting in some of the most inhospitable and inaccessible regions of the world continued throughout 1948 but finally a ceasefire was signed on 1 January 1949 and on 27 July 1949, a ceasefire line (CFL) was agreed by both sides along the broad lines described above.

Kashmir and the United Nations

Attention to the Kashmir dispute was now one of the first tasks for the newly established United Nations Organisation (UN) in New York. The world was still reeling from the Second World War and there was little appetite from any of the permanent members to take any firm position in favour of either India or

Pakistan. The consensus among the Security Council permanent members was that this was an issue that should be resolved peacefully between the parties and the UN should assist in finding a solution acceptable to the people of Kashmir through a referendum; this was a position accepted in principle by both India and Pakistan.

In contrast to later Indian hostility to the UN having any involvement with the Kashmir issue, it was in fact India that on 31 December 1947 officially raised the Kashmir issue in the UN. This may seem surprising to neutral observers given that Pakistan has always felt itself to be the aggrieved party in the Kashmir dispute, but it is a matter of record that it was India that raised the issue, to try to use the international forum to bring attention to what it saw as Pakistani military involvement in a state which had legally acceded to India. India, led with passionate and eloquent arguments from Nehru, put forward a number of arguments as to why India had been within its rights to act in the manner it had and why it had referred the matter to the UN. India maintained that the accession instrument was a legal document and that as the Maharaja had opted for India, the legal case was closed. After that, Pakistan's encouragement and use of force to try to impose a solution, and then its alignment with Western powers and particularly the USA, gave India the opportunity to renege on its promise to hold a plebiscite, and the Kashmir issue remained a matter in which the UN was now involved, yet relatively helpless to resolve. Even if the permanent Security Council members had all decided to accept Pakistan's case, short of full sanctions or war with India, the UN was not going to be able to persuade India to part with an area to which it believed it had a legitimate claim.

Over the coming years the UN Security Council was to pass a number of Resolutions on Kashmir. The first, on 17 January 1948, called upon both parties to improve the current situation and not to do anything to aggravate the military conflict any further. This led three days later to the establishment of a committee by the name of United Nations Committee for India and Pakistan (UNCIP). Resolution 47 followed on 21 April 1948, this called for an immediate ceasefire in order that a plebiscite might be held to determine the wishes of the people of Jammu and Kashmir. To ensure the impartiality of the plebiscite, it recommended that Pakistan withdraw all tribesmen and nationals who had entered the region for the purpose of fighting and India should leave only the minimum number of troops needed to keep civil order. The UN was also to send as many observers into the region as it deemed necessary to ensure that the provisions of the resolution were carried out.

Pakistan was naturally reluctant to vacate the part of Kashmir it controlled, as it wanted to ensure the arrival of a UN force first and not leave Kashmir open to India after the fighting that had taken place. This gave India the opportunity to refuse to implement the resolution and its call for a plebiscite by claiming that the withdrawal of Pakistan forces was a prerequisite under the resolution. The resolution stated 'that the final disposition of the State of Jammu and Kashmir will be made in accordance with the will of the people expressed through the democratic method of a free and impartial plebiscite conducted under the auspices of the United Nations'.

Over the next few years the UN Security Council passed four new resolutions, revising the terms of Resolution 47 to include a simultaneous withdrawal of both Indian and Pakistani troops from the region. To this end, UN arbitrators put forward eleven different proposals for the demilitarisation of the region; each one was accepted by Pakistan, each one rejected by the Indian government. Because of the diplomatic impasse, the territorial position in Kashmir remained largely static after 1 January 1949 when the ceasefire took hold. It is probably fair to say that India was not seriously interested in trying to move into Azad Kashmir

16

nor move the ceasefire line (CFL) nor challenge the status quo once the CFL was signed.

The CFL left the most populous and richest parts of the state of Kashmir, including the Kashmir Valley, and the greater part of Jammu, in Indian hands; this area will now be referred to as Indian controlled Kashmir (ICK). The remainder of the state was predominantly two areas known in Pakistan as the Northern Areas (the area bordering China) and Azad (Free) Kashmir (AK) from the area of Kashmir that Pakistan had managed to hold on to. The CFL separating the two Kashmirs was almost 500 miles long, passing for over a half its length through inhospitable mountainous terrain. The UN mediators and representatives who were sent out to try and resolve the impasse soon realised this and within a few years, it was Pakistan that had the stronger sense of grievance. It was increasingly frustrated by the UN's inability to force or persuade India to accept any proposal that would risk India losing the Kashmir Valley, and began to lose faith in the UN as a means of resolving the situation.

'The most allied ally'

As Pakistan had come into being as an avowedly Muslim state, it was unsurprising that its first search for allies would be within the Muslim world. Pakistan tried to appeal for Islamic solidarity from other Muslim countries but found little or no support on these grounds and soon gave up on this approach. As far as the communist world was concerned, a state formed on the basis of religious belief was not going to evince much sympathy or interest from the communist states of the USSR or the Peoples Republic of China (which came into being in 1949). Even if Pakistan had sought help from the Eastern Bloc, it would almost certainly have been met with a cool reception as Pakistan at the time of independence was viewed by the communist world as a state based on religion and therefore naturally reactionary, and Partition as little more than an attempt to divide and rule the Indian subcontinent by the British.

That effectively left the United States as Pakistan's main hope. The US had emerged from the debris of the Second World War as the undisputed economic and military victor. In 1945, it had gold reserves of $20 billion out of the world total of $33 billion, with more than half the world's manufactured goods being produced there, and it also had half the world's shipping. Militarily, the US was also overwhelmingly dominant with by far the largest navy in the world, with 1,200 warships, more than 2,000 long-range bomber aircraft and a monopoly of nuclear weapons. No country in the world could match the American combination of economic and military might and it was an era of world domination by one country that had rarely existed in historical terms; little wonder that the USA was soon dubbed not just another great power but a superpower (Paul Kennedy, *The Rise and Fall of the Great Powers*, London: Fontana Press, 1988, 461).

Early attempts by Pakistan to obtain American aid were unsuccessful as the Americans initially had little interest in South Asia; the focus of American attention was very quickly to become the containing and fighting of communism in Europe and the Far East. It was not until the accession of General Eisenhower as president in 1953 and the emergence of communist China and the Korean War that the US changed its attitude towards countries willing to sign up to an anti-communist agenda. There is no doubt that Pakistan's leaders in the 1950s were not remotely pro-communist, but equally little doubt that they were far more concerned about India than communism. However, the Pakistan government in the mid-1950s realised that by signing up to anti-communist pacts such as the South East Asia Organisation Treaty (SEATO, formed September 1954) and the Central Eastern Treaty Organisation

(CENTO, formed in 1955) they would be entitled to a large-scale infusion of American economic and military aid. The political price was one the Pakistani leadership at the time felt was worth paying and by 1958, Pakistan was dubbed the US's 'most allied ally'.

As a result of large-scale US aid, Pakistan was able to record high levels of economic growth in the 1950s and by 1960 the massive flow of US weapons had enabled Pakistan to build up a sizeable, well equipped army. Pakistan was given some of the latest American weaponry, superior to anything the Indian armed forces possessed at the time, and this slowly developed Pakistani military confidence with regard to India.

The price that Pakistan had to pay (and arguably is still paying) is that the scale and expense of US aid led to a situation whereby the Pakistan armed forces were equipped and financed well beyond the means of the government of Pakistan's own resources. By 1960 this had led to an almost total dependence by the Pakistan Army on the US for military equipment and, arguably, a closer relationship between the Pakistan Army and the US than between the Pakistan Army and its own people. In return for this aid, Pakistan lent valuable diplomatic support to the US position in Asia during the 1950s and permitted the US to establish military and air bases in West Pakistan.

The issue of whether US military equipment would or could be used by Pakistan against India seems to have been dealt with implicitly rather than explicitly. Although the military aid was explicitly provided for Pakistan's defence against communism, there was no clear prohibition on Pakistan using the equipment in any future conflict with India if Pakistan was acting in self-defence. By 1959 (later to be viewed as the high point of the US-Pakistan alliance) the US was also willing to assure Pakistan that it would not stand by and let it be overrun by India in the future. The real question, which was posed in 1965, was what the US position would be when Pakistan initiated a war against

19

India and India retaliated in such a manner that Pakistan needed external assistance. Many thoughtful Pakistanis knew in their hearts what the answer would be but preferred to wishfully hope that the US would at least prevent India from conquering Pakistan and would not cut off all assistance to Pakistan.

By 1960, however, although the US was as implacably anti-communist as before, the US administration had begun a re-examination of its South Asia policy and its military alliance with Pakistan and had begun to question whether the massive amount of aid given to Pakistan from 1954 to 1961 could really be justified strategically. An increasingly pervasive American view of South Asia was that India was a much larger state than Pakistan and that the critical focus of the Cold War, because of the Korean and Vietnam wars, was now Asia and not Europe, and it made eminent sense for the US to improve relations with the largest non-communist state in Asia. By comparison Pakistan was much smaller, and given the hostility between India and Pakistan, running the risk of diplomatically upsetting Pakistan in order to bolster India against China seemed a risk worth taking. In addition, Pakistan was seen in 1961 as having little alternative to US support; China was not in a position to replace US aid and the USSR was seen as too wedded to India to ever seriously contemplate switching support to Pakistan—even assuming the Pakistan military wished for such an alliance.

This review of the US military aid to Asia was undertaken towards the end of Eisenhower's presidency and its policy conclusions were followed by presidents Kennedy and Johnson; the outcome was that the suspicion and hostility with which the US had viewed non-aligned states, of which India was a leading player, were now replaced with a view that India was a critical counterweight to China. The US was now going to provide India with greater access to US products and aid, the most important part of which was aid for food security, not only to prevent the spread of communism within India but also to try and obtain a long-term strategic understanding with India.

Under the new policy, amongst the methods used to contain communism there was now to be a focus on economically strengthening non-aligned states and ensuring that communism would be a less attractive option. In 1959 J. F. Kennedy had publicly spoken of the great importance he gave to India's place in this policy and argued that no struggle in the world deserved more attention than the struggle being waged between India and China for the leadership of Asia. Unsurprisingly, therefore, India was to benefit substantially from the change in American policy once Kennedy became president in 1961. In the years from 1951 to 1962 total US economic aid to India was $155.3 million, but by the third Five Year Plan, 1961 to 1966, US aid had reached an annual average of $457 million. By contrast, on 16 July 1964 the average annual American aid authorisation for Pakistan's Five Year Plan in 1965 stood at $210 million.

This change of policy and focus was bound to cause resentment in Pakistan, particularly in the army which had become accustomed to large amounts of US military aid. As early as July 1961, after comparing the amounts of economic assistance received by India and Pakistan, President Ayub stated that some of the reasons given by the US for assisting India were spurious and India did not need such a large army to protect it from China. Similarly, Pakistani newspapers began to complain in editorials that the paltry sums that Pakistan received in aid would not meet its development needs. With the armed forces equipped almost wholly by American military assistance programmes and the government allied to the US by various treaties, Pakistan was watching the transformation of American foreign policy with increasing dismay and concern. The most allied ally of the US was now forced to look quickly for new friends.

FROM KUTCH TO TASHKENT

India's Kashmir and foreign policy

The first Prime Minster of independent India, one of the giants of
the independence movement, was Jawaharlal Nehru. Descended
from a Kashmiri Hindu family (though settled in central India),
he had a special affinity for Kashmir. Nehru directed a large
amount of thought and effort to this topic, as evidenced by the
large volume of documents and correspondence he left behind.
Nehru was very concerned by what he felt might be the
permanent loss of a large and strategic state in an area that he
saw as his ancestral home. In late September 1947, Nehru had
written to his Interior Minister, Vallahbhai Patel, that 'something
must be done before these winter conditions set in…We definitely
have a great asset…and things must be done in a way so as to
bring about the accession of Kashmir into the Indian Union as
rapidly as possible' (Wolpert, *Nehru*, 413).

It appeared to a senior British journalist who met
Mountbatten in October 1947 that the former Viceroy, now
Governor-General of India, had lost his objectivity in his
dealings with Pakistan and now saw himself as the defender of
India alone, he seemed to be have 'become wholly pro-Hindu'
(Ian Stephens, *Horned Moon*, Indiana University Press, 1955,
109). As far as Jawaharlal Nehru was concerned, he did not
even pretend to be neutral or unconcerned about Kashmir. In
October 1947 Nehru wrote to the then prime minister of Jammu
and Kashmir, Mr C. Mahajan, on the subject of the future
accession of the state: 'For me it is both a personal and public
matter. It would be a tragedy, so far as I am concerned, if
Kashmir went to Pakistan' (Wolpert, *Nehru*, 414).

With such a firm and clear objective and with a much larger
army and air force at its disposal, any military confrontation in
Kashmir was very likely to end in India's favour. It was only due
to the stubborn fighting of some Pakistani irregular units backed
up by some local fighters that Pakistan was able to prevent the

Indian Army in 1947/48 from taking over the whole of the former State of Jammu and Kashmir.

Although this was generally a popular position in India, it is also true that for most Indians in 1947/48, Kashmir was generally not a burning issue, and the decision to send Indian troops into Srinagar was criticised by Mahatma Gandhi who said in a prayer meeting:

If the people of Kashmir are in favour of opting for Pakistan, then no power on earth can stop them from doing so. But they should be left free to decide for themselves…If the people of Kashmir, in spite of its Muslim majority, wish to accede to India no one can stop them…If the people of the Indian Union are going there to force the Kashmiris, they should be stopped too, and they should stop by themselves. About this I have no doubt (Wolpert, *Nehru*, 418).

It was soon clear, regardless of what even Gandhi thought on the matter, that Nehru was not willing to compromise on the issue of Kashmir despite the voices of caution and restraint from Mountbatten, Attlee, Gandhi and the Indian High Commissioner to Pakistan. As far as Nehru was concerned Kashmir was always a part of India and always would be, and it was soon clear that his commitment to hold a plebiscite in Kashmir would never be more than a means of placating Mountbatten and international world opinion and he found one reason after another never to honour the commitment. As Nehru was to remain prime minister of India and the unchallenged towering figure of Indian politics until his death in 1964, India's Kashmir policy never deviated much from his view. It therefore became very difficult if not impossible for any future prime minister of India to alter the status quo in Kashmir, whatever their private views.

This stance on Kashmir, and the fact that India was now in a virtual state of war with its smaller neighbour, did not sit easily with the elevated view the world had of India during its independence movement. Despite this Nehru had charisma and

India was a large enough state for few countries to take an openly hostile stance on the subject of Kashmir, either at the UN or in other forums such as the Commonwealth. The fact remained, however, that India's position on the subject of Kashmir was never popular internationally and even Britain, one of India's closest friends, urged India to treat the UN missions with some degree of seriousness and be prepared to give Pakistan some concessions in order to resolve the situation there. However, throughout the 1950s Nehru refused even to enter into any serious negotiations with either the UN mediators or Pakistan, thereby not only damaging the moral high ground he sought to occupy but also leaving Pakistan to feel it had little choice but to explore any and all means of forcing a change in India's stance.

In contrast with Pakistan's keen, not to say desperate, need for allies and military support, India under Nehru was soon to emerge as one of the leaders of the Non-Aligned Movement—those countries that wished to remain free of both the Western and Eastern military pacts. There is little doubt that this was a popular decision within India, but the fact that India was willing to be on friendly terms with both the USSR and China in the 1950s meant that India appeared to America as being 'soft' on communism and thereby removed many lingering American doubts about the wisdom of large-scale military assistance to Pakistan.

It was not until the election of Kennedy that this changed; not only was India's non-alignment overlooked, but it was now viewed as an essential bulwark against communism in Asia. That was bad news for Pakistan and became even worse when the previously close friendship between India and China broke down with dramatic consequences. By 1960, relations between the Asian giants had cooled over border issues in the two main areas where China's and India's land borders met: near Kashmir, in the area known as Aksai Chin, and north of Burma, near the

Tibetan border. In the latter area there was a dispute over the British-drawn McMahon Line of 1914. At first, both sides attempted to resolve the border issue peacefully, but from 1961 there was an increasing number of violent border incidents along the McMahon Line. In the mountainous terrain there was some real doubt on both sides as to exactly where the border was, but Nehru's orders to aggressively patrol the border as claimed by India during the summer of 1962 led to armed clashes along the border.

The 1962 Sino-Indian war and its impact

On 20 October 1962, the Chinese launched a strong attack on the McMahon Line along the north-east India/China border. Within four days the Chinese army had achieved all its military objectives by pushing the Indians back and were then ordered by Beijing to stop their advance. There then followed a lull in the fighting with the Chinese situated well within territory claimed by India, but diplomatic attempts to resolve the issue proved fruitless. The fighting resumed with the Chinese Red Army advancing again on the north-eastern front, and reaching within 30 miles of Assam. By 19 November, China had advanced as far as it wished and declared a unilateral ceasefire, and the Chinese army was ordered to withdraw a further 20 miles behind the border claimed by Beijing. The fighting was brief but the fallout was to be long-lasting.

As the implications of a resurgent China, capable of easily defeating India, sent shockwaves throughout world capitals, the fallout for Pakistan was momentous. This was mainly because of Nehru's increasingly volatile behaviour. As it became obvious that China was advancing with ease, Nehru appealed for immediate Western military support, abandoning the non-alignment which he had championed for over a decade with his official request for large amounts of US military aid. Nehru requested that the US send twelve squadrons of supersonic aircraft to be based in India in order to fight the Chinese on a long-term basis (*Foreign Relations of the United States* [hereafter FRUS], *1961–1963, Volume XIX: South Asia*, 397). The US ambassador to India, John K. Galbraith, noted that this request meant 'that the Indians are effectively pleading for military association' (J. K. Galbraith, *Ambassador's Journal*, London: Hamish Hamilton, 1969, 486). Although in the event the US planes did not arrive in time, as China unilaterally called a halt to its advance, the speed and volume of US military aid sent to India during the conflict alarmed Pakistan. Even the previously staunchly pro-American Ayub was constrained to write a stiff letter to Kennedy on 17 December 1962 saying that such large-scale arms transfers appeared to be unnecessary from a military point of view and India was merely using the Chinese threat as an opportunity to have the Americans fund their military expansion against Pakistan (*FRUS*, Document 228, 442).

For the Americans, however, this was too good an opportunity to try and wean India away from the USSR and to bolster India in relation to China. In addition, Kennedy was in no mood to apply any pressure on India to relinquish Kashmir or even part of it merely to please Pakistan, and agreed with Galbraith that any attempt to do so would be seen by India as blackmail. The most that Kennedy requested was that India should agree to have talks with Pakistan on Kashmir once the war was over (Galbraith, 486, 501).

Pakistan was now forced to confront the bitter reality that the Americans were prepared to arm India without any preconditions or any pressure on India to make concessions on Kashmir. It must have been a bitter moment for Ayub and the Pakistan establishment that a decade of pro-US alliance was being ignored by the US in favour of its most bitter enemy. However, the silver lining as far as Pakistan was concerned was that it now awoke to the reality that its northern neighbour, China, was more than capable of standing up to India and that there was a common enemy for both states. After tentative feelers were sent out by Pakistan in 1962, China indicated that it was willing to change its earlier attitude as far the Pakistan/China border was concerned. In October 1962 negotiations to demarcate their common border began between Chinese and Pakistani officials, and within a few months, on 2 March 1963, the border between the two states was agreed. Pakistan agreed to cede to China territory claimed by India north of Ladakh, while China agreed that around 750 square miles around Hunza was now within Pakistan.

Although Pakistan achieved more from the territorial exchange itself, the real benefit was the realisation that China was very keen on improving relations with Pakistan. For China, it was an excellent chance to neutralise an Asian state which had been part of anti-communist blocs and US military pacts that for the last decade China had viewed as hostile. For China there was an added strategic benefit in having a friendly neighbour along one of its borders. For Pakistan, however, the potential benefits were even greater as China had proved itself militarily in Korea and now in a direct head-on clash with India, as a rising great power. It gave Pakistan the chance to widen its strategic options and lessen its dangerous over-dependence on the US for economic and military aid just as the US was now providing both to India.

While China-Pakistan political relations prospered in the aftermath of the India-China conflict, so too did commercial relations, and agreements were signed in January and September 1963 which helped make China the biggest purchaser of Pakistani cotton in 1963. Of greater symbolic and political significance was an aviation agreement concluded in August 1963 which allowed Pakistan International Airlines to become the first non-communist airline to secure landing rights in China. In exchange the Chinese received landing rights in Karachi and Dhaka which enabled them, if they so wished, to fly to Europe and Africa without passing through Moscow. After the inaugural

Pakistan International Airlines flight to Shanghai the Chinese Foreign Minister was able to say with satisfaction that those who tried to isolate China had failed.

It was not until 1964, however, that China openly modified its position of neutrality on Kashmir in Pakistan's favour. Then, on a visit to Pakistan, the Chinese Premier Zhou Enlai expressed the hope that the Kashmir dispute would be resolved in accordance with the wishes of the people of Kashmir. This was the exact position Pakistan had on Kashmir, and a veiled reference to the UN resolutions of 13 August 1948 and 5 January 1949.

Pakistani politics

The war of 1965 cannot be fully appreciated without a brief explanation of the internal political state of play within Pakistan and the people in charge at the time. In 1958, the Pakistan Army under the command of General Ayub Khan declared martial law and assumed control of the country. Ayub had passed out of the Sandhurst Military Academy in the UK in 1928 and had risen rapidly through the ranks in both the British Indian Army and the newly created Pakistan Army. He was not expected to become the first Pakistani Commander-in-Chief, but following the death of the senior-most general, Ayub became the Commander-in-Chief of the Pakistan Army after Gracey stepped down in 1951. Ayub was not renowned as a great thinker but was widely known and respected as a competent and straight-talking general. He was also known for his pro-Western views and was seen as genuinely anti-communist by both the British and the Americans.

Although it was a military regime, there was also a constant search by the army for bright political leaders who could support the regime without posing a threat to it. Zulfikar Ali Bhutto was to become the international face of Pakistan when he became the Foreign Minister in 1962 at only thirty-four years of age, and the eloquent voice of a basically military regime. Bhutto came from a different class to Ayub, who was not from a wealthy family, whereas Bhutto's father had been knighted by the British and owned substantial land holdings in Sindh province. Bhutto was an Oxford graduate who had been called to the Bar in London. Ayub was known to be very impressed by Bhutto and gave him a large degree of latitude in his dealings, and on becoming Foreign Minister Bhutto made it one of his priorities to lessen the international perception of Pakistan's status as a US client state and improve relations with China and the USSR. Despite his Western education, Bhutto was very much a product and representative of the left-wing, nationalistic and non-aligned movement prevalent in many Third World countries at the time, and was soon to emerge as one of the strongest advocates within Pakistan of taking some action in Kashmir to try and wrest it from India's control.

Ayub sought some legitimacy for his presidency, since he had assumed power through the coup of 1958, and so devised an un-threatening system of 'indirect democracy'. In 1962 a new constitution was introduced by Ayub which meant that future assembly and presidential elections would have an indirect franchise of 80,000 'Basic Democrats'. These were people handpicked by the local civil and military officers for their loyalty to the regime, and could be trusted to vote in the manner chosen by the regime. The first test came in a referendum in 1960 on the rather disingenuous sole question of whether they had confidence in Ayub. Unsurprisingly the result of that referendum was that over 95 per cent of the Basic Democrats said they did. This cleared the way for elections to the provincial assemblies and national assembly, and again there were no surprises in the elections of 1962, with pro-Ayub figures easily elected, in many cases, such as Bhutto and some other ministers, without even facing an opposing candidate.

The only election now left under the terms of the new 1962 constitution was the presidential election, which was set for

2 January 1965. There was no organised political opposition; the former set of politicians from the 1950s had either retired or been disqualified, and the economic growth of Pakistan under Ayub meant that the regime was confident enough even at the outset of the campaign to maintain a dignified silence. It was therefore a shock to Ayub when in September 1964 the opposition announced that its presidential candidate to challenge Ayub was none other than Miss Fatima Jinnah, the elderly sister of the founder of Pakistan.

This announcement caused a degree of panic within the regime as the Jinnah name still carried enormous clout and Miss Jinnah had remained above the fray of Pakistan's politics since the death of her brother in 1948, and was therefore untainted by any scandal or controversy. The fact that Fatima Jinnah was a relatively frail seventy-one-year-old seemed irrelevant; her charisma and standing meant that she drew huge crowds during the campaign in both West and East Pakistan. Even the staunchly conservative Islamic parties threw their weight behind her and the sheer size of the crowds she was able to attract caused deep unease amongst Ayub's cabinet.

The government of Ayub Khan took no chance of losing the election, ensuring that the army controlled the polling stations, but despite large-scale vote rigging Miss Jinnah still managed to obtain 38,691 votes to Ayub's 49,951 out of the 80,000 people entitled to vote—a very respectable result given the degree of intimidation and rigging carried out by the military regime. Even Ayub was painfully aware that without the rigging and manipulation he had in reality lost the presidential election, and Altaf Gauhar, the Information Secretary and close confidant of Ayub records that the 'dazed look did not leave Ayub's face for several hours' after the election results (Altaf Gauhar, *Ayub Khan: Pakistan's First Military Ruler*, Lahore: Sang-e-Meel Publications. 1993, 286).

With a manipulated election behind him, Ayub now attempted to regain some popular support. It was from this time onwards (early 1965) that, it is believed, the 'Kashmir hawks' within the Pakistan government, who had already been meeting since 1964 to discuss how Pakistan could take the initiative in the Kashmir dispute, now also began to advise Ayub that his way to achieve not just regained popularity but political immortality in Pakistan was by securing Kashmir for Pakistan. The recent poor showing of the Indian troops in 1962 and the qualitative edge in advanced weaponry that Pakistan possessed, argued the hawks, meant that Pakistan was now in a position to force the military solution in Kashmir that it had been unable to in 1947/48.

A number of factors seemed to favour Pakistan taking action in Kashmir at this time:

i) India had lost its best known statesman, Nehru, in 1964; Ayub was unimpressed by his successor, Lal Bahadur Shastri and did not consider him a man capable of facing down a war or to possess the same international standing as Nehru;

ii) Pakistan was prospering economically and recording food surpluses while India was facing local famines and serious economic difficulties;

iii) India's rearmament programme was in full swing following the defeat at the hands of the Chinese and India was now also receiving US military aid, and so the qualitative edge Pakistan possessed could be lost within a few years;

iv) ICK was in a state of flux with the Holy Relic Action Committee (HRAC) and other bodies demonstrating their ability to bring Srinagar to a standstill. In addition, Sheikh Abdullah was now viewed with suspicion by India and it was seen as a politically opportune time for Pakistan;

v) The international situation was viewed as more favourable to Pakistan, their relations with China were rapidly improving to the point of a *de facto* alliance. The USSR was less hostile than for many years.

For all these reasons, plus a desire to recover lost ground politically, by early 1965 Ayub was beginning to be persuaded by an increasingly influential group around him that a localised war in Kashmir was the only way to settle the issue once and for all. It was an argument that Ayub was becoming increasingly convinced by.

2

STATUS QUO ANTE BELLUM

Kashmiri politics

Soon after India had accepted the accession from Maharaja Hari Singh, Sheikh Abdullah was appointed by Nehru to head the new government in May 1948. In 1952 Sheikh Abdullah announced the end of the Dogra dynasty and Hari Singh's son was declared the first constitutional head of state. The legal status of ICK in the new Indian Constitution was special with Article 370 of the Indian Constitution declaring that the State of India was effectively limited to issues of defence, foreign affairs and communication in respect of Jammu and Kashmir. This was reaffirmed by Article 152 of the 1956 amendment to the Indian Constitution. India was aware of the need to placate both international and Kashmiri opinion in the aftermath of the events of 1947/48, and so ICK was initially allowed a degree of autonomy not accorded to other areas controlled by India.

Sheikh Abdullah was increasingly mistrusted by Nehru, and once his role in giving India some legitimacy in ICK was achieved, his usefulness was deemed over. On the night of 8/9 August 1953 Sheikh Abdullah was dismissed from office on Nehru's orders and placed under arrest. The new leader of ICK (also handpicked by Nehru) lost little time in declaring that

Kashmir was an inseparable part of India, and Sheikh Abdullah was now to spend almost all the period between August 1953 and April 1964 under arrest and in jail. His arrest had the effect, of the government of Pakistan now hailing Sheikh Mohammed as the legitimate voice of the Kashmiri people.

During the night of 26/27 December 1963, it was discovered that a relic deeply venerated by the Muslims of Kashmir, a hair (Hazrat Bal) believed to be that of the Prophet Muhammad was found to be missing from its shrine. This shrine was situated about five miles from the centre of Srinagar, and news of the relic's disappearance led to large processions of angry Kashmiri Muslims taking to the street. A general strike was called with all shops, offices and educational institutions closing while public transport also ceased to operate. The demonstrations soon turned violent with buildings being set alight and senior members of the ruling party being manhandled by an angry crowd.

On 1 January 1964 a committee was formed by the name of the Holy Relic Action Committee (HRAC) in an attempt to co-ordinate the campaign of protest and to demand the recovery of the relic. The leaders of the HRAC were representatives of political and religious organisations and its leaders initially sought to confine the committee's demands to matters related directly to the recovery of the relic. However, during the large and widespread demonstrations anti-Indian sentiments were also widely aired and for several days there was a complete administrative breakdown in Srinagar with the HRAC virtually in control. The Indian government was now forced to send the Home Secretary of India to assume direct control.

On 4 January 1964, All India Radio reported that the relic had been discovered, a claim that the HRAC initially regarded with scepticism as the director of the Indian Central Intelligence Bureau refused to allow the committee to examine the recovered relic, and the Indian government would not return the relic to the shrine. The HRAC demanded that it be restored to the shrine and authenticated by a group of Muslims to be chosen jointly by the committee and the authorities. On 10 January the first demand was met, but when the Indian government refused to concede the second demand, the HRAC ordered the ongoing protests to continue.

Only after the arrival of Lal Bahadur Shastri (then a minister without portfolio but soon to be prime minister), sent by the Indian government to negotiate with the HRAC, was a group of fifteen scholars allowed, on 3 February, to see the recovered relic. It was unanimously agreed by the scholars that it was the genuine relic and three days later it was once again publicly exhibited at the shrine. On the day following the verification, however, the HRAC announced that it would not be disbanded and would continue its campaign for investigation of the relic's disappearance and punishment for those responsible. In the weeks that followed the HRAC increasingly assumed a political character and became the focus of activity for parties and individuals sharing anti-India sentiment (*Times of India*, 29/1/654).

Realising the level of public discontent in ICK, the Indian government moved to lessen tension with restrictions on civil liberties loosened and permission granted to hold public meetings. On 8 April 1964, Sheikh Abdullah and his twenty-five co-defendants were released on the orders of Nehru and the state withdrew the charges against him in a trial which had lasted nearly six years and in which the prosecution had failed to secure a single conviction. After his release from jail and in a triumphant return to Srinagar, Sheikh Abdullah was warmly welcomed by large crowds and now began to openly challenge the official Indian claim that Kashmir's accession to India was the final word on the subject. He insisted that the people of Kashmir were yet to exercise their right to self-determination as had been jointly agreed by India and Pakistan—statements which were highly unpopular in Delhi but received with pleasure in Rawalpindi.

In 1964/65, the government of India initiated a series of legal and political measures designed to integrate ICK fully into the Indian Union politically and legally and to increase the powers of the Indian central government. On 4 December 1964 it was announced in the Indian Parliament that, with the ICK government's 'consent', the Indian government intended to extend certain provisions of the Indian constitution to ICK. This was done while there was an ongoing debate inside the Lok Sabha (the Indian parliament), which sought to abrogate Article 370 in order to bring about Kashmir's integration into India.

Kashmir, which had been the only state within the Indian Union with its own constitution, was now pressured to change its constitution to allow for the designation of the head of state as governor and the prime minister as chief minister, to conform to the practice of other Indian states. The ICK Assembly passed this Bill unanimously on 30 March 1965, followed by the Legislative Council on 3 April.

The diplomatic repercussions of the Indian unilateral changes were that Pakistan immediately objected in the UN and emphasised India's repudiation of its obligations under the UN resolutions claiming this was further evidence of India's intentions to solve the Kashmir dispute not through a plebiscite or negotiation but by unilateral decisions. If these moves went unchallenged, argued Pakistan, India would in the future claim that there was no longer a dispute and thereby hope to leave Pakistan with a *fait accompli* in accepting the CFL as the permanent border. In a letter to the UN Security Council, Pakistan argued these measures were 'designed to tighten Indian stranglehold over Kashmir and to deny the right to the people to decide their own future' (Letter from Pakistan Representative to Security Council, 20/4/64, quoted in Antony Wright, 'The Indo-Pakistan War 1965', unpublished PhD thesis, Australian National University, 1972, 51). Pakistan warned that the UN resolutions, the ceasefire order effective from 1 January 1949 and the Karachi Agreements establishing the ceasefire line constituted an interdependent system of actions and that it was therefore not open to either party to treat any single element as defunct without upsetting the whole framework. Fortunately for Pakistan, developments both within Kashmir and internationally meant that the issue was taken more seriously by the international community than it might otherwise have been, and not only the USA and Britain but also the USSR were all privately concerned by the Indian moves.

The release of Sheikh Abdullah meant that in May 1964 he was able to visit Pakistan for the first time and meet Ayub—obviously with Nehru's approval. There were meetings between Ayub and Sheikh Abdullah in Rawalpindi, and although full details of the talks are unavailable, it appears that towards the end of his life Nehru was rethinking his inflexible approach to Kashmir. To pretend that there was no dispute and the Kashmir issue was simply being kept alive by Pakistan was a fiction Nehru knew he could not maintain if he was to keep a credible foreign policy alive. In addition, Pakistan's closer ties with China and already close ties with the US were factors that inevitably concerned the Indian prime minister. Finally, Nehru had always hoped to have India viewed as a beacon of morality and principle in world politics through the Non-Aligned Movement and the UN. The Kashmir issue was a blemish on India's international image which, however hard he tried, would simply not go away. Nehru sent his daughter Indira Gandhi to Washington on 15 April to inform President Johnson that her father intended to hold a summit in Delhi with Ayub and Sheikh Abdullah to try and reach a permanent solution to Kashmir.

Before any serious negotiations could begin, Nehru passed away on 27 May 1964 while Sheikh Abdullah was in Pakistan. This effectively put an end to what little hope there was for any swift negotiated solution in Kashmir. For an Indian politician to be able to surrender (from an Indian point of view) any part of the Valley was something only someone of Nehru's stature could do and survive. It is of course ironic that no one had done more to ensure the Indian hold on ICK more than Nehru, and yet no one else was potentially capable of making any serious concessions to Pakistan over it. The new prime minister of India, Lal Bahadur Shastri, lacked the popularity and stature of Nehru, and Kashmir was a low priority for his new government as India had serious issues of food security to deal with.

Sheikh Abdullah took advantage of his newfound freedom by embarking on a world tour in early 1965 following a visit to Mecca, and in Algiers he met the Chinese Premier Zhou Enlai and accepted in principle an invitation to visit Beijing. This invitation was not made public by the Chinese but by Bhutto, on 27 March in Karachi at a dinner with China's Vice-Premier and Foreign Minister. The Indian government was already outraged by Abdullah's overseas speeches and interviews and was further enraged by the Algiers meeting, even more so at the proposed visit being announced by Bhutto.

Some Indian politicians began to demand that Sheikh Abdullah's passport be cancelled and that on return to India he should be indicted for treason. The new prime minister Shastri announced that Abdullah would never be allowed to visit China legally, and on 5 April the validity of Abdullah's passport and those of his party was cancelled by the government of India with effect from 30 April. It was only towards the end of their tour to several countries that the group was granted an extension which enabled them to legally return to India up to 8 May. On his arrival back in India in May 1965, Sheikh Abdullah was rearrested, and he was to remain in jail in Tamil Nadu, 2,000 miles from Kashmir, until 1968 (Victoria Schofield, *Kashmir in Conflict: India, Pakistan and the Unending War*, I. B. Tauris, 2000, 106).

Diplomatic moves

After the visit of Mountbatten to Lahore in October 1947 to try to resolve the Kashmir issue, there was a number of half hearted attempts by India and Pakistan to try resolving the issue bilaterally. There is little doubt that after 1949 the issue of Kashmir was largely resolved to India's satisfaction. Although the loss of Gilgit was a blow to those in the Indian Defence and Foreign Ministries who hoped to continue the British policy of playing a role in Central Asia, the gain of Ladakh and its approach to Central Asia was compensation enough. The effort that India put into capturing the town of Kargil—on the road from Srinagar to Leh—in 1948 shows that India was very conscious of the potential future role Kargil could play in Central Asia. In addition, the fact that India was also in possession of the Valley and its capital Srinagar meant that India was not unhappy with the status quo, and many leading figures in the Indian government expected the new state of Pakistan to be a temporary phenomenon; so the Indian attitude became one of consolidating the gains of 1947/48 in ICK and not trying to force a settlement in AK.

For Pakistan, on the other hand, Kashmir became nothing short of a national obsession and the cornerstone of its foreign policy, and at the risk of boring its new friends in the international community, Pakistani diplomats talked of little else for the first decade after independence. When India therefore suggested in 1949 that there should be an agreement between the two states that future issues should be resolved peacefully and without recourse to force, Pakistan's response was indignant. India, as far as Pakistan was concerned, had used force to obtain what it now possessed in the old State of Jammu and Kashmir and now wished to obtain an agreement from Pakistan not to disturb the status quo by force. Pakistan replied that such an agreement was only possible if India agreed to binding arbitration on Kashmir, something that Nehru was in no mood to consider. Liaquat and Nehru met in Delhi in July 1950 to discuss the possibility of a 'No War Pact' but without any agreement on Kashmir, the situation remained unresolved. Despite a few international discussions, the next major round of talks was in 1953/54, in which India reaffirmed the principle of a plebiscite in August 1953 and there was some discussion on the principle of regional votes so as to allow the multi-religious community of the State of Jammu and Kashmir a vote independent of the other regions. Nehru later dropped the idea of regional plebiscites and even cooled publicly on the idea of holding a plebiscite at all. The official reason given by India was the acceptance by Pakistan of US military aid under the April 1954 military assistance agreement signed with the US.

Nehru soon began to forge close ties with the Soviet Union, which in turn was anxious not to see Pakistan host large US military bases in the same way as Japan, West Germany and South Korea had done since the Second World War. By 1955, the USSR began supporting India not simply with military aid but even more crucially in the UN Security Council with diplomatic assistance, as the Soviet veto prevented any effective UN pressure being placed on India. Nehru was now emboldened enough to publicly give up on the idea of a plebiscite, and the official Indian line changed to stating that as the Jammu and Kashmir Assembly in November 1956 had voted to ratify the accession of the former ruler, the people of Kashmir had now expressed their opinion.

What was curious and inconsistent about the Indian position was the ease with which it was prepared to accept the existence of Azad Kashmir with Pakistani control over that territory. If India genuinely believed that the accession of the Raja in 1947 was a valid legal document, then India ought logically to have pressed for the area of Azad Kashmir, almost half of the former state of Jammu and Kashmir, to be brought under its control. Instead, from 1956 onwards, the unofficial Indian position was for both sides to accept the CFL as the legal boundary of Kashmir. This was obviously not a position that Pakistan was willing to consider as a solution and the matter reached a diplomatic impasse.

Soon after assuming the presidency in 1958, Ayub offered India a pact for the joint defence of the subcontinent against both China and the USSR. Nehru refused to take the idea seriously and Ayub was then to observe the defeat of India at the hands of China in 1962. Despite the apparent opportunity available at the time, politically Ayub was simply unable to undertake military action in Kashmir. To have done so would certainly have led to a complete cut-off of all US economic and military aid to Pakistan and might well have led to a direct confrontation with the US military on the side of India if the Americans felt that a joint Pakistan-Chinese attack was posing a serious threat to India's security and independence.

The US, having succeeded in applying pressure on Pakistan not to take advantage of India's militarily parlous position in 1962, now prevailed on Nehru to reopen talks with Pakistan on Kashmir. These began in December 1962 in Rawalpindi between the two Foreign Ministers, Bhutto and Swaran Singh. In January 1963, the venue was moved to Delhi, then in February 1963 to Karachi, in March to Calcutta and in April back to Karachi again and finally in May back in Delhi. It was during these talks that India made its first territorial concession on Kashmir, in offering official recognition for Pakistani control of Azad Kashmir and even more importantly, for the first time, offering Pakistan some further territory in Kashmir and Poonch. The Indian offer of territory in ICK was rejected by Pakistan as inadequate and the talks were finally stopped in 1963. On 26 May 1964 Sheikh Mohammed Abdullah announced in Rawalpindi that President Ayub and Prime Minister Nehru were to meet in New Delhi in the third week of June 1964 to discuss Kashmir, and it appeared that a further and possibly decisive round of direct negotiations was about to begin. It seemed to some international observers that finally Nehru had a change of heart regarding Kashmir, and he was expected to announce further concessions to Pakistan in the Valley itself (Wolpert, *Nehru*, 496–7). The very next day Nehru died, and it became obvious from the actions of the new prime minister Shastri that the faint hopes of some accommodation over the state of Kashmir had all but died with Nehru.

Pakistan's consistent position over the Kashmir issue was to insist that the solution lay in a free and impartial plebiscite to be held under the auspices of the United Nations, a position which by the early 1960s India was unwilling to discuss. In 1964 the Indian Representative in the UN Security Council was arguing that with the passage of time and various factors intervening, the UN resolutions were now obsolete, and under no circumstances would India agree to hold a plebiscite on Kashmir which was now an integral part of the Indian union. This was a provocative position and reflected Indian fears that any fair plebiscite would very likely result in accession to Pakistan. Another argument often used by India was that a plebiscite in favour of Pakistan could lead to large-scale and violent disturbances which could disturb India's delicate communal balance. Pakistan was indignant and argued that the people of Kashmir could not be held hostage for the security of India's Muslim population.

By 1964, successive attempts by the Security Council, to which India had first referred the Kashmir dispute on 1 January 1948, had all failed. Unsurprisingly Pakistan now viewed the UN as unable or unwilling to apply pressure on India thanks to the Soviet veto, and the Pakistani military and foreign policy establishment had now begun to consider other ways of resolving the conflict.

Pakistan's communist overtures

The United States was watching Pakistan's efforts to improve its relations with the two leading communist powers with some alarm, and took great offence in particular at Pakistan's improved relations with China. The United States considered China a greater threat to its interest in Asia than even the Soviet Union, and although the early stages of the China/Pakistan rapprochement were described by an American official as 'a series of pinpricks', Washington responded by making minor reductions in the aid programme to Pakistan. One of the most noticeable displays of American irritation occurred when the US unsuccessfully opposed the 1963 China/Pakistan civil aviation agreement, which it regarded as giving China access to Asia and beyond through air services to and from China. In retaliation, the United States indefinitely deferred the granting of a $4.3 million loan which was earmarked to modernise Dhaka airport.

By 1963 President Johnson began to remark pointedly that there was nothing permanent about the level of US aid to Pakistan. Furthermore, during 1964 and early 1965 the US repeatedly expressed concern, both publicly and privately, at the improvement of relations between Pakistan and China and made clear to Ayub that this process could jeopardise the continued flow of large-scale American aid. Ayub continued however with this policy of 'normalisation' of relations with China, and also continued to explore the limits of US tolerance with Pakistan's mildly critical attitude towards the growing military involvement of the US in Vietnam and refusal to commit any Pakistani troops to the war there. Fortunately for Ayub, the US was also offended by India's muted criticism of US involvement in Vietnam, and so India was unable to benefit from the distinct cooling of US-Pakistan relations.

The obstacles to normalising relations between Pakistan and the Soviet Union were far more difficult than those between China and Pakistan, for a number of reasons. With Pakistan's entry into the US-sponsored alliance system from 1954, the Soviet Union began to provide economic and military assistance to India, and between 1955 and 1964 Pakistan was viewed as a

US puppet. The Soviet Union also supported the Afghan government's demand that the Pakhtun people living within Pakistan should be permitted to decide through a plebiscite on whether they wished to accede to Afghanistan, remain within Pakistan or form an independent state.

In addition, Pakistan was not only a member of the Western military alliance system but also host to US air bases which were used to spy on the USSR. This was demonstrated in spectacular fashion on 1 May 1960 when a U2 high altitude reconnaissance aircraft of the CIA took off from a US air base near Peshawar and was shot down by the Soviets. Under agreements valid until July 1969, personnel from the US Air Force, the National Security Agency and the CIA had since 1958 spied on the Soviet Union from installations and bases within West Pakistan. There were four US bases inside Pakistan at this time, and one more had been agreed in principle but its exact location was to be finalised. The four sites were Malir Cantonment in Karachi for the USAF, Lahore Cantonment for the USAF, US Signals Corps in Badaber, Peshawar, and Army Signals Corps in Model Town Lahore (14/8/65, Karachi to Washington, 45-Pak US Natioanl Archives [hereafter NA]).

The Soviet Union was well aware of the aerial surveillance from these US bases within Pakistan, in particular of the U2 flights from Peshawar. After the shooting down of the U2, the USSR warned Pakistan that further espionage flights taking off from Pakistan would lead to Soviet retaliation directly against Pakistan.

The Soviet position as regards Kashmir up to 1955 was one of favouring a direct settlement between India and Pakistan but with due regard to the legitimate right of self-determination of the people through a plebiscite. After Pakistan's integration into the Western alliance system in 1955, the Soviet position changed to stating that by voting in Indian elections, the people of Kashmir had decided to remain within India. The Soviet position took no account of the fact that the 1951 elections were confined to ICK or that in seventy-three of the seventy-five constituencies members of the ruling or pro-India National Conference were returned unopposed and with widespread allegations of irregularities, with Sheikh Abdullah unable in 1954 to participate in the assembly's proceedings. Following the statement of this Soviet policy, Moscow then twice vetoed Security Council draft resolutions on Kashmir, which were opposed by India but acceptable to Pakistan and supported by the US and Britain.

The first veto in 1957 prevented the UN Security Council from approving in principle the dispatch of a UN force to Kashmir, where the council hoped the presence of such a force might help to bring about the demilitarisation of the state which was a prerequisite for a plebiscite. The second Soviet veto was cast in June 1962, preventing the passage of a draft resolution which reminded India and Pakistan of the principles contained in the previous resolutions and urged them to enter into negotiations on the Kashmir question.

By the end of 1962, however, there were several indications that the Soviet attitude towards India and Kashmir was undergoing a subtle shift favourable to Pakistan. When Kashmir was debated in the Security Council in 1962, the Soviet representative refrained from any criticism of Pakistan, which had been the previous Soviet practice, and the Soviet ambassador to the UN stressed that the India-Pakistan dispute must be resolved directly through bilateral negotiations. During a visit to New Delhi in June 1964 the Soviet president went as far as to suggest to Shastri that it was time to seek a settlement of the dispute. When Shastri visited Moscow, it was reported in the Indian press that in contrast with previous statements there was no reference to Kashmir in the final communiqué. The Soviet Union however continued to supply India with military aid such as transport planes, helicopters and supersonic interceptors, which coupled with its diplomatic support meant that India still relied on the USSR heavily during this period.

Growing US anger

With the assassination of Kennedy on 22 November 1963 and Vice-President Lyndon Johnson's succession as president, Ayub was initially delighted to see an old friend in the White House. Ayub and Johnson had been friends since Ayub's visit to Johnson's ranch in Texas in 1961. Ayub had diplomatically ignored the fact that pork ribs were on the menu and the two men became friends. Johnson later said that Ayub was a 'man's man', which Johnson considered the ultimate stamp of approval (Warren Cohen and Nancy Bernkopf Tucker (eds), *Lyndon Johnson Confronts the World*, Cambridge University Press, 1994, 136). Johnson had visited Pakistan earlier that same year as part of an Asian tour and had publicly stated that Pakistan was the best friend the US had in Asia. Ayub hoped, no doubt, that the Kennedy's pro-India tilt would now be replaced with a return to the more pro-Pakistan line of Eisenhower. Ayub was soon to be disappointed as Johnson was more anti-communist than pro-Pakistan, and Pakistan's moves from 1962 onwards to improve ties with China while the US was fighting in Vietnam had infuriated Johnson. Bhutto was to be at the receiving end of this anger when he arrived in Washington for the funeral of Kennedy.

Johnson met Bhutto on 29 November 1963 in Washington at the latter's insistence, and Bhutto must have wished with retrospect that he had not made the effort. Johnson lost control of his temper and in no uncertain terms warned Bhutto of the danger to good relations with the US if Pakistan continued with its new China policy. In a raised and angry tone, Johnson said that the US was indeed a true friend of Pakistan and would continue to be 'if Pakistan would let him'. He went on to say that the US government had always viewed Pakistan as staunchly anti-communist and yet he understood that Pakistan was soon going to host a state visit by leaders of communist China. Johnson wanted Bhutto 'to know that there would be a serious public relations problem here if Pakistan should build up its relations with the communist Chinese', and that he was fundamentally 'pro-Free World' and a state visit by a Chinese leader would make things difficult. Bhutto tried to point out to Johnson against this torrent that the US had to appreciate Pakistan's concern about Indian antagonism. Johnson swept that aside by saying that Pakistan knew the US would not let India attack Pakistan and assurances had been given to Pakistan on this point in the past. Johnson said that the strongest supporters of Pakistan in Congress were the same people who were the most anti-communist (Cohen and Tucker (eds), 138). Philips Talbot from the State Department saw Bhutto off at the airport that evening and reported that Bhutto 'showed himself deeply upset and disturbed by the turn the conversation had taken'. Bhutto was reported to have regretted not having replied better to Johnson's statements and said he could not understand why the Chinese visit had been raised in this way. Talbot explained the 'corrosive effect' of Pakistan's relations with China and said Johnson had pointed out that he and the US remained a friend of Pakistan and would not allow India to attack Pakistan. Talbot reiterated the US line which was that 'when Pakistan got itself mixed up with communist China, this tied our hands domestically and also of course removed any leverage we might have had to influence India in direction of accommodation with Pakistan' (2/12/1963, Telegram from Washington to Karachi, *FRUS 1961–1963 Volume XIX South Asia*, Doc 341).

This incident was later reported in the book *Lyndon Johnson and the World* by Philip Geyelin, and even in June 1968 Bhutto was still sensitive enough about the incident to write to the author to put his version of events across. Bhutto claimed that although he was familiar with the phrase 'to break bread', he could not follow Johnson's accent and so when Johnson said 'you are going to break bread with Zhou Enlai, Bhutto claimed he had not understood Johnson's accent (4/4/68, Pakistan Bhutto Correspondence, Box 43 LBJ). The strain placed on the US-Pakistan relationship by the new rapprochement between China and Pakistan was obvious when on 9 December 1963 Johnson wrote to Ayub and clearly warned him that the US policy of trying to improve relations with India would not be sacrificed for Pakistan's sake. Ayub replied to this letter on 21 January 1964 explaining why Pakistan wanted to raise the issue of Kashmir in the UN again. The previously close relationship between the superpower and its 'most allied ally' was now under obvious strain (Cohen and Tucker (eds), 139).

The US ambassador to Pakistan during this critical period was Walter McConaughy, who was a close confidant of Dean Rusk, the US Secretary of State, and had been appointed to the post during Kennedy's presidency. McConaughy was a professional diplomat and had served as US ambassador to Burma and South Korea before becoming ambassador to Pakistan from 1962 to 1966, and was viewed by many in Washington as 'too soft'. The US ambassador to India, J. K. Galbraith, complained that 'The Pakistanis would not be aware...that he [McConaughy] had talked to them' (Galbraith, 437). It was an open secret in Washington and Rawalpindi that Ayub was not pleased by Kennedy's choice of ambassador, as he was said to have preferred someone who was closer to the president, such as Galbraith in Delhi. An amusing story in this regard was told of an occasion when Jacqueline Kennedy, the president's wife, visited India and Pakistan in 1962 and was asked by Galbraith (a genuinely close friend of Kennedy) to impress on Ayub when she visited Pakistan that McConaughy was a close friend of the president. When Jacqueline Kennedy took the first opportunity to inform Ayub that the ambassador was an old friend of her husband's, she was corrected by McConaughy who factually if undiplomatically stated that he had 'only recently become acquainted with the president. The effect was further spoilt when she presented a photograph to McConaughy from Kennedy with the message inscribed 'To my old friend William McConaughy' (Galbraith, 340).

In 1965 both Ayub and Shastri were due to visit the US on official invitations, and on 2 April the State Department prepared a memorandum outlining why Ayub's and Shastri's visits were due and what the US hoped to gain from them. The memo began by stating that the US alliance with Pakistan 'has been coming apart since the Chinese attack on India in 1962 when we initiated our military aid to India'. A face-to-face meeting between Ayub and Johnson was therefore vital to 'halt the drift in our relations with Pakistan'.

The meeting with Ayub was seen as important for informing him that his efforts to widen Pakistan's circle of friends were exceeding the 'speed limits' as far as the US was concerned, particularly as regards China. The ambition was to make Ayub appreciate the new 'tolerable, if watered down, alliance relationship'. As far as military aid to both Pakistan and India was concerned, the US position was going to be one of continued support for military modernisation for both armies provided that the two countries (i) continued to rely on the West as their key supplier, (ii) remained committed to resisting communist aggression, (iii) tried to resolve their differences peacefully and (iv) refrained from actions which conflicted with US anti-communist actions. India was seen as being in the midst of the 'traumatic experience' of having to deal with the Chinese threat, and therefore it was seen as important to assure Shastri of US support and 'sympathetic understanding' (Outline for Ayub/Shastri Visits 2/4/65, Pakistan Memos 12/64—7/65 Johnson Presidential Library [hereafter LBJ]).

In 1964, Rusk informed Johnson that he had reviewed with General Maxwell Taylor the results of a trip the general had made to India and Pakistan. The conclusion was that General Taylor would fix the responsibility on the Indians of coming up with a satisfactory five-year defence plan which would limit the Indian need for Soviet aid and hold to a minimum the diversion of Indian resources from economic development. Provision of a limited number of high-performance aircraft from the US was seen as a possible part of such a plan. Rusk therefore recommended the following course of action: i) inform the British and other Commonwealth aid donors about the US plans for military assistance, ii) inform the Indians that the US was willing to provide military assistance if the Indians worked out a satisfactory five-year defence plan, iii) inform the Indians they could use a planning figure of about $50 million from the USA. However, in conclusion the Secretary of State noted that providing a long-term military programme for India, including some supersonic aircraft, would probably create in Pakistan and India 'an initial storm in each country about our policy in the other. We shall have to find ways of riding this out' (Dean Rusk to the President, Memo 16/1/1964, DEF 19 US-India).

In May/June 1964, US relations with Pakistan had a temporary lift when the Indian Defence Minister, Y. B. Chavan, arrived in the US to request military aid. Johnson was not generous when faced with a lengthy and detailed Indian request for a fixed commitment for military assistance, as he was irritated by India's constant criticism on the subject of Vietnam and continued military assistance from the USSR. On 7 July 1964, Ayub sent a letter to Johnson complaining of US military aid to India and repeated that he believed it was highly unlikely that the weapons would be used against China. On 15 July McConaughy met Johnson and recommended that the president invite Ayub to Washington to iron out the problems in the US-Pakistan relationship, but Johnson rejected this proposal and instead told McConaughy to deliver an oral message to Ayub. The content of the message has been heavily redacted by the US government to this day, which implies that it was blunt and highly sensitive (Narrative and Guide to Documents, South Asia Review, LBJ).

On 16 September 1964 McConaughy reported a private conversation with Mohammed Shoaib, the Pakistan Finance Minister, who was seen by the US government as the most pro-American member of the Pakistan cabinet. Although there is no doubt that Shoaib was trusted by the Americans, it appears that Ayub was conscious of this position and often used Shoaib and Bhutto as conduits for messages Ayub wished to convey unofficially to the US government, depending on the message and tone. The US ambassador said it was important in the course of planning ahead for the State Department to bear in mind the delicacy of Shoaib's position in the Pakistan government and to avoid overloading him. Shoaib was seen by McConaughy as providing an indispensable balance within the Pakistan government not only on economic matters but also in the whole foreign policy area where he served 'as a brake on the disengagement trend' (16/9/64 US Embassy to Washington, Karachi 559 NA).

On 20 September McConaughy reported that he had made President Ayub aware of the difficulties Ayub had caused the US with 'unnecessary and unfortunate gestures of friendship and goodwill' between Pakistan and China. The US ambassador described the gestures as particularly regrettable when there was an appearance of some possible negotiations of a secret nature. President Ayub defended the goodwill gesture as necessary and assured McConaughy that there had been no substantive talks, and chided the US for being hypersensitive and over-suspicious. Ayub said the trip of the Chinese premier only lasted as long as it did because of the flight schedule and the wait for a return flight (20/9/94 Pol 15–1 PAK NA).

On 21 September the US Embassy reported on a private lunch meeting of Shoaib and Phillips Talbot, the Assistant Secretary of

State, in which Shoaib had given his private and personal views on a variety of subjects. The central consideration of Pakistan foreign policy was still seen as India and after the 6 June announcement of further US arms aid to India, there seemed to be a strong urge within Pakistan to show its displeasure. Bhutto had wanted to make some gesture of friendship with China and Shoaib said that unfortunately there was some truth in the Indian prime minister's comments about differences between Bhutto and Ayub. Shoaib said that Bhutto had inherited this China policy from the previous Pakistan Foreign Minister (Manzur Qadir) but was keen on pursuing this further (23/9/64 Karachi 351 NA).

Pakistan's 'New Foreign Policy'

1965 was to be the year of the 'New Foreign Policy' for Pakistan as it sought to lessen its dependence on the US, improve relations with the USSR and cement relations with China. Ayub was to visit China from 2 to 9 March, the Soviet Union from 3 to 9 April and the USA on 25 and 26 April. It appears with hindsight that this schedule was arranged by Bhutto and Ayub with plans for a possible military conflict with India looming, and so the intention must have been to see what assistance the Chinese might provide in the event of a war, how neutral a position the Soviet Union could be persuaded to take, and how to keep American aid flowing while improving relations with China. It was an impressive schedule for an Asian leader, to meet the leaders of the two superpowers and an increasingly important Chinese leadership within the space of a few months.

A memorandum was sent to Rusk before he and Bhutto were due to have lunch in January 1965. Bhutto had arrived in America for a United Nations session and had travelled via Moscow, Bonn and London. It was recalled in the memorandum that McConaughy had recently had a fairly extensive conversation with Ayub on 14 January in which Ayub had confirmed the strength of Pakistan's alliance with the US and expressed his hope that he could have a moderating influence on the Chinese communists. Bhutto had appeared at a press conference in Moscow in January and seemed to have made a deliberate effort to emphasise a Pakistan-Soviet common identity of views on many issues. This press conference was seen by the Americans as bidding for a change in the Soviets' pro-Indian stance on Kashmir and possibly also trying to slow down Soviet arms shipments to India. In these private talks in Bonn and London, Bhutto appeared to be trying deliberately to create an impression of uncertainty as to what further steps the Pakistan government might take because of US/UK policies in India. The State Department said that the British saw this talk as 'bluff'. By contrast, in talks with the US diplomats at the UN, Bhutto was seen as unusually warm and co-operative (24/1/65 Memo from P Talbot to S of S, POL 7 Pak NA).

Bhutto's travels resulted in a telegram from McConaughy to the State Department on 27 January in which he reported on what he saw as a damaging trail of 'unfortunate' foreign policy pronouncements Bhutto had left in the wake of his current visit to the Soviet Union; this implies that the US ambassador was not inclined like his British counterparts to take a relaxed view of Bhutto's 'bluff'. McConaughy felt that the trip was a succession of ill-considered public comments which were contrary to US interests, as in both public and private statements Bhutto was unmistakably seen to be going beyond the limits that the Pakistan government had hitherto stayed within. The US ambassador stated that some of Bhutto's recent statements 'constituted sheer blackmail' and felt that there were grounds for suspicion that he was using the trip to try to signal a major change in Pakistan's foreign policy. McConaughy felt the best way to approach Ayub on this issue was by indirectly sowing the seeds of suspicion in Ayub's mind that Bhutto was a clear liability to him, but the ambassador warned that this would need to be done with care as it could bring about a protective reaction from Ayub (27/1/65 Karachi to Washington, Karachi 1422 NA).

Prior to Ayub's visit to Beijing, the State Department directed McConaughy on 19 February 1965 as to the US official position regarding this visit. The main point was that the US should refrain from appearing to sanction the trip by accepting Ayub's offer to act as a middleman, but in addition the US did not wish to appear totally disinterested or negative towards the trip and it was seen as desirable that McConaughy should see Ayub before his departure. The following points needed to be made to Ayub by McConaughy:

   i) the US was glad to have Ayub's assurances that the Pakistan-Chinese relationship was limited to one of non-provocation in good neighbourliness;

  ii) Ayub must have no doubt as to US determination to resist Chinese threats to peace and stability in Asia;

 iii) regardless of what Pakistan's motive was, it was inescapable that the Chinese had derived encouragement and national prestige from the apparent success of the Pakistan link. This was of considerable importance to the US at a time when the US confrontation with the Chinese communists had reached a new high;

 iv) the US believed it had a right to expect from Pakistan as an ally that it would not allow itself to be manoeuvred into support for the Chinese position on issues in which US vital interests were involved. The last was a clear hint regarding Vietnam and India (POL 7 Pak 19/2/65 NA).

McConaughy met Ayub on 26 February to deliver Johnson's invitation to visit the US and at the same time to give Ayub the above message regarding the US view of the forthcoming visit to China. Ayub read the invitation immediately and said that he would acknowledge it in writing and also that he wanted to re-establish personal contact with President Johnson in order to reaffirm the closeness of their official and personal relationship. After saying that Pakistan considered the US 'her best and closest friend', Ayub then said that he would like to meet Johnson alone for a brief period and would also like to have an opportunity to call on Mrs Jacqueline Kennedy if that was possible.

Ayub and McConaughy then moved on to the thorny subject of China, and the ambassador said that following the meeting Ayub clearly understood that he was not authorised to act as a spokesman for the US and that the Americans did not consider the visit to China as being in any sense undertaken for the US interest. Ayub denied that the Pakistan government had in any way changed essential foreign policy decisions, and repeated his view that the US was overestimating the importance and influence that Pakistan had if it felt that modest gestures made by Pakistan had any appreciable effect on the international standing of communist China (27/2/65, Rawalpindi to Washington, POL 7 Pak, NA).

On 24 March, McConaughy provided the State Department with some background to Ayub's forthcoming trip to Washington. The embassy recognised that the 1962 war marked the major turning point in US-Pakistan relations. The Western response to the war had been to send military aid to India and refuse Pakistan's request to use the leverage gained to press India to make real concessions on Kashmir. Pakistan had feared that India would use this major expansion of the Indian armed forces against Pakistan and not China, and had reacted to this by developing differing strands of foreign policy which in turn had further aggravated relations with the US, already strained by fundamental differences about policy towards India (24/3/65, Karachi to Washington, 1-DL Pak NA).

The first stop on Ayub's international travel after his election was China—setting a precedent, as almost every Pakistani leader since then has made China their first overseas destination after coming to power. This was always going to be the easiest but in many ways the most critical part of his international tours as the Chinese government viewed Pakistan as an important ally and was determined to continue its charm offensive. It is unclear whether any military action against India was discussed or if Ayub took China into confidence regarding the planning of some military action in Kashmir; subsequent events would indicate that while no detailed discussions took place (to judge from the polite criticism China levelled at Pakistan during and after the war) there were apparently some general Chinese promises of assistance to Pakistan in the event of war with India. Both sides used the visit to emphasise the new close relationship, and a film of Ayub's visit was made by China and shown throughout Pakistan. However well the images and film may have gone down in Pakistan, they were badly received by the Americans who had expressed their private displeasure at the trip from the outset.

On 2 April there was a memorandum to Johnson by Robert Komer of the State Department following on from Ayub's China visit. Komer was a former adviser to Kennedy who had been retained by Johnson as a special adviser on South Asia. Komer was known to be a keen advocate of Kennedy's belief that India was the key to anti-communist action in Asia. Komer wrote that Bhutto had the 'gall' to state publicly that there was no inconsistency in Pakistan being friends with both the US and the Chinese communists since both were 'peace-loving nations'. The remark that US aid to India after the 1962 war with China had shattered the whole concept of alliances with the US was very unhelpful, and Komer said the Pakistanis appeared to have arrived at the conclusion that they could 'have their cake and eat it too' despite the fact that Washington had just provided around $450 million in the financial year 1964 as aid to Pakistan. Komer said Ayub should be informed that equating the US with China was going down very badly in Washington, and the US should also make known its annoyance at the fact that while Dean Rusk was in Tehran, Bhutto and Ayub were both in Moscow. Komer said that Ayub still knew in his heart that he could not do without US assistance, but he was going to try to play the Chinese off against India. Shoaib, who was again described as the US government's 'best Pakistani friend', was reported as saying Ayub believed that accommodation with China could be carried much further without jeopardising the flow of US aid. Therefore Ayub's forthcoming visit to Washington was seen as a critical opportunity to tell Ayub that unless he pulled back from his friendship with China, Pakistan would be carried beyond the point of no return and Congress might not approve the $400/500 million a year in aid currently provided to Pakistan, and at that stage the US intelligence facility at Peshawar could also be lost. The memorandum concluded by saying that the only way to get through to Ayub appeared to be a direct face to face meeting between Ayub and Johnson at which these points would be spelt out to Ayub bluntly (2/4/65 Memo Komer to President NA).

After the highly successful visit to China, Ayub and his team flew to Moscow on 3 April—the first visit ever by a Pakistani head of state to the USSR. Ayub was concerned by the generous diplomatic and military support India had received from the USSR and by the use of the Soviet veto in the UN Security Council to support India over the issue of Kashmir. After the carefully orchestrated welcoming crowds in China, the Pakistani delegation received a cold but polite welcome from the Soviet government. The talks were initially held in a tense atmosphere as the Soviets had a list of grievances with Pakistan—not least the US bases inside Pakistan which were used to spy on the Soviet Union, and the listening posts and US military advisers. The Soviets viewed the Pakistan Army as one armed and equipped by the Americans to fight anti-communist wars, and it was hardly surprising that Ayub was not accorded a warm welcome. In addition, relations between the communist giants of the USSR and China were strained and one of the few common interests the USSR and USA had in 1965 was a common desire to limit Chinese influence in Asia, in particular a determination not to allow China to bully India and team up with Pakistan in doing so. From that unpromising premise, Ayub struggled to make any headway in persuading the Soviets that Pakistan's relations with China and the US were based on the need to defend itself against India and that it had no aggressive intent with the membership of military pacts. According to Gauhar who accompanied Ayub on this visit, Ayub made a bold and relatively straightforward offer to the Soviets: in return for Pakistan ensuring that US bases left Pakistan, the USSR would not use its veto on Kashmir in the UN to protect India. The Soviets were no doubt taken aback by the offer, but in private talks with Ayub, they were reported by Ayub to have been seriously interested in the offer, and as a gesture of good will the Soviet leader, Leonid Brezhnev, hinted that Soviet military aid might be available to Pakistan (Gauhar, 300–1). There is no doubt in view of later events that Ayub's trip had gone some way to persuading the Soviets that Pakistan was amenable to reasonable offers and Ayub was not irredeemably anti-communist. The Soviet position on Kashmir, which had become more nuanced since 1964, further softened and the visit did succeed in moderating the hostile anti-Pakistan stance the Soviets had displayed throughout the previous decade. Ayub therefore returned to Pakistan pleased that the trip had gone as well as expected on 9 April, and could now start planning his state visit to the US.

On 15 April (just ten days before the scheduled visit was to take place) McConaughy met Ayub with a difficult message to convey; Johnson had decided to 'postpone' the visits of Ayub and Shastri to America, due to take place within weeks. The ambassador detailed his meeting with Ayub Khan in Rawalpindi to break the news of the trip's cancellation to him, with only one other person recorded as being present at the meeting, the Foreign Secretary Aziz Ahmed. McConaughy set out the reasons for the president's decision to postpone the trip and reiterated the official line that the postponement was not a cancellation as Johnson wanted the visit rescheduled when the time was more opportune. McConaughy reported that Ayub took the postponement well and responded amicably, although he seemed to be slightly taken aback and did not appear to have any evidence of any forewarning from Shoaib or any other source (15/4/65 POL 7 Pak NA). Ayub's carefully planned tour of major world capitals was now brought to a juddering stop, as Johnson had finally lost patience with Pakistan during Ayub's carefully orchestrated visits to the communist capitals of Beijing and Moscow. Ayub's visit was to have taken place in April and Shastri's visits to the US had been scheduled to take place on 2 and 3 June. There was no doubt that the 'postponement' was aimed at Ayub rather than Shastri, but the US could not invite Shastri while cancelling Ayub's trip, as this would risk another mini-crisis in Pakistan-US relations. While this came as an unpleasant shock to Ayub, it had the unexpected benefit of helping to convince the Soviets that there was a genuine difference of opinion between Pakistan and the USA, one that they might be able to exploit. Johnson's decision caused great offence in India, where Shastri declared that he would not accept another invitation to visit the US, but Ayub remained publicly restrained, believing that the US had no option but to tolerate Pakistani moves towards its communist neighbours.

Following on from the cancellation of Ayub's visit, in July 1965 there was an even bigger shock for Ayub when the US postponed the Aid to Pakistan consortium meeting due to be held in Paris on 27 June. This meeting was to plan the level of aid to Pakistan for the next few years and its postponement effectively left Pakistan's future aid pledges uncertain. On 9

June, Johnson held a meeting in the White House with Rusk, McNamara and USAID officials. Johnson clearly stated that there had to be a fundamental rethink of US aid and strategy in South Asia. There were to 'be no additional decisions, authorisations or announcements without his approval pending passage of the FY 1966 foreign aid authorisation'. Johnson also ordered that all US aid should be reviewed in the light of questions about whether the US should be spending such large amounts of money in either country and what leverage the US was getting in terms of encouraging 'self-help and...political purposes' (Bundy to Rusk, 9 June 1965 NSC LBJ). In effect, Johnson had decided to withhold all aid promised to Pakistan for 1966; a decision which obviously hit Pakistan harder as India had already been promised its aid for 1966 but now Pakistan's aid meeting due to take place on 27 June had been postponed. Johnson was now playing the aid card and making US displeasure at Pakistan's 'New Foreign Policy' public (Cohen and Tucker (eds), 157).

McConaughy reported that the news of the aid postponement, following on from the cancellation of Ayub's US visit, meant that 'Ayub took the news quite hard—worse than I had anticipated'. Ayub was now genuinely offended and spoke out more harshly than ever before. He described the Americans as 'power drunk' and said that on his recent trips he had gone to find 'new friends, not new masters'. This phrase was later to be the title of Ayub's autobiography (Cohen and Tucker (eds), 158).

The situation was so serious that on 10 July, Shoaib met McConaughy and said he would like to take advantage of an old offer to use the US Embassy telegraphic facilities if ever he had a 'message of special importance and sensitivity' to deliver to Rusk. The message sent by Shoaib was that the improvement in relations with the US which had been under way in Pakistan was now 'threatened by the shift in the US government approach to the consortium pledging session. I ask your help in finding some way out so that a crisis does not arise' (01/7/1965, Karachi to State, Vol III 12/64—7/65 LBJ).

On 23 July the State Department received reports of the wave of indignation coming out of Pakistan and reacted by sending a lengthy message to the US ambassador to Pakistan to clarify its position following the two recent US snubs. McConaughy was told to inform the Pakistan government that the US regretted that Pakistan had 'over-reacted' to the delay in the aid pledges. It even appeared to US that 'Ayub at least initially followed the anti-American line of Bhutto and other extremists'. The tactic of whipping up public anger appeared to be little more than pressure tactics and the US treated Pakistan 'with courtesy and politeness'; the US needed to make it clear that 'abuse and attack' would only leave an 'extremely bad impression'. What was also of concern to the State Department as well was the impression that Ayub seemed to have that the US wished Pakistan to play a subservient role to India. McConaughy was told to make it clear to Ayub that this idea was 'totally false'; the US' position was that it wished to treat both countries as friends and hope for a peaceful solution to Kashmir. The ambassador was also told to remind Ayub that the military alliances were specially designed to protect Pakistan against communist aggression and Pakistan had received 'massive investment' from the US—which was proportionately far higher than India had received. In fact, Pakistan was the second largest recipient of US aid in the world and as the US had become more concerned with the growth of communism in south-east Asia, Pakistan was seen as becoming less and less co-operative.

Despite this, the US respected Pakistan's right to choose its friends and allies whom Pakistan believed to be best suited to help, but in turn, the US expected Pakistan to allow the US the same freedom to choose its friends and allies. Differences could certainly be discussed, but there was 'no obligation to maintain a particular level of aid in any country or indeed any aid at all'.

Foreign aid was 'a privilege and not an obligation' and therefore the US would reject any accusations of using aid to apply 'pressure'. Open and extreme criticism of US policy, particularly by recipients of aid, had made the idea of convincing Congress to approve any further aid appropriations 'a real problem'. Owing to the Pakistan's government's 'strong and unfriendly reaction' to the aid postponement, the US did not propose sending any senior official to Pakistan in the immediate future and understood that Pakistan likewise did not appear to have any delegations due to visit the US. The State Department had decided that the 'best and most effective communication channel for time being is through US ambassador', and so McConaughy was given authority to convey as much of this message to Ayub as he deemed helpful (23/7/65, Rusk to Karachi, *FRUS 1964–1968*, Volume XXV South Asia, Document 266).

The fact that by the summer of 1965 all the signals coming from Washington regarding Pakistan's 'New Foreign Policy' were negative, if not positively hostile, seemed to be either ignored or viewed as a temporary pressure tactic by Ayub and Bhutto. Although Pakistan had succeeded in improving relations with China and the USSR, the fact was that the Pakistan armed forces were equipped almost exclusively by US weaponry and US financial aid had been responsible in a large part for Pakistan's last decade of economic growth; the Americans believed that Ayub was rational enough to realise that Pakistan had no alternative but to keep up excellent relations with them. Relations with the US by mid 1965 had now reached the point where on 30 July 1965 McConaughy was only able to meet Bhutto as Ayub refused to meet the US ambassador. Bhutto was described by McConaughy as being in a 'personally cordial mood but substance remarks reflected hard GOP (Government of Pakistan) position encased in velvet glove'. Bhutto said that he regretted that Ayub had not been able to meet the ambassador despite repeated requests and gave a 'new and candid reason' for this. Ayub feared that 'in his anger he would lose control of himself and make some undiplomatic statement to me' and so was waiting until the situation had become clearer. McConaughy said that he was used to plain language and that Ayub could 'speak to him as bluntly as he wished'; the more important thing, he said, was for a dialogue to be started, and 'diplomatic niceties' should not stand in the way. Bhutto said that he would pass on this message but in the meanwhile he had been authorised by Ayub to meet McConaughy and deal fully with him on Ayub's behalf.

McConaughy said that the US greatly regretted the Pakistan government's decision to publicise the current problems and that he 'specifically deplored' Bhutto's decision to stress in the National Assembly the existence of 'certain other factors' which had led to the aid consortium postponement. McConaughy said that this made a diplomatic resolution to this issue very hard. Bhutto claimed that the tradition of candour in the Assembly made it necessary for him to say that, and that news of the postponement needed to be broken by the Pakistan government to its parliament. Bhutto said the government was resolved to prevent anti-American violence and Ayub's sense of grievance was aggravated by the fact that this was the second US snub, following on from the postponement of his trip to the US. Bhutto said that these two events had 'convinced' Ayub of an 'unsympathetic and indifferent US attitude' towards Pakistan.

McConaughy said he informed Bhutto in confidence that India's aid consortium meeting was also going to be adjourned and the official Pakistan government reaction was only making the situation more difficult and harder to resolve. Bhutto took this to be the US 'hard line and said that if the US did take a hard line, Pakistan would immediately take a harder line'. This would escalate, according to Bhutto, like Vietnam, except that it would be peaceful. Bhutto said he was aware of Johnson's request on 25 July to Ayub for Pakistan's assistance with troops in Vietnam and Ayub would respond in the next few days to the request. Bhutto ended by saying the Pakistan government would be willing to pass on any message that the US might have for China. This offer appeared to have backfired as McConaughy took the offer to be that of a 'friendly neutral' rather than that of an American ally (2/8/65, Karachi to Washington, *FRUS 1964–1868* Volume XXV South Asia Doc 161).

In the period from 1954 to 1962, US-Pakistan relations had prospered and Pakistan had been seen by the US as a trusted and reliable ally. Relations had first faltered in 1962 when the US had begun to provide military aid to India, but until 1964 were still close enough for Pakistan to continue receiving large amounts of military and economic aid. From the beginning of 1965, however, Pakistan-US relations were now stretched to their limits. The 'most allied ally' was now being viewed with a degree of suspicion, bordering hostility, by sections of the US government; which was also its main military and economic aid donor. This was a far from ideal position for Pakistan to be in on the eve of war, and yet one which Ayub and Bhutto were confident of handling.

3

FIGHTING IN KUTCH

The Rann of Kutch

When most histories of the 1965 war are written, for obvious reasons it is usually the fighting in Kashmir and the Punjab which tend to dominate the narrative. But it was in the relatively unknown and inhospitable terrain of the Rann of Kutch that the military hostilities really began in 1965, and without the events there it is highly unlikely that a full-scale war would have broken out later that year. With the obvious exception of Kashmir, India and Pakistan had by 1963 demarcated their entire western boundary except for the southernmost stretch on the West Pakistan/India border, separating the Pakistani province of Sindh from the former princely state of Kutch. After Partition in 1947, the whole of the princely state of Kutch had become the Kutch district in the Indian state of Gujarat, but Pakistan and India had from the outset always disagreed over the location of the boundary as Pakistan continued the claim of the province of Sindh to some territory in the area known as the Rann inside Kutch district. From 1948 until 1965 (except for a short localised clash in 1956) neither side had sought to resolve the border dispute by anything other than peaceful means. During the 1950s there were intermittent Diplomatic Notes exchanged between India and Pakistan stating their respective claims, with India laying claim to the whole Rann and Pakistan claiming a portion of the northern territory of the Rann.

The territory of the Rann of Kutch was an unlikely battlefield to fight over for two armies as it was an inhospitable desert (and deserted) territory. The Rann lies to the south and east of the Indus Delta and was further subdivided into two areas, the Great Rann in the North and the Little Rann in the southeast. The dispute in 1965 between India and Pakistan was confined to the Great Rann which measures just over 160 miles from east to west, 80 miles from north to south, with a total area of just over 7,000 square miles. In 1965, the Great Rann was inhabited only seasonally by shepherds and border forces manning check posts and was rarely crossed by anyone except police patrols. It is a low-lying, salt marsh which could grow little except coarse grasses and the only animals found there are wild asses, gazelles and seasonally grazed livestock, including camels and cattle. Within the flat landscape, there were a few pockets of higher ground called *bets* that stood no more than a few feet above the general level and varied from a few square yards to more than 20 square miles. From November to the outset of the southwest monsoon, which usually takes place in early June, the Great Rann was mostly dry, but during the monsoon it would flood, which meant that the *bets* became islands and the few roads across the Rann would become virtually impassable.

If the Rann of Kutch is viewed as a potential battlefield into which both India and Pakistan wished to deploy a large volume of troops and military equipment, then the region's terrain and communications network greatly favoured Pakistan. Pakistan had a railway connection at Badin, 26 miles north of the Indian claim line and only 113 miles east of Karachi, where Pakistan's 8 Division was based. There was also a bridge over the river Indus at the Pakistani city of Hyderabad, north of Badin, which meant that although the distance by rail from Karachi to the

Rann was 186 miles, there was a shorter road link between Karachi and Kutch of 130 miles by way of a ferry crossing the Indus near Thatta. The distances involved and the terrain meant that Pakistan could quickly and easily move troops from Badin to any point along the Kutch border while other routes could facilitate the troop deployment southward into the disputed area.

All of the approaches to the Rann of Kutch from the Indian side were much more difficult than those from Pakistan, as the nearest Indian regular military formation was the 31 Infantry Brigade which was stationed in Ahmedabad, 180 miles east of the railway station at Bhuj, a small town located in the Rann but 110 miles from the disputed border. There was a road from Bhuj to the town of Khavda, approximately 44 miles away from Bhuj, and although Khavda was closer to the Rann/Sindh border, the road from Bhuj was almost impassable in the monsoon season. The road and rail links from India into the Rann therefore followed long routes and India's military posts inside Kutch were dependent on vulnerable lines of communication and supplies.

It is impossible to state with accuracy the *de facto* border between the two sides at the Rann border as well as the precise location of police posts and pickets in January 1965, but a clue emerges from the fact that on 12 May 1964, an Indian patrol arrested three Pakistani nationals near the abandoned fort at Kanjarkot in the north-western corner of the Rann, where the future flashpoint was to be. India claimed that Kanjarkot was 1,500 yards south of the Sindh/Kutch border on Indian maps, and so it claimed the Pakistani nationals were inside an area controlled by India. The three men were returned quickly on the grounds that they appeared to have strayed by accident. The fact that this incident was reported indicates that this was a rare occurrence, but the Indian reaction was mild given the seriousness with which incidents like these were treated by both sides along the CFL and along the Bengal border. This shows that both sides generally observed scrupulously the *de facto* border and the ground rules agreed by both sides.

Flashpoint at Kanjarkot

In 1965, the Indian side of the border was patrolled by a paramilitary police force called the Special Reserve Police (SRP) whose recruitment and training came under the Indian state government of Gujarat, while it was the West Pakistan and Indus Rangers who were responsible for patrolling the Pakistan side. From November 1962 the 31 Infantry Brigade was responsible for the military protection on the Indian side of the border, but the day-to-day patrolling was left to the SRP. On 25 January 1965 an SRP patrol noticed what it regarded to be a freshly made track in the vicinity of Kanjarkot, the abandoned fort. Pakistan placed Kanjarkot just to the north of its line and thereby claimed it was outside the disputed area. However, as Kanjarkot was in the area of the Great Rann, it was therefore regarded by each side as being a part of its territory and so it was certainly not, as Pakistan claimed, 'indisputably' within Pakistan's territory. The SRP patrol in January also noticed a freshly made track linking two small hamlets, Ding and Surai, whose location inside West Pakistan was not disputed—they were north of the Indian claim, as Ding was four miles to the north-west of Kanjarkot and Surai eleven miles to the east. The problem for the Indians was that for several miles the 18-mile track passed south of the main feature at Kanjarkot and ran more than 1½ miles south of the Indian claim. In addition, it appeared to the Indians that the track was made by the passage of heavy motor vehicles through the sandy area, and the patrol's discovery was taken seriously enough for the District Magistrate of Kutch to be sent to make an inspection and confirm its findings (Indian Note, 12/2/65, K-SBQ 138–139, Wright, 30).

The SRP was then ordered to undertake 'vigorous patrolling' in the Kanjarkot area right up to the Indian claim line. The Pakistanis later claimed that India was trying to take the whole Rann by default by patrolling with impunity throughout the territory and often passing very close to long-established

Pakistani posts. On receiving Pakistani protests, the Indians later claimed that they had always patrolled that area. On 30 January an Indian patrol was challenged near Kanjarkot by the Pakistani Rangers, and on 3 February another Indian patrol was sighted near Kanjarkot and a formal protest was lodged with the Indians by the Government of Pakistan (Pakistani Note, 1/3/1965, K_SBQ, 142, Wright, 32).

After attempting and failing to secure a meeting with the Pakistan Rangers, the Indians decided to continue to probe away and try to see the Pakistani reaction near Kanjarkot. On 5 February a Pakistani patrol intercepted an Indian party in four jeeps, two of SRP and two of regular Indian soldiers. On being asked to do so, the Indian patrol returned to the Indian post of Chhad Bet and the local Pakistani commander now concluded that the SRP's continued probing indicated an attempt by the Indians to occupy the area of Kanjarkot. When a small SRP patrol approached the fort the next day its way was blocked by a large party of Rangers.

Finding Kanjarkot cordoned off from its patrols, the Indian government sent a protest note to Pakistan on 12 February. In this note the Indians protested at the forcible intrusion of Rangers across the international border into Indian territory in and around Kanjarkot and urged Pakistan to withdraw them immediately. On 15 February a meeting was finally held between the local commanders, the Indian Deputy Inspector General, Rajkot Range and the Commandant, Indus Rangers. The Pakistanis again repeated their country's claim that the area around Kanjarkot had been under its *de facto* control since 1947, but found the Indian side had an identical claim, and the meeting broke up without any resolution (Lt Gen. Mahmud Ahmed, *History of Indo-Pak War—1965*, Services Book Club, 2006, 1).

As the Kutch-Sindh border was not fully demarcated and was now actively disputed on the ground, the Pakistan Rangers and the SRP used the local ground rules to try to decide a working boundary. The Pakistan side insisted that Kanjarkot fell within Pakistan's *de facto* control and had been patrolled by Pakistan for many years, and went on to assert that Pakistan had patrolled the Ding-Surai track for many years. The Indian side claimed that Indian patrolling had always been south of its control line, which included Kanjarkot. The Indians' position meant claiming that even before Pakistan began to move towards Kanjarkot, the area around that fort was normally patrolled by India, but neither side mentioned the precise date when its forces had begun to patrol Kanjarkot, and if both sides were being truthful, it is surprising that neither had encountered the other until January 1965. On 18 February another Note was sent from India to Pakistan asking for a withdrawal of Pakistani forces and a meeting of the two countries' respective Surveyors-General. On 19 February these demands were reiterated by the Indian High Commissioner to Pakistan at a meeting with Bhutto. The Pakistanis replied by claiming that Indian aircraft had recently violated their airspace and ignored the suggestion of the Surveyor-General's meeting.

Operation Kabadi

On 21 February 1965 the Indian GHQ forces authorised Operation Kabadi to force the Pakistan evacuation of Kanjarkot; the Indian 31 Infantry Brigade Group under Brigadier S. S. M. Pahalajani was tasked with this operation and authorised to cross the international border if necessary to secure this objective, and Indian forces began to assemble at Bhuj (Chakravorty, 21) Despite these orders, it appears that Indian troops on the ground realised they were inadequate to force a Pakistani withdrawal from Kanjarkot and maintained a largely defensive position, but now decided to proceed with more regular and aggressive patrolling. Pakistan realised that there was now a major move under way by Indian regular forces, and on 22 February the Pakistani Indus Rangers were ordered by Major General Tikka Khan, GOC, 8 Infantry Division to occupy Kanjarkot Fort in strength (M. Ahmed, 1). This means that whether Pakistan admitted it was in control of Kanjarkot before 22 February or not (and it seems likely that it was), there is no doubt that it was after this date. Despite the order being given for strong and aggressive patrolling to be carried out in Kabadi, Indian forces did not appear to take the initiative despite the order and remained relatively defensive, no doubt conscious of the relative strength of the Pakistani forces available in the border area. Pakistan now ordered 51 Brigade under Brigadier Azhar from 8 Division to patrol the area claimed by Pakistan and its brigade headquarters was established at Badin. 51 Brigade had three battalions, 18 Punjab, 6 Baluch and 8 Frontier Force, in addition to the Indus Rangers placed under its command.

On 24 February the political stakes were also upped by the Gujarat Home Minister who gave the Indian version of events and stated that India was ready 'to accept the challenge if the situation worsens' (24/2/1965 PREM 13 393, UK Public Record Office [hereafter PRO; later renamed The National Archives] PRO). On 1 March Pakistan sent a Note to India stating that the area around Kanjarkot had been in Pakistan's *de facto* possession since 1947 and rejected the Indian request for a meeting of the two Surveyors-General on the grounds that the alignment of the border was a matter for political discussion between the two governments. Pakistan added that although the Pakistan police were patrolling the area around Kanjarkot Fort, they had not occupied the Fort itself; which appears to be at variance with General Tikka Khan's orders of 22 February.

On 4 March the Indian Foreign Minister, Swaran Singh, gave a press conference in which he stated that Pakistan had never been in *de facto* possession of the area and that the Rann of

Kutch was a disputed area whose borders had not been demarcated. During March, India decided on patrols to 'show the flag' and military exercises were held in the Kutch area to demonstrate Indian resolve towards the dispute. By 6 March troops from Pakistan's 8 Division, 8 Frontier Force and 18 Punjab, each with its supporting artillery including a battery of 25 pounders, had moved to Kanjarkot but apparently not south of the Indian claim line. They were under orders not to allow the Indians to edge forward but not themselves to advance beyond the line already held by the Rangers (M. Ahmed, p. 2). On 30 March Pakistan sent an *aide mémoire* to India describing the Indian military actions as provocative and warlike. While these talks were going on, India had begun reconnaissance flights over Kutch in March and had, even by its own admission, begun to patrol some areas for the first time. Operating from the Chhad Bet post, the Indian patrols began during March to patrol closer to the Pakistani tracks. Although the patrols were within India's area, they were in violation of Ground Rule 9 which stated that the status quo was to be maintained. The new patrols inevitably drew strong Pakistani protests requesting that India should stay on the old patrolling tracks.

There was now both military and diplomatic deadlock in the Rann of Kutch, and India's seemingly meek response to what was viewed by the Indian population as Pakistan's attempts to claim Indian territory by force now drew fierce criticism in the Indian parliament and the Indian press. For some Indian politicians, the parallel between the situation at Kanjarkot and that faced by India during 1962 in the conflict with China was depressingly similar. Swaran Singh argued in the Indian parliament, the Lok Sabha, that it was inappropriate and inaccurate to draw parallels between Kanjarkot and the incidents on the India-China border as the Chinese had built a properly engineered road whereas the track near Kanjarkot was only a track left by impressions through the passage of Pakistani trucks. Angry members of the Indian parliament accused the Indian government of bungling inefficiency and of compromising India's position, while other members of parliament thought that negotiation with Pakistan was cowardly and asked why the Indian government was not sending in military reinforcements (A. D. Mani, RSD, Third Series, L1:11, 3/3/65, col 2370). On 11 March India proposed a very early meeting, at any level acceptable to Pakistan, where at least a solution to the problem of patrolling could be discussed. The Indian government admitted that by 13 March it had established Sardar post which was almost 5,500 yards to the south west of Kanjarkot and was intended to block the Pakistani route to Kanjarkot. In retaliation Pakistan now set up a military post at Ding, to the north-east of Sardar. The Indians responded to this with the establishment of yet another post close to the Sardar post at Vigiokot (B. C. Chakravorty, *History of the Indo-Pak War, 1965*, History Division, Ministry of Defence, New Delhi, 1992 (Chief Editor S. N. Prasad), 22). By the middle of March, therefore, both sides had established new standing posts in the Kanjarkot vicinity in areas which had previously only been patrolled, and Pakistan had also sent regular infantry battalions to reinforce the Rangers along areas claimed by Pakistan. The fact that India now decided to create new posts suggests that the Indian intention was to be able to mount patrols as strong as those hitherto used by the Pakistan Rangers, but it seems India did not anticipate that Pakistan would respond by reinforcing its border police with regular military units. That is precisely what Pakistan's GHQ had ordered and there was now a stand-off with neither side ready to move and with only a trigger needed for fighting to break out.

The opening shots are fired

Despite the build-up of tension during March, Pakistan claimed it was the creation of new Indian posts inside the Rann that led to the first outbreak of fighting. Tikka Khan ordered Brigadier Azhar on 6/7 April to carry out the removal and destruction of the Indian post at Sardar and other smaller posts by last light 9 April. The attack was due to have been launched on 7/8 April but was delayed owing to movements of Pakistani troops to the required positions, and so it commenced at 0200 PST on 9 April. 18 Punjab was ordered to take Sardar post and 6 Baluch was to capture the Indian posts named Jungle and Shalimar. Pakistani troops advanced in the dark and achieved the desired surprise factor they had hoped for, and with covering fire from medium machine guns, heavy mortars, 51 Brigade attacked India's Sardar post which was manned by SRP positions. Although Shalimar post was captured without much resistance, Sardar post saw heavy fighting during the night and through to the next afternoon. The attack did not lead to the swift success that 51 Brigade had hoped for and despite mortar and artillery fire which became heavier during the afternoon of 9 April, the Indian defenders succeeded, by and large, in holding their position. Just as Brigadier Azhar had decided by the late afternoon of 9 April to call off the attack, nearly fourteen hours after its start, the Indian troops defending Sardar post withdrew to retreat two miles south to their Vigiokot post. Having succeeded in driving the Indians from Sardar post, the Pakistani forces did not realise it had been vacated and were already in the process of their own withdrawal to their original positions. By the evening of 9 April, after a day of heavy fighting, the Indian forces realised that Sardar post was still unoccupied by Pakistan and then reoccupied it without any fighting. A later Indian government report into the war described this episode with some accuracy as proving that 'Commander of Pak 51 Brigade handled the operations as ineptly as Brigadier Pahlajani of 31 Indian Infantry Brigade' (Chakravorty, 26).

The attack had not gone according to plan for Pakistan, as although its forces had eventually forced the Indian troops out (without realising it), co-ordination between the attacking forces had been poor and it had been shown that with a determined defence, the Indian posts were going to be harder to remove than GHQ in Rawalpindi had imagined. Brigadier Azhar was now to be effectively sidelined for the duration of the conflict as a result of the rather botched operation, but the real significance of the operation was that for the first time since 1948, Pakistan had now initiated the use of force in a dispute with India—evidence of real confidence in its military strength by this time.

Both sides realised that the situation on the ground was escalating and both armies now reinforced their respective positions. Major-General P. O. Dunn was now appointed commander of the region by the Indian government, and he moved his HQ from Bombay to Khavda, while 50 Para Brigade was sent to Kutch on 9 April, comprising 2 and 3 Para battalions, which meant that by 18 April India had two regular army brigades inside Kutch; these were now designated as 'Kilo Force' by Indian GHQ and Dunn was now GOC Kilo Force (Chakravorty, 26). It appears from Dunn's orders that the Indian position was still essentially defensive, as the orders were to maintain the Indian positions at Sardar and Vigiokot posts rather than remove Pakistani border posts, but India was still not ready to concede any territory to Pakistan. Pakistan meanwhile moved the whole of 8 Infantry Division to Hyderabad from Karachi as Pakistan's GHQ was now expecting a strong Indian reaction to the Pakistani attack on Sardar post. The Pakistan 8 Infantry Divison consisted of four brigades, 6 Brigade under Brigadier Iftikhar Janjua, 51 Brigade under K. M. Azhar (which had already seen action at Sardar post), 52 Brigade under Brigadier Sardar Ismail and Divisional Artillery under Brigadier S. M. Aslam. It was the arrival of the artillery brigade with its armour and artillery that was to pose a real threat to the Indian posts inside Kutch.

On the diplomatic front, Pakistan replied to the Indian Note of 10 April by rejecting the Indian allegations and renewed its demands for a ceasefire and high level political talks. Shastri stated in the Indian parliament that India would insist on Pakistan leaving the position at Kanjarkot before India would enter into discussions on border demarcation. On 14 April India announced that it agreed in principle to Pakistan's three point plan of 9 April but would not agree to a ceasefire until Pakistan vacated Kanjarkot; this was rejected on 15 April by Bhutto who issued a statement reiterating Pakistan's claim that the northern half of the Rann of Kutch was disputed territory and asserted that Kanjarkot fell within Pakistan's territory and therefore there was no question of accepting any conditions as to its evacuation. On 14 April the Pakistan High Commissioner to India, Mr Arshad Hussain, called on the Indian Foreign Secretary, Mr C. S. Jha, and stated that as Kanjarkot lay within Pakistan, his government could not order its evacuation, and as long as India insisted on this as a precondition to meaningful negotiations, Pakistan would neither begin them at an official level nor agree to order a formal ceasefire. The diplomatic front was therefore not able to progress; both sides were not ready to concede an inch at this stage in the border dispute, and negotiations could not even begin. In addition, for political reasons India was reluctant to be seen as yielding to Pakistani military pressure and Pakistan was keen to press ahead with full knowledge of its local advantage.

On that same day, 14 April, the Commander-in-Chief of the Pakistan Air Force (PAF), Air Marshal Asghar Khan, telephoned his counterpart in the Indian Air Force (IAF) to make the extraordinary suggestion that both air forces should stay out of this dispute in order to avoid escalation. Although the exact details are unclear, it appears that the suggestion was accepted by his Indian counterpart with the caveat that the air forces would be permitted to supply front line troops (Chakravorty, 26). Whether this suggestion of Asghar Khan had been cleared with Ayub or GHQ in Rawalpindi is doubtful, and it is interesting that Asghar Khan does not mention this episode in his book about the war, *The First Round: India-Pakistan War 1965* (Islamic Information Services, 1979). This offer was apparently unknown to General Mohammad Musa, the Commander-in-Chief of the Pakistan Army, and was doubtless one of the factors that persuaded Ayub to allow Asghar Khan to retire soon afterwards despite planning for further military action taking place.

The Indian government kept the door open for negotiation and it appears from the relatively moderate tone and measures taken by the Indian government that it did not want the Kutch dispute to escalate into war and wanted to defuse the situation while trying to persuade Pakistan to evacuate Kanjarkot. Secondly, the Indian Army and government were fully aware of the difficult lines of communication and of India's military disadvantage in the Kutch region and so could not, without a large risk, take the military offensive there. Pakistan was obviously enjoying the local military advantage and so maintained the pressure on India through Bhutto, who again stated clearly that there was no chance of Pakistan accepting any condition as to the evacuation of Kanjarkot. He repeated a request for India to cease all the military preparations and asked for clarification on whether or not India was prepared to talk without preconditions (*Dawn*, 16 April 1965).

Operation Arrow Head

The next phase of military activity now became inevitable as diplomatic attempts had failed, and in fact, since the last major clash of 8/9 April at Sardar post, both sides had built up their respective military forces inside Kutch. With the Indian infantry now occupying the high ground around Sardar/Vigiokot, the Indian paratroopers had established posts on tracks leading across the Great Rann to Biar Bet, around 25 miles east of

Kanjarkot. Chhad Bet was also reinforced but India did not have armoured vehicles at its disposal in the region. The task of these units was obviously to assist the SRP in establishing a network of posts in the northern part of the disputed area and try to present Pakistan with a tough defensive position. By 17 April, Tikka Khan's plan for dominating the border area was complete and the objective was the removal of the Indian posts close to the Pakistani positions and also to bottle up the Indian forces in the Rann by cutting off the only road available to them. This was codenamed Operation Arrow Head and was ambitious enough to threaten all-out war as it was aimed at nothing less than the capture and/or destruction of the two Indian brigades inside Kutch, which India was unlikely to accept without some retaliation in Punjab or Kashmir.

On 18 April, Tikka Khan ordered 6 Brigade Group under Brigadier Iftikhar Janjua to move to the Rahimki-Bazaar-Jat Trai area and, with the help of the armoured regiments at its disposal, to 'dominate no-man's land' (M. Ahmed, 5). This was a more aggressive posture than before and the Pakistani build-up of troops across the border, particularly tanks, did not go unnoticed by India. General Dunn's request for more troops and armour could not be met by the Indian GHQ as it was aware of the difficulty in large-scale troop movements to Kutch, and Dunn was ordered to hold his ground rather than plan any offensives (K. C. Praval, *India's Paratroopers*, Thomson Press (India), 1974, 244). On the night of 19/20 April the Pakistani battalions of 6 Punjab and 15 Punjab began to aggressively patrol the region towards Vigiokot, and on 20 April Pakistani artillery began to shell Indian positions at Point 84 (also known as Sera Bet) in the Chhad Bet area. The shelling was heavy enough for the Indians to abandon the posts at Point 84 on 20 April. Raiding parties were sent out by Brigadier Iftikhar on 20/21 April to probe at Indian positions near Sera Bet and Gullu Talao. Dunn now ordered 3 Para with mortar and artillery support to reoccupy Sera Bet, but India was still confident that no major move would be made by Pakistan. The prevailing logic for the Indian commanders was that Pakistan's moves would be essentially defensive due to the relative failure of the attack on Sardar post, and Indian commanders also expected any Pakistani attack to occur after 15 May when the monsoon rains would force India to withdraw the bulk of its forces to the southern part of the Rann, and so they were not at the high state of alert against a possible Pakistani attack as they should have been (Chakravorty, 29–31).

On 23 April General Musa, the Commander-in-Chief of the Pakistan Army, gave the green light for Arrow Head with orders for 6 Brigade to move forward from its current position and clear Indian positions around and including Sera Bet; the order was to be carried out by first light on 24 April. This was potentially a large-scale concerted military push for the capture/destruction of Indian troops within Kutch. Within hours of receiving the order, Brigadier Iftikhar finalised plans for the capture of Biar Bet and Chhad Bet, with the timing of the attack fixed for 0230 hours on 24 April. Following shelling by Pakistani artillery and (so the Indians claimed) tank fire, by 0730 PST 24 April Sera Bet (also known as Point 84) had been captured by Pakistani forces. The Indians were surprised by the scale of the assault which they claimed involved two tank squadrons, armoured personnel carriers and artillery, and it was unsurprising that Sera Bet was captured relatively quickly and without much resistance from the Indian defenders (M. Ahmed, 7).

The next day, 25 April, Pakistan turned its attention to the capture of Biar Bet, which was first attacked in the afternoon of that day. Fighting went on intermittently throughout the night and India managed to send some reinforcements overnight to Biar Bet, but it was to prove of no avail as the *bet* was virtually indefensible against the Pakistani attacking force. Although a company of the Indian 3 Paratroopers held Biar Bet, the

Pakistani assault using both tanks and artillery was too much and by 0730 hours, 26 April, Biar Bet and a large quantity of arms and equipment were also captured by Pakistani forces (Chakravorty, 34). Pakistan added to India's public discomfort by flying national and international journalists to Biar Bet to show the arms and ammunition left behind by the retreating Indian soldiers.

India was humiliated in the fighting and now had to decide its next move with public opinion calling out for some reaction to the latest Pakistani offensive. Pakistan's GHQ now felt they had the measure of the Indian Army—purely on the basis of a limited border clash involving no more than a couple of brigades on either side. Ayub was now made aware through Western channels of growing Indian public anger and the likelihood of all-out war if Arrow Head was carried to its planned conclusion, and therefore ordered all plans for further advance movements in Kutch to cease with immediate effect. Ayub was effectively cancelling Operation Arrow Head without the public of either India or Pakistan even being aware of its existence.

Diplomatic pressure for a ceasefire

Although the capture of Biar Bet marked the end of 8 Division's offensive operations in Kutch according to the Pakistani version, the Indians were now increasingly convinced that Pakistan was going to move against other Indian posts inside the Rann, and tensions rose. The capture of the Indian military posts in the *bets* and the use by Pakistan of both armour and artillery in the area (despite increasingly incredible Pakistani denials) led to widespread anger and concern in India. On 24 April General J. N. Chaudhri, the Indian Army Commander-in-Chief, called senior US military officers based at the American Embassy in Delhi and began by stating dramatically, 'Gentleman, I am faced with a crisis'. He then gave an outline of the military position at

Kutch and said that the Pakistan attack at Biar Bet was launched using US Chaffee tanks in squadron force. General Chaudhri said that he did not have any armour in the area, nor could he employ any as it would need to be moved long distances by rail and then road, after which his tanks would be useless. Chaudhri said it was his clear understanding that if either India or Pakistan used US weapons on each other and not against communist threats, then the US would intervene, and he wanted to know what the US planned to do (Delhi to State, POL 32–1 India-Pak, NA).

On the same day in the White House, a memorandum was prepared on exactly this matter, the facts and regulations regarding the use of American weapons by Pakistan; it was emphasised that although hard facts were difficult to come by, it appeared clear that Pakistan had a military advantage thanks to the terrain it was exploiting and was using forces equipped by the US (Read to Bundy, POL 32–1 India-Pak NA). It did not however criticise the use of American weapons, nor did it suggest any action to prevent their use.

The Indians feared that Pakistan was now planning to move deeper in Kutch and there were sufficient concerns as to Pakistan's long-term intentions in Kutch, that on 26 April Y. B. Chavan, the Defence Minister, ordered a general mobilisation of India's army and the deployment of Indian troops along the Punjab border (Chakravorty, 34–5). The Indian Foreign Secretary, C. S. Jha, informed John Freeman, the British High Commissioner to India, that there was now a danger of a general war with Pakistan. India was conscious of its local disadvantage in Kutch and now began a large-scale movement and concentration of its troops along other sectors of the India-Pakistan border, particularly in the Punjab where India was confident that its larger troop numbers would count. In messages sent to both the Indian Prime Minister and the Pakistan President on 28 April the British Prime Minister, Harold Wilson, expressed his deep concern at the situation that had developed in the Rann of Kutch and offered to help resolve the issue by the offer of mediation if both governments so wished. In the messages Wilson proposed an immediate ceasefire followed by a withdrawal of troops to the positions occupied on 1 January 1965 and a negotiated determination of the frontier. Shastri accepted Wilson's proposals but stated in the Indian parliament that if Pakistan persisted in its aggressive activities then the Indian Army would defend the country and would 'decide its own strategy and the employment of its manpower and equipment in the manner in which it deems best' (Sir Morrice James, *Pakistan Chronicle*, Oxford University Press, 1993, 124).

This was reported in the Pakistani press of 29 April under the headline 'India to choose its own battleground' (*Dawn*, 29 April 1965) None of this could disguise the fact that India was unlikely to win back Kanjarkot, Biar Bet and Point 84 militarily, and the Pakistani claim of having inflicted heavy losses on the Indian troops had a plausible ring of truth even to Indians (Gulzar Ahmed, *Pakistan Meets Indian Challenge*, Al Mukhtar Publishers, 1967, 70). What concerned the British—who seemed to be more involved and concerned than the Americans—were the possible ramifications of the fighting, how it might spread along the Punjab border and lead to all-out war. The British High Commissioner to Pakistan, Sir Morrice James, said that he spent 28 and 29 April trying to impress on Bhutto and others the real anger in India at what they saw as Pakistani aggression and 'the very real risk that they would decide to retaliate elsewhere' (James, 124).

With India having accepted the offer of mediation from Wilson, on 29 April Ayub replied to Wilson's proposals by saying that since India did not acknowledge the existence of a territorial dispute, the ceasefire must be followed by a withdrawal of forces from the disputed area, but did not rule out an immediate ceasefire. On 30 April Wilson sent a further message to President Ayub suggesting that he should order an unconditional ceasefire for seven days while the British government tried to clear up misunderstandings about the Indian attitude. A similar message was delivered to Shastri and James flew to New Delhi on 30 April and convinced him that a peaceful solution could be found to the conflict. Ayub and Shastri now agreed to the idea of British mediation and Ayub ordered his troops not to advance any further, which meant there was now a *de facto* ceasefire in place.

Thanks to Wilson's timely intervention, a practical ceasefire was achieved without being made public and Pakistani forces were ordered not to push forward and execute Arrow Head as envisaged, which would have led to Pakistan trying to capture or remove the Indian brigades in the Rann. The order by Pakistan's GHQ to effectively scrap Arrow Head and not to move further into Kutch 'astounded' Brigadier (later General) Gul Hassan who was Director Military Operations (DMO) at GHQ; he stated later that he learned of this order from Tikka Khan rather than from GHQ where he was located. Had Arrow Head been executed in its entirety, Tikka Khan would have attempted not only the capture of much territory of the Rann claimed by Pakistan but also the plan to 'destroy the enemy trapped' between 6 Brigade and 51 Brigade (G. Ahmed, 6). Gul Hassan felt that if Pakistan 'had bagged the bulk of the invading force, which was within our grasp, I doubt they would have opposed us so confidently in Kashmir a little later' (General Gul Hassan, *Memoirs*, Oxford University Press 1993, 165–6). While it is quite possibly true that Pakistan could have exploited its military position in Kutch further at this point as India was unable to deploy either armour or artillery to the region, Gul Hassan seems not to have appreciated the mood within India and the build-up of Indian forces along the Punjab border factors, nor the international pressure on Pakistan to stop provoking India and to settle the dispute amicably. Ayub was, as mentioned previously, more aware of the real possibility of all-out war if India had been pushed further, and he decided that his troops had shown enough of their superiority for peace moves to continue.

In an effort to assist with Wilson's plea for a ceasefire, on the morning of 30 April McConaughy met Ayub to inform him that the United States was unhappy with the use of American aid equipment in the Rann of Kutch, and later on the same day the Pakistan government learned from its ambassador in Washington that the US was officially, if privately, objecting to the fact that US military equipment was being misused in a dispute between India and Pakistan (Cohen and Tucker (eds), 156). Although the Americans had remained publicly silent and non-committal during fighting in Kutch, they wished to see tension reduced in South Asia, and so the intervention was timed to assist the British initiative, and although it was not well received in Pakistan, it was seen in the context of the desire to stop the fighting in Kutch from escalating, and as a reminder to Pakistan of its reliance on US weapons.

British mediation

The hard slog of patient diplomacy now began, with James and Freeman tasked by Wilson with trying to find mutually acceptable proposals for both sides while trying to ensure that the uneasy peace was not disturbed. The negotiations were orchestrated by the Commonwealth Office in London and in Pakistan James dealt with Aziz Ahmed, the Foreign Secretary, while Freeman dealt with Jha. James said that he was forced at certain sticking points to appeal directly to Ayub when Aziz Ahmed was too inflexible, and at one point James was frustrated enough to suggest to Aziz Ahmed that he should communicate directly with his Indian counterpart: at which suggestion 'Aziz reacted almost with horror'. Although the British took the lead in the negotiations, James confirms that the Americans were kept fully informed of the mediation efforts and gave the British initiative their full support and had stated their willingness to become involved if needed (James, 125–6). On 4 May the first draft of the British government proposal was put to both sides, but almost immediately rejected by Pakistan. On 5 May the Pakistan government said in response to the proposals that if the Indians were to keep a post in Chhad Bet, then the Pakistanis must also keep a post at Biar Bet. Despite this unpromising start, it was on 5 May that a public announcement was made in Pakistan of the *de facto* ceasefire.

On 6 May McConaughy reviewed all the agreements between the US and Pakistan and India to see what assurances had been given by the US to both countries in case the Kutch talks were unsuccessful and both sides appealed to the US for help. The first agreement was the military aid treaty signed with Pakistan in 1954, which had stipulated that the military aid equipment provided by the USA was to be used for self-defence purposes by Pakistan, and there was an assurance in that treaty that Pakistan would not undertake an act of aggression against any other country. The issue of a US promise to Pakistan to protect it against Indian aggression was given in explicit assurances by following US aid to India, given in an *aide-mémoire* on 5 November 1962 stating that the 'US will come to Pakistan's assistance in the event of aggression from India against Pakistan'. On 17 November of the same year, the State Department had stated that if US aid to India was misused and directed at Pakistan, then the US 'would undertake to thwart such aggression'. Similar assurances had been given to India in 1954 by President Eisenhower who stated that if Pakistan used its US weapons against India in an act of aggression, he would undertake to intervene (6/5/65 POL 32–1 India-Pak NA). It was these assurances that both India and Pakistan were now relying on to pressure the US to support its position, but so far, in

Kutch, it was India alleging use by Pakistan of American weapons. The US response had been subdued thus far; it is interesting to speculate how a hard US line with Pakistan on the use of its equipment during the Kutch dispute might have discouraged Ayub from later action, but it appears that in April/ May 1965 the US was bogged down with Vietnam and other issues and did not want to provoke Pakistan further after an already bruising few months.

India's continued military build-up along the border with Pakistan was causing some concern to Ayub and his government, and on 7 May Pakistan complained to the UN Security Council that the bulk of the Indian armed forces had been moved to Pakistan's Punjab border and were poised in offensive formations. India did not deny this allegation and Pakistan detailed the complaint by stating that four infantry divisions, one armoured division and an armoured brigade had been deployed within 25 miles of Indian Punjab and another Army unit had moved closer to the Kashmir ceasefire line. A British military review later stated that the Indian 1 Armoured Division was moved from Jhansi to east of Amritsar, 15 Infantry Division was moved from Dehra Dun to Amritsar, 4 Mountain Division from Ambala to Ferozepur, 6 Mountain Division from Bareilly to Jullundur, 2 Armoured Brigade from Patiala to south of Amritsar, 116 Mountain Brigade was moved from southern India and ordered to come under the control of 4 Mountain Division. 7 Infantry Division was normally stationed along the border and was now concentrated in Ferozepur. Therefore, by May 1965, India had moved one armoured division, one independent armoured brigade, and four infantry/mountain divisions under the operational control of 11 Corps at Jullundur. Along the Kashmir border, the Indian troops remained much as before, namely three infantry divisions (25, 26 and 19) and independent infantry brigades under 15 Corps at Udhampur (*India-Pakistan War*, May 1966 Ministry of Defence, PRO

British military review, 4–5). The Pakistan Army had far smaller resources at its disposal and had traditionally stationed the bulk of its forces close to the Indian Punjab/Kashmir border. Along this border Pakistan had 1 Armoured Division stationed at Kharian, 15 Infantry at Sialkot, 10 Infantry at Lahore; the latter two divisions being of four brigade strength. Along the Kashmir border, the 12 Infantry Division comprised one regular brigade and around 18 Azad Kashmir infantry battalions. Apart from 6 Armoured Division and some elements of 8 Infantry Division, Pakistan had no real reserves.

On 10 May, revised British government proposals were put to both sides and again these were rejected by Pakistan because there was no reference to the two sides' claims as to what constituted the dispute. Pakistan also objected as it did not consider that the arbitration procedures laid out in the proposals were tight enough, but Ayub made it clear that Pakistan was prepared to drop its insistence on retaining a post at Bair Bet, thereby accepting the principle of a return to the status quo. Bhutto also expressed concern about the concentration of troops elsewhere along the India-Pakistan border and suggested a separate and possibly confidential agreement on disengagement.

Weighing in behind the scenes, but with heavy diplomatic pressure, were the Americans who on 12 May informed both India and Pakistan officially that they were prohibiting the use of American weapons in the Kutch area. Although both sides were informed of this decision, it was Pakistan that was always going to be more affected as not only had it managed to send tanks and artillery to the Kutch front, but almost the entire Pakistan Army equipment was of American origin, and banning US equipment from the area effectively meant that Pakistan could not officially use much of its military equipment in Kutch. The decision put further strain on an already fraught relationship and Bhutto warned that the US decision would have 'profoundly negative effects' on Pakistan's relationship with America (12/5/65 Read to Bundy NSC History of South Asia, NSC LBJ).

On 13 May the US State Department considered the use of American weapons by both sides in the Kutch dispute. The summary of the analysis was that Pakistan had admitted the use of some US weapons and American observers had witnessed the use of US vehicles, communications equipment and 106mm recoilless rifles. The presence of such weapons on the Indian side was also observed but there was no hard evidence of their use. The conclusion was that although the weapons had been supplied for 'legitimate self defence' both sides appeared to have used the weapons, which explains the decision to warn both sides. The issue was recognised as complicated and difficult as both India and Pakistan were using US weapons supplied to them; it opened up the whole issue of separating US-supplied equipment from non-US equipment in military action. It appears that the Americans had not seriously contemplated this scenario and knew that such a directive was hard to enforce, and were merely making their position and displeasure known to both sides (Hughes to Acting Secretary, 13/5/1965 Pakistan Memos Vol III 12/64—7/65 LBJ). Despite the prohibition, by this time both sides had effectively stopped fighting and although the ban came too late to have any effect on the fighting, it assisted the British mediators, which was no doubt the objective of the intervention.

On 15 May new British proposals were put to both sides including a non-specific formula on patrolling, the preamble containing a watered-down reference to disengagement. A proposal was made that both sides' claims to the disputed area should be dealt with by reference to what both had said in letters sent to the United Nations, but on 18 May the Indian government reply rejected the 15 May proposals, mainly because the wording on patrolling was deemed unacceptable. On 27 May the British suggested to both sides that there should be a separate and simultaneous agreement on disengagement, a principle which was accepted by Ayub but refused by Shastri.

The main obstacles to the agreement at this stage were Pakistan's reluctance to withdraw forces from the Rann of Kutch, thereby restoring the position as at 1 January 1965, and India's reluctance to agree to submission of the dispute to an independent tribunal. From 1 to 15 June, detailed negotiations continued on the mechanism for a face-saving and dignified end to this conflict. By mid June, the Indian government was losing patience with the whole process and Shastri instructed B. K. Nehru, the Indian ambassador to the US, to inform the Americans that India had reached its limit in concessions to Pakistan and if Pakistan would not move diplomatically, then India would have to stop diplomatic means and move to military ones. The Americans must have been concerned by this message, and replied that another break out of hostilities would lead to dire consequences (James, 126).

The exhausting and tedious negotiations then received a boost when both Ayub and Shastri visited London for a Commonwealth summit. On 15 June Wilson met Shastri who complimented the British High Commissioner in Delhi, Freeman, on his role in helping to arrange the ceasefire. Shastri said that India could not go further than Wilson's letter of 12 May and if the question of patrols on the Ding-Surai track could be resolved, there was little else outstanding. Wilson asked if Shastri had contemplated a meeting between himself and Ayub, to which Shastri replied that he had not as he doubted the value of such a meeting and would prefer to continue the indirect diplomacy using the two British High Commissioners. Shastri said that a resolution of the issue was now urgent and Pakistan must give up the issue of patrols, particularly now that the area was flooded and so the notion of patrols was unreal. As for the Indian forces moved to the Pakistan border, Shastri said that once the Kutch issue was resolved, this matter would also be settled. He said that his position was clear; he would not agree to a single document dealing with both the Kutch issue and the withdrawal of forces. Shastri felt that a time limit on talks should be set by the British, but Wilson said he was reluctant to do this as it would cause a crisis if the matter was not resolved within that time frame. Shastri ended the meeting by saying that although he had 'great respect' for Ayub, the latter had caused him great harm and his connection with China was 'particularly damaging' (15/6/65, Downing Street Notes, PREM 13–190 PRO).

The next day it was the turn of the Pakistan delegation to meet Wilson. On 16 June Ayub Khan, Bhutto and the Pakistan High Commissioner in London, Agha Hilaly (brother of Agha Shahi, also in the Pakistan Foreign Ministry) met Wilson at 10 Downing Street. Ayub Khan started the talks with reference to Rhodesia rather than the Kutch issue, which seems surprising given the urgency and seriousness of the situation in Kutch and along the Punjab border. Ayub thanked Wilson and the British government for their assistance to date and was complimentary regarding James' efforts in securing a ceasefire. Wilson said he understood that the issues had narrowed down to patrolling on a single track. Ayub produced a map showing the disputed territory and a track that India wished to continue to patrol. Ayub claimed that Pakistan only wished to patrol the track around Kanjarkot to prevent both smuggling and incursions. Wilson stated that Shastri had agreed to binding arbitration on the condition that it did not prejudice Indian patrols. Ayub stated that without patrolling rights being the subject of arbitration, there seemed little point to the arbitration. Ayub did, however, reiterate that negotiations needed to continue and if they could not settle all the issues in London, then the talks could continue in Karachi or Delhi. Ayub said that he was even prepared to meet Shastri, even though he 'disliked and despised him'. Ayub then produced another map which claimed that Indian forces on the ICK side were now up to seven divisions including armoured and mountain divisions—the latter equipped with British and American weapons.

Wilson said it was his impression that Shastri might be willing to move Indian forces back to positions before the recent outbreak of fighting in Kutch and wanted to know if Ayub was willing to give such an undertaking in principle. Ayub said that he was, although he believed that the Indians would 'try to cheat'. He said Pakistan knew very well which Indian troops had recently moved into previously unoccupied areas and the Indians might not play fair on this. Ayub continued that Pakistan would do its best but he did not hold out much hope as he believed that 'all Indians were dishonourable rascals'. Ayub repeated that the proper solution for Kutch was for both sides to give up patrolling and Pakistan, was even prepared to give up Kanjarkot, not out of right but as a gesture of goodwill (16/6/65, Downing Street Notes, PREM 13–190 PRO).

The Kutch Agreement

As a result of patient and inexhaustible British diplomacy, American pressure and the reluctance of both sides to begin a war over 'the possession of various ruined forts on sandbanks in a tidal marsh', (British military review), (4) there was finally an agreement on the mechanism of resolving the Kutch dispute on 30 June. The Kutch agreement was signed simultaneously in Delhi and Karachi and the ceasefire was to be effective from 0530 hours PST, 1 July 1965. The mediation process had taken nearly two months to reach a successful conclusion, but even during the hostilities which were to follow, the ceasefire in the Rann held firm.

The Kutch Agreement was a relatively short document considering the painstaking diplomacy it had taken to agree it: a preamble and three articles. Under Article 1 the ceasefire was to take effect from 0030 GMT 1 July, whereupon all troops on both sides would immediately begin to withdraw to positions in the area of Gujarat/West Pakistan which were occupied on 1

January 1965, and this process was to be completed within seven days.

Article 2 then defined the status quo which was to be restored, that of 1 January 1965, as well as the procedure for maintaining it. Upon the completion of the withdrawals the Indians could reoccupy Chhad Bet post in strength no greater than that employed on 31 December 1964, and Indian and Pakistani police could patrol the tracks which they had patrolled prior to 1 January 1965. Article 3 acknowledged that on 11 January 1960 both India and Pakistan had agreed that the Rann border was still disputed and a Tribunal would study all relevant material before holding talks with both sides and then try to arrive at a settlement which took into account the rival claims.

Article 3 concluded by providing that within one month of the ceasefire Indian and Pakistani ministers would meet to seek agreement on the determination of the border and to arrange fresh demarcation. The next provision set down a timetable for the establishment of a three-member Tribunal, which would be constituted within four months of the ceasefire and whose decisions would be binding on both India and Pakistan. No member of the Tribunal could be from either India or Pakistan, but each side could nominate one member from another country and the chairman would be appointed by the UN Secretary General if a choice had not been agreed. Each government was free to develop its case before the tribunal, whose decision was not to be questioned on any ground, and its findings were to be implemented in full as quickly as possible. Any differences in opinion over the implementation would be referred to it for a final decision. For this reason, the tribunal had to remain in being until its findings had been implemented in full.

The agreement was generally welcomed in Pakistan and Ayub Khan described it as a victory for common sense and a model for the resolution of all India/Pakistan disputes should other means fail. He was, of course, thinking of Kashmir, and Ayub and

Bhutto were delighted by the mechanism in Article 3 of the Agreement which provided precisely for the binding nature of the independent tribunal's award. At one point in the negotiations, Aziz Ahmed was said to have turned to Ayub and said, 'I think we have found our Kashmir negotiator' (James, 125).

In India, however, the agreement was denounced by opposition political parties and some political critics of Shastri described the whole Kutch affair as a disaster for India. They also alleged that Shastri had violated the undertaking given to parliament to make no territorial concessions to Pakistan, and they objected to India's evacuation of posts in the Rann of Kutch within areas regarded as Indian territory. Even worse, in those critics' view, Pakistan would continue to patrol some of the supposed track that partly ran through the territory; while Indian acceptance of independent determination of the issue of sovereignty over what they (the critics) deemed to be Indian territory was seen as a bad precedent. Furthermore, while Pakistan regarded the agreement as a model for the settlement of India/Pakistan disputes, Indian politicians were anxious that they should not be seen as establishing a precedent and were determined to resist any attempt to extend the principles of the Kutch dispute to the Kashmir dispute.

As set out in the Kutch agreement, a Tribunal of three was established to demarcate the border. The Pakistan government nominated Nasrollah Entzam, a former Iranian Foreign Minister, the Indians nominated Ales Bebler, a Yugoslav judge, and the UN Secretary-General nominated Gunnar Lagergren, a senior Swedish judge, as Chairman of the Kutch panel. The Tribunal began its deliberations soon after being established but the final award was not announced until 19 February 1968. Under it Pakistan was awarded Kanjarkot and Chhad Bet in a total award of 828 square miles; Biar Bet, Point 84 and Sardar post remained with India.

Kutch reviewed

The whole Kutch episode was perceived by Ayub and GHQ as evidence for the widespread patronising and racist assumption that 'the Hindu has no stomach for a fight', which even Altaf Gauhar admits now had become 'a belief, if not a military doctrine' (Gauhar, 312). This was to have a disastrous bearing on the future dealings in Kashmir and with Shastri, as it induced a sense of false confidence regarding future military clashes. The Indian military build-up was seen as a bluff, and although the Pakistan government had complained of the large build-up of Indian forces on the Punjab border, it noted that no Indian military action had been taken. Pakistani newspapers published interviews with senior Pakistani commanders who stated that the fighting had been easy as the Indians 'would hardly ever allow themselves to get too close to the Pakistanis. Even at the sight of the Pakistanis they fled the field in much disorder'. During his visit to London during the Commonwealth conference, Ayub told a meeting that the Indians were 'squealing like they did after their conflict with China' and if war was to break out 'we shall hurt India beyond repair' (Russell Brines, *The Indo-Pakistan Conflict*, Pall Mall Press, 1968, 290).

Ayub, Bhutto and an increasing number of senior figures within the Pakistan government now began to be convinced that India was not serious in launching an offensive across the international border against Pakistan and did not want a general war. This was one of the many errors of judgement for which Pakistan was to pay a heavy price in the events that unfolded. Although he was a military man, Ayub also did not appear to realise that in Kutch, Pakistan was fighting in an area where the terrain was heavily in Pakistan's favour with armour available to the Pakistan side and with India at a huge local disadvantage as its forces were unable to move artillery or armour to the area. Ayub also failed to realise that whatever Shastri's misgivings over the manner in which he had agreed to settle the Kutch dispute, no Indian politician, with the possible exception of Nehru, could survive major concessions over the Kashmir issue, particularly concessions in the face of Pakistan's use of force. The final ominous sign that Pakistan chose to ignore was the studied silence of the US as it stayed quiet during the fighting and left the diplomatic manoeuvring to the British. The fact that the US only objected to Pakistan using American weapons after the fighting was over encouraged Ayub to believe that the US would turn a blind eye to their use in any future conflict too. All of these conclusions and assumptions were soon to be put to the test.

As far as the military campaign was concerned, it was undoubtedly a local and limited win for Pakistan whose local advantages had been put to good use and, like China in 1962, had achieved its immediate and local objectives; Pakistan was delighted that international pressure had helped persuade India to agree to binding arbitration. Whether the Kutch clashes would be a useful pointer to fighting in Kashmir or Punjab was another matter. For Ayub, however, Kutch helped convince him that India would succumb to military pressure from Pakistan and international diplomatic pressure from the West. Time would tell if these assumptions were correct, but drawing such wide ranging conclusions on the basis of a few days' localised fighting was always going to be risky.

4

OPERATION GIBRALTAR

De-freezing the Kashmir issue

Having viewed with satisfaction the Pakistan Army outgunning India, especially in the use of armour and artillery in the sand dunes of Kutch, Ayub was now a receptive listener to those who had been urging for some time that 1965 was an ideal time for a military solution to Kashmir. Ayub was by nature a cautious man who liked to weigh up and consider options presented by close advisers before making a decision. One of Ayub's cabinet ministers of the time, G. W. Choudhury, describes how the critical decisions were made by Ayub. A few cabinet ministers such as Bhutto were described as having some influence, 'but usually the cabinet would discuss peripheral issues such as a civil aviation pact...But the vital decisions—whether related to defence, foreign affairs or economic policy—were decided in the Presidential House with the help of an inner cabinet'. Rather than having a genuine debate in parliament or cabinet, Ayub's technique was to have senior military officers 'make a careful analysis of the pros and cons of the proposed course of action, one group presenting the case, while the other group acted as opponents of the proposed action'. In the case of proposed military action against India, 'this well-established practice was not allowed' (G. W. Choudhury, *The Last Days of United Pakistan*, Oxford University Press, 1993, 17–20). The arguments and voices of those in favour of the use of force in Kashmir, led by the Pakistan Foreign Ministry and a group of generals, became stronger and louder. The absence of genuine debate within the cabinet in Pakistan or even with all senior military officers led to obvious problems being overlooked or simply ignored.

Planning ways to reactivate the Kashmir issue and to consider a military solution went back as far as 1964. Ayub asked the Intelligence Bureau to consider ways of keeping the Kashmir issue alive, and in early 1964 Aziz Ahmed was made Chairman of the newly formed 'Kashmir Publicity Committee' with the rather vague instruction of 'keeping the Kashmir issue alive' (G. Ahmed, 21). With its meetings held in the home of the Education Secretary to ensure secrecy, the deliberations were not recorded on paper; the Director of Military Intelligence would also attend the meetings as a member. The Foreign Ministry, led by Bhutto and Aziz Ahmed, was convinced that if given military and political direction, the population of ICK would rise up in popular revolt against India, and it appears that the group agreed with this conclusion. It was soon apparent, however, that the Commander-in-Chief of the Pakistan Army, General Musa, was opposed to the idea as he felt that inadequate preparations were being made inside the Valley to organise armed resistance and that it would lead to a general war for which Pakistan was ill prepared and outnumbered. Musa also said that he wanted his opposition to the proposals noted for the record and for Ayub, and he claims that he ensured that he had a note sent to Ayub following one of the cell meetings in which he expressed his opposition to any premature military action. Ayub, Musa claimed, returned the note with the comment that 'he [Ayub] agreed with GHQ'. Musa also wrote of Bhutto's meeting with General Akhtar Malik, GOC 12 Division and other military officers, at the former's house where Bhutto would try and urge the 'indispensability of launching raids as soon as possible'. Musa says that he complained to Ayub about this 'brainwashing' by Bhutto and was assured by Ayub that he would put a stop to it (M. Musa, *My Version: India-Pakistan War 1965*, Lahore: Wajidalis, 1983, 5–10). The arguments used by the Foreign Ministry and Pakistan's Military Intelligence, both of which were broadly in favour of military action, were:

First, the recent military action in Kutch, which as discussed in the previous chapter had led Ayub to a number of military and diplomatic conclusions—all of which seemed to Ayub to point in favour of a successful limited military action by Pakistan. The feeling among some senior Pakistani generals was not only that the Indian Army was an ineffective fighting force in reality despite its large size, but also that the better quality US weapons gave Pakistan a military edge which could be exploited.

Second, late 1964 had seen a surge of anti-Indian feeling in the Valley of Kashmir and there were reasons to think, after Sheikh Abdullah's visit to Pakistan and the Hazrat Bal general strikes, that the political mood inside ICK was receptive to Pakistan's move into the area. The hope was that if Pakistani trained and armed irregular and regular forces and made a decisive move into Kashmir, the population would rise up and place the Indian government in a difficult position of suppressing a popular revolt in Kashmir and simultaneously fighting a war with Pakistan. Even the fact that Sheikh Abdullah was in prison could be an advantage as he could serve as a reminder of Indian repression.

Third, in the mid-1960s India was going through a difficult time politically and economically. A visit to South Asia by Talbot in 1964 reported that he had seen 'the sharpest contrast in years' between India and Pakistan, with Pakistan self-confident and with a 'new-found buoyancy' that was in stark contrast with India which was facing serious economic problems. India in early 1965 was coming to terms with communal riots, food shortages and slow economic growth under an inexperienced and unknown prime minister (Cohen and Tucker (eds), 145).

Fourth, India's rearmament programme post-1962 meant that Pakistan was going to face a very different Indian Army in terms of both size and training in 1970 than it would in 1965. If Pakistan was ever going to mount a serious military challenge to India in Kashmir, according to the hawks in the Pakistan establishment, it could not be left later than 1965/66. In 1965 Pakistan was seen as having more modern weapons and superior armed forces morale, and time was seen as being on India's side as its rearmament programme would mean that challenging it would be an almost impossible military proposition by 1970. Bhutto made no attempt to hide the fact that he urged Ayub to act quickly. He told his biographer that 'I wrote to Ayub Khan saying that if we wanted to pursue a policy of confrontation with India, time was running out. We had to act now or it was too late' (Salman Taseer, *Bhutto*, London: Ithaca Press, 1979, 60).

Fifth, Pakistan's 'new' foreign policy meant that of the major powers, Britain was on friendly terms with both India and Pakistan but unlikely to be much of a factor to consider in the event of a war. The three major powers that now counted in Asia were China, the USSR and the USA. China was now on extremely friendly terms with Pakistan as there was a common enemy in India and China was keen to make friends with a large Muslim state in Asia. In fact it is very likely that had the US not supplied weapons to Pakistan in the 1950s, Pakistan would have been requesting Chinese arms and equipment by 1965, but fear of the US reaction prevented such a request.

The USSR was still far from being pro-Pakistan in 1965, but it is fair to say that it was also a far less hostile presence at the UN. The Soviet leadership seemed receptive to Ayub on his visit earlier in the year and was increasingly convinced that there was a growing rift between the US and Pakistan which it might be able to exploit at some time in the future. Relations with the US had rarely been cooler since 1954 when Pakistan joined the military aid pacts of the US, but Ayub was still sure that the US bases inside Pakistan gave Pakistan enough leverage with the US to be able to befriend China and also threaten India without too hostile a US reaction. On the issue of Kashmir, the US position had generally been sympathetic to Pakistan since 1948 and US diplomats had consistently expressed their private view that Pakistan held the moral high ground in Kashmir and some irritation that India's refusal to make any concessions was threatening the stability of South Asia.

Finally, Ayub had been badly shaken by the recent presidential election which he knew (and had ensured) had been rigged in his favour to ensure victory over Miss Jinnah. The result meant that he felt the need to regain popularity at home, and it is true to say then as now that nothing united West Pakistan like the issue of Kashmir. Success in Kashmir would have meant that the election and its dubious result would almost certainly be forgiven and forgotten if Ayub could somehow wrest Kashmir out of Indian control.

In February 1965, a plan of action formulated by the Kashmir Publicity Committee was placed before the intelligence committee of the Pakistan cabinet with Bhutto, Aziz Ahmed, Musa and Gauhar present but in the absence of the heads of the Pakistan Air Force and Navy. After a presentation recommending the use of Pakistani soldiers sent into ICK disguised as Kashmiri guerrillas, Ayub asked who had given authority to the Foreign Ministry and ISI (Inter-Services Intelligence) to force a military campaign on the government of Pakistan. There was said to be some embarrassment around the table as Bhutto and the Committee were seen as having overstepped the mark, and Gauhar felt that was the end of the plan. This, however, turned out not to be the case (Gauhar, 320–21).

On 20 April the Americans learned of a private meeting in Rawalpindi chaired by Ayub following his visits to China and the USSR, from which the press was excluded but at which there was a briefing given to ministers, military officers and civil servants. Ayub said that he was 'more than satisfied with his visit to China' because the Chinese leadership 'had assured all-out support to Pakistan'. He said that he was attempting to undo the mistakes of the past by trying to befriend the USSR but it would take a long time to mend the damage from the past; however, he felt that the USSR might not veto a future Kashmir resolution if the issue were raised again in the Security Council. Ayub, it was reported, was asked by an audience member how Pakistan could survive as a small country in the position of a lamb between lions; he replied that he was not a lamb and that he knew how to live peacefully amongst lions by setting one lion against another. Ayub also said that he would retain Pakistan's membership of CENTO and SEATO and also friendship with the USSR and China (Pakistan Memo, Vol III 12/64 7/65, May 1965 LBJ Library).

Operation Gibraltar—the background

By the early summer of 1965 Ayub had secretly approved military planning for a limited war in Kashmir, despite opposition from Musa and a few other military senior officers, and his own reservations. Later General Akhtar Malik, GOC 12 Infantry Division and the man given the task of preparing a plan to reactivate the Kashmir issue, was to confirm, 'Ayub was fully involved in the enterprise. As a matter of fact it was his idea. And it was he who ordered me to bypass Musa while Gibraltar, etc. were being planned' (G. Ahmed, 553). Evidence from other senior military and civilian figures at the time tends to confirm that this was indeed the case. The decision to give Malik and 12 Division the authority to plan and execute military action inside ICK was now taken in great secrecy and was known only to a handful of Ayub's closest political and military advisers. Even some senior generals who it was thought might oppose the plan were unaware of what was going on and the Pakistan Air Force and Navy were not informed or consulted about this decision. Gul Hassan admits that the air force was never taken into full confidence by the army during this time as the PAF senior command was not considered to be 'as security minded' as the army. As for the navy, Gul Hassan says that GHQ was 'aware that we had such a service in the country and that it was located somewhere near Karachi.' (G. Hassan, 177–8).

The exact date is unknown, but it appears that after Ayub's first negative reaction to the plan in February 1965, in the spring/early summer GHQ directed Major-General Akhtar Hussain Malik, GOC 12 Division, to prepare a draft plan 'for deep raids' into ICK. This planning was to be done in consultation with GHQ and within the parameters defined by GHQ (Musa, 35). There is little doubt that the order to plan for 'deep raids' came from Ayub himself and despite Musa's objections, it was now for Malik to prepare and present a workable plan for Ayub's consideration. On 15 April Malik sent the Chief of Defence Staff an outline of a plan of military action inside ICK as requested, with a more detailed plan being sent on 9 May, and it was arranged that formal presentation of the plans to Ayub and other senior officers would be on 13 May 1965 at Murree, the headquarters of 12 Division. Also present at this briefing were General Mohammed Musa, the Chief of General Staff, Brigadier Irshad, the Director of Military Intelligence, and Brigadier Gul Hassan, the Director of Military Operations (G. Ahmed, 29).

The plan to be presented to Ayub by General Malik was not in essence very different from the one earlier outlined by the Kashmir Publicity Committee in February, but the planning was now more refined and consisted of two separate but interdependent moves: Operation Gibraltar and Operation Grand Slam. The fact of the presentation to Ayub was obviously known to those familiar with those close to the president, and a letter was sent from Bhutto to Ayub a day before the briefing urging him to approve the plans. Bhutto wrote that India was in 'no position' to risk a general war and Pakistan had either to act bravely now or to allow the initiative to pass to India which would launch an attack on Pakistan at a time of its choosing. Bhutto ended by saying, 'This is our hour of decision and may God guide us on the right path' (White Paper, Ministry of Foreign Affairs, Government of Pakistan, quoted by Gauhar, 322). There is some doubt as to whether Bhutto was present at the briefing; Gauhar maintains he was but Musa states that no civilian official attended the meeting (Gauhar, 322; Musa, 35).

Gibraltar was a daring plan to send thousands of Pakistani soldiers and paramilitaries from AK into ICK disguised as Kashmiri guerrillas, to engage Indian forces in ICK as well as leading a popular civilian revolt against Indian rule. Gibraltar itself was planned to be executed in two phases. The first phase was to create a shock wave by launching raiding parties on selected targets and areas and thereby preparing the ground for a civil uprising and causing a degree of chaos inside ICK. The second was the fusion of the civil uprising with the guerrilla operation, and was naturally reliant on the first phase being successfully carried out.

The aims of Operation Gibraltar were clearly laid down, with the objective given to 'create large-scale disturbances in Indian Held Kashmir which would force India to take major political and military steps to meet the situation and which in turn nullify her pretentious stand before the world that no political problem exists in Kashmir'. The armed fighters were meant to tie Indian forces down in a protracted guerrilla war in the way that US forces had been forced to fight a war of attrition in Vietnam. If India decided to widen the conflict by all-out war then 'a dangerous situation would be created in South Asia, which would force the Security Council and the United Nations and in particular the big powers, to take urgent steps to bring about a solution of the problem instead of treating it as a dead issue' (12 Division Final Report on Gibraltar, quoted in G. Ahmed, 29).

That, in essence, was the strategy which advocates of military action believed would unfold, as encapsulated in a few sentences. Because of the recent fighting in Kutch and the successful British mediation in bringing about not only a ceasefire but also a solution to the border issue in Kutch, there was real confidence amongst the advocates of action that the plans were, if not foolproof, then at least blessed with a very high chance of success and were a gamble worth taking with little apparent risk. The second part of the strategy to 'de-freeze' Kashmir presented that day by Malik was Operation Grand Slam. It is worth emphasising, in fairness to Malik, that he never appears to have envisaged that Gibraltar alone would succeed in driving India to the negotiating table over Kashmir, and he envisaged Grand Slam as a natural second part of the plan to create real pressure on India inside ICK.

Grand Slam was the code name given to the plan for an armoured thrust by 12 Division against Indian forces across the CFL at Akhnur, which was a critical supply line for Indian forces from India to Srinagar. The original plan as presented by Malik to Ayub was designed to be limited to a push across the Chhamb sector towards the town of Uri and to threaten Akhnur without any plan to take the town. It was obviously assumed by the military planners that the armoured thrust would be sufficient to create an international crisis in which India would be placed under pressure to return to the negotiating table with a view to making some serious concessions on Kashmir. At the briefing, however, Ayub pointed to Akhnur and said, 'But why don't you go for the jugular?' The fact that it was Ayub himself who suggested that targeting the town of Akhnur should become the main plan for Grand Slam is confirmed by almost every source present. It was in fact an excellent choice in purely military terms, as there is little doubt that Akhnur had real strategic value as the conduit to Srinagar and its capture would have put India under huge pressure inside ICK. Malik replied that he had not been able to plan for a push towards Akhnur because it would require more resources in terms of both money and men. Ayub sanctioned the necessary resources needed immediately, which meant that Grand Slam was now on a bigger and bolder scale than previously envisaged (Gauhar, 322; G. Ahmed, 82; Musa, 36).

The first indication that Altaf Gauhar claims that he (despite being a close confidant of Ayub's) to have received of Ayub's decision to try and push for a military solution in Kashmir was on 24 July when he met the president in the cabinet office and was told by him that 'a great deal will depend on how we handle the propaganda front'. Gauhar says that he was not immediately aware of the significance of the remark but Ayub then left the meeting and Bhutto took the chair and dramatically stated that the people of Kashmir were locked in a life or death struggle and Pakistan would not be forgiven if it remained 'an idle spectator'. Gauhar said he was asked by the Director of Military Intelligence to provide two Kashmiri speaking broadcasters for radio broadcasts and was told he would be given 24 hours notice 'before the curtain went up' (Gauhar, 315–16).

Ayub was convinced that military action was now the way by which Pakistan could solve the Kashmir issue once and for all, and the stage was set for him to test his convictions and conclusions.

Gibraltar—the preparation

Detailed planning for Gibraltar now had the green light and commenced on 17 May, just a few days after the Murree briefing and the go-ahead from Ayub. General Malik sent a note to all sector commanders telling them that it was time to:

discard hopes of peaceful settlement and adopt more aggressive measures which will compel India to either come to the negotiating table in chastened mood or face a growing menace in Kashmir imposing an ever increasing burden on her economy…Violent actions, if properly planned and conducted and these are launched with sufficient dispersion will create a shock wave which with continuous nourishment can engulf the whole of Indian Held Kashmir (Gibraltar Planning Directive 17/5/65, quoted G. Ahmed, 29).

This was a bold statement from the commander of 12 Division as his troops were badly outnumbered along the Kashmir border, but it was symptomatic of the confidence felt by some Pakistani generals at the time.

The Gibraltar forces were divided into six groups, each given a suitably inspiring Muslim military code name: Tariq, Qasim, Khalid, Salahuddin, Ghaznavi and Babur. Babur was the smallest of the groups with a force of only 34 men; the others were made up of approximately three platoons of 34 men each and a company headquarters of seven men with five to six officers per force to command the companies. Each of the five forces was provided with another 20 men and an officer from the Pakistan Army's elite Special Services Group (SSG). Apart from the SSG and some of the company officers, few regular Pakistani soldiers were used in the Gibraltar forces according to General Ahmed. The exact numbers involved in the Gibraltar forces were provided by General Ahmed and are the most detailed provided by anyone on either side of the conflict, estimates of 5–7,000 being provided by General Musa; no other precise figures are provided. The later Indian claim of tens of thousands appears to be an exaggeration and although the precise number may never be known, the figure of 5,000 provided by General Ahmed does not appear an unreasonable estimate. The bulk of the force was made up of Azad Kashmir soldiers, Northern Scouts and a local paramilitary group in Azad Kashmir known as Mujahids. All the Gibraltar forces were ordered to operate in civilian dress rather than military uniform.

The training of the force had been designed to prepare them for independent operations in enemy-held territory, with an emphasis on organising raids on formation and unit headquarters as well as attacking supply and ammunition dumps, laying ambushes and disrupting communications by blowing up bridges. Each man carried five days' cooked and five days' dry rations, and the troops were armed with light machine guns (one per section), Sten guns, rifles, 2 and 3 inch mortars, and grenades (four per man), 83 mm rocket launchers, anti-personnel mines and plastic explosives (200 pounds per company). Each force commander had a two-way wireless set, while the company was issued with four transistors, one each for the company and platoon commanders, on which orders could be received at a given frequency and at fixed times. They were also instructed to listen at fixed times to the Azad Kashmir radio for coded signals. Messages between platoon commanders, company commanders and force commanders were only to be sent by runner (G. Ahmed, 30).

Tariq force was to operate in the extreme north of the Kashmir Valley and was tasked with damaging Indian military communications in the area and holding the surrounding area. Qasim force was to the west of Tariq force and was to demolish strategic bridges in the area and then liaise with Salahuddin force.

Khalid force was to operate in the area west of Wular lake; aside from damaging communications and bridges, it was also to attack Indian Army forces in the area as well as the local power station. After carrying out the initial tasks, it was to operate south of the river Jhelum. The largest of the Gibraltar forces was Salahuddin, which comprised six companies. This force was to operate in the main Valley of Kashmir and was to isolate Srinagar by demolishing tunnels leading to it, and to disrupt telecommunications and the local airfield. The fifth force was Ghaznavi which was to operate near the CFL and base itself at Sunartop and to assist Salahuddin force. The sixth and smallest of the forces, Babur, was to raid the Headquarters of XV Corps at Udhampur.

After their initial orders and targets, all the Gibraltar teams were expected to remain in ICK and lead the second phase of the operation, the popular uprising. To facilitate the Gibraltar forces, another group was organised by the name of Nusrat, comprising fourteen groups each of 350 men. Nusrat forces were to harass Indian forces along the CFL immediately before the infiltration and assist the Gibraltar forces in their move into ICK. The Gibraltar forces were engaged in intensive training in July, and on 10 July a meeting at 12 Division HQ finalised the exact routes and plans for the force. On 13 July the final plans were presented by General Malik to both Ayub and Musa and approved. 7 August was fixed as the date of the move into ICK. The entire training and detailed planning for Gibraltar lasted therefore a total of ten weeks (G. Ahmed, 32).

The issue of whether any political and intelligence groundwork was done to prepare the local population for this large-scale infiltration has proved to be one of the most contentious matters, and the facts indicate obvious failures of planning. Unsurprisingly the military officers reviewing the operation have blamed the Foreign Ministry and intelligence services for this failure while Bhutto and political leaders blamed the military officers responsible for the plans. The simple fact was that no senior Kashmiri leader within ICK appears to have been taken into confidence as to the planning, no groundwork was done to prepare the local population in the event that assistance was required once inside ICK (which it inevitably would have been), and no account appears to have been taken of the fact that the Indians had developed an effective means of repressing the population of ICK, which meant that any support given to the Gibraltar forces would have incurred serious punishment. It was a surprisingly naive approach and one which was to cost the Gibraltar forces dearly, and for which Malik took personal responsibility:

Not informing pro-Pak elements before launching Gibraltar was a command decision and it was mine. The aim of the op was to defreeze the Kashmir issue, raise it from its moribund state and bring it to the notice of the world. To achieve this aim the first phase of the op was vital, i.e. to effect undetected infiltration of thousands across the CFL. I was not willing to compromise this in any event. And the whole op could be made stillborn by just one double agent (Letter to brother, quoted in Ahmed, 552).

As the Gibraltar forces would have to move many miles through mountainous terrain to reach their allotted areas, the move to the AK/ICK border began around 24 July and was able to progress without any Indian alarm bells ringing. Lt General Harbakhsh Singh, in charge of Western Command of the Indian Army, later regretted this as a 'poor reflection' on Indian intelligence (H. Singh, 1991: 29). An indication of how unaware the Indians were of Gibraltar was provided at a press conference in Srinagar on 3 August by India's Defence Minister Chavan. After a three-day inspection of Indian positions in the Kargil and Uri sector of the CFL, Chavan seemed blissfully unaware of any imminent threat, declaring that he was returning to Delhi with 'a sense of confidence and happiness'. He went on to say that he was satisfied with the border defences in Kashmir and also that the number of Pakistani violations of the CFL was now far less since the Kutch ceasefire agreement had been signed (*The Hindu*, 5/8/65).

Gibraltar—the execution

Although 7 August was the date specified by General Ahmed as D-Day for the Gibraltar force to begin its infiltration of ICK, it seems to be have been brought forward by two days as it was on 5 August that the order was given for the move across the CFL to start Operation Gibraltar. On the night of 5 August an Indian patrol was attacked by a group of approximately seventy men at a point 8,000 yards from the CFL in the Galuti sector of Jammu. On the same night on the northern slopes of the Pir Panjal range near Gulmarg, a hill station about eight mountainous miles from this CFL and 23 miles west of Srinagar, there was a second clash with Indian troops. The Home Minister of ICK, D. P. Dhar, visited the Gulmarg area and concluded that the men who had clashed with the Indian patrol had crossed the CFL from AK. This information was passed on to Delhi quickly, but it appears from the slow response that the central government seemed to think the ICK government was exaggerating the seriousness of the situation as anti-government protests were due to take place on 9 August in Srinagar and other towns in the Valley. Sadiq, the Chief Minister of ICK, flew back to Srinagar on 8 August with Indira Gandhi to try to impress on Delhi the gravity of the situation. Only after an exchange of fire within five miles of Srinagar were armed police units quickly flown in from Delhi.

On 8 August, following a meeting of the emergency committee of the Indian Central Cabinet, an official Indian spokesman gave his country's interpretation of the events. It was claimed that since 5 August there had been extensive infiltration by a considerable number of armed men from AK along several points all along the CFL and at other points which India regarded as the international border between Indian Kashmir and West Pakistan. The operation had been planned and organised in Pakistan and it was alleged that most of the infiltrators belonged to the Azad Kashmir forces and that their purpose was to carry out acts of sabotage and create disturbances in Indian Kashmir (*Times of India*, 9/8/65).

The Pakistani spin on the events had been pre-planned and the propaganda offensive was quickly launched. Bhutto declared that the people of the state of Kashmir had been driven to rebellion by Indian repression and tyranny and that their action should be understood as part of the fight for freedom which was taking place all over Asia and Africa. He stated that Pakistan had nothing to do with the 'uprising' (*Dawn*, 13/8/65). It is fair to say that the Indian account was more widely believed as not only did it have a ring of truth about it but UN observers on the ground quickly informed the UN Secretary-General, U Thant, that the Indian version was more or less accurate. Lieutenant-General Nimmo (the chief military observer UNMOGIP) reported to U Thant that a large-scale infiltration of armed men from Azad Kashmir was under way and the Indian complaints which started after 6 August were credible. U Thant acted on this report on 9 August by conveying to the Pakistan ambassador to the UN, Syed Amjad Ali, his 'very serious concern about the situation that was developing in Kashmir…involving the crossing of the CFL from the Pakistan side by numbers of armed men and their attacks on Indian military positions on the Indian side of the line…' (S/6651, Part 1 para 9 quoted Wright, 112–13).

On 8 August Srinagar was expected to be especially tense as it would be crowded with villagers coming to the city to attend the annual fair and devotional ceremonies held in celebration of the saint revered by Kashmiri Muslims, Syed Abdul Qadir Gillani, popularly known as Pir Dastagir Sahib. The following day was the twelfth anniversary of Sheikh Mohammed Abdullah's dismissal from the State premiership and his subsequent arrest. The significance of these dates could explain why Gibraltar was launched 48 hours earlier than originally planned. The anti-Indian forces in the Valley—the HRAC, the Plebiscite Front and the Awami Action Committee—had all joined forces for this period and collectively called for a general strike and demonstrations in support of their demands, for the release of all political detainees and a plebiscite to determine the future of Kashmir. Under the direction of the HRAC, many Kashmiris had been carrying out civil disobedience twice weekly in Srinagar since 5 June in defiance of a ban on public meetings. From 9 August, the HRAC planned to extend these activities to other urban centres along the Valley.

Salahuddin force had planned to slip into Srinagar with the large number of villagers coming into the city, and then on the next day planned to seize the radio station and government secretariat during the demonstration. Srinagar was to be isolated to prevent the movement of Indian reinforcements into the city by seizing the airport, while forces to the south-west and north-east would cut the road between Srinagar and Jammu. Having achieved these objectives, the plan was then to establish a ruling Revolutionary Council and a national government which was to include figures from the ranks of the anti-Indian parties, and appeal for recognition and assistance from all countries, especially Pakistan. It was not until the evening of 10 August that significant numbers from Salahuddin force were able to reach the western outskirts of Srinagar. Meanwhile, inside the city, individual infiltrators had been politically active in trying to secure increased participation in their activities by local people. Influential opponents of the Indians within Srinagar seemed however to have declined to provide any support to the infiltrators and the general strike passed off without any major incidents, which meant that Salahuddin force had failed to secure its immediate objectives.

Undeterred, Azad Kashmir radio operating from Muzaffarabad reported that on the evening of 8 August it had monitored transmissions from a radio station located inside ICK calling itself *Sada-i-Kashmir* (Voice of Kashmir) radio, which had announced the establishment of a Revolutionary Council. The Voice of Kashmir had proclaimed a 'War of Liberation' and 'the Revolutionary Council' announced the formation of a National Government without specifying who the members of this new government were. The Council promised, amongst other things, to fight the armed struggle until all the 'usurpers are expelled from our land, our leaders now in jail are freed and that the will of the people is allowed to determine the future in our land'.

Although it was only expected that the Muslim Kashmiris were to revolt against India, the general tone of the proclamation was non-religious, even though the members of the Revolutionary Council explicitly identified themselves as Muslims by stating that Kashmir had been sold to India in 1947. It also went on to say that acts of sacrilege were being perpetrated in the state of Kashmir under the shadow of Indian guns and bayonets, but there was no call for a proclamation of *jihad* as Indian sources claimed. It was emphasised that the call was not directed against the people of India but against the Indian government and army and its local agents. The Revolutionary Council went further and appealed for assistance to three specific groups within India—South Indians, Sikhs and Rajputs—thereby conjuring up the vision of an India dominated by a Hindi-speaking centre which was intolerant, not only of the rights of Kashmiri Muslims, but also of other castes and language groups.

This idea of India as a Hindu state was obviously a crude vision of Indian political life; it was an official Pakistan stereotype which it hoped would strike a chord within India. As recently as 2 August 1965 the Sikh leader of Indian Punjab, Master Tara Singh, had reiterated the Sikh demand for the creation of a Punjabi-speaking state within the Indian union, and he also referred to the continuous attempts made to try and stifle the true aspirations of Kashmiris. At the same time the language issue within India between north and south over the official status of Hindi and southern languages was well-known. The reason for including the Rajputs was not clear but could only have been intended to undermine morale within India and the Indian Army. The people of Pakistan were mildly rebuked in the proclamation for not having done enough to assist the Kashmiris in the past and were invited to rectify this now. There was no mention of the situation within Azad Kashmir and the Revolutionary Council pledged itself to fight until 'the will of the people was allowed to determine the future of our land'. It declared that all agreements between India and ICK were annulled and constituted itself as the sole lawful authority of the State of Kashmir, thereby adding to the list of non-elected governments in both parts of Kashmir. The tone and language bore the unmistakable hallmarks of Bhutto's speeches and writings and there is little doubt that the Pakistan Foreign Ministry was involved in drafting of the proclamations of the Revolutionary Council.

India lost little time in declaring that the Voice of Kashmir radio station was based within Pakistan and that the frequencies were registered in Pakistan's name with the International Frequency Registration Board (*Kashmir Answers Pakistan*, Government of India, 20). This, as Gauhar later confirmed, was indeed the case. On the morning of 8 August, Gauhar says, he was approached by the Director of Military Intelligence, Brigadier Irshad, apologising that they had not given him the 24-hours notice they had promised and saying there was an urgent need for a mobile transmitter. Gauhar recalls that none was available, and so the 'Voice of Kashmir' had to be broadcast on the same frequency as the Pakistan-government run 'Azad Kashmir Radio'. It would not and did not in fact take the Indian government very long to discover that fact and publicise it widely, adding to the general feeling within Pakistan that Gibraltar was not exactly going according to plan.

Things were to go from bad to worse for the Pakistani planners when on the evening of 8 August, All India Radio broadcast interviews with four prisoners captured by Indian forces from the Gibraltar force. They provided a detailed account of the planning and execution of Gibraltar. Irshad, on hearing a summary of the interview from Gauhar, was reported to have said, 'Oh my God, the bastards have spilt the beans' (Gauhar, 318). Harbakhsh Singh claims that not only did the two captured officers give a detailed account of Gibraltar on the radio, they also had documents in their possession which 'revealed that the plot for massive infiltration was hatched as early as January 1965' (H. Singh, 26). Whether those documents existed in reality and were carried by Gibraltar forces is unclear, but if so it would add to the general perception of a rushed operation, without proper training or groundwork.

The Gibraltar forces therefore struggled from the date that they were confronted by the large numbers of Indian forces based within ICK. Tariq force tried to blow up a couple of bridges within ICK but was unable to make much impact and withdrew from ICK on 10 September having suffered casualties. It is believed that the force commander and twenty-one men died for lack of acclimatisation (Gauhar, 324). Qasim force managed to hang around in northern Kashmir until the fourth week of September but then withdrew with some 16 casualties. Khalid force seemed to have lost contact with its command structure soon after moving into ICK and had to be withdrawn and then sent back in the second week of September. This force did manage a degree of success with an attack on the Indian Army base of 4 Kumaon in which the Indian commanding officer was killed and his second of command was injured on 13 August.

Salahuddin force was the largest and most important of the Gibraltar forces, and as previously stated was tasked with trying to enter Srinagar and direct the uprising from there. The Salahuddin forces managed to enter the city by 8 August, and their presence was enough for the government of ICK to request Delhi to declare martial law, a request which, although refused by the Indian government, was an indication of the level of concern within the ICK government (H. Singh, 29). On the night of 10/11 August there were exchanges of fire around various areas in the western outskirts of the city where the city began to merge into marsh and paddy fields. The presence of the attacking force within and on the outskirts of Srinagar was not only a military irritant for India but also a political embarrassment. While enclosed in Batmalu, traditionally a Pathan stronghold, elements of Salahuddin force directed harassing fire on the secretariat and police lines. House-to-house searches that were instituted had real difficulty clearing out the entire area. Finally, on the night of 14/15 August Indian forces burned Batmalu to the ground, and on the following day an all-night curfew was imposed on the whole city of Srinagar (*Times of India*, 12/8/65).

Salahuddin force was also tasked with disrupting Indian forces in the use of the roads towards Srinagar. *Sada-i-Kashmir* radio claimed that by 13 August the infiltrators had sealed off Srinagar from the surrounding countryside by cutting off twelve roads including three major arteries, the ones leading to Jammu, Baramula and Leh. This was almost certainly not the case as the Gibraltar forces were not large enough to be able to hold these roads in force. Instead Salahuddin force resorted to the attempted demolition of bridges and the ambush of moving columns. India reported ambushes along the road and at a village 40 miles to the west of Srinagar on the Tanmarg Road, where on 10 August, 12 Indian policemen were killed. Nimmo confirmed reports of attacks on the bridges of Baramula on the night of 7/8 August and Kargil on 10 August, as well as on the Srinagar-Leh road where an attack on the bridge was combined with an ambush of an Indian convoy on 1 September (S/6651, Part II quoted by Wright, 112).

Ghaznavi force was later to be deemed the most successful by the Pakistan Army. It operated in the area of Budhil in north Kashmir and claimed by 18 August to be in control of the area having inflicted Indian military casualties. Ghaznavi force claimed that local Kashmiris of this area joined it enthusiastically and an air drop of rifles by the PAF meant that additional rifles were available to the local population, making Ghaznavi force appear larger than it was. The force was able to stay in place until 23 September when it was ordered by GHQ to withdraw (Ahmed, 34–40).

The fact was that the majority of the Muslims and their leaders in ICK did not rise up and participate at the behest of the infiltrators as the Kashmir Cell had expected, not least because they had received no request or warning prior to the infiltration. However, individually and in small groups, some Kashmiris did give some assistance to the infiltrators by providing information and shelter or simply by concealing from the Indian authorities the fact that there were infiltrators in their areas. A later British review of the war simply noted that 'the inhabitants of the Valley, noted more for the beauty of their women than the martial valour of their men, did not revolt' (British military review, May 1966, 11). The lack of local Pakistani intelligence was demonstrated when it was realised that rather than discovering a population ready to fight the Indians, when the Gibraltar forces arrived in the Valley, 'they were met by a frightened, hostile population' (Gauhar, 325).

There is no doubt that a general uprising within ICK would not only have made the task of the infiltrators infinitely easier, it would also have had the immense value to Pakistan of bestowing a degree of international legitimacy to Operation Gibraltar; the obvious lack of support within ICK damaged Pakistan's international credibility as it claimed from the outset that the Kashmiri population had risen up themselves and were simply waiting for liberation. The denial by the Pakistan government of any involvement in the infiltration also convinced no one and it seems that only a general lack of international sympathy with India's stance on Kashmir since 1947 allowed Pakistan to escape serious international censure and UN condemnation. By 30 August Nimmo had presented his report on events along the CFL since 5 August and said that of the twenty-three violations of the line, nineteen were committed by Pakistan and four by India, whose violations had been from 14 to 24 August. U Thant's report to the Security Council was presented on 3 September but as the Pakistan government objected to its release, it was kept secret until 6 September (Second Report of the UN Secretary-General 3/9/65, cited Indian Official History 91).

Reaction to Gibraltar

Within the Indian government, the initial hope was that the infiltration could be dealt with by operations confined within ICK and that there would not be any need for troop reinforcements as there was a large number of Indian soldiers inside ICK, which was the reason for this confidence. There were four Indian infantry divisions inside ICK with three independent brigades and a large number of paramilitary and irregular forces. On the Pakistan side there was only 12 Division comprising eighteen infantry battalions, mostly of Azad Kashmir troops and irregular companies (Ahmed, 26). This disparity of forces gave the ICK government and the central Indian government confidence that not only could the troops available inside ICK deal with the infiltration without too much difficulty, but also that there was also little risk of Pakistan launching any military offensive of its own.

The Information Minister of the government of ICK, Ali Mohammed Tariq, stated on 10 August that many of the raiders had been captured or killed and others had fled to Azad Kashmir, while the army had encircled the remainder who would not be allowed to escape (*The Times*, 13/8/65). On the same day, also in Srinagar, Indira Gandhi described the situation as serious but under control (*Times of India*, 11/8/65). The Indian government seemed by 11 August to feel that the initiative had been regained by the Indian security forces; it was reported that the army had managed to seal off all the exit points along the CFL, and with the assistance of armed police, India was confident of being able to locate all the infiltrators within a week (*Times of India*, 13/8/65). On the same day, the Indian cabinet decided that for the time being the Indian Army would not cross the CFL, either in pursuit of the infiltrators or to block the main infiltration attempts (*The Times*, 13/8/65). In a radio broadcast to the nation, Shastri stated that mopping up operations were now in progress and whilst India was told to be vigilant, the general tone was one of confidence (Lal Bahadur Shastri, *When Freedom is Menaced*, 5–6).

Meanwhile, the US State Department was requesting clarification of the fluid situation in Kashmir from the Karachi embassy. This resulted in a telegram from Karachi to the State Department on 11 August in which it was revealed that the UNIMOGIP Station Commander, Colonel Graham, told American diplomats it was clear to them that a sizeable number of non-local, well-armed personnel were operating inside ICK. Graham thought the number might be as high as one thousand and their objectives appeared to be military ones such as bridges and trucks, and went on to say that the groups of armed men were too well-organised, well-disciplined and well-drilled to have been very recently trained (Karachi to State Department, 11/8/65, POL 32–1 India-Pak, NA).

Between 9 to 22 August the estimate, by the Indian government, of the number of infiltrators involved in Gibraltar was revised upwards in five stages; from several hundred to between 1,000 and 1,200, 1,500 to 3,200, 3,000 to 4,000 and finally 1,100 killed or captured with 3,000 to 5,000 still at large (*Times of India*, 22/8/65). The true figure was probably closer to 5,000 and that is broadly agreed between the two sides now, but the casualties suffered by the Gibraltar forces are not (General Ahmed, 30 and Indian Official History, 60). In diplomatic exchanges during the first phase of the infiltration, India and Pakistan repeated their views about the development of the situation. The Indian High Commissioner to Pakistan, Kewal Singh, was instructed to call on Ayub and inform him of the grave consequences which would follow if Pakistan did not immediately order the withdrawal of the infiltrators. Although the appointment had been arranged well in advance, when the Indian High Commissioner arrived to meet Ayub on 10 August he was unable to see the president but was instead received by

Bhutto who stated that Pakistan knew nothing of the massive aggression across the ceasefire line and that it was an internal revolt of the people of the state against India (Security Council Official Records, UN Department of Public Information, 20th Year, 1237th Meeting, 4/9/65).

Two days later, while still denying any Pakistani involvement, Bhutto clearly set out the diplomatic objective which Pakistan hoped to achieve with the reopening of the Kashmir question, by stating that India had chosen to close all the doors to a peaceful settlement and the integration of the occupied territory, and therefore had only itself to blame (*Dawn*, 13/8/65). Ayub spoke in a similar vein and said it was time for India to recognise the gravity of the situation and try to bring about an honourable settlement (Ayub Khan, *Speeches and Statements*, Lahore: Mohammad Ali Academy, 1966) (VIII, 13). Shastri claimed Pakistan had made a thinly disguised armed attack on India which would be met forcibly, and stated firmly that under the circumstances there was absolutely no scope for talks and he would not even contemplate them (Shastri, 10).

On 14 August Chester Bowles, the US ambassador to India, reported on the perspective from Delhi regarding Pakistan's actions in sending guerrilla/military fighters into Kashmir and the setting up of a 'bogus' radio station, which had created a very serious situation that 'may get worse before it gets better'. Bowles also said that if Pakistan had hoped that its infiltration and propaganda would lead to an uprising then its intelligence was 'woefully inept and planning and operation of this gambit equally so'. The US Defence Attaché based in Delhi, who had recently returned from ICK, was reported to have said that the Kashmiris were in no mood to welcome the Pakistanis as they 'never had an appetite for violence and have traditionally feared the Indians'. Bowles went on to say that the danger now was that either the Indians would be tempted to teach Pakistan 'a lesson' after Kutch where they were forced to fight at a disadvantage, or Pakistan, 'frustrated by the blatant failure of their ambitious effort will embark on direct military action'. The last comment was perceptive as it suggested precisely what Pakistan's GHQ was now considering. Bowles said that he was doing his best to prevent India from escalating the situation and it would be helpful if the US government did not 'equate their (India's) position in this particular affair to that of Pakistan'. In other words, Bowles was requesting clear-cut condemnation from the US government of Pakistan's actions and support or at the very least some understanding if India reacted with military force (14/8/65, New Delhi to State, India Cables, Vol V LBJ).

During the crisis inside ICK due to Gibraltar, the government of Shastri was being placed under political pressure as the extent of the infiltration became more clear. The Lok Sabha was summoned for a special meeting due to begin on 16 August, with the Indian opposition leaders advocating the cancellation of both the Kutch ceasefire agreement and the meeting scheduled for 20 August between the Pakistani and Indian delegations. A future prime minister of India, Atal Behari Vajpayee, demanded that India should attack the bases of the infiltrators across the ceasefire line (*Times of India*, 16/8/65). The Indian government faced a debate on the Kutch agreement and with eight no-confidence motions tabled by the opposition in which the Indian government was accused of failing in the defence of India, bungling in foreign affairs and failing to ensure the integrity of the country's borders. Although the government had a substantial majority in parliament and there was no real danger of defeat, it was noteworthy that no minister or parliamentary secretary appeared in Parliament to speak in support of the prime minister. Shastri announced that India had cancelled the forthcoming Indo-Pak ministerial talks due to be held on 20 August, and the motion that the House approve the Kutch agreement was carried by 269 votes to 28 (LSD Debates, Third Series XVLV:1). The cancellation of the talks avoided a potentially difficult law-and-order situation for the Indian government which could well have resulted from Bhutto's scheduled arrival in New Delhi.

By 14 August, India felt that it should now use its numerical superiority to try and cut off the supply lines to the Gibraltar forces and take the fight across the CFL. India had much larger forces in the area than Pakistan, under XV Corps commanded by Lieutenant General Kashmir Singh Katoch. Within ICK there were four infantry divisions: 19 Division, 25 Infantry, 10 Infantry were under the command of XV Corps and 3 Infantry was based at Leh. There were also three independent infantry brigades and three artillery brigades based in ICK as well as several battalions of Jammu and Kashmir militia.

On 16 August the Indian 121 Brigade took control of three Pakistani posts north of Kargil. Although the second occupation of the Kargil pickets marked the first open crossing of the CFL by regular army units from either side during the August fighting, it was not in fact a major escalation of the conflict. In the context of the infiltration launched by Pakistan all along the CFL, and of the attacks carried out on bridges and along major roads which were all verified by the UN, India's response was militarily measured and within the limits expected by the Pakistan military (Ahmed, 50).

On 19 August the US embassy in Pakistan informed the State Department that it was hard to obtain exact information regarding the 'dimensions and character of the infiltration' but it now revised the number of infiltrators up to several thousand. The embassy felt that despite Indian claims of minimal local support, there must have some participation by locals to establish arms drops and operations (19/8/65, Karachi to State Department, POL 32–1 India-Pak, NA).

On 21 August, India attacked three further Pakistani posts across the LOC in the Tithwal area the Uri-Poonch bulge. The Indians claimed that the push was defensive rather than offensive as it was merely designed to prevent further crossings to supply and reinforce the Gibraltar forces. The Tithwal operations which began on 21 August were directed against a track running along the valley of the river Neelum and linked Muzaffarabad to other towns in Azad Kashmir. Indian forces now dominated the Muzaffarabad-Kel tract, and although the declared Indian aim was simply to disrupt a further wave of infiltrators from operating across the CFL from Muzaffarabad, the fact was the Indian forces were now threatening the Neelam valley.

The main route across the CFL for the infiltrators operating in the area of the valley was the Haji Pir Pass in the Uri/Poonch bulge. Indian units crossed the line south of the Uri during the night of 25/26 August, and in a flanking movement captured the Haji Pir Pass on the morning of the 28 August. The Haji Pir Pass was a critical strategic point for Pakistan as it was through there that most of the logistical support for Pakistani troops in the valley had to pass and it was undoubtedly a route used by Gibraltar forces. The British were unimpressed by the speed of the Indian advance, noting that 'the capture of the Pass took four days despite a somewhat half-hearted defence' (British military review, 12). It may have taken four days but the capture of Haji Pir Pass was a serious blow for Pakistan as it left the Gibraltar forces within ICK isolated and with potentially no route from which to exit. It is reported that on news of the capture of the pass, Musa rushed to Bhutto's residence and by means of a map, demonstrated how it left the Gibraltar forces isolated and shouted, 'My boys have nothing but stones to fight with' (Gauhar, 326).

While claiming that its army had crossed the CFL and had seized ground within Azad Kashmir and the Northern Areas in order to minimise the threat posed by infiltrators, India used the opportunity not only to seal off the escape routes of infiltrators operating in the southwest of the valley and prevent reinforcement by the infiltration of fresh elements which were said to be gathering in the vicinity of the Haji Pir Pass, but also to improve its military position along the CFL. There is little doubt that India, confident with the vast number of troops at its disposal that were able to deal with the Gibraltar force, was also taking advantage of the opportunity to take control of passes and military posts which were of long-term strategic value. Pressure within Pakistan was now mounting for the launch of Grand Slam. It appears that the lack of response within ICK and the poor showing of the Gibraltar forces dented Ayub's confidence in the whole project. There was now a question of whether Ayub would accept the failure of Gibraltar and cut his losses or would press ahead with the plan until international intervention came about.

Review of Gibraltar

A later British military review of the war said that the Pakistani planning and execution of Gibraltar was in effect 'calling "heads" with a double-headed coin'. If all went well and there was a full scale revolt, Pakistan could claim that it was an indigenous revolt and if it went badly, the prolonged guerrilla war would help convince the international powers to intervene in order to prevent an all out war (British military review, May 1966, 5).

Although it is accepted by Pakistani generals and writers that Operation Gibraltar was far from successful and failed to achieve its objectives, it was not a total failure in purely military terms. An Indian writer later admitted that in areas of Jammu 'it took considerable effort to get rid of the administration which the infiltrators had set up there' (B. M. Kaul, *Confrontation with Pakistan*, Delhi: Vikas Publications, 472). Another Indian writer admitted that throughout the month of September there was fighting in a wide region of western and south-western Jammu and the Indian troops found it difficult to dislodge the infiltrators until after the ceasefire following the end of the war (D. R. Manekar, *Twenty-two Fateful Days: Pakistan Cut to Size*, Bombay: Manaktalas, 1967, 69). Such tenacity implies some degree of local assistance and support, although nowhere was there the level of support that the planning had hoped for. Even the Indian official history of the war concedes that Gibraltar achieved at least 'one indirect success. They tied down about four Indian divisions in Jammu and Kashmir in mopping up the Pak infiltrators during the whole of September 1965' (Chakravorty, p. 93).

The simple fact remains that there were some fundamental problems with Gibraltar, amongst which were:

i) Lack of time and preparation. However intelligent a concept may be—and even Harbakhsh Singh conceded that the 'plan of infiltration was brilliant in conception' (H. Singh, 26)—it takes successful insurgencies and guerrilla wars years to plan and succeed. The troops sent in were assessed by the British military review as 'neither physically fit, prepared as to morale or briefed as to their targets' (British military review, 11). It is said that some men died of cold and others simply lost the will to fight. There was the highly embarrassing broadcast of 8 August in which the Indians were able to force two members of an allegedly elite force to disclose the full plans and training on Indian state radio.

ii) Failure to establish links inside ICK and lack of/faulty intelligence. This was a critical failure and however much the Foreign Ministry and GHQ in Pakistan blamed each other, the ultimate responsibility rests with Ayub as he approved the plan and must have been briefed by his military intelligence on what if any contacts had been made within ICK to ensure that the Gibraltar forces would not be forced to hide in the forests but would be able to melt into the local population and establish safe houses. Algeria and Vietnam should have served as examples of how long-term planning was necessary to defeat a larger force, and however discontented the population of ICK was, political groundwork was vital and it was missing. Better intelligence from the ground would have warned the Pakistan government that the recent Indian crackdown and rearrest of Sheikh Abdullah had succeeded in dampening public protests. Regardless of the reason put forward by Malik, that fear of a double agent might compromise the mission, the result was even worse as the troops went there with no local intelligence and were badly exposed against superior forces.

When this point was put to Bhutto later, he claimed that the fault was that of the army, as it had sent in regular soldiers instead of his recommended use of guerrillas from Azad Kashmir: 'You know the fish in water theory'. It was again put to him that guerrillas had to be from the same village as even non-local villagers would be spotted, to which he replied 'Well maybe'. Bhutto however maintained in the same interview that it had been the army's job to ensure the infiltrators were properly trained and led and the army had obviously failed (Taseer, 61). It was precisely this casual attitude towards the planning of a 'guerrilla' operation that points to the reasons for its ultimate lack of success, and once Gibraltar failed to meet its objectives, no one wanted to accept any responsibility for it.

The kindest thing that can be said for Gibraltar was that it was a bold and imaginative operation and if it had been followed up within fourteen days by Grand Slam, the second part of the operation as outlined by Malik, it would not have given the Indian forces time to pick off the Gibraltar forces as they did and the Gibraltar forces would then not have had the full weight of the Indian divisions based in ICK on them. The decision whether to launch Grand Slam was still in the balance by the time the majority of the Gibraltar forces had either been killed, captured, withdrawn or were in hiding. It was not a good start in 'de-freezing' the Kashmir question and the dilemma facing Ayub was now whether to cut his losses or proceed with Grand Slam. The stakes were high and about to get higher whatever Ayub now decided.

5

OPERATION GRAND SLAM

Hesitation and delay

Within Pakistan's GHQ there was now some real pressure building for the immediate launch of Operation Grand Slam, phase two of General Malik's plan. If the Indian Army was allowed to have a free hand for much longer in dealing with the Gibraltar forces and capturing posts across the CFL, the situation in Kashmir would be much worse for Pakistan by 1 September than on 5 August and all Gibraltar would have achieved would be some publicity and a few hundred deaths and injuries. Malik's fear now was that without Grand Slam being launched, or an order given for all Gibraltar forces to withdraw (assuming they could still safely do so), it was now only a matter of time before all the Gibraltar forces still operating within ICK would be killed or captured. Although south of the Pir Panjal Mountains pockets of Gibraltar forces remained active, there was a real danger at this stage of Pakistan completely failing to secure its main political and diplomatic objective, which was the reopening of the Kashmir question and some form of international intervention with India being placed under some pressure. To make matters worse, the population of Kashmir stayed relatively silent, thus exposing the Gibraltar forces to Indian counter-measures.

There now appears to have been a combination of loss of nerve and second thoughts by Ayub in giving the go ahead for Grand Slam. It was without doubt a serious step to order the launching of an armoured thrust by Pakistan to capture a strategically vital town based within ICK. Not only did it mean that the Pakistan Army would have to cross a small part of the international border between Sialkot and Jammu, it also made the prospect of an all-out war very real. Kutch had been a series of small-scale skirmishes with relatively few troops used by either side, and that too in a desert that few people had heard of before the fighting had begun. Fighting in Kashmir was another prospect altogether and Ayub hesitated, aware of the magnitude of the decision that he was being asked to make as he now appeared to belatedly realise that a general war with India could have very serious international and national implications. Ayub now did what he had done at other critical times in his life, he disappeared to the Swat Valley where he was almost unreachable. Malik and other senior officers were painfully aware that every day's hesitation meant more ground lost in AK along the CFL and another day for India to continue the decimation of Gibraltar forces within ICK.

The US Central Intelligence Agency (CIA) was well informed as to the details of discussions going on within Pakistan's GHQ, as it reported that on 28 August General Akhtar Malik arrived by helicopter to meet General Musa, General Sher Bahadur, the Chief of General Staff, and the Director Military Operations, Brigadier Gul Hassan. It was reported to the CIA that it was decided at this meeting to order Pakistan's army in Kashmir to stop the Indian military violation of the CFL. The Pakistan Army was to pursue the Indian Army into ICK, and it was acknowledged that if the army failed, 'the Pak position in Kashmir would be extremely serious'. The Lahore-based 10 Infantry Division was ordered to Kasur-Wagah field position to protect Lahore. The CIA source stated that there was obvious tension at the meeting between the older and newer officers, with the younger officers such as Malik and Gul Hassan pushing for action and 'full Pak army commitment' and the older officers being more cautious and trying to delay the operation and contain the Indian move along the CFL. Malik was said to have accused some senior officers of obstructing support for the Kashmir forces and the conference was said to have ended on the conclusion that the use of irregular forces such as the Mujahids, Scouts and Pathan tribesman was 'useless' and only regular Pakistan Army forces should confront the Indian Army (31/8/65, CIA Cable, Pakistan Cables Vol IV Box 151 LBJ).

This CIA account is largely corroborated by Gul Hassan who says that from 24 August he began to receive urgent requests from Malik for permission to launch Grand Slam. Gul Hassan replied that there was no need to seek explicit permission as 'the president had himself suggested an attack on Akhnur...so all he [Malik] had to do was fix the date for the offensive and I would inform all concerned'. Akhtar Malik was said to have laughed loudly in response and said that Gul Hassan had been in GHQ too long and had a lot to learn yet about such matters. Malik was proved correct as despite Gul Hassan's urgent requests for the necessary clearance, Ayub had disappeared to Swat, weighing up his options. The date of the meeting at Murree described by the CIA is given as 27 August by Gul Hassan but otherwise the accounts largely match each other, and given the seniority of the people present in Murree at the meeting, the CIA source must logically have been very highly placed. Gul Hassan says that he was thrilled when initially informed of news of the meeting as he and Malik now assumed that the go-ahead was to be given for Grand Slam at the briefing by Musa on Ayub's orders, but instead, 'the meeting developed into a briefing session'. The problem of course was that Musa did not have the authority to go ahead and would only have done so if so ordered by Ayub. As Ayub had not yet decided on the next course of action, no decision was possible at the Murree briefing. Gul Hassan added that he and Malik were now becoming additionally concerned that the forces assembled for Grand Slam along the border could be detected any day by the Indians as they could not remain unnoticed for long along the heavily-patrolled and watched border (Gul Hassan, pp. 183–4).

Bhutto had been the foremost champion of military action for some time and he was made aware by Malik and other advocates of Grand Slam of the need for urgent action if the Gibraltar forces were to have any chance of rescue and if further losses along the CFL were to be avoided. Bhutto himself needed little persuading and had written to Ayub around this time that 'Time is therefore of the essence in striking a few hard blows against India in Kashmir' (Wolpert, *Bhutto*, 90). It was perhaps only Bhutto at this stage who could persuade Ayub to act as Musa was still unconvinced of the wisdom of the whole plan, and so Bhutto flew to Swat in order to obtain the clearance for Grand Slam from Ayub, which he obtained on 29 August. Ayub's directive to give the green light was odd for a number of reasons, not least because it was addressed to the Foreign Minister and the Commander-in-Chief, and as it was the document which began a war, it is worth quoting extensively. The aim was:

to take such action that will defreeze the Kashmir problem, weaken Indian resolve and bring her to the conference table without provoking a general war. However the element of escalation is always present in such struggles. So whilst confining our action to the Kashmir area, we must not be unmindful that India may in desperation involve us in a general war or violate Pakistani territory where we are weak. We must, therefore, be prepared for such a contingency. To expect quick results in this struggle when India has much larger forces than us would be unrealistic. Therefore our action should be such that can be sustained over a long period. As a general rule Hindu morale would not stand more than a couple of hard blows at the right time and place. Such opportunities must therefore be sought and exploited' (Gauhar, 328).

This is a fascinating document which encapsulates the strategy and thinking behind Ayub's decisionmaking. It demonstrates at least that Ayub was aware that Pakistan could not sustain a long war (whether he was aware of the exact number of weeks or not is unclear), but still gave an oblique green light for Grand Slam. It also shows that Ayub was fully aware of the likelihood of an Indian attack in Punjab but was obviously persuaded by a combination of assurances from Bhutto and others that India would not dare to cross the international border and also that 'Hindu morale' would not last a few hard blows. No doubt historians and psychologists could analyse the document further but the simple fact was that now General Akhtar Malik was finally given permission to launch Operation Grand Slam.

Whatever Ayub's hope of a short war and Bhutto's hope of India confining the war to Kashmir, there was little doubt in the minds of 12 Division and its commander that the launch of Grand Slam would lead to general war with India. In a briefing to his senior officers before its launch, Malik was told by an obviously startled brigadier that 'This would mean war with India'. Malik replied sarcastically, 'You've been paid long enough to make a war.' (Ahmed, 83). Malik wrote later that:

Bhutto kept insisting that his sources had assured him that India would not attack if we did not violate the international border. I however was certain that Gibraltar would lead to war and told GHQ so. I needed no op intelligence to come to this conclusion. It was simple common sense. If I got you by the throat, it would be silly for me to expect that you will kiss me for it. Because I was certain that war would follow my first choice objective for Grand Slam was Jammu. From there we could have exploited our success either towards Samba or Kashmir proper as the situation demanded. In any case whether it was Jammu or Akhnur, if we had taken the objective, I don't see how the Indians could have attacked Sialkot before clearing out either of these towns (Letter to brother, quoted Ahmed, 553).

The delay in obtaining clearance for Grand Slam had a potential silver lining according to Malik, as Indian troops were now focused on the Gibraltar forces and capturing various passes, and after their capture of the Haji Pir Pass Malik thought that 'Indian concentration in Haji Pir could only help us after Akhnur and they would have to pull out troops to counter the new threats and surrender their gains' (Major General Malik's letter to brother dated 22/11/67, quoted in General Ahmed, 70). Grand Slam was aimed squarely at the capture of Akhnur and as Indian defences around Akhnur were weak, Malik had been eyeing this area as a potential Indian weakness since May 1965 and had urged that some military pressure be applied on India there irrespective of Gibraltar from that time (Ahmed, 81).

Forces for Grand Slam

The forces assigned to Grand Slam were small given the task they were to undertake, made up of little over three brigades and two armoured regiments. The forces available to Malik were two armoured regiments, the 11 Cavalry and 13 Lancers (under the normal command of the newly raised 6 Armoured Division); Artillery 4 Corps under Brigadier Amjad Ali Khan Chaudhry; 102 Brigade under Brigadier Zafar Ali Khan; 10 Infantry Brigade under Brigadier Azmat Hayat and Divisional Artillery under Brigadier Khurshid Ahmed Khan under the normal command of 7 Division.

An outline of Grand Slam was given to brigade commanders on 28 August and a final co-ordination meeting was held on 31 August at HQ 7 Division. At that meeting the first signs of tension between Akhtar Malik and Yahya Khan, GOC 7 Division, surfaced when Yahya 'kept on saying that his brigade (10 Brigade) cannot go into the attack because they had just come from Bhai Pheru and he kept repeating this again and again'. Akhtar Malik lost patience eventually and snapped at Brigadier Zafar, commander of 102 Brigade, 'Alright Zafar we will launch the attack without their help!' (Interview with

Brigadier Iqbal Shahmim, Ahmed, p. 83). Yahya was probably motivated by a combination of professional jealousy and pique as his 7 Division had been virtually split up between 12 Division and 6 Armoured Division, leaving him with little to do. Grand Slam was envisaged to be carried out in three phases; the first phase was the capture of territory up to the Tawi river by 102 Brigade, the second phase, which was to begin later on 1 September, was for 10 Brigade to cross the Tawi and capture Akhnur. In the third phase, 102 Brigade was to link up with 25 Infantry Brigade at Naushahra and capture Rajauri, a town on the far to the north of Akhnur, whereas Jammu, the most strategic point for Indian troops in ICK was to the south of Akhnur. Although these were the written orders for Grand Slam, Malik had informed his commanders that once they had reached Akhnur, he would tell them whether to head for Rauauri or Jammu, but it appears from his later correspondence quoted above that Malik always intended to head for Jammu and had not wished to alarm Ayub or Musa unduly by declaring Jammu as his objective (Ahmed, 84–5).

The Indian forces inside ICK (as outlined earlier) were much larger, comprising in total four divisions, and so the forces at the disposal of Malik were not only meagre in comparison, but they also suffered from the problem of being assembled from other divisions and being used to operating under different commanders. For Grand Slam to have any chance of success, it was vital to move with speed in an area suited to Pakistan before India's greater numbers would begin to take their toll, and to obtain a locally advantageous strategic position where those greater numbers would not be able to be brought to bear for some time. It was not difficult to see why the route towards Akhnur was a tempting target for Pakistan. Bhimbar in Azad Kashmir and Chhamb in Indian Kashmir are positioned at the very southern end of the CFL at its junction with Azad Kashmir and ICK. In 1965, the Bhimbar sector was within easy reach of the major Pakistani military base of Kharian and the single Indian line of communication with the Chhamb sector was extended and therefore vulnerable. These foothills and the river Chenab, which flows from Akhnur in a south-westerly direction into Pakistan, sealed off the Chhamb sector from the north and east so that it became a virtual island, dependent for practical links on the bridge at Akhnur. Had Grand Slam managed to capture or destroy the Akhnur bridge, it would have cut the practicable supply line of the Indian units stationed in the south-west sector of the CFL while leaving the right flank of the Pakistan forces protected from attack from the east by the river Chenab. Capturing the town of Akhnur, 24 miles inside ICK, would also have cut off Naushera, Rajauri and Poonch from Jammu and Pathankot and all Indian forces stationed north-west of the front would have been effectively cut off. It would then have been possible from Akhnur for the Pakistani armour to continue another 18 miles and capture the town of Jammu, the second city of ICK, and this appears to have been the target in Akhtar Malik's mind. The capture of Jammu by Pakistan would have been a strategic nightmare for India as it was on the main route from India to Srinagar, and even the Indian commander of the region admits that 'had it succeeded, a trail of dazzling results would have followed in its wake and the infiltration campaign would have had a new lease of life. The troops of 25 Infantry Division Sector would have been bottled up and those north of Banihal completely isolated' (H. Singh, 57).

On 31 August, a day before the launch of Grand Slam, Musa addressed all the divisional commanders at Kharian, the new operational HQ of 12 Division which had relocated from Murree to be closer to the field of operation. Grand Slam was clear in its military objective of capturing the town of Akhnur but there was still some ambiguity about where the Pakistani troops were to go next following its capture, or whether they were merely to hold Akhnur. If the idea was to sever India's land links with Srinagar and place India under real military pressure, then the objective should have been the town of Jammu from the outset, as that would have cut the lines of communication between India and ICK thoroughly rather than merely threatening to do so. Malik hinted even at the time that his next target after Akhnur would have been Jammu—still confident that not only would his offensive succeed, but he would also be given as much operational freedom by Ayub as he needed. Malik was sure that as war with India would follow even from the capture of Akhnur, his objective of Jammu after the capture of Akhnur would not have been any more dangerous and would have been even more strategically vital for Pakistan.

Whatever the grand strategic plans agreed by Ayub earlier with Malik, Musa later claimed that Grand Slam's aims were nothing more than 'a view to reducing pressure in the north by capturing Chhamb and threatening Akhnur which was to be the limit of our exploitation' (Musa, *My Version*, 39). That is certainly not the case, as the written orders of Grand Slam published by the Indians were clearly for the capture of Akhnur. Grand Slam's plans were also hamstrung at the outset by political rather than military considerations. If placing India at a military disadvantage and striking a 'few hard blows' by the swift capture of Jammu had been the plan at the outset, then the logical direction for Grand Slam would have been from Sialkot and not along the route via Akhnur, which meant crossing the river Tawi; not only was the route from Sialkot to Jammu the shortest and easiest way to reach Jammu from Pakistan, it also had fewer physical obstacles. The obvious political problem with this route was that it would have meant an assault across the international border and not from the CFL, which conflicted with Ayub's concern to try and prevent an all-out war with India and try and retain the moral high ground. Having political considerations such as these for Malik to be concerned about must have been frustrating, but he remained confident that advancing along the route to Jammu from Akhnur would still succeed.

Launch of Grand Slam

Malik had ensured that Operation Grand Slam had plenty of firepower and had assembled a formidable array of artillery and the heavy field guns with the task of preparing the ground for the armoured and infantry assault. There were ten field, seven medium and two heavy batteries, totalling 110 pieces, belonging to 7 Division and 4 Corps Artillery. H-Hour was set for 0500 hours, 1 September 1965. The Indian forces facing them in this sector were the 191 Independent Infantry Brigade which not only manned the CFL but was also charged with guarding the line of communication back to Akhnur. 191 Brigade was supported by a squadron of around 15 AMX-13 light tanks, a regiment of field artillery (25 pounders), a medium battery and a machine gun company. Pakistani historians claim that India also had units from its 93 Infantry Brigade in the area and had constructed a proper defensive line of three-storey concrete bunkers with medium and light machine gun and the recoilless rifle positions which were interlinked with covered trenches and protected occasionally by minefields (Gulzar Ahmed, 89–91).

At 0330 hours, 1 September, the Pakistan artillery under Brigadier Chaudhry, commander of IV Corps Artillery, opened Grand Slam with an intense bombardment which continued for over an hour until the armoured brigades were ready to advance. The sheer weight and ferocity of the artillery shelling was described by the Indians as 'staggering', and so it was little surprise that at 0500 hours, when Grand Slam's three-pronged attack led by Pakistan's 102 Brigade was launched in the Chhamb sector, it advanced quickly against a shell-shocked Indian defensive position (H. Singh, 59). 191 Infantry Brigade fell back in some disarray as the massive Pakistani artillery bombardment had succeeded in causing real panic and disruption in the Indian defences. The Indians now withdrew all their available tanks around Chhamb to try to prevent Pakistani troops from crossing the Tawi river. By noon on the first day of Grand Slam, Pakistani tanks had broken past the first line of Indian defences in the area and were now surrounding the town of Chhamb, and the Indian positions in the area were quickly overrun or bypassed. The river Tawi (or Munnawarali Tawi, a tributary of the Chenab) was reached by the afternoon; this was the only natural obstacle between the attacking force and the bridge over the Chenab at Akhnur.

With Chhamb under severe pressure, it was at this point that General Chaudhri, the head of the Indian Army, decided to ask Chavan for permission to launch air strikes as they were necessary to relieve the pressure on his hard-pressed forces in the Akhnur sector (Y. B. Chavan, *1965 War, The Inside Story*, Atlantic Publishers, 2007, 3–4). The Indian government having sanctioned air strikes, the first Indian flight was airborne at 1700 hours and before sunset the Indians claimed that the Indian Air Force (IAF) had destroyed thirteen Pakistani tanks and between thirty and forty vehicles with the loss of two Indian Vampires shot down by the Pakistani forces (*Times of India*, 2/9/65). Despite later claims by some Indian writers that this air strike saved Akhnur and the whole course of the war, the air attack was too late as the Pakistani attacking forces had entered Chhamb, and some of the advance units of Grand Slam were now so close to Indian defensive positions that some of the IAF bombing hit the Indian ammunition lorries and supplies in the area. The Pakistan Air Force (PAF) was now also called on for assistance by the Pakistan Army and claimed to have shot down four IAF Vampires on that day. It appears that delays in air support on the Indian side were due to the time taken for the Indian cabinet to sanction the use of air power, which had not been employed in April in the Rann of Kutch fighting. India's decision to use the Indian Air Force marked the beginning of the use of air power in this war, but the initial foray by the IAF was far from impressive.

By nightfall on 1 September, Grand Slam had advanced quickly and decisively along several axes on a 14-mile-wide front and some Pakistani tanks had in places reached the west bank of the Tawi, which in this area flows variously between about four and eight miles east of the CFL. To their rear some Indian posts which had been bypassed were still holding out, but Grand Slam had allowed for these to be bypassed and mopped up by Pakistani infantry following the armoured attack. Although there had been some pockets of resistance by units of 191 Infantry Brigade, on the whole the first day had gone roughly according to plan and had caused real concern in Delhi. The speed and direction of the assault had caught the Indians off guard and Harbakhsh Singh admits that Pakistan 'had got one over on us...Our intelligence service had once again failed to penetrate the fog of war' (H. Singh, 58).

The fact that India was taken off guard is surprising given that India was warned by UNMOGIP observers that the Pakistan infantry and armour were moving towards the CFL in the Chhamb sector; it appears that the Indian command was still surprised by the number of tanks employed and had not reinforced the area despite the tip-off (Manekar, 94–5). Heavily outnumbered in Grand Slam as well as outgunned, the lighter armoured and faster French-built tanks used by India (although specifically designed as tank-destroyers) were no match for the Pakistan Army's American Patton tanks. Even if any of India's heaviest tanks, the 50 ton Centurions with their 84 mm guns, had been within the area, they could not have been sent into battle against the Pattons because of the low load-bearing capacity of the Akhnur bridge (S. R. Johri, *The Indo-Pak Conflict of 1965*, New Delhi: Himalaya Publications, 1967, 19, 42, 109). The lack of Indian preparation would not, however, have surprised a UN official who had remarked in July 1965 that 'the Pakistanis are assembling a massive tank force in the Punjab. The Indians are asleep and they won't know what hit them' (Brines, 303). The Indians appear to have been confident towards the end of August that they had not only contained the Gibraltar forces but also, by taking ground across the CFL, reduced the threat of war. Indian complacency and lack of military intelligence very nearly cost the country dearly, as at least two Indian generals on 31 August were reported to have said that even if Pakistan did try to attack Chhamb 'it would not get very far' (Indian Official History, 114).

International reaction to Grand Slam

Although Malik believed that the silver lining to India's capture of the Haji Pir Pass and other posts across the CFL was that it distracted India from Grand Slam, the really positive aspect of India's reaction to Gibraltar was that it distracted the world from the fact that Grand Slam was too well prepared to have been a pure reaction to India's capture of strategic passes and must have been prepared well in advance, regardless of India's actions or reactions. Because of the widespread belief that Pakistan had launched Grand Slam in reaction to India's moves across the CFL, Grand Slam did not attract much international criticism or condemnation. Even the Indian public reaction was surprisingly muted as Indians had been aware of Grand Slam and appeared also to believe that this was Pakistan's reaction to its own moves.

The US embassy in Pakistan reported on 1 September that the situation on the CFL was now 'changing rapidly' and Pakistan was now reacting to Indian moves across the CFL as there was a fear of an Indian attack on Muzaffarabad. The embassy was unable to define 'Pak intentions with certainty' but felt that the situation was now being determined by military rather than political considerations. McConaughy felt that although Pakistan 'never expected to win Kashmir by military means' and even now did not have that intention, there was a real danger that the situation could escalate as both sides were now committing 'national prestige in expanding operations' (Karachi to State, 1/9/65 Pakistan Cable, Vol IV 8/65–9/65 Embtel 333 LBJ). In Washington, Komer explained the situation as he saw it to Johnson on 1 September by stating that all-out war might now 'be imminent' as the Pakistan infiltration had failed and the Indian retaliation had now forced Pakistan to use its army. Komer said that the US had managed to 'prod U Thant into moving' to appeal for a ceasefire, but that the only leverage it had now was aid and there would be growing political and public pressure on Johnson to use this lever. The real issue for the US and Johnson to consider was whether this lever would work or just alienate both sides. McConaughy was said to believe that the aid threat would not work on Pakistan and was concerned that the fragile relationship with Pakistan could be at 'breaking point' if aid was cut off, and Ayub was described as 'out for blood'. India was seen as likely to be more understanding of the need to use aid as leverage; indeed it would demand the cutting off of military supplies to Pakistan. The summary was that Komer believed the best option for the US was to back the UN in order to prevent action by China 'who probably have some kind of understanding with the Paks'. Aid suspension was seen as the ultimate weapon but one which 'may not work and will certainly get both sides highly incensed with us' (1/9/65, Komer to President, Pakistan Memos IV LBJ). In the event Johnson decided to wait and see how events would unfold before deciding whether or not to suspend aid.

On 2 September Johnson convened a special meeting on the Kashmir situation and summoned his most senior advisers relevant to the conflict: Rusk, Bundy, Komer, Vance and senior military officers. Rusk described how Kashmir had the potential to erupt into a major conflict, and hence every effort had to be made to stop the fighting. Rusk said that the situation had escalated from Pakistani infiltrators inside ICK to Indian moves across the CFL and now the Pakistan Army's own offensive, and the US needed to persuade both sides to respect the CFL and return to it.

Johnson listened to Rusk but had his own approach to the situation already formulated despite the recommendations of the State Department. Johnson said that he wanted everyone to be 'very cautious about anything we said'. Firstly, either side could look like a martyr if threatened by the US, and secondly, both sides would use US equipment regardless of what the US said. Johnson said the US should 'get behind a log and sleep a bit' as he had become aware over the last few months how little influence the US had with either India or Pakistan, and although both sides claimed to be threatened by the US, they had not been. Johnson therefore did not want to apply any pressure on either side, nor to take the diplomatic lead, and wanted someone else, such as the British government or the UN, to lead the call for a ceasefire, Johnson repeated that he did not want to intervene and would 'like to sit it out a little bit'. Rusk pointed out that once Pakistan's use of US equipment was confirmed the Indians would complain. Johnson repeated that the UN should be used as the means of trying to achieve a diplomatic solution and the US 'should hide behind that log' (2/9/65 Memorandum for the Record, Pakistan Memos LBJ). Had news of this attitude of Johnson reached Ayub, he would have been bitterly disappointed as the main rationale of using force was having the superpowers, particularly the US, intervening and pressuring India. Instead of the US government intervening directly, Johnson had decided to use the UN as the means of trying to pressure both sides, and coincidentally the US assumed the presidency of the UN Security Council for the month of September. The US ambassador to the UN was Arthur Goldberg, a former judge of the US Supreme Court, who was persuaded by Johnson to take up the position at the UN. Goldberg was told to work with the other countries, even the USSR, to avoid China exploiting the situation and ensure a ceasefire as soon as possible.

On 3 September, the Karachi embassy reported a conversation between the head of the PAF, Nur Khan, and the Italian ambassador to Pakistan. Nur Khan stated that unless the US was going to assist Pakistan in replacing fighter aircraft, then the PAF would look to China for replacements. Nur Khan also revealed that the Kashmir infiltration plan (Gibraltar) had been presented to Ayub and had been approved by him, and that the Pakistan government was involved and had originally sent in 1,000 men but had followed this up by another 3,000. Nur Khan went on to state that Pakistan had remained loyal to the US in its agreements, providing an air base at Peshawar. The US embassy commented that much of this conversation had been repeated by Nur Khan to a US embassy official on 28 August and so not much of the material was original, but that it confirmed the US suspicion that the Pakistan military action was meant to be limited in military nature and was meant mainly for political effect (3/9/65, Karachi to State Department, DEF 19-B, US-Pak, NA). This conversation provides a partial explanation of why the Pakistan Army did not consider the PAF to be 'security minded'.

On the same day (3 September) the State Department sent a telegram to its embassies in New Delhi and Karachi informing them of a conversation between Rusk and the Indian ambassador to the US, Braj Kumar Nehru. Nehru had stated that infiltrators were attempting to cut the Jammu-Poonch road and if they succeeded, India would lose contact with Kashmir. If Pakistan succeeded in doing this, then India would be forced to cross the international boundary in the Punjab. Nehru went on to say that the Indian government saw no distinction between the infiltrators and the Pakistan Army but was prepared to respect the CFL if Pakistan did the same. Nehru then touched on the use of US equipment by Pakistan, which was giving the latter the military advantage in Kashmir. He said that speaking personally, he was not sure how a ceasefire was to be achieved unless the US applied pressure on Pakistan to desist. Rusk emphasised that the US had raised the issue of the use of US military aid to Pakistan but still hoped that India would respond positively to the UN Secretary General's appeal for a ceasefire (3/9/65, State Department to New Delhi, Karachi, PO1 32–1, India-Pak, NA).

The US, which was less than delighted at news of the escalation of hostilities, was even more offended on 4 September by the arrival in Pakistan of Marshal Chen Yi, the Foreign Minister and Vice-Premier of China. Marshal Chen Yi publicly declared China's support for Pakistan's 'just action' inside ICK and spent six hours with Bhutto discussing the situation (Shastri, 235).

Bhutto later claimed that his advice to Ayub that India would not attack Pakistan across the international border was based on the assessment given to him by Chen Yi at this meeting (Asghar Khan, 76). Even if Chen Yi had in fact given this assessment— and it has to be said that other than Bhutto's recollection there is no evidence of it—it does not explain Bhutto's recorded enthusiasm for both Gibraltar and Grand Slam, both of which had been launched before Chen Yi's visit, and both of which Ayub had hoped would not lead to general war with India. Such a hope was at least partially based on prior advice from Bhutto, but it does not excuse Ayub as the final decision maker.

On that day, the UN Security Council asked both sides to return to the CFL and order an immediate ceasefire, but this was ignored by both India and Pakistan and Indian plans for its own retaliation were now advanced and ready to execute. U Thant, the UN Secretary-General, had initially decided not to publish the report prepared by UNMOGIP which was critical of

Pakistan's infiltration into Kashmir, but it was now presented to the Security Council, at least partially because of a decision by Goldberg to push for its publication. That in itself would have indicated to Ayub and the Pakistan delegation that the US was not going to protect Pakistan in the UN and was in fact going to use the UN as a means for pressuring Pakistan into accepting an immediate ceasefire; the resolution asked both sides to observe an immediate ceasefire and withdraw to the CFL.

On 5 September, a telegram was sent from Rusk to the Karachi embassy with instructions for McConaughy's imminent meeting with Ayub. The instructions from Washington were that McConaughy needed to clearly spell out to Ayub that the US had refrained from condemning Pakistan publicly despite clear evidence that they had begun this conflict, but had been placed in an awkward position by the misuse of US arms in the Rann of Kutch, and the Pakistan government had over-reacted to postponement of a US aid pledge. The blunt message was that President Johnson was not going to agree to any resumption of US aid unless there was a face-to-face meeting between him and Ayub at which there needed to be a basic examination of US-Pakistan relations. The US president was said to believe that a mutually beneficial relationship could grow out of this meeting. Pakistan was viewed by the US as being at 'a crossroads' now, and although the US believed that Pakistan was fundamentally well-disposed to the US, it needed clarification on the direction in which Pakistan was heading. Ayub was also to be told in no uncertain terms that until and unless Pakistan agreed to a ceasefire, there could be no possible resumption of US aid. If McConaughy was asked if India was receiving the same message, McConaughy was to reply that he was 'without instructions' (State Department to Karachi, 5/9/65. POl 327 India-Pak, NA).

It was an uncompromising and clear message from Johnson, and the US position did not fundamentally change during the war. Johnson was now of the opinion that rather than ignoring

Ayub by not receiving him in Washington, as had happened in April, he now needed to see him face-to-face and decide on future aid to Pakistan and other matters after that meeting. The level of mutual mistrust was now such that Johnson felt that he had to hear assurances as to Pakistan's intentions with regard to future ties with China and its tactics inside Kashmir before any future commitments could be made. The diplomatic ball was now in Ayub's court, but before he could respond, the Indian Army took the military initiative.

Within Pakistan, the justifications for Grand Slam were provided by a senior Pakistani official who gave three reasons for launching the operation: first, to retaliate for repeated Indian aggression across the CFL into Azad Kashmir since May 1965; secondly, to forestall further aggressive Indian moves; and finally, to prevent further aggravation of the conflict. The Pakistan military informed UNMOIP on 2 September that the operation was a purely defensive measure and Pakistan was forced to take action to stop the Indians from conquering AK (S/661, 6/9/65). This assertion was developed in the Security Council by the Pakistani Law Minister, Mr S. M. Zafar, who warned against the 'Indian propaganda line' saying India had seized posts in Azad Kashmir with the limited objective of stopping further infiltration was 'a trick...and Pakistan had reliable information that at the end of August India was preparing to mount a big offensive with a view to capturing Azad Kashmir' (SCOR, 20th Year, 1240th Meeting, 18/9/65).

On 15 November 1965, in a speech to the Pakistan National Assembly, Ayub Khan added a further explanation about Pakistan's actions. He said that simultaneously with the shelling of the West Pakistan village of Awan Sharif, the Indians were preparing the ground for launching a direct offensive against Pakistan from the Chhamb sector, and that the Pakistani forces had moved in support of the Kashmiri forces into the Chhamb sector and destroyed the aggressive positions which the Indian

Army had taken for an attack on Pakistan (Ayub Khan, *Speeches and Statements*, VIII, 75–6). Pakistan's argument that it had acted in self defence given recent Indian military activity across the CFL did elicit some international understanding, but had it been known that Grand Slam was planned in any event to complement Gibraltar, there would have been a very different international reaction.

Change of command

Although Grand Slam had not gone according to plan in some ways, it had still managed to punch a large hole in the Indian defences and was still on track to take the town of Akhnur in the next 24 hours. Unknown to Pakistani forces at the time, the Indian 191 Brigade had evacuated its defensive positions around Chhamb overnight (1/2 September) and had been ordered to fall back east of the Tawi towards Akhnur. As the Indian commander of the region himself admits, 'By last light 1 September it became evident that 191 Brigade was not in a position to withstand much longer the steam roller action of the enemy'. The Indians now rushed all available troops in the vicinity to defend Akhnur, which now became the critical focal point and the priority rather than the town of Chhamb. These included troops from 163 Mountain Brigade, 20 Lancers and 28 Infantry Brigade (H. Singh, 60).

Within 24 hours the Pakistani forces had managed to use their local advantage in artillery and armour to capture virtually all the area west of the river Tawi. Although Grand Slam had not succeeded in reaching Akhnur on the first day as Malik had hoped, this was still a definite success for the operation, and by first light on 2 September Akhnur was now within reach and Chhamb had been taken. The Indian government and GHQ now waited for the onslaught to begin again and for the inevitable push on Akhnur on 2 September with real trepidation.

News of the Pakistani advance had been downplayed by the Indian media and government as there was real fear in the Indian government of the effect it could have on both civilian and military morale. The 'sudden collapse' of 191 Brigade had caused 'a critical situation', (H. Singh, 61) and another Indian account admits that 41 Infantry Brigade was 'anxiously awaiting' the expected onslaught when the Indian defenders were saved by what must have appeared to be divine intervention (Praval, 225).

It was in the early afternoon of 2 September 1965 that one of the most controversial incidents of the war took place. With Akhnur within reach and Chhamb abandoned by the Indian forces, Musa flew to 7 Division HQ under the command of Major-General Yahya Khan and summoned Malik to meet him there as well. Musa asked Yahya to take command of Grand Slam with immediate effect in the presence of Malik at 1300 hours, 2 September, and even more dramatically, Malik was flown back with Musa to GHQ in Rawalpindi and then sent on to Murree, the HQ of 12 Division. This change of command was confirmed in a flash message from GHQ: '7 Division assume control of Operation Grand Slam with immediate effect...Further orders to be issued in accordance (with) plans discussed by Commander-in-Chief with commander 7 Division' (Gauhar, 333).

Malik had suspected that something was wrong as:

The de facto command changed the very first days after ops after the fall of Chhamb when Azmat Hayat (commander 10 Brigade) broke off wireless communication with me. I personally tried to find his HQ by chopper and failed. In late afternoon I sent Gulzar and Vahid, my MP officers to try and locate him but they too failed. The next day I tore into him and he sheepishly and nervously informed me that he "was Yahya's Brigadier". I had no doubt that Yahya had reached him the previous day and instructed him not to take further orders from me, while the formal change of command had yet to take place. This was a betrayal of many dimensions (Letter to brother, quoted Ahmed, 552).

It was a decision that, without exaggeration, may well have decided the course of the war. There is no doubt that this was a fundamentally flawed military decision, and so it can only be explained by some political motivation. As the decision was so critical to the war it is worth examining the possible logic and reasoning behind it. Such a momentous decision could simply not have been made by Musa on his own initiative; he was as always the messenger for Ayub, and whatever the later denials and silences, there is no doubt that the decision was made by Ayub and executed by Musa. As Ayub never took any of the many opportunities available to him in order to explain this decision, even years after the war, others close to him during the war, especially Musa and Gauhar, did so on his behalf, and they offer different explanations.

Musa claimed that the change of command from 12 Division to 7 Division—from Malik to Yahya—was a pre-planned move; that once Malik had secured Chhamb and territory east of the Tawi river, Yahya would take over. Musa also claims that it was not just Malik and Yahya who were aware of this plan, but other senior commanders also knew about this change of command strategy. Musa says that Yahya took 'over command on my orders and issued instructions for the resumption of the advance while I was there, since the first phase had been successfully, although belatedly, completed'. Musa's highly improbable explanation continues by saying that it would have been 'unsound' to allow Malik to continue fighting across the Tawi as he would have been too far removed from his HQ. The change of command, therefore—according to Musa—was because Malik's return to his HQ was an 'imperative operational necessity' and 'catered for in our plan'. Malik was blamed for not having exercised proper control over his troops on the front during 1 September, and Musa also charged Malik with having stretched the communication links between himself and his troops as well as between himself and GHQ. Musa claims that on visiting the 12 Division at Kharian, the staff officer there was unable to brief Musa as to the latest battle situation, to Musa's 'amazement' (Musa, *My Version*, 39–41).

Gauhar focuses on Malik's alleged lack of control of his troops during the first 24 hours, leaving no option for Ayub but to remove Malik from his command. Gauhar says that Ayub was briefed by Musa on his return from Swat to Rawalpindi on 30 August that Gibraltar had been a failure and now Grand Slam was not producing the 'spectacular breakthrough' that had been expected. Ayub, according to Gauhar, then decided 'the time had come to cut the losses and wind up the operation' and the decision to wind up was given to Yahya 'who was hitting the bottle' as he had been given a marginal role till now (Gauhar, 332). If this account is to be taken seriously, it begs a number of obvious questions. First, there is no mention by Gauhar of the 'well known' decision to change commanders once the river Tawi had been reached, as claimed by Musa. Secondly, Grand Slam had been launched on 1 September and had gone as well as could have been expected and so, if the decision was made on 30 August, then Grand Slam had not failed militarily; in fact it had badly damaged Indian morale and was poised to take the town of Akhnur, even according to Indian sources. Logically, therefore, Ayub's decision must have been taken on 1 September when Grand Slam was going well and had met little resistance, justifying Malik's line of attack, and so the claim of military failure is palpably not true. Thirdly, if the decision to wind down was taken, why was it entrusted to a man who, even according to his friends, was 'hitting the bottle' and had a reputation as an alcoholic, General Yahya? Finally, why was the man responsible for both Gibraltar and Grand Slam, Akhtar Malik, not asked by Ayub directly what the true nature of the operation was and given a chance to provide an explanation of the real picture on the ground? Neither Gauhar nor Musa claims that Malik was given any chance to meet or discuss the progress of Grand Slam with Ayub, and so it appears that none of the reasons provided stand up to scrutiny.

Musa's explanation has been contradicted by a number of senior army officers including the future Commander-in-Chief, Gul Hassan, who was the Director of Military Operations (DMO) inside GHQ and would certainly have been aware of the change of command plan had one existed. Instead Gul Hassan described himself as 'stunned' by the disclosure and said that Malik had spoken to him about wanting to capture Akhnur within 72 hours of launching Grand Slam, and that there was no reason to think the timetable was not still feasible. Gul Hassan also states that knowing Malik as he did, he was sure that Malik would have declined the command of the operation if he was only to lead it as far as the Tawi river (Gul Hassan, 186–7). The definitive evidence that Musa's assertion was simply not true is provided by Lt General Mahmud Ahmed who was given almost unfettered access to military papers in writing his account of the war, and who quotes from a GHQ order issued just before Grand Slam got under way. It reads: 'Depending on the development of these offensive operations 7 Division is expected to assume control on orders from GHQ of troops in Akhnur... On Orders from GHQ, 7 Division will assume control of troops in Akhnur area with the task of denying enemy line of communication Akhnur and Riasi towards Rajauri/Poonch (Ahmed, 96). In other words, only once Akhnur had been taken by 12 Division was it to relinquish control of that area to 7 Division, and there is no mention of a 'planned' change any earlier in any other document that General Ahmed or anyone else was able to find. Interestingly, even Yahya himself contradicted Musa when he later stated in an interview that, 'Since I was to take over the operation after capture of Akhnur... Change of Command should have taken place after the capture of Akhnur...General Akhtar Malik failed to cross Tawi until midday 2 September. This probably annoyed the C-in-C of

Pakistan Army who himself came on to the scene and ordered me to take over immediately' (Interview with Yahya Khan, quoted in M. Ahmed, 97).

There are also eyewitness accounts of the drama unfolding that day by, amongst others, Brigadier Chaudhry, Commander 4 Corps Artillery, responsible for the heavy artillery pounding of the Indian defences on 1 September. He recounts that he heard that Musa had arrived at the HQ of 25 Brigade (part of 7 Division) and wished to see him. Chaudhry says that he struggled to the area as it was a long distance from his location, and when he was informed of the change of command and that the reason given was the breakdown of the command structure, he was 'surprised' as he had not experienced that during the fighting of the previous day. In the event, he did not get an opportunity to meet Musa and explain this to him face-to-face, as he was informed by other officers that his presence was 'not required' (Brigadier A. A. K. Chaudhry, *September 1965*, Ferozsons, 1977, 55).

General Akhtar Malik as a professional soldier did not speak out at the time or later, and the only record from him of his feelings about what occurred is contained in a remarkable letter to his brother written in 1967, which was never intended for publication but was given to General Ahmed by Malik's son with permission to publish it. Malik says that 'At no time was I assigned any reason for being removed from command by Ayub, Musa or Yahya. They were all sheepish at best. I think the reasons will be given only when I am no more'. Malik goes on to say that 'I reasoned and then pleaded with Yahya that if it was credit he was looking for, he should take the overall command but let me go up to Akhnur as his subordinate but he refused' (Letter to brother, 22/11/1967, quoted Ahmed, 552). That does not appear be to the reaction of a man who either expected or wanted to be removed from command.

To this day there is still no credible official explanation for the change of command taking place when it did, and so it is left to historians to examine a number of the most likely reasons. One possible explanation is that Yahya was a close friend of Ayub's and known to be on unfriendly terms with Malik. With the capture of Akhnur apparently imminent, either Yahya had lobbied to be given command of Grand Slam and capture the prize of Akhnur, or Ayub had decided to help an old friend take the glory.

Secondly and highly controversially, it has been claimed by some that as General Akhtar Malik belonged to the Ahmadiyya sect (which was in 1974 declared by the Pakistan government under Bhutto to be non-Muslim), he was not to be permitted to become a war hero with the capture of Akhnur. Although this is widely believed in Pakistan to be the reason, it seems unlikely to have been a large factor in Ayub's mind. Despite his limitations, Ayub was not known for religious bigotry and was unlikely to have been swayed by this argument, if it was ever put to him, of which there is no evidence.

The third and most likely explanation appears to be that Ayub's doubts and hesitations about the whole operation and the risks involved with Grand Slam had reared up again. Apart from Malik and Gul Hassan, there seem to have been few senior army officers in the Pakistan army keen on the idea of all-out war with India and Musa was known to be sceptical about the chances of Gibraltar and Grand Slam achieving their objectives. Ayub had hesitated even before the launch of Grand Slam, and news that it was moving towards Akhnur meant that Ayub now decided to follow the advice of Musa rather than Malik and limit the offensive so as to avoid all-out war with India. Ayub must have felt that Pakistan had yet again demonstrated its military superiority over India and now was the time to wait for international pressure and India's overtures for peace. If that is what Ayub believed would follow he was to be sorely mistaken, and Malik would surely have been entitled to ask, if Ayub believed that war with India was inevitable with the capture of

Akhnur, why had this not occurred to Ayub in May 1965 when he (Malik) was given the green light by the president rather than mid-battle with operational success in sight? In any event, Malik accepted the decision with the discipline of a professional soldier and after his replacement was on 7 September awarded Pakistan's second highest gallantry award, the citation stating that he attacked a well-prepared and well-held garrison. Malik was moved to a non-operational command at the Pakistan army's military academy at Kakul (despite Musa's claims that he was needed along the LOC) and later to Ankara as the Pakistani Military Attaché at the embassy to Turkey. Akhtar Malik was one of the few senior generals from 1965 who did not write their accounts of the war in order to present their version of events. He wrote later that he had given

serious considerations to writing a book but given up the idea. The book would be the truth. And truth and the popular reaction to it would be good for my ego. But in the long run it would be an unpatriotic act. It would destroy the morale of the army, lower its prestige among the people, be banned in Pakistan and become a textbook in India. The first day of Grand Slam will be fateful in many ways...The book is therefore out (letter to brother, quoted Ahmed, 553).

Go slow

Evidence that Malik was removed from command simply for fear that his operation would succeed, amid serious concern about India's declaration of all-out war, comes from the immediate change in tempo of Grand Slam from 2 September. With the Indian defences in some disarray, the first orders of the new commander to his troops were to consolidate their position 'with a view to meet enemy counter-attacks'. There was nothing more than a negligible chance of an Indian counter-attack on 2 September and all the senior officers involved in Grand Slam must have known it. It must have been with considerable relief that the Indians realised that on 2 September 'the enemy probed forward with comparative caution' (H. Singh, 61).

Only the town of Jaurian now stood between the forces of Grand Slam and Akhnur, and not even the Indian soldiers tasked with holding Jaurian expected to be able to hold out against what must have appeared to be an imminent assault. At 1530 hours, 2 September Yahya ordered the 10 Infantry Brigade to establish a bridgehead across the river Tawi, this was carried out without any real Indian resistance. The 102 Brigade crossed unopposed at 1930 hours, 2 September but was ordered to consolidate the position there rather than push on. Yahya's next move was to order troops to capture Jaurian by last light on 3 September. This delay enabled the Indian 41 Mountain Brigade to strengthen its position by two further infantry battalions. The formidable Pakistani artillery was once again called upon to assist the advance towards Jaurian. Their fierce assault had such a demoralising affect on the Indian troops that the Indian 161 Field Regiment abandoned its guns and retreated in disarray on 4 September. Harbakhsh Singh described the abandonment of weapons on a battlefield as 'shocking conduct' by 161 Field Regiment and said that despite his explicit orders to retrieve the guns, they were unable to do so. This abandonment of the guns and the failure to retrieve them was said to remain 'a blemish on the fair name of the 161 Field Regiment as well as 10 Infantry Division'. Despite what appears to have been deliberately slow progress to Jaurian, the pressure from Pakistani armour and artillery was beginning to tell on 41 Mountain Brigade defending the town, and so the Indian high command gave the order on the night of 4/5 September for the troops to withdraw to Akhnur and abandon Jaurian (H. Singh, 62). The slow pace also surprised the authors of the British military review of the war which said that it was not 'until 4 Sep that the second wave of the attack fetched up against Jaurian, time having apparently been wasted effecting a scorched earth policy on the way.

Subsequent visits to the battlefield showed little evidence on the ground of severe fighting in country good for defence' (British military review, 13). On 5 September, Jaurian was finally taken by Pakistani troops.

The leisurely pace of the advance also frustrated some of the troops involved in Grand Slam, and Brigadier Chaudhry writes that on 5 August, Musa visited the front at midday and met Yahya; after the meeting, Chaudhry says that he was informed by Musa after the conference 'that there was no point in taking Akhnur' and the troops should take up positions on the high ground between Jaurian and Akhnur. Chaudhry says he was 'stunned' by the revelation, and 'the decision did not make sense to me. Akhnur was within our grasp...Yahya could have taken it without undue losses' (Chaudhry, 56).

India now placed the defence of the town in the hands of 10 Infantry Division which was also bolstered by the arrival of fresh regiments, but Pakistani troops were by the afternoon of 5 September reported to be within four miles of Akhnur. With Akhnur now seriously threatened (but whether Yahya intended to push on is a moot point), the Indian government had to decide how best to defend Akhnur or whether to open another front to relieve the pressure on this sector where Pakistan had the territorial advantages. The possible fall of Akhnur and the situation in Chhamb sector were described by the most senior Indian general in the region as a situation 'slipping into disaster', and so India now did what it had threatened to do for some time—attack in a place of its own choosing. In the early hours of 6 September, Indian forces crossed the Punjab border and a general all-out war was now under way. As news of the attack came through to Yahya and the forces operating in Grand Slam, orders followed for the redeployment of artillery and infantry to the Lahore front. Grand Slam, according to a senior Indian general, was 'checkmated just in the nick of time' (H. Singh, 63). This would not have come as news for Malik, and one can only wonder what he must have felt watching his carefully laid offensive grinding to halt.

Review of Grand Slam

How much long-term difference the swift capture of Akhnur would have made if Malik had been able to capture the bridge and town by 2 September is still debated. Malik himself thought that capturing Akhnur would have prevented India from opening a second front as it would have been threatened in Jammu and Kashmir and would have had to deal with the threat before it could risk opening a second front.

The British military assessment of the war believed that if the Pakistani troops had pushed on to Akhnur, 'it is difficult to see how they could have failed to capture Akhnur. Whether they would have held it, however, after the Indians took the inevitable step of further escalation is very doubtful' (British military review 1966, 13). The British obviously felt that the Indians would inevitably have attacked across the Punjab border where the terrain meant that their greater numbers would tell, and Akhnur would have had to be abandoned in the defence of Lahore or Sialkot.

In the event, the proposition was never put to the test as Malik was prevented from capturing Akhnur and Yahya made little or no effort to do so. After the war, Brigadier Chaudhry of the Artillery 4 Corps asked Yahya why he had not taken the town of Akhnur when he had the chance to do so: 'His reply was short and crisp. "You know I was told not to do so"' (Chaudhry, 63). This reply is entirely credible and can be the only logical explanation of a change of command after an initially good start to Grand Slam and the surprisingly slow speed at which Pakistani troops had advanced after the fall of Chhamb under as to Yahya's command. As Ayub was the only person who could have given this order to Yahya, it is only Ayub who could have offered his reasons for this decision, but unfortunately no explanation was ever given by him and historians can only speculate as to why it happened. The most credible explanation is that Ayub had worries about a general war in South Asia and the widespread ramifications once Grand Slam was under way and wanted to pull back from Akhnur, with international pressure on India not to open another front sufficient for him to claim victory.

Despite its bold objectives and initial success, Grand Slam failed in both its military and its political objectives. Militarily, Grand Slam was to result in the capture of the vital town of Akhnur which was a clear and stated objective of the operation, the only question mark being what troops of the 12 Division would do next. Although the capture of Akhnur would not have been as much of a fatal blow as that of Jammu, it still would have placed the Indian troops inside the Valley in danger of being choked off from the rest of India and would have been a major blow to the Indian army and government. Politically, too, Grand Slam failed in its primary objective; the application of military force inside ICK had failed to convince either the Indian government or the international community that it was time for India to accept arbitration or a plebiscite in Kashmir to resolve the issue once and for all. Indeed, Grand Slam appears to have had the opposite political effect within India; it united Indian politicians in determination not to give in an inch to what they perceived as Pakistani bullying, and there appears to have been no time during the offensive when India suggested any compromise on the issue of Kashmir. The international reaction was also far from encouraging. Although the Security Council and its permanent members were muted in their criticism of Pakistan's actions because of Indian movement across the CFL, there was no support either for Pakistan's actions, nor any international pressure on India to try to resolve the Kashmir dispute.

6

OPERATION RIDDLE

The Indian strategy

From as far back as 1949, the Indian cabinet had approved military plans based on the hypothetical situation of the Pakistan army having taken the military initiative in launching an attack in Kashmir. In the event of such an offensive, Indian troops in Kashmir would seek to contain the Pakistani forces while the main Indian Army would attack across the Punjab border towards Lahore and Sialkot, and a diversionary secondary action would also be launched towards Rawalpindi or Karachi to prevent a concentration of Pakistani forces in the major theatre of West Punjab. The Indian plan also talked about a possible occupation of Lahore in order to compel the Pakistan government to accept peace (Lorne Kavic, *India's Quest for Security: Defence Policies*, Berkeley and Los Angeles: University of California Press, 1967, 37). This plan indicates that India had always factored in the principle of attacking West Pakistan in response to a possible Pakistani attack in ICK, and although it does not clarify whether Indian retaliation was inevitable, it strongly indicates that it was highly likely and an Indian offensive in the Punjab would be preferable to trying to fight purely in Kashmir.

Once Gibraltar was launched, India was initially confident that it could contain the Pakistani operations inside ICK and limit its response to border posts and strategic passes along the LOC. After carrying out these successful operations, India did not seek to reinforce the Chhamb sector in anticipation of any Pakistani retaliation, and seemed completely taken aback by Pakistan's use of its armour and artillery. The initially rapid advance of forces from Grand Slam on Akhnur reduced the possibility of India being willing to accept the risk involved in attempting to hold the Pakistan advance solely by action in Kashmir, as the cost of such a failure could be very high for India and Akhnur was increasingly hard to defend, despite the half-hearted attempt to surround the town by Yahya. The Indian plan to launch an offensive across the Punjab border was updated and reiterated on 9 August 1965 when India's GHQ decided that if ICK was threatened by a Pakistani attack, then India's XI Corps would be given the task of executing an all-out assault on Lahore. Therefore, when on 1 September Operation Grand Slam was launched, the Indian troops in Punjab had already been placed on high alert and told to be ready for 'imminent hostilities'. It appears from this account that it was on 3 September that the go-ahead for the invasion was given and H-Hour for the attack was fixed at 0400 hours, 6 September (Chakravorty, 144).

After the ceasefire, Shastri described a cabinet meeting at which the decision was made but did not give a date. He stated that Pakistan's attack was 'so swift and formidable' that India could not afford merely to talk of defending itself, but had to take decisive action with all haste, and he had told his generals firmly that they must go ahead and not flinch (Shastri, *When Freedom is Menaced*, 55). The Indian Defence Minister Chavan's statement on 2 September supported this view as he declared that the necessary countermeasures had been initiated and that militarily it was a developing situation (LSD, Third Series, XLV:13, 2/9/65).

There were a number of factors which made the Indian attack on Lahore inevitable, and the only surprise was the obvious lack of Pakistani preparation for or expectation of the Indian response. Given the terrain of the Punjab plain, the Indian army was likely to attack either Lahore or Sialkot. Sialkot was important strategically as it was close to Kashmir and capture of that town would not only endanger Lahore and Rawalpindi, but also help choke off Grand Slam. Lahore's advantage as far as India was concerned was that it had held huge symbolic importance as the historic cultural and educational centre of northern India since Mughal times and was only 14 miles from the Indian border. If Lahore had fallen to India, it would have propelled the Indian army and Shastri to hugely popular status and would have helped the Indian army silence its critics since its poor showing in the war with China and the Kutch fighting.

Lahore (the second largest city of Pakistan) in 1965 had a population of just over 1.3 million, and was Pakistani Punjab's capital. It was located at the northern end of a 50-mile-wide land gap between the rivers Ravi and Sutlej. This gap was protected but not completely sealed off by the Bamanwala-Ravi-Bedian-Diplapur (BRBD) Canal which runs north-south between Lahore and the border. This was known to the Indians as the Icchogil Canal, and it linked the Upper Chenab and the Dipalpur Canals. According to the Indians, the BRBD Canal was between 80 and 140 feet wide, up to 15 feet deep, steep walled and lined (Lt Gen. P. S. Bhagat, *The Sword and the Shield—India 1965*, New Delhi: Vikas Publishers, 1974, 29). The dimensions described are an exaggeration, but the fact remains that there was a large canal running a few miles to the east of Lahore which would undoubtedly provide some cover against an armoured Indian attack. It is ironic that construction of the BRBD Canal which offered Lahore some measure of protection started in 1949 as a direct result of unfriendly Indian action affecting the supply of water to Pakistan in 1948 at a time when there were still hundreds of thousands of Muslim refugees in camps in West Pakistan. India had cut off water supplies to the canal in Dipalpur from the Ferozepur headworks, an action that left 5 per cent of West Pakistan's main agricultural areas without water at the main sowing time and also left Lahore without its main source of municipal water. Supplies were later resumed under an agreement signed on 4 May 1948 which was later superseded by the Indus Waters Treaty. However, in 1948 Pakistan considered it necessary to provide alternative supplies to the area, which meant the construction of the BRBD Canal, completed in 1958.

From Indian East Punjab, there are three main approaches to Lahore. The shortest is from Amritsar to Lahore on the Grand Trunk Road (GT Road). The GT Road, also known as the *Sadak-e-Azam*, was one of the longest and oldest roads in Asia and linked Peshawar in the north-west of Pakistan to Bengal in the east. The second route is along the Harike-Khalra-Barki approach and the third is from the town of Kasur which the Indians could approach from either Ferozepur or Khem Karan. Despite Lahore's proximity to the Indian border, it did enjoy some protection against an Indian attack. First, there was the BRBD Canal already mentioned; this was equidistant from the city of Lahore and the border and would not be easy for an armoured attack to cross. Secondly, at the northern end of the canal, there was the river Ravi, one of the great rivers of the Punjab plain, which was an even more formidable obstacle than the canal to an Indian armoured offensive. Thirdly, all roads leading to Lahore narrowed as they approached the city, which meant the defending forces could concentrate their fire there knowing that the offensive forces would have to pass that way if they intended to reach Lahore. Fourthly, the border had been mined since the 1950s, which meant that although the minefields were never likely to halt an advance, they would at least slow down any invading force while mines were cleared and would buy the defending forces some time.

The issue of the minefields was to prove controversial as it was later claimed by Gauhar that in the summer of 1965 Pakistani minefields were removed from the border at the request of some generals who owned land on the Indian border, following the ceasefire over Kutch, in order to allow the land to be farmed (Ashgar Khan, *The First Round*, xiv). The fact that mines were cleared from the Pakistani side of the border is not disputed by General Ahmed, but the explanation offered is different as he claims that the mines and defence works along the BRBD Canal were removed to prevent them being damaged by the monsoon rain (Ahmed, 155). Gauhar's assertion was indignantly denied by Musa who said that any such request from a general would have been refused and that general would have been removed from the army and told 'to go and live in his mine-infested land' (Musa, *My Version*, 31). Some confirmation that mines were not in place by September comes from another general's account of the war, based on interviews and documents available from military officers. He states that on 3 August General Sarfraz (GOC 10 Division) asked General Rana, the Corps commander, if they should occupy defensive positions along the border. 'The answer was "Negative". Sarfraz persisted, "Please allow us to lay mines". The answer was "No. We do not want to provoke the Indians"' (Major General Shaukat Riza, *The Pakistan Army War 1965*, Lahore: Services Book Club, 1984, 191). Whatever the truth about the mine removal, the fact remains that Pakistani forces along the Lahore/Sialkot front were not expecting a full-scale invasion by India and were not on a war footing despite the fighting in the Chhamb front.

Comparison of forces' strength

The Institute of Strategic Studies provides a neutral picture of the two armies' strength on the eve of war. The ISS stated that the Indian Army had six infantry and nine mountain divisions at full strength, with a further four divisions under formation;

one armoured division and armoured brigade armed with Centurion and Sherman tanks; and four light tank regiments. India may also have had additional regiments of Centurions and Shermans which were integral to some of the infantry divisions. An official US estimate was that of the fifteen full-strength infantry/mountain divisions of India, six were stationed in the central and eastern sectors along the Chinese-Indian border and on the East Pakistan-India border and three were in the Kashmir Valley. If this was accurate, then there remained just six infantry/mountain divisions and units of four under-strength divisions and all of India's armour except for an unknown but possibly smaller number of light tanks available for use in the Punjab. This estimate roughly matches the Pakistan government's, which claims that India deployed four infantry divisions (the 7th, 14th, 15th and 26th) the two mountain (the 4th and 6th) divisions, the 50th parachute regiment, the 41st Mountain Brigade, the 1st Armoured Division, the 2nd Independent Armoured Brigade and two tank regiments (the 2nd Lancers and the 62nd Cavalry). According to a Pakistani source, these formations collectively added up to 77 infantry battalions, of which there are normally nine in an infantry division (G. Ahmed, 103) India claimed that this estimate was too high and Indian historians have generally omitted from the tally the two infantry/mountain divisions in reserve, the mountain and parachute brigade and the two tank regiments (Bhagat, 19–20). However, the estimate of neutral observers such as the Institute of Strategic Studies and the US was that India would be able to deploy more forces than it admitted.

As far as Pakistan's forces are concerned, the ISS estimated that on the eve of the war, Pakistan had six infantry divisions, one of which, 14 Infantry, was based in East Pakistan while another, 8 Infantry, had fought in the Rann of Kutch and was still in that area, which left four divisions along the Punjab/ Kashmir border. Pakistan was estimated to have around ten armoured regiments armed with M-47 and M-48 Pattons and M-4 Shermans, and two or three reconnaissance regiments armed with M-24 Chaffees. According to the ISS, the armoured regiments were probably formed into one armoured division and a separate independent armoured brigade while each infantry division was estimated to have one integral armoured unit. General Ahmed states that the Pakistan Army's strength in 1965 was eight divisions, which included 1 Armoured Division and the newly-formed 6 Armoured Division. 11 Division had only been running for three months when war broke out in September and so was still under formation. The rough parity in armoured units conceals an advantage in numbers in favour of India, which was estimated to have 1,100 to 1,400 medium and light tanks while the Indians claim that Pakistan had between 800 and 900 tanks, including about 360 Patton tanks. It is impossible to say to what extent India's numerical advantage was offset by the allegedly superior design of Pakistan's main battle tank, the Patton, over India's Centurion. The Patton outguns (90 against 84 mm) and outranges the Centurion (1,800 against 1,200 yards) and is also faster; it is also equipped with infra-red gunsight which enables it to fight at night. Furthermore, Pakistan's artillery was superior to India's but again India had the numerical advantage of around 2,500 pieces to Pakistan's 900, though Pakistan's heavy artillery had a greater range than India's at 25,000 to 18,000 yards.

As far as air strength was concerned, it is widely accepted that the PAF force's strength in the west of the country when the war began was approximately eighty-five Sabres and twelve Starfighters. Assuming that 60 per cent of the Indian Air Force's interceptors and fighter-bombers were allotted to the Western command, then India had at its disposal about sixty Mysteres, sixty Gnats, ninety Hunters as well as some Vampires, or an advantage of 210 to 97, which could easily be reinforced up to 300 by transferring planes from other parts of India. Because of

India's numerical superiority, the PAF had to refrain from combat wherever feasible as there are risks inherent in aerial combat and defeat there would have increased the overall vulnerability of Pakistani ground forces to air attack.

Since 1947, the task of defending the city of Lahore had been given to 10 Division, under the overall command of 1 Corps of the Pakistan Army. A newly created 11 Division (of which more later) was by this time (in the summer of 1965) given the task of defending the southern approach to Lahore near Kasur. 10 Division comprised a mixture of infantry battalions and armoured regiments, which had one squadron of M-47 Patton tanks, the other tanks were Shermans. 11 Division was little more than three infantry battalions and was later bolstered by the arrival of Pakistan's main armoured force, 1 Armoured Division, in its sector.

Order of battle

Although the whole Indian strategy and offensive were under the overall supervision of the Indian Chief of Army Staff, Lt General Jayanto Nath Chaudhri, the precise direction and day-to-day tactical decisions were usually finalised by Lt General Harbakhsh Singh, GOC Western Command. Under Harbakhsh Singh, there were three army corps: the XVth under Lt General Kashmir Singh Katoch in the Kashmir Valley, the I[st] under Lt General P O Dunn, who had his troops in northern Punjab facing Sialkot, and the XIth under Lt General Joginder Singh Dhillon, who was tasked with leading the assault against Lahore.

The plan as finalised by Harbakhsh Singh, codenamed Operation Riddle, involved a three-pronged attack on Lahore from all the three possible routes described above, by the XI Corp. The forces operating in Riddle were:

15 Infantry Division—Major General Narinjan Prasad.
38 Infantry Brigade—Brigadier Pathak.

54 Infantry Brigade—Brigadier Rikh.

96 Infantry Brigade—Brigadier Malhotra.

50 Para Regiment—Brigadier Nambiar.

4 *Mountain Division—Major General Gurbakhsh Singh.*

9 Deccan Horse.

7 Mountain Brigade—Brigadier D. S. Sindhu.

33 Mountain Brigade.

62 Mountain Brigade—Brigadier H. C. Gahlaut.

4 Mountain Artillery Brigade.

7 *Infantry Division—Major General SK Sibal.*

29 Infantry Brigade—Brigadier Pritam Singh.

48 Infantry Brigade—Brigadier Shahaney.

65 Infantry Brigade.

Opposing them on the Pakistan side were:

Pakistan's 10 Infantry Division—Major General Sarfraz Khan.

22 Brigade—Brigadier Qayyum Sher.

103 Brigade—Brigadier Asghar.

114 Brigade—Brigadier Aftab Ahmad.

10 Division Artillery—Brigadier Jamil Akhtar Aziz.

11 *Infantry Division—Major General Abdul Hamid Khan.*

21 Infantry Brigade—Brigadier Sahib Dad.

52 Infantry Brigade—Brigadier S. R. H. Rizvi.

106 Infantry Brigade—Brigadier Nawazish Ali.

The Pakistan Army also had at its disposal on this front two armoured regiments, the 15 Lancers and 32 Tank Delivery Unit and divisional artillery.

Riddle envisaged the offensive commencing with 15 Infantry Division under Prasad which was to advance along the Amritsar–Lahore route, while 7 Infantry Division headed by Sibal was to move on the Harike–Khalra–Barki road and 4 Mountain Division under Gurbakhsh Singh was to enter Pakistan along the Khem Karan–Kasur route. These forces had been assembled from various parts of India during the standoff

169

over Kutch but now had to be moved to the front and be ready to move by 5 September. It is recognised as a major failure of Pakistan's military intelligence that it ignored or misinterpreted Indian intentions as regards the build-up of forces, and the last-minute movement of troops therefore achieved what the Indian GHQ had hoped for—complete surprise. The last-minute and long-distance troop movement did take its toll, however, as some Indian troops arrived exhausted and were unable to join in the offensive because of exhaustion and lack of supplies. The Pakistani 10 and 11 Divisions were still under strict orders not to do anything that could be viewed as provocative and despite occasional warnings that they should be prepared for an Indian invasion, the reality was they were not ready, either mentally or physically, to face Riddle. The war diary of 114 Brigade of 5 September shows that although the 10 Division commanders did receive orders to move into battle location, 'GHQ feel that no war expected on the Lahore front and that this move was taken as a precautionary measure' (Ahmed, 164). Facing India's XI Corp were the two infantry divisions mentioned and 1 Armoured Division belonging to Pakistan's 1st Corps under Lieutenant-General Bakhtiar Mohammad Rana. On the northern and central axis of the Indian advance, the 10th Infantry Division under Major-General Sarfraz Khan, based at Lahore, was tasked with holding the line extending southward from the Ravi to a small tributary which is crossed by the Khalra–Lahore Road south-east of the BRBD Canal. On the right of 10 Division, covering the southern axis of the Indian advance, was the newly raised 11th Infantry Division under Major-General Abdul Hamid Khan with its HQ at Kasur, which held the line south of and including Ganda Singhwala. The Pakistani 1 Armoured Division was able to reach the front by 8 September in support of 11 Division but was not to play any role in Operation Riddle.

Operation Riddle: the Amritsar—Lahore border

Operation Riddle began on schedule at 0330 hours with a thrust along the Grand Trunk Road at Atari-Wagah border to Lahore. This was led by 15 Infantry Division under General Niranjan Prasad, who planned the attack in two phases. In the first phase, 54 Infantry Brigade with three infantry battalions, the 3 Jat, the 15 Dogra and the 13 Punjab, under Brigadier Rikh led the assault.

54 Infantry Brigade overwhelmed the paramilitary Pakistan Rangers unit at the village of Dial with some ease and advanced to the village of Dograi. This village was five miles from the border and ten miles from the centre of Lahore, and was the first target of Riddle west of the BRBD Canal. There is no doubt that the attack took the Pakistan 10 Division by surprise; the British High Commissioner said 'the Pakistanis were taken by surprise. Their troops had not been alerted and were asleep in their barracks' (James, 136). Some of the first panicked reports received from the Pakistani troops at the border expressed hope that the fighting was nothing more than nervous Indian troops opening fire. (Ahmed, 166). Pakistani troops on the east side of the BRBD Canal were quickly overwhelmed by the large oncoming Indian force and the Pakistani troops fell back behind the canal.

At 0700 hours the PAF made its first major air attack of the war by attacking Indian troops near Wagah, which not only caused losses to the Indian side in men and equipment but also slowed the Indian attack down by an estimated two hours. The PAF was able to operate with relative freedom and its bombing resulted not only in ammunition losses for the Indian troops, the 3 Jat regiment also lost its second-command and heavy guns and mortars (Chakravorty, 148). The PAF intervention bought invaluable time for General Sarfraz to rush troops to the front and the Indian advance was further slowed by 3 Baluch Regiment which fought hard along the BRBD Canal. The Indian battalion leading the attack, 3 Jat, had only personal weapons and no armoured support. Even more dangerously the Indian battalion, was now outside the range of its own artillery protection which was therefore unable to provide supporting fire. The battalions of 3 Jat and 13 Punjab advanced under Pakistani air and artillery attacks and managed to get to within 500 yards of the railway bridge over the BRBD Canal by 1030 hours, but were unable to move from the railway station area until 1400 hours that day. At 1420 hours 3 Jat was ordered to fall back to the village of Gosal Dial held by the 15 Dogra, as it was unable to advance and had used up most of its ammunition.

Harbakhsh Singh was very disappointed by the failure of 54 Infantry Brigade's commander to keep in contact with 3 Jat once it had reached the canal. He blamed Brigadier Rikh for not only losing contact with the advancing troops but also failing to maintain the pressure, and a 'brilliant success was allowed to slip away unexploited'. Brigadier Rikh also lost contact with his division's HQ, which seemed to be unaware of the exact location of the battalion and therefore ordered it to pull back to the village of Gosal Dial. In subsequent recriminations over the order to 3 Jat to withdraw, Rikh later said that the withdrawal was made with the permission of the GOC 15 Infantry, though this was denied by Prasad, but the argument was now academic as Riddle had lost its edge and momentum and was 'throwing away a cheap victory...for want of aggressive and enterprising leadership' (H. Singh, 90–91). All India Radio and the BBC had broadcast news of the city of Lahore having fallen to the Indian offensive on the morning of 6 September; both reports were proved wrong and the morale of the civilian population of Lahore was reported to be excellent.

Fighting now focused on Batapur bridge, south of 3 Jat's field of operation, and one of the major canal bridges past Dograi. The Indian assault here was led by 13 Punjab and they got to within 500 yards of the railway bridge at around 1000 hours.

Military planning by the Pakistani forces was meant to have ensured that all such major bridges were wired for demolition in the event of an Indian attack, but this bridge's demolition charges were not ready on 6 September. Pakistani sappers had begun work frantically up on news of the attack but Indian forces managed to get close to the bridge on the morning of 6 September when the explosive charges were not yet complete. The result was that the first demolition attempt failed to blow up the bridge, but it was rendered unfit for armoured crossing. In any event, the Indian troops were met by fierce shelling under the command of 114 Brigade and were said later to have shown 'an inexplicably lethargic attitude to command'. 13 Punjab's performance was judged to have been 'depressing and deplorable' especially in comparison to the more daring moves of 3 Jat regiment (H. Singh, 91).

In this sector, therefore, Riddle forces were now facing some determined defensive fighting by the defending 10 Division, and by the late afternoon the initial assault had resulted in the Indian troops not only being halted but also giving up some of the main gains of the offensive, including Dograi. The afternoon reverses seem to have dented the morale of the GOC 15 Infantry as Prasad reported at 1300 hours that 'his position was desperate on account of heavy casualties and no further offensive action was possible'. Harbakhsh Singh says that he found this account hard to believe and so went to see with his own eyes the military state of affairs on the ground, and concluded that the only thing seriously damaged was the will to fight of General Prasad. Harbakhsh Singh said of Prasad that 'there was the unmistakeable air of the defeatist about him', but he decided to give Prasad an opportunity to pull himself together and redeem himself (H. Singh, 92).

Another attack was ordered on the afternoon of 6 September by the Indian 38 Infantry to capture the bridge near Bhasin— which, unknown to the Indian forces, had already been blown up by the Pakistani sappers. 38 Brigade began its move around 2030 hours, 6 September but was soon bogged down by accurate Pakistani artillery fire and took up defensive positions and was unable to advance at all. During the fighting 38 Brigade lost contact with headquarters of 15 Division and so Prasad set out himself in the afternoon of 7 September to try and locate its whereabouts with a small group. Unfortunately for the hapless Prasad, Pakistani forces ambushed the team and not only captured twelve men and four jeeps but also, even more embarrassingly for the Indians, captured Prasad's briefcase and notebook and then broadcast the contents on Pakistan Radio (Chakravorty, 151). This episode was the last straw for Harbakhsh Singh whose patience was already wearing thin, and he now decided that Prasad's continued command of 15 Infantry Division was 'most harmful'; this last fiasco was to cost Prasad his command (and later his service), and at 2300 hours, 7 September, he was replaced by Major General Mohinder Singh. The harsh but inescapable conclusion was that, 'By the evening of 7 September 1965, 15 Infantry Division had accomplished none of its tasks' (H. Singh, 92–4). 54 Infantry Brigade had dug in at Gosal Dial, just inside Pakistan, and 38 Infantry Brigade was based at Sadhanwali; both were now in defensive mode.

By midday on 7 September, Sarfraz was feeling confident enough to start planning a counter-offensive as it appeared that the Indian offensive had petered out and it would be an opportune moment to strike back. The main problem facing such an audacious plan was the lack of forces available to 10 Division as they not only faced much larger forces spread out against them, but had few reserves available in case the counter-offensive failed. Nonetheless, 22 Brigade under Brigadier Qayyum Sher was tasked with attacking Riddle forces across the BRBD Canal at Chahiwal. By the evening of 7 September, troops from 23 Cavalry, 18 Baluch and 15 FF were in position and ordered to move across the canal and attack Indian troops at

Bheni at 0400 hours, 8 September. In contrast with the criticism Indian commanders faced of showing a lack of leadership, Brigadier Qayyum Sher gallantly led the attack from the front in a jeep with his 'plate and pennant visible' (Riza, 203).

The reality of a Pakistani counter-attack appears to have caught the Indians completely by surprise, and Bheni was recaptured by the daring offensive by 0830 hours. The extent of the shock became apparent when the 13 Punjab and 15 Dogra 'broke the line and abandoned their defences'. The Indians were totally taken aback by the fact and speed of the counter-attack so soon after the launch of Riddle; their senior general described how Pakistan's 10 Division 'reacted viciously...and it began to exert heavy pressure' (H. Singh, 94). The 13 Punjab and 15 Dogra regiments were temporarily rallied and told to hold firm, but it was obvious they were in no position to continue the fight and they had to be replaced by 96 Infantry Brigade on 9 September. The Indian forces were particularly surprised by the fact that Pakistani forces had managed to attack across the BRBD Canal, a direction they had not believed to be possible because all bridges along the canal had been blown up and damaged in the first phase of Riddle on 6 September. The Indians began to imagine that the only way this was possible was that Pakistan had built secret underground tunnels for the BRBD Canal which it was now using. This was almost certainly not the case, and no Pakistani writer has ever claimed this engineering feat; it appears to have been the use of temporary bridges put up by the Pakistani engineering corps that enabled the canal crossing (Ahmed, 182).

On 10 September the Indian offensive surrendered more of its early gains when 1 Jat and 6 Kumaon regiments were also pushed back after heavy fighting, and Indian GHQ was now becoming sufficiently concerned for the protection of the Indian city of Amritsar for additional Indian reinforcements now to be sent to the front simply to protect the route to Amritsar and ensure that Pakistan's counter-offensive did not develop any more dangerously.

The success of 10 Division in pushing the Indians back to the international border raised the brief but fleeting possibility of Sarfraz trying to march on past the international border into India itself and, potentially, all the way to Amritsar. This was simply unrealistic given the very limited troops at the disposal of 10 Division, but the counter-offensive ordered by him had hugely raised morale within the Pakistani army and GHQ and, with the exception of the loss of Dograi in a later Indian counter-offensive, this particular front was to remain fairly stable until the conclusion of the war. Despite having been taken by surprise on the first morning of 6 September, 10 Division had acquitted itself with some honour and fulfilled its role of protecting Lahore.

The Khalra-Barki axis

The Khalra-Barki-Lahore road was the central axis of the Indian offensive towards Lahore and the defence of this particular front was the responsibility of Pakistan's 103 Brigade commanded by Brigadier Mohammed Asghar. The Indian troops tasked with capturing the bridge on the BRBD Canal and push on were the Indian 7 Infantry Division led by Major-General S. K. Sibal, who had two brigades under his command, 65 Infantry Brigade and 48 Infantry Brigade.

The main obstacle after the crossing was the village of Barki, which was protected by units of 103 Brigade and was about a quarter of a mile from the BRBD Canal, only 7 miles from the border and 14 miles from Lahore. Around 4 miles south-east of Barki, the road crosses the Hudiara Drain whose south-eastern approach passes Hudiara and Nurpur, and yet another water obstacle for the advancing troops was the Bhuchar Kahna Distributary, a water channel originating in India but passing through this area.

48 Brigade was tasked with leading the offensive and its orders were to capture Barki and secure the bridge over the BRBD Canal by last light on 6 September. Along the same front, 17 Rajput and other troops were to cross along the Wan-Bedian and to secure Bedian by last light on 6 September. As with the Atari border crossing, the Indian attack achieved an initial degree of success as the Pakistani Sutlej Rangers were quickly overwhelmed in the early morning of 6 September when the offensive commenced at 0330 hours. Much to their surprise, the Indian troops from 7 Infantry did not encounter much resistance at the Bhuchar-Kahna Distributary, but they were held up at the Hudiara Drain. At 1000 hours the Indian advance was temporarily halted as the Indian tanks trying to cross the bridge at Hudiara Drain were hit with anti-tank fire. Despite this, the leading Indian battalion from 48 Infantry Brigade had covered the 3 miles to Hudiara within 90 minutes, but it now came under Pakistani artillery fire from across the canal.

The bridge at Hudiara Drain was not ready for demolition by the Pakistani defenders, but by 1000 hours a partial demolition attempt made the bridge difficult for Indian tanks to cross. Pakistan's artillery used its heavy guns from both the villages of Hudiara and Nurpur to shell the Indian forces and caused some delay. As 48 Infantry had suffered casualties during this assault, Sibal decided to switch 65 Infantry into the lead to try and secure the village of Barki and continue the advance. Pakistani forces in the village of Nurpur, across the Hudiara Canal, were under continuous pressure from Indian shelling and the company pulled back across the Hudiara Drain at about 1500 hours and blew up the bridge behind it. By 1700 hours the village of Nurpur was in Indian hands, but 65 Infantry Brigade could not continue its advance until a temporary bridge was installed. Sibal ordered the erection of a usable bridge by first light on 7 September but owing to administrative difficulties and constant Pakistani shelling, the Indians troops did not manage to get a temporary bridge across until 1400 hours. Even then, when a bridge was in place and the advance resumed, 65 Infantry Brigade spent three days trying to clear the ground around Barki by capturing surrounding villages instead of making a frontal attack on Barki. It was not until a direct order was received from Sibal that a determined frontal assault was made to take the village of Barki on 10 September. The Indian delay meant that Pakistani troops had a few days to lay mines and prepare for the assault.

A fierce defence of Barki took place on 10 September, led in the most part by Major Aziz Bhatti (later decorated posthumously with the highest Pakistani military award); the village was described by the Indians as 'a prestigious objective of great tactical importance' (H. Singh, 96). The village does not appear to have been given that level of strategic importance by Pakistani GHQ, but there is no doubt that the defence of Barki was fierce and tenacious. The village was eventually captured after some heavy hand-to-hand fighting during the night of 10/11 September; ironically Major Bhatti survived the assault on Barki, having led an orderly withdrawal from the village, but was killed the next day by an Indian tank shell. After the capture of Barki, 48 Brigade was ordered to undertake a mopping up operation on the eastern bank of the BRBD Canal and capture and destroy the bridge at Jahman. No real progress was made and the orders were carried out so poorly that the Indian brigade commander was relieved of his command on 14 September. The new commander was also unable to make much headway, and as on the Amristar-Lahore front the Indians were unable to make any real progress in this sector until the end of the war. The attack on Bedian, also, did not go according to plan for the Riddle as Indian troops were unable to take this village and it remained in Pakistani hands for the duration of the war.

However, on the whole, 7 Division did manage to hold on to most of its early gains and was deemed to have performed better than the other Indian divisions involved in Riddle. Harbakhsh Singh felt that the performance of 7 Infantry Division 'compensated in large measure the reverses suffered by us in the rest of the Corps zone' (H. Singh, 98). Although it is true that 7 Division had some tangible success to show for its offensive, it had moved slowly and failed to break through the defensive positions of the Pakistan Army despite facing only brigade strength opposition. For the duration of the war, 7 Infantry did not manage to advance further and so did not pose any serious threat to the defence of Lahore. It was really seen to have performed well relative to other units involved and its main achievement was later deemed to have been the capture of Barki, described by the Indians as 'a virtual fortress' as it was said to have concrete pill boxes and tunnelling (Chakravorty, 168). This seems to have been an exaggeration, but at least the advancing troops had something to show in this sector.

The Khem Karan-Kasur axis

The Khem Karan-Kasur road was the southernmost route of India's three-pronged assault on Lahore. The outskirts of the town of Khem Karan (in Indian Punjab) extend to within 1 mile of the international border, while the town of Kasur (in Pakistani Punjab) lies around 7 miles due west of Khem Karan. From Kasur, a road runs 30 miles north-west and about 8 miles south-east to the Sutlej towards Lahore. To the north of Kasur, between Bedian and Ballanwala, the BRBD Canal runs, like the road, very close to the border.

The Indian forces tasked to carry out the offensive in this sector were those of 4 Mountain Division under the command of Major General Gurbaksh Singh. This division had been raised recently and so had some organisational weaknesses in collective training and equipment, as it was primarily designed to fight in the Himalayan mountains rather than the Punjab plains, but it was still a formidable force and one which Pakistani intelligence had little idea of. The initial orders for this division were to occupy the territory between the border—irrespective of casualties—and the eastern bank of the BRBD Canal and destroy the bridge on the canal. Facing it was the—also newly raised—11 Infantry Division under Major General Abdul Hamid Khan.

At 0430 hours, 6 September, India's 4 Mountain Division moved across the border at several points on a 16-mile-wide front stretching from Bedian to Rohiwal, south of the Khem Karan-Kasur road. This area was defended by only five Pakistani infantry battalions and it appears from later well authenticated accounts that the HQ 10 Division was so preoccupied with defending Lahore that it failed to inform 11 Division that all-out war had begun. (Ahmed, 240). As was the case all along the Punjab border, it was the border forces of the Pakistan Rangers and paramilitaries who had to face the unequal task of facing a full-scale invasion and they were simply not equipped or designed to do so. In addition to being ordered to capture all the territory up to the BRBD Canal and destroying the bridge at the crossing, 4 Mountain Division was to protect and hold the area against any possible Pakistani counter-attack. After the initial thrust in with little opposition (as was the case in the other two sectors), troops from 62 Mountain Brigade leading the invasion began to face serious resistance within hours and as an Indian account phrases it, 'The enemy temporarily paralysed into inaction by the tactical surprise...quickly regained balance and reacted sharply against the positions captured' (H. Singh, 99). 4 Mountain Division was now held at the BRBD Canal and was unable to advance.

By 1400 hours 13 Dogra was attacked with heavy shelling and some tank fire from 7 Punjab from 11 Division at Rohi Nala, as a result of which, the Indian unit 'gave way and broke rank. The remnants of 13 Dogra were ordered back by senior

Indian officers to hold the line but by the evening, when the commander of 62 Mountain Brigade went to inspect the front, 'he found that with the exception of the Commanding Officer and Subedar Major (an NCO) the rest of the battalion had again left the line' (H. Singh, 99). It was to get worse for 4 Mountain Division as by first light it was discovered that 7 Grenadiers and two companies of 1/9 Gurkha Rifles had also abandoned their positions owing to overnight shelling.

On the right of 62 Mountain Brigade, 7 Mountain Brigade was tasked with the capture of the east bank of the BRBD Canal from Bedian to Ballanwalla. Offensive operations were to commence at 0700 hours, approximately an hour and a half after those of 62 Mountain Brigade. The first phase of the operation went relatively smoothly and troops from 4 Grenadiers managed to reach the BRBD Canal. The next objective was the capture of Ballanwala, and this was initially delayed. Eventually, on the night of 6/7 September, 7 Mountain Brigade made a rather chaotic attempt to attack and capture Ballanwala but was again forced back in the face of Pakistani artillery fire.

Within 24 hours of attack, in this sector too Indian hopes of securing any of their offensive objectives for Riddle had failed. Even Indian sources admit that a few regiments appear to have lost their nerve in the heat of the battle, (H. Singh, 99–100) and the official Indian history of the war claims that 4 Mountain Division suffered as it was facing the full force of Pakistan's 1 Armoured Division (Chakravorty, 171). This was not in fact the case—it was the newly raised 11 Division that was able to hold and even push back 4 Mountain Division with surprising ease. By the afternoon of 7 September, thirty-six hours after Riddle was launched in this sector, 4 Mountain Division's position was described as 'desperate'. Out of six battalions which had led the offensive, two and half had 'ceased to exist as fighting units' and the remaining three and half were under pressure and unable to advance, and 'the situation was rapidly slipping out of control'. The GOC of the division, Gurbakhsh Singh, now sought permission to pull back to Khem Karan, in other words to retreat back into India, as there was a real danger that the division would simply be destroyed piecemeal if it tried to continue the offensive in Pakistan. This was agreed by the Corps Commander and 4 Mountain Division was the shortest lived of the three offensives in Operation Riddle, as by 8 September it was back inside Indian territory (H. Singh, 100). For Pakistan's newly raised 11 Division, however, it was a triumph and one which convinced Pakistan's GHQ that of the three fronts which the Indians had used to attack Lahore, 4 Mountain Division was the weakest link, and it was against that division that the main Pakistani counter-attack was now planned.

Riddle—a mystery

The Indian government and military were both initially reluctant to define Operation Riddle's territorial objectives, and it was not until a few days after the offensive began that the Indian Defence Ministry stated that the destruction of the Pakistani armour was more important than the occupation of towns. After the ceasefire, General Chaudhri declared that the occupation of Lahore had never been an Indian objective and that once pressure on Akhnur had been eased, India's objective was to degrade Pakistan's armour and capability of offensive action by drawing its forces into a battle and destroying them. In support of this statement, he said that India would have needed a very large number of troops to garrison Lahore, which it did not have (*Times of India*, 10/9/65). Although the statement regarding the large number of troops is true, the fact is that Riddle did involve an offensive of three full Indian divisions and so was hardly a small force. Other Indian historians have stated that the objective was to position Indian troops on the eastern bank of the BRBD Canal and, from there, contain any possible Pakistani attack in this direction (Bhagat, 34–5).

Some Pakistani historians have rather improbably claimed that India planned to invade West Pakistan in any event and that Riddle was not launched in response to fighting in Kashmir, but merely brought forward from 15 September when Riddle would have been launched in any event. Interrogation of Indian prisoners of war is alleged to be the source of this information; they were supposed to have said that Indian troop movements began in the border areas as early as mid-August (G. Ahmed, 76–8). However, these movements are well known to have taken place during the Rann of Kutch crisis as a warning to Pakistan and were almost certainly not moved for a planned invasion later in the year, and so this seems implausible.

There is little doubt that the real reason for the launch of Riddle was the relief of Akhnur and that it was squarely aimed at relieving pressure in Kashmir. The fact that the Pakistanis had advanced more than 5 miles into ICK from 1 to 5 September was concealed from the Indian public, and in a radio broadcast to the nation on 3 September Shastri declared that Pakistan's initial thrust had been halted (Shastri, 16). The Pakistanis' crossing of the Tawi was not reported until 5 September, and then with the implication that it had taken place on 4 September and not on 2 September. The mood in India at this stage was such that wider military action against Pakistan would have been welcome in any event, but awkward questions might well have been asked about whether it was necessitated by the situation in the Chhamb sector. No doubt the Indian government withheld information about having lost ground in Chhamb in order to prevent a repeat of the drop of army morale that occurred in 1962. After the ceasefire, General Chaudhri acknowledged that civilian morale was volatile and stated that if initial failures had been known it could have resulted in morale dropping (Gen. Chaudhri, 42). Bowles had described the mood in India immediately prior to Riddle as one of 'frustrated militance' and by 4 September was hinting that India was likely to invade any day (Shastri, 233).

India's need for a good explanation was due to international pressure for a ceasefire, exerted particularly by the 4 September UN Security Council call for the immediate cessation of fighting in Kashmir and the withdrawal of all armed personnel of each party to their respective sides of the CFL. With the UN Security Council calling for a ceasefire, an all-out Indian offensive across the international border in Punjab was hard to justify to some in the Security Council. The purpose of these explanations was therefore to try to justify to India's economic and military donors that a significant escalation of the conflict was needed, and to try and keep the moral highground India had after Gibraltar. India used two main arguments to justify its offensive; first, that Pakistan had already crossed into India and, by crossing the international border with regular forces, had in fact begun this war; second, that Pakistan had been about to attack India, not just in ICK but also in the Punjab, and therefore India was acting in self-defence.

After announcing the invasion of Pakistan to the Indian parliament on 6 September, Chavan claimed that on 5 September, Pakistan Air Force planes had crossed the international border near Amritsar and fired rockets at an Indian Air Force unit. He also claimed that in order to forestall the opening of another frontier by Pakistan, Indian troops had to cross the border to protect it (Foreign Affairs Record, Government of India, Ministry of External Affairs, External Publicity Division, New Delhi, XI:9 (September 1965), 254XI: 254). Shastri also claimed that Pakistan wished to open another front and that the Indian attack was a pre-emptive one (*Indian Information*, New Delhi, 8:17, 1 October 1965, 549). The Indian government said Pakistan had amassed an armoured division and two infantry divisions in the Sialkot area and an identical force of one armoured and two infantry divisions in the Lahore area ready to launch an offensive (B. G. Verghese, *India Answers Pakistan*, Bombay: Times of India, 1965, p. 9). It was not until a day after the ceasefire that India admitted the truth; Chaudhri emphasised that the Indian Army had to march into West Pakistan to relieve the pressure on the Chhamb sector, as it was necessary to open up another front to save Akhnur (*Times of India*, 25/9/65).

Within 48 hours of launching Riddle, the Indian offensive had not only been halted, in some areas it had been pushed back. The precise aims and objectives have been debated ever since. With time only a few credible explanations have appeared, but it is worth discussing some of the justifications given at the time. The different objectives suggested for Riddle are:

1. Delaying or preventing a Pakistani attack along this region towards Amritsar. This idea was one of the original reasons given by the Indian government at the time, but with the passage of time it seems highly unlikely to be the main reason or even a real fear at the time. There was no military evidence at the time to suggest that Pakistan was planning an attack across the undisputed international border, and so the explanation appears to be little more than an official justification for military and economic donors in the Security Council. Chavan also tried to claim in the Lok Sabha on 6 September that a PAF plane had attacked an IAF base as a prelude to a wider attack, but this was an unconvincing argument and did not appear to persuade the international community even at the time.

2. Destroying/damaging the Pakistani war machine. This explanation has been given more importance after the war by Indian generals and ministers, as the loss of armour and ammunition did no doubt deprive Pakistan of a large part of its future offensive capability. As a primary reason for launching Riddle, however, it again appears to stretch

credibility, as there was little assurance that this aim could be achieved and little planning appears to have gone into this military objective.

3. Relieving pressure on Akhnur. This appears to have been the true objective and one that India's generals and politicians are more comfortable with admitting with the passage of time—just as Pakistani generals were with admitting the planning for both Gibraltar and Grand Slam later. The Indian military had been conscious during both the 1962 war with China and the Kutch clashes that it often found itself at a physical and strategic disadvantage when the fighting was ongoing, because of the location of the fighting. During the Kutch fighting, India had begun to move troops to the Punjab border, where it obviously felt that it would easier for Indian troops to fight. The fact that India did this in the summer of 1965 means that it perceived Lahore's proximity to the Indian border as a pressure point for Pakistan, and when Akhnur's loss seemed imminent, Riddle's launch was an obvious riposte.

4. Capturing Lahore. This is hotly denied by the Indian leadership as ever having been an aim of Riddle, but if it was not an aim then, the obvious question would be, why not? To attack a target without having the objective of capturing it seems as illogical as Grand Slam's attack offensive on Akhnur by Yahya once he took over command from Akhtar Malik. If the Indian army was ordered to attack Lahore along a wide front on three separate pressure points, the obvious conclusion has to be that the objective was the capture of Lahore, and if it was not, then apart from relieving pressure on Akhnur, the operation appears to have been badly thought through. It leaves the question open, if the Pakistani 10 and 11 Divisions had not put up a good defence, where were the Indian forces due to halt? There is still no clear answer to this but logically it appears that at the very least the encirclement

of Lahore would have been an immediate and desirable objective, even if the capture and occupation of Lahore were not. The lack of clarity on this issue could not have helped the Indian offensive if it appears to have been launched without any clear medium- to long-term aim.

Riddle—a military retrospective

Apart from the obvious success of the main objective of relieving pressure on Akhnur and finally fighting a war on territory 'of India's choosing', Riddle was a military failure. A large attacking force of three divisions was held with some ease by a much smaller and initially unprepared defensive force. Apart from the obvious advantage that most defensive forces have by virtue of being on familiar home ground, and the fact than an offensive force needs to be much larger, some serious deficiencies in the Indian military were exposed within forty-eight hours of the operation.

These were:

i) Poor leadership from some senior commanders in the Indian army. Even aside from the obvious example of the unfortunate Prasad, other senior commanders seemed either hesitant or incompetent in their military operations and tactics. Despite having achieved the advantage of surprise and despite being faced with a smaller force, brigade and battalion commanders often lost touch with their senior officers and were unsure what to do when faced with determined defence or when things did not go exactly according to plan. There seemed also to be a prevailing culture of hesitation and 'safety first' amongst the Indian senior officers, and any serious resistance was often followed by requests by Indian brigade commanders and even generals to be allowed to withdraw rather than digging in to fight in order to hold on to hard-won territory within Pakistan.

ii) Poor co-ordination between the infantry, armour and artillery on the Indian side. On a number of occasions, the Indian infantry divisions advanced only to find themselves unsupported by artillery or armour. There seemed also to be a complete lack of co-ordination with the IAF which could have played a vital role in both reconnaissance and support in attacking Pakistani armour and artillery on the ground. Even when Indian tanks were used they were often led by the infantry, contrary to almost all principles of military tactics as tanks were usually used as battering rams to create the space for the following infantry. This led to the defensive forces having an easier time than they ought to have had.

iii) Inferior artillery. In the defensive battles fought between Pakistan and India, the superior range, quality and use of Pakistan's artillery meant that the Indian big guns rarely had an opportunity to break up the enemy lines in the same way as Pakistan had managed in both the Chhamb and the Riddle offensives. Not only were the Indian guns inferior in range, their handling was also inept and they were usually if not always outgunned by the Pakistani counterparts. As the later British military review of the war pointed out, 'Even Indian observers were impressed by the speed and accuracy of the retaliatory fire' (British military review, p. 27).

iv) Riddle was too thinly spread. Although the wide front along three invasion points was originally seen as a strength, as it forced the smaller Pakistani forces to meet an attack from three different fronts, it actually resulted in the Indian attacks at each of the three points being more easily contained and the Indian attacks therefore being weaker at each point. When the defending Pakistani forces were able to halt the offensive, it left India vulnerable to Pakistani counter-attacks as there were insufficient reserves at each point to support the offensive troops and the overall effect of the large-scale offensive was lost. In simple terms, India pulled its punch and it was easier for Pakistan to fend it off.

v) Lack of strategic vision. Leaving aside the diplomatic fallout from India's decision to cross the international boundary, in purely military terms objective of Riddle appears not to have been defined (at least from the documents and material available to date). If it was to capture and hold land east of the BRBD Canal, then why were so many determined efforts made to cross the bridges over that canal? If it was to capture Lahore, then why were more troops not committed to this objective, as the Indians must have been aware that the city would be defended hard? This ambiguity, however useful in diplomatic terms, could not have been helpful to soldiers fighting on the front without a clear direction from the senior commanders.

In summary, although Riddle achieved its major objective of halting Pakistan's capture of Akhnur, as a military operation it was far from encouraging for India. It exposed some of India's military weaknesses and failed to damage Pakistan's military capability except in the most general terms. In fact, India now faced the prospect of a Pakistani counter-attack on its own territory with some trepidation. There was, by 7 September, serious concern in India that the war that had now been taken to a new level could in fact backfire and result in Pakistan taking the military initiative. The initiative had surprisingly been handed back to Pakistan and now Pakistan had one (as it transpired, final) further chance to try and gain the military advantage.

7

OPERATION MAILED FIST

Pakistan's counter-attack

By 7 September the shock of the Indian invasion had worn off, the Pakistan Army had recovered its balance and had pushed Indian troops back. Pakistan now had the opportunity to launch its main armoured attack and counter-offensive which it hoped would be a *Blitzkrieg* style movement, smashing through Indian defences and forcing India to sue for peace. By that afternoon, Pakistan had managed with relative ease to push the Indian forces of Riddle to a safe distance from Lahore and plans for a major counter-attack by Pakistan into Indian Punjab were hurriedly finalised. The Pakistan Army, proud of its qualitative edge over India in armour and artillery, had, since at least 1964, planned that in the event of war with India across the Punjab boundary, once Indian forces had been held Pakistan should go on a rapid counter-offensive deep into Indian territory. Previously agreed directions for the possible deployment of 1 Armoured Division were given by GHQ to the commander of Pakistan's 1 Corps, stating that in the event of a planned Pakistani offensive in the Ravi-Beas corridor, one armoured brigade from the armoured division would support 1 Corps operation. 1 Armoured Division was told by GHQ to plan for both defensive operations in the area of 11 Division and also to prepare for offensive operations in the Ravi-Beas corridor (Ahmed, 223).

The detailed planning for an armoured thrust in the Ravi/Beas corridor began in the summer of 1965 between General Nasir Ahmed Khan (GOC 1 Armoured Division) and Major General Altaf Qadir, GOC 7 Division (Diary of 1 Armoured Division, Ahmed, 225). In the event, it was later decided by GHQ to use 7 Division to take part in Grand Slam and so 1 Armoured Division was now to operate with 11 Division instead, but with brigades from 1 Armoured Division to be placed under the control of either 10 or 11 Division. The plans were kept at an impressive level of secrecy from the Pakistan side, but with the resulting disadvantage that not even senior brigade commanders of 1 Armoured Division or other divisions were aware of the date planned for the offensive or where this was to take place. It was not until the morning of 6 September that maps of the Khem Karan area were distributed to senior officers; this last-minute rush meant that a large water obstacle just past Khem Karan by the name of Rohi Nala was missing from the Pakistani maps; the Pakistani troops only discovered this discrepancy on reaching it during the battle. The commander of 3 Armoured Brigade, Brigadier Moin ud Din, said later in an interview that the first he heard of an operation in the Khem Karan sector for his Division was on 6 September, from General Nasir, and as a result he was unable to plan or prepare at all for the operation (Ahmed, 224). Indian intelligence again failed as the Indians were completely ignorant of 1 Armoured Division's location and movements. In May 1965 1 Armoured Division had been based at Changa Manga, a forest area around 100 miles from Lahore, and at the outbreak of the war during August 1965 Indian intelligence believed that this was still the case. Subsequently the Indians believed it had been moved to protect Sialkot and was not in the Lahore sector.

In keeping with the bold strategy of counter-attacking planned by GHQ, Riddle had barely been stopped in its tracks by 7 September when Operation Mailed Fist was finalised and ordered to be launched on the Khem Karan front, with 10 and 11 Division to lead the attack with the support of 1 Armoured Division. GHQ had a temporary period of what can only be described as hyperactivity as it began by 7 September to send orders to move brigades around the entire front, only to frequently change its mind within a few hours and then order them either to another location or back to where they had been previously. In the first phase of Mailed Fist, 10 Division was to secure the town of Bhikkiwind while 11 Division was to secure Harike, on the river Sutlej, for which purpose 5 Armoured Brigade from 1 Armoured Division would come under the command of 11 Division. Both these targets were well inside Indian Punjab, and once these areas were securely held, the next target was Jandiala Guru, a small town close to Amritsar and astride the GT Road (GHQ Operation Instruction Number 49/65 dated 31/8/65, Ahmed, 223).

In these military moves with very high stakes the importance of success for Pakistan could not be overestimated as neither Gibraltar, nor Grand Slam, nor fear of China had yet forced India to the negotiating table. Even though Riddle had been a military failure for India, it had taken the fight to Pakistan and had resulted in the threat to Akhnur being lifted. Mailed Fist had to be executed successfully for Pakistan to exert real military pressure on India. Pakistan to date had not committed the bulk of its armour to the war and its formidable 1 Armoured Division was now ready to be unleashed on India when and where Pakistan's GHQ felt it could have maximum impact. A large force of Pakistani armour moving towards Amritsar would pose a deadly threat to Indian forces operating in Punjab and ICK, and given the manner in which India's 4 Mountain Division had performed on 6 September, the decision to launch

Mailed Fist at Khem Karan looked like a stroke of great fortune as it would be directed at the sector held by that division. The GOC XI Corps, Lt General J. S. Dhillon, wrote that on visiting 4 Mountain Division's HQ on the afternoon of 7 September, his impressions, apart from finding the officers 'generally uninterested', were that 'the strength of the six infantry battalions had been reduced to an overall total of about three and half battalions in twenty-four hours of action commencing 0400 hours 6 September. This reduction was partially due to enemy action but mostly due to desertion'. The 13 Dogras were blamed for starting this trend but the 'rot quickly spread to other infantry units'. Only 4 Grenadiers and 1/9 Gorkha were seen as 'intact'. The Commanding Officer of 9 J&K Rifles had 'left his position, without orders, on the night of 6/7 September taking a company of infantry with him'. 18 Rajputana Rifles were seen as suffering from desertions and its own commanding officer felt that the unit was 'cracking up'. Because of this state of affairs, the division had failed to carry out a single task allotted to it and had retreated to a defensive position in the Asal Uttar area, and 'any defences held by the present infantry units in 4 Mountain Division cannot withstand even the slightest enemy pressure'. The recommendation was that the entire division be replaced and all units except 4 Grenadiers and 1/9 Gorkha Rifles disbanded.

This letter delivered by special courier was 'very dark and gloomy', and alarming enough for Harbakhsh Singh to rush to the front and see for himself what was happening; he met Gurbakhsh Singh and after seeing for himself the state of affairs, he felt that although 'the situation was serious, it did not call for a recourse to the recommendations made by GOC XI Corps'. In any event, the fact was, as admitted by Harbakhsh Singh, that even if he had wanted to replace the entire division as recommended by the corps commander, 'We had no reserves available'. The visit by Harbakhsh Singh was vital from India's point of view as he was able to restore a degree of fighting spirit to a demoralised unit and left with an assurance that the mauled 4 Mountain Division 'would not budge' from their positions (H. Singh, 100–3). These positions by the afternoon of 7 September were that 1/9 Gurkha Rifles were placed near Bhura Kuhna covering the Khem Karan-Bhikkiwind road, 18 Rajputana Rifles were close by on the left just south of Asal Uttar, and behind these two battalions were 4 Grenadiers south of Chima, while the remnants of 9 J&K Rifles were placed behind Asal Uttar to assist 18 Rajputana Rifles.

The plan

Across the Pakistani district of Kasur and close to the border, is the small Indian Punjabi town of Khem Karan. Various roads lead out of this town; one heads north-east towards Amritsar and then on to the GT Road eastwards to the bridge over the river Beas, which was the objective of the first phase. The most western of these roads runs for 36 miles in a straight line to the western suburbs of Amritsar, intersecting along the way the Harike-Khalra-Barki Road, which was one of the routes used by India for Operation Riddle. Because all these roads run between the great rivers of the Punjab, tank movement from Khem Karan to the GT Road was not expected to be hindered by too many natural obstacles, and this was a terrain that the Pakistan armour was looking to exploit. As mentioned earlier, detailed knowledge of the man-made obstacles such as water channels and canals was lacking, as were details of the Indian defensive position. The distance from Khem Karan to Bhikkiwind was around 15 miles, and from Bhikkiwind by the straight road, Amritsar was another 23 miles away. A successful armoured thrust supported by infantry would have meant a deep penetration by the Pakistan Army into Indian territory and would have given Pakistan, assuming it was able to hold on to the gains made, the power to dictate the terms of peace in the way China had done three years earlier.

The success of Mailed Fist was dependent on its armour and artillery being able to smash through Indian defences at a speed that would allow the armoured brigades to temporarily ignore the danger posed by the exposed flanks which could be attacked by Indian infantry divisions. Speed was critical as Pakistan's GHQ would have had reservations about being able to protect itself against the much vaunted Indian 1 Armoured Division whose location was as yet unknown. Next, the lines of communication and supply would have to be secured, which would largely depend on the extent to which Indian troops were demoralised by finding their supply lines cut and being cut off from Jullundur and the other cantonments east of the Beas.

Had the Pakistani attacking force been able to reach the Grand Trunk Road, with its right flank protected by the rivers of Sutlej and Beas, then both Indian and Pakistani generals fantasised (although for different reasons and outcomes) about what could happen next. 1 Armoured Division and 11 Division could then theoretically have been able to push north towards Madhopur, which was the Indian railhead for Kashmir, surround Amritsar and even, in some wild fantasists' minds, threaten Delhi. Later Indian writers have speculated that Pakistan would have wished to push on from Khem Karan all the way to Delhi, which was claimed to be almost undefended, but this was almost certainly not the Pakistani plan as 1 Armoured Division did not appear to have the means to cover the 244 miles to Delhi and it would have needed to cross the river Beas once it reached the GT Road. However, even for the Pakistanis to take or surround Amritsar would have had a major demoralising effect on India and placed the Indian government in a dilemma over whether to transfer its armour back from Sialkot or reach a political settlement with Pakistan over Kashmir. In terms of morale, the news that Pakistani tanks had reached the GT Road would have been impossible for the Indian government to conceal from the Indian public in the way it had managed to hide its difficulties in the Chhamb sector. The capture or even siege of Amritsar would have been a huge symbolic win for Pakistan, and might well have caused problems for India given the large numbers of Sikhs serving in the Indian army.

The execution

The composition of 10 and 11 Division involved in Riddle has already been given. 1 Armoured Division was under the command of Major-General Nasir Ahmad Khan; the division's composition was as follows:

12 Cavalry—a Division reconnaissance regiment of Chaffee tanks.
Division Artillery—under the command of Brig. A. R. Shami.
3 Armoured Brigade—commanded by Brigadier Moin-ud-Din.
19th Lancers—a Patton tank regiment.
7th Frontier Force—an armoured Infantry regiment.
4 Armoured Brigade—under the command of Brig. 'Tony' Lumb.
4 Cavalry—a Patton tank regiment.
5 Horse—a Patton tank regiment.
10 Frontier Force—an Armoured Infantry regiment.
5 Armoured Brigade—under the control of Brigadier Bashir.
6 Lancers—a Patton tank regiment.
24 Cavalry—a Patton tank regiment.
1 Frontier Force—an Armoured Infantry regiment.

Facing them were the remains of 4 Mountain Division (already specified) under the command of Major General Gurbakhsh Singh and additional troops sent during the operation:

9 (Deccan) Horse—a regiment of Sherman tanks IV/V with three squadrons.

7 Mountain Brigade—under the command of Brigadier Sidhu.
62 Mountain Brigade.
2 Independent Armoured Brigade under Brig. T. K. Theograj.

From the outset there were a couple of major flaws with Mailed Fist. First, as 1 Armoured Division was not normally under the command of 1 Corps, the offensive required 1 Armoured Division to be placed under the command of HQ 1 Corps during the operation, something which was described as far away 'from the intention or capability of HQ 1 Corps' (Riza, 215). In turn, I Corps decided that Major General Hamid of 11 Division was to be the overall commander of Mailed Fist but without the staff or rank needed to act as a corps commander. This meant that on many occasions GHQ was often sending direct orders to 1 Armoured Division and 11 Division was unaware of those orders or countermanded them. In addition, units from 1 Armoured Division were placed under the control of 11 Division, which naturally resulted in 1 Armoured Division being less formidable as a force. Secondly, although Mailed Fist is often criticised for being too hasty, there was no reason why 11 Division had not pushed home its advantage on 7 September in the face of the retreating 4 Mountain Division. That was the time to have carried the offensive into Indian territory, and the parlous state of the Indian division facing them must have been known to advance units of 11 Division. The failure to attack on 7 September evening gave the 4 Mountain Division time to plan its defences and await the assault rather than being kept off balance and unable to plan—which would almost certainly have been the effect on 7 September.

Whatever the shortcomings, the morale of 11 Division and units from the 1 Armoured Division was high and they were keen to progress when ordered to do so overnight on 7/8 September. The first phase of Mailed Fist was to secure the town of Khem Karan and use it as the launchpad for the armoured thrust to follow. Once the bridgehead created at Khem Karan was secure and ready to be used by first light on the morning of 8 September, there was to be a two-pronged attack led by the two armoured regiments of 5 Armoured Brigade, the 6 Lancers and the 24 Cavalry. The left flank led by 24 Cavalry was to head to the village of Chima and the right flank led by 6 Lancers was tasked with the capture of the strategically placed village of Valtoha; the idea obviously being of two armoured hooks bypassing villages but advancing along canal and railway lines so as to make heavy tank progress possible.

11 Division launched its attack on Khem Karan at 0430 hours, 8 September and the town was firmly in Pakistani hands using 1FF (an armoured infantry battalion) by 1100 hours and ready to be used as a springboard for Mailed Fist. Although some Indian snipers were left behind, the town had been largely abandoned by the Indian forces by the time the Pakistani troops had arrived. Given the fact that only one infantry battalion had created the bridgehead for the armoured break out, there was an inevitable crush of armour as the road and space for movement were simply inadequate. In some cases, some tank crews had to wait for up to two hours, consuming valuable fuel and daylight hours, while they waited for their turn to be able to move.

Day 1 of Mailed Fist

Brigadier Bashir issued his orders to 5 Armoured Brigade at 0430 hours, 8 September, an inexplicably late time as he had been given at least twenty-four hours' notice of the launching of Mailed Fist. 6 Lancers were ordered to advance along the Khem Karan-Valtoha railway line and capture Valtoha. 24 Cavalry was to advance along the Khem Karan-Bhikkiwind road and sit astride the Khem Karan-Bhikkiwind-Uttar road at the village of Chima. Both these tank regiments were to be supported by a company from 1 FF which was ordered (minus the two companies given in support of the 2 armoured regiments) to advance in support of 6 Lancers and reach Valtoha to capture the Indian HQ which was believed to be based there. The direction of the armoured thrusts was chosen as it was believed that the tanks would be able to progress more quickly if they moved parallel to existing routes such as railway lines and roads, as there would be less risk of having to cross canals or other water channels.

Very little appears to have been known by the Pakistani forces about either the strength or location of the Indian troops facing them; it was assumed that the GOC 4 Mountain Division was located close to Valtoha, from the limited intelligence gathered from prisoners of war, but in fact Pakistani forces moving forward had no idea where the Indian defensive positions were located or their strength. This was another inexplicable failure as scouting missions and aerial reconnaissance are a vital part in any battle, and it showed a dangerous sense of complacency among the Pakistani troops who obviously felt they could deal with whatever Indian positions they came across.

6 Lancers began their move out at 0700 hours, 8 September and the first phase went relatively smoothly despite the long queues of tanks leaving Khem Karan; the bridgehead was secure and although the advance was delayed for a couple of hours with Indian fire from different directions during its push, the force was fully on the move by 1000 hours. The advance of 6 Lancers was then delayed for around three hours between 1200 and 1500 hours by some defensive resistance in villages and positions along the railway line, but they pushed on until they reached the Machhike Minor, another canal in the area. That too was crossed without too many mishaps and the CO of 6 Lancers, Lt Colonel Gul, was able to report that by 1500 hours advance units of 6 Lancers had reached Valtoha railway station which was seven miles from Khem Karan. By 1600 hours other units of the regiment had caught up at the railway station. At this point the picture becomes confused. 6 Lancers now wanted

to push on to the town which was within reach, but were told to wait as they had outrun their infantry support and were also told to await a PAF strike on Valtoha which would ease the capture of their target. It was later claimed that 6 Lancers were also low on fuel and there was no artillery or infantry support available to assist. Brigadier Bashir was becoming increasingly convinced that Valtoha was well defended and refused a request by Gul to be permitted to proceed to Valtoha—which was in fact his ordered target for the day. The early evening of 8 September was therefore spent by 6 Lancers awaiting an air strike which did not materialise. Brigadier Bashir now ordered 6 Lancers to also return to Khem Karan to laager there for the night (Ahmed, 273).

24 Cavalry, the other armoured regiment to break out from Khem Karan, had been ordered to take the village of Chima by last light of day one of Mailed Fist. It too left Khem Karan without major difficulty and the village of Manawan was reached by 1130 hours. The village of Chima, which was the regiment's final objective of the day, was now only a few miles away, and it must have appeared to the CO of the regiment, Lt Colonel Imam, that he would reach it without any dramatics, but a squadron on 24 Cavalry then drove straight into a defensive ambush prepared by Gurbakhsh Singh the day before by the village of Bhura Kuhna. This was the position held by the 1/9 Gurkha Rifles immediately before Asal Uttar and had been chosen well, as the fields on either side of the road in this area along which 24 Cavalry was advancing were cultivated with sugar cane which was tall enough to protect the defending Indian troops. The defending Indian troops now opened fire from all directions; Gurbakhsh Singh had ensured that fields without crops were left unoccupied, and infantry and tanks were placed in fields of sugar cane and other crops which provided vital camouflage and protection from air and artillery raids, while a gap south-east of the village of Valtoha was flooded with

water from the nearby canal and land mines were laid (H. Singh, 103) Another squadron from the 24 Cavalry was also approaching Chima from a different road and that too was attacked by the waiting 18 Rajputana Rifles.

Unknown to the commander of 5 Armoured Brigade, Lt Colonel Sardar Ali Imam, the tanks of 24 Cavalry had in fact managed to drive a wedge between the Gurkha regiment defending Bhura Kuhna. By the afternoon, the Gurkha regiment simply abandoned its positions and retreated behind Chima and the situation became desperate for 4 Mountain Division, its own history admits that the situation was 'critical. Enemy tanks had infiltrated the headquarters of 7 Brigade and 18 Rajputana Rifles were under attack' (K. C. Praval, *The Red Eagles—History of the Fourth Division of India*, Vision Books, 1982, 327–8).

Two hours of daylight remained, 24 Cavalry had managed to survive the ambush without too many casualties and was keen to press on. However, radio communication had broken down not only with the brigade commander and the CO of the regiments but also between unit commanders. The second in command of 24 Cavalry was sent in a jeep to urgently request infantry support from Brigadier Bashir. The officer returned after only fifteen minutes to inform Lt Colonel Imam that although he had not been able to communicate directly with Brigadier Bashir, he had been intercepted by the brigadier's liaison officer who had ordered 24 Cavalry to return to Khem Karan to laager for the night. That meant that 24 Cavalry, which had fought hard to advance to Chima before the end of 8 September, had to withdraw and effectively surrender the eight miles of territory they had captured. The return journey did not begin for one of the squadrons until early evening and it did not arrive back in Khem Karan until 2330 hours as it had advanced the full eight miles and now had to move back to its morning starting point.

Laager for night

The decision by Brigadier Bashir to order both his armoured regiments to withdraw back to Khem Karan for the night was one more decision by an advancing Pakistani force that saved the Indians; a decision almost on a par with the change of command during Grand Slam when Pakistani forces were within in sight of Akhnur. Having fought through ambushes and fulfilled their orders, both 24 Cavalry and 6 Lancers had been ordered back to Khem Karan to 'laager' for the night. Laager or 'leaguer' is a German/Dutch word used to describe a (usually) night time defensive formation of tanks enabling them to refuel and rest. The order had come as the 6 Lancers were at the outskirts of Valtoha and occupying the railway station, 12 miles from Khem Karan, and squadrons of 24 Cavalry were on the outskirts of Chima, 8 miles from Khem Karan, and had bypassed the village of Asal Uttar.

For the tanks and their crews, it must have been a depressing order as the hard-fought ground they had crossed that day not only had to be surrendered, it would also have to be regained the next day. The order to return to camp by Brigadier Bashir proved to be one of the turning points of the war, but it would be unfair to blame him alone for this decision. The fact that 5 Armoured Brigade was sent into battle without sufficient logistical support was an error from the outset. If, as proved to be the case, the two units had done the job asked of them and advanced to the areas they had been ordered to reach by nightfall that day, then the fuel, ammunition and infantry support that they would inevitably need to push on should have been in place before they set off. If none of this was in place because of a lack of available supplies and troops, then Mailed Fist should have been delayed a day or so until the supplies were ready. Generals Hamid and Nasir must also share the blame as neither countermanded the order and obviously neither had thought through the logistics of the move; Pakistan's GHQ too must share the blame for the fiasco. After the war Nasir, when asked why such a hastily planned and executed counter-offensive had been launched, astonished his audience of Pakistani military officers by replying, 'No sooner had the Indians attacked than GHQ began pestering me with such orders as "For God's Sake do something!" So I said do something'. This extraordinary answer was confirmed in essence by Major General Sher Bahadur, Chief of General Staff during the war, who also later stated 'The armoured division was lying in Changa Manga—it had to do something!' (Ahmed, 223).

The decision is even more unforgivable as advancing or fighting at night was an obvious thing to have planned for, given that one of the main advantages over the Indian tanks that the Patton tanks used by 5 Armoured Brigade had was infra-red night vision technology equipment which should have enabled the Pakistani armoured regiments to carry on advancing and fighting during the hours of darkness. With some logistical support such as fuel and ammunition and back-up in the shape of infantry, 5 Armoured Brigade would have laid the foundation for the possible success of Mailed Fist and the armoured regiments would have done what they had been asked to do. Gul Hassan also criticised the decision by writing later, 'Surely the Division Commander (General Nasir) was aware that what his only committed Brigade Commander (Brigadier Bashir) was doing on the afternoon of 8 September was not militarily acceptable?' Gul Hassan believes, as did some other Pakistani officers, that General Nasir was incapable of commanding 1 Armoured Division, and also blames General Hamid of 11 Division for not stepping in when it was obvious that Nasir was 'incapable of stopping the rot' (G. Hassan, 204). Even Musa describes the decision to withdraw as 'inexplicable' (Musa, 36). As he was Commander-in-Chief of the army, nothing should have been inexplicable to him and he should have known the rationale behind the decision at the time, and if he was not satisfied with the explanation, then he should have held the responsible officers to account. Given that Musa was able to fly to Chhamb during Grand Slam and effect a change of command, military historians will surely wonder whether this was not the time for a more justified repeat performance of that day.

Later Pakistani historians have said that the decision to laager in Khem Karan for the night was based on the assumption that by 8 September, India's 4 Mountain Division was beaten and in flight and that the numbers of Indians killed and taken prisoner on day one meant that Mailed Fist should have met even less resistance the next day. There was also huge, in fact disproportionate, importance given to the power of the Patton tank possessed in abundance by 1 Armoured Division and its alleged ability to sweep aside the less well equipped Sherman and Centurion tanks used by India. Be that as it may, the fact was that the initiative was indisputably lost and the Indian 2nd Independent Armoured Brigade which was to play a vital role in containing this offensive now reached the front on 9 September (Manekar, 114). Not only did the delay allow for Indian armoured reinforcements to arrive, it also gave invaluable time for the Indians to lay minefields and once again prepare the defences again along the route taken on 8 September.

Day 2—Mailed Fist

On the night of 8/9 September, Brigadier Bashir was asked to report to HQ 11 Division to receive orders and report on the events of 8 September. During the briefing General Hamid of 11 Division was persuaded by Bashir of the need for 5 Armoured Brigade to rest, and it was not until 1200 hours, 9 September that detailed orders for the day were passed on by 5 Armoured Brigade to its regiments. 6 Lancers with 1 FF were to repeat their advance to Valtoha along the railway line and 24 Cavalry with

5 FF were to advance along the Khem Karan-Bhikkiwind axis with the time of the advance fixed at 1300 hours, 9 September.

The Indian position was still serious as 1/9 Gurkha Rifles had simply abandoned their post due to the previous days' fighting, but 18 Rajputana Rifles, although now pulled back slightly, were in defensive positions and 7 Grenadiers were now placed at Valtoha. As mentioned earlier, the 2nd Independent Armoured Brigade had arrived at the front at 0400 hours, 9 September and was placed under the command of 4 Mountain Division; the sight and sound of Indian tanks must have raised Indian morale considerably. On the Pakistan side there was some good news for 5 Armoured Brigade in the shape of the arrival of the main force of 1 Armoured Division. The command from Pakistan's GHQ to 1 Armoured Division on the night of 7/8 September was to 'over run maximum enemy territory', and this rather strange vague order was left to Nasir and the commander of 4 Armoured Brigade, Brigadier Lumb, to interpret (Ahmed, 283).

It was decided this time to send out two armoured brigades rather than do what had been done on the previous day when 5 Armoured Brigade had been ordered to move alone with its two regiments divided. Now the attack was to be of brigade strength along different routes as on the day before, but this was due at least partially to the losses suffered by 5 Armoured Brigade on 8 September. The battle orders for 9 September were for 4 Armoured Brigade to advance along the axis towards Chima along the Sobroan Canal, which was to be its objective for that day. 5 Armoured Brigade was to advance from Khem Karan towards Amritsar and 12 Cavalry was to advance along the Kasur Canal. The scope was ambitious but there appears to have been little or no co-ordination between 4 and 5 Armoured Brigades (perhaps because the two brigadiers were reputed not to be on speaking terms with each other) and still little or no knowledge of the Indian redeployment or strength, despite the previous day's fighting. 5 Armoured Brigade now reverted to the operational control of 1 Armoured Division from 11 Division, but the change of orders and direction was a shock to the artillery and armoured commanders, and even the *History of the Pakistan Artillery* admits that it 'tried the tempers of artillery commanders...In order to support [the] advance, field guns had to be repositioned' (Quoted by Cloughley, 101–2).

By the afternoon of 9 September Mailed Fist was underway for the second time, setting out again from the bridgehead at Khem Karan as on the morning before. 6 Lancers were again tasked with the capture of Valtoha but on reaching Asal Uttar they ran into the full defensive positions of 18 Rajputana Rifles and the CO of 6 Lancers was killed in action. During the fierce fighting that ensued, 6 Lancers were unable to break through the defensive position of the Rajputana Rifles despite a fierce battle lasting into late evening/nightfall. Again, the lack of infantry support handicapped 6 Lancers who found their heavy Patton tanks a liability in the soggy fields of the battlefield. 6 Lancers and 1 FF began to fall back in confusion and the loss of control with the death of the commanding officer began to tell, as instead of 6 Lancers digging in around Asal Uttar overnight and waiting for reinforcements in the morning, there was again an order to withdraw with valuable ground lost leaving the regiment demoralised and battered.

4 Mountain Division's own history records that the Pakistani tank commanders, following the gallant but dangerous traditions of cavalry officers, advanced with their heads above the tank cupola and provided easy targets for Indian riflemen. 'The enemy finally broke off the engagement around 10pm... There had been very anxious moments during the battle when the fate of the battalion hung in the balance' (Praval, 330). While it is clear that 9 Lancers as a regiment were unable to break through the Indian defences at Asal Uttar, the fact is that some of their tanks had reached Valtoha again, and there has never been a clear answer as to who gave the order for the regiment to return to Khem Karan to laager for the night.

The other attack of 5 Armoured Brigade fared little better. 24 Cavalry and 5 FF set off at 1600 hours (the late departure is still a mystery) and then reached a similar area as the day before, the territory between Bhura Kuhna and Chima, which is where the Indian 4 and 7 Grenadiers were waiting. This time 24 Cavalry laagered overnight near Major Meher Chand, but this was done without any camouflage along the main road, almost inviting an Indian response. The laager was inevitably shelled by the Indians at around 0430 hours, 10 September and both men and armour suffered casualties. 5 Armoured Brigade was now a spent and exhausted force as Brigadier Bashir had managed to send his troops straight into the most heavily defended and predictable route possible. 4 Armoured Brigade, although it had managed to capture some ground, was not threatening any major Indian position as it was advancing into abandoned villages and strategically unimportant areas. This allowed 4 Mountain Division to fight 5 Armoured Brigade without having to worry about Brigadier Lumb's forces.

The lack of overall direction and control was demonstrated by the GOC 1 Armoured Division Nasir, who remained divorced from his main headquarters during the entire period of 1 Armoured Division's commitment in Khem Karan. GOC 11 Division Hamid, who was the overall commander of Mailed Fist, seems to have receded into the background after the arrival of 4 Armoured Brigade into the bridgehead on 9 September morning. In the absence of unity of command, each division and brigade acted independently of the other (Ahmed, 291). Harbakhsh Singh says that 'the assault fizzled out and the enemy who expected an easy breakthrough withdrew in frustration. So far the enemy thrusts had appeared in the nature of impetuous thrusts as if it was expecting a rout' (H. Singh, 107). Yet again the offensive had petered out and the result was that by the evening of 9 September chaos and confusion reigned within the Pakistani troops, the only certainty being that Mailed

Fist was not on track. Musa philosophically said later of the chaos, 'Such is the fog of war' (Musa, 57). With better planning and tactics, however, Mailed Fist need not have been labelled as 'the fog of war'.

The final push

Around midnight on 9/10 September General Nasir planned his next and, for all practical purposes, final move, as now all the armoured regiments at his disposal were to be thrown into battle and if they could not succeed in breaking through then, there was not only little point in attempting it again, there was no realistic chance of another attempt. The orders this time were for a push from 5 Armoured Brigade along to Bhikkiwind to capture Chima and for 4 Armoured Brigade to move up to Milestone 32.

Brigadier Lumb, commander of 4 Armoured Brigade, ordered H-Hour to be 0500 hours, 10 September for 4 Cavalry and 10 FF to carry out a sweeping manoeuvre to cut the Khem Karan-Bhikkiwind Road at Milestone 32. 4 Cavalry set off at 0520 hours and reached Duhal Kuhna in around two hours without encountering any fighting. With its right and left flanks resting between two water channels, the Indian 2 Independent Armoured Brigade had been deployed to block all the routes running north-east from Khem Karan. The first line of defence was in front of and around Asal Uttar and was manned by well dug-in and camouflaged infantry reinforced by Sherman tanks. The Divisional Artillery was located behind the infantry, between the villages of Valtoha and Chitti Khui, with its left flank covered by a minefield. Mobile armoured squadrons which included Centurions were well positioned behind minefields and Indian tanks were concealed in thickly sown fields of ripening sugar cane and maize. The route of 4 Armoured Brigade in reaching Milestone 32 (that is, 32 miles from Amritsar) was to move behind the Indian positions by an outflanking swing to the north and then to attack from the rear. 4 Cavalry under Lt Colonel Mohammed Nasir spearheaded the attack and moved through Manawan and pushed on towards Asal Uttar, outrunning its supporting infantry who were not fully mobile.

The Indian defensive positions were exactly where the Pakistanis advanced; given the predictability of the advance, the defences were now well prepared and dug in. Once the heavy armoured regiments had moved into the areas prepared, the Indian troops breached the Rohi Nala, and as a result many of the advancing heavy Patton tanks were bogged down in the mud by Mahmudpura. As the rest of the regiment advanced it came under fire from Indian tanks concealed in high cane fields in the surrounding villages. Because the Indian positions were well concealed they were able to offset the superior range of the Patton's main gun and in this situation could more easily fire against the rear and sides of the Pattons, which were less heavily armoured on the side than in the front. Moreover, the moving Pakistani Pattons with waving aerials were easily spotted by Indian troops lying in wait. 4 Cavalry was without any real infantry protection, and the absence of Pakistani infantry also allowed Indian tank killing teams using 6 mm recoilless guns mounted on jeeps to operate freely. An Indian Muslim Grenadier, Havildar Abdul Hammed, was awarded India's highest decoration for destroying three Patton tanks with his recoilless rifle.

By the time 4 Cavalry staggered on to Assal Uttar, it had already lost a large number of tanks and was said to be low on ammunition and fuel. The M-47 Patton has a full tank range of 100 miles and the M-48 tank of 160 miles. Asal Uttar is only eight miles from Khem Karan, and 10 September was only 4 Cavalry's first 24 hours of action; so, even if the regiment had moved by road from Raiwand to Kasur, its tank engines would have moved at most 40 miles. Therefore the tanks probably started out with less than full fuel tanks and did not replenish them, or their slow pace had meant that their engines had already been running for hours. The last known radio contact was at 1400 hours on 10 September just after the CO reported his position as 1,000 yards from the 32 milestone on the Kasur/ Amritsar road. Around 40 to 70 Pakistani tanks were destroyed that day by India's 3 Cavalry, and as a distinguished military historian phrases it, to all intents and purposes '4 Cavalry ceased to exist' (Cloughley, 105).

5 Armoured Brigade was no more successful than 4 Armoured Brigade on this final push for Mailed Fist. The constant withdrawal from the front of regiments and brigades meant that on the nights of 8 and 9 September, troops from 6 Lancers, 24 Cavalry and 1 FF arrived late into the night and were in no shape to start the break out at first light, as a result the advances of both 9 and 10 September began late in the day. The immediate objective on 10 September for 5 Armoured Brigade was the village of Chima, and the task was entrusted to 24 Cavalry with 6 Lancers in reserve. The precise timing of the offensive's commencement is not known but it was almost certainly after the visit of the Chief of General Staff, Major General Sher Bahadur, who was in Khem Karan at 1100 hours on that day.

24 Cavalry was to capture Asal Uttar as its first objective and, once secure, to advance on Chima in two squadrons. Surprisingly unknown to the Pakistani troops even after the previous days of fighting, Asal Uttar was the headquarters of 4 Mountain Division, and so although the attack was begun with determination, it ran straight into the prepared defences of 9 Deccan Horse. After one of the squadron leaders of 24 Cavalry was killed in the offensive, a second attempt was scheduled to start at 1700 hours, but the death of Brigadier Ahsan Rashid Shami, the commander of Artillery 1 Armoured Division, led to the second offensive being aborted. News of Brigadier Shami's death and rumours of the death of Brigadier Bashir caused some

panic in 5 Armoured Brigade, and such was the confusion within the ranks that had 4 Mountain Division chosen to counter-attack on the evening of 10 September, it is unlikely they would have faced much organised resistance.

On 11 September, General Hamid called a conference of all brigade and unit commanders to discuss the failures to date and asked the commanders what had gone wrong. For twenty minutes Hamid was given a number of blunt explanations of what had been wrong with the planning, including complaints that the area was unsuitable for armour and also that the entire bridgehead available had been created by one infantry battalion. Hamid listened and admitted, 'There is some truth in what you have said. Mistakes have been made. We have suffered serious set backs', but tried to reassure them that the Indians were far from invincible (Riza, 241). It is unsure whether Hamid or Nasir were aware of the extent of the losses that their forces had suffered the day before, but this was soon made apparent. Of 4 Cavalry it is reported that only seven tanks returned. More humiliation was to follow for the proud division as nine Patton tanks were captured intact near Mahmudpura by the Indians with their engines running and were driven back in triumph to the headquarters of 3 Cavalry. That day the CO of 4 Cavalry was also taken prisoner along with his senior officers and his battle plans were also captured. General Ahmed describes 11 September as the 'gloomiest and the worst day of the war for the Pakistan Army'. Not only was Mailed Fist well and truly stopped in its tracks by the events of 10 September around Asal Uttar, in addition the awaited armoured attack by India's 1 Armoured Division had been launched on the Sialkot front, and so what was left of the Pakistani 1 Armoured Division was given orders on the evening of 10 September to move to the Sialkot front. The three-day Mailed Fist offensive was now over and from 10 September onwards, with all hope gone inside Pakistan's GHQ of regaining the military initiative, the Pakistan Army was now fighting a defensive war.

Gauhar records how the news was broken to Ayub by his military secretary, General Rafi, on 11 September. Ayub had been confident that Mailed Fist would succeed and 'had personally approved the offensive and was extremely optimistic about its outcome...General Rafi walked into the room in a state of great agitation and almost shouted that the Indians had breached the Madhupur Canal...The Khem Karan counter-offensive ran aground on 11 September and with it collapsed Pakistan's entire military strategy' (Gauhar, 343). Even Bhutto said, 'We thought our armoured divisions would cut through like a knife through butter...and then of course Khem Karan was a disaster' (Taseer, 61).

Mailed Fist—a retrospective look

After the war had ended, the American military carried out an extensive examination of Mailed Fist and the failure of the Patton tanks, said to be qualitatively superior, to punch their way past Indian defences. A number of factors were apparent indicating that it was not the tanks in themselves but the manner in which they had been operated which had led to their failure, proving yet again the old adage that it is not the gun itself, but the man behind the gun which counts. For the Indians, the fact that they had succeeded in blunting Pakistan's main armoured force was a huge relief. The possibility that Mailed Fist might have succeeded in its aim of reaching the GT Road near Amritsar led the senior Indian commander of the region to admit to 'a nightmarish feeling even when considered in retrospect' (Harbakhsh Singh, 161).

The obvious reasons for the failure (although many theories abound) are:

i) Failure to support the advance. On 8 September 5 Armoured Brigade managed to capture territory and achieve the objectives it had been set for that day, and given the requisite support to continue the offensive, it is more than likely that it could have covered the 20 miles to reach the outskirts of Amritsar by the night of 10 September. This would have meant that it would have physically outflanked the Indian 15 Division while it was still unprepared and placed the other Indian divisions operating in Punjab at risk as they could potentially have been attacked from the rear by the advancing 1 Armoured Division. The lack of co-ordination not only between unit commanders and brigade headquarters but also between different squadrons of the armoured brigades meant that there was little to no coordination between the advancing units, and this led to subsequent failure to drive home the advantage. The poor co-ordination may be explained by a startling claim by Gul Hassan who says that not only was there minimal communication between the GOC and brigade commanders, 'the three Brigade commanders were not on speaking terms with each other' and that he had 'not known such fragile and dangerous climate to pervade any formation' (G. Hassan, 213).

ii) Failure to adapt. Many retired military officers have written with commendable honesty about the tactical and practical shortcomings of Mailed Fist with only a small minority refusing to accept that it was a major assault or that the failure was due to anything other than underhand Indian tactics. It appears that the Pakistani armour commanders were following tactics from the World War II tank operations and operating in large sweeping arcs without consideration for infantry support or for a few miles of territory. Many of the tank officers had been trained or may even have seen action in the British Indian Army during the battle of El Alamein, and had studied the great tank battles of the Eastern Front between Soviet and German tanks. In those terrains space was not an issue and tanks, like the cavalry regiments which were their forerunners, were able to operate with freedom and space and engage each other. In such a battle, the great firepower and armour of the Patton tank would undoubtedly have tipped the balance in Pakistan's favour, but in the narrow confines of Punjab with irrigation ditches, fields providing camouflage and advancing without proper intelligence the advantages of the Patton became liabilities as the tanks were often obliged to advance in straight lines, making them easy targets. Their size also meant that they were hard to miss, and close up they were as vulnerable to recoilless rifles as the Indian tanks. The British military review said later, 'Tactics used were of World War II vintage...the tanks were the principal arm supported or not, as the case may be, by infantry' (British military review, 27).

iii) Poor leadership. Much criticism has been levelled at Generals Nasir and Hamid and Brigadier Bashir, much of it justified because of the way they handled the powerful weapons at their disposal, and because the urgency which General Nasir tried to inject on 10 September was absent on 8 September; in other words, it came 48 hours too late. It was a failure that was to cost General Nasir his command after the war. Blaming those officers, however, would be to allow not only Pakistani GHQ but also Musa and Ayub to escape their fair share of responsibility. Pakistan in 1965 had only one corps headquarters over a front stretching from Kashmir to Kutch. This was plainly inadequate, but this problem was not dealt with in time; at least one more corps headquarters could have improved the communication and command immeasurably. The absence of a clear-cut plan of action, and failure to appreciate the need to keep the initiative on the battlefield and to bring overwhelming force there rather than piecemeal operations, meant that poor command decision went unpunished during the war; unlike what happened on the Indian side, when General Prasad was removed from command for his poor performance, there was no such move against either General Nasir or Brigadier Bashir during the war, when it might have made a difference. In addition, many of the commanders had never seen active duty before and were inexperienced in planning and executing large-scale armoured attacks.

iv) Lack of preparation. Despite being a well funded and large division, 1 Armoured Division seems to have fallen into the same trap as other Pakistani Army divisions (with the exception of 12 Division under General Malik), of apparently not taking the prospect of war seriously until Operation Riddle was launched. There had been some years since its creation, and given the limited terrain in India into which it could ever have been expected to operate in, the Khem Karan axis should surely have been one in which it was familiar. Even the existence of a major obstacle such as the Rohi Nala was unknown to the senior commanders until it was encountered during the advances. Given also that Grand Slam was highly likely to result in war with India, the fact that 1 Armoured Division barely reached the front by 7 September was a major failure of both GHQ and divisional level preparation. There seems to have been a complete absence of patrolling before and after the fighting and whenever a skirmish was over, there seems to have been little attempt to gauge the full strength of the Indian defensive forces and their positions. In addition, given the fact that 7 Division had originally been the unit with which 1 Armoured Division had always planned the assault into India, it should have been allowed to remain as co-ordination was obviously hasty and faulty with 11 Division.

v) Piecemeal attack. The full force of 1 Armoured Division, which was to execute Mailed Fist, was never brought to bear on the Indian defence. GHQ had ensured through its meddling that 5 Armoured Brigade was initially placed under 11 Division and 3 Armoured Brigade was kept in reserve and unused throughout Mailed Fist. Ahmed says that Mailed Fist was not so much 'mauled by foes as it was by friends' (Ahmed, 303). In addition, artillery was massively underused by Mailed Fist, though it had at its disposal during the operation Artillery I Corps with formidable firepower, which was more than capable of breaking up Indian defensive formations if given proper direction. Even the PAF, which had already shown its worth in both offensive and defensive operations, was not called upon to assist.

Despite the ineptitude on the Pakistan side with which Mailed Fist was executed, the operation was hard fought and got closer to success for Pakistan than was known at the time. The operation has attracted a fair share of conspiracy theories but it appears that it was nothing more than the factors outlined above, and the tenacious and brave defence by 4 Mountain Division, that led to its failure. The performance of the Indian division is all the more commendable as it was considered a spent and beaten force on 7 September and yet it saved India from a major crisis. The final word should go General Kaul who later summarised by stating: 'It had been a matter of touch and go...we should thank God for his mercies and the enemy for his mistakes for saving us from a grim situation' (B. M. Kaul, *Confrontation with Pakistan*, Vikas Publications, 1971, 41).

8

EARLY POLITICAL AND DIPLOMATIC MOVES

Reaction to Riddle

News that on 6 September India had crossed the international boundary in a large-scale offensive launched against Lahore, thereby giving a whole new dimension to the limited fighting to date, was of huge concern to governments around the world. However serious the fighting in Kutch and Kashmir had been, the fact that all-out war had broken out between two large Asian countries sent shockwaves not just through Western capitals but also to the USSR. It was not only other world leaders who were taken aback by the Indian decision, as in Pakistan news of the Indian offensive caused something close to panic. According to Gauhar, following news of Riddle's launch 'the most surprised person was Ayub Khan'; this, he says, was because Ayub had taken 'noticeable steps' to wind down Gibraltar and Grand Slam by 5 September and had hoped that the Indians would take the hint that Pakistan did not want a general war. Ayub could hardly say that he was not warned as Shastri had explicitly stated on 3 September that the Indian people should prepare themselves for the 'hard days ahead', but this statement was viewed by Ayub as yet more bluster by the Indian government.

Gauhar goes on to make a serious allegation against Bhutto and Aziz Ahmed by saying that the Pakistan High Commissioner to India, Mian Arshad Hussain, had managed to send a message via the Turkish embassy in Delhi to the Pakistan Foreign Ministry on 4 September that India was planning an invasion on 6 September. Gauhar alleges that Bhutto and Aziz Ahmed concealed this message from Ayub, contrary to the rule that all cipher telegrams from ambassadors must be copied to the president (Gauhar, 335–6). In fairness to Bhutto, however, even if this allegation is true it was not the only warning Pakistan received, as Gibraltar forces operating in Chhamb had managed to intercept Indian military orders outlining plans for Riddle on the night of 4/5 September and these had been flown to GHQ— but had then been apparently ignored by GHQ in Rawalpindi (Ahmed, 116).

Pakistan now faced an unpredictable war against a much larger army, and the hard fact was that the assurances given by Bhutto and Military Intelligence that India would not escalate the conflict by crossing the international boundary now turned out to be incorrect, which disturbed the whole strategy. Bhutto now turned his fertile imagination to trying to explain why India's move could not have happened 'without positive United States complicity'. It had become 'increasingly clear' to Bhutto that the US now had a 'positively malicious' attitude towards Pakistan and was trying to secure a foothold in India. Bhutto urged Ayub to 'issue a denunciation of the United States' complicity with India' and said Pakistan had to realise that the US 'requires nothing short of capitulation from Pakistan'. Bhutto then continued in this vein, ending with a flourish in predicting that 'The next inevitable step will be in the direction of liquidating our national leadership which would then find itself in no position to offer effective resistance'. Ayub was obviously unimpressed by this rather far-fetched analysis and although there is no record of his immediate reply, a clue to his reaction came in a later conversation between Ayub and Mumtaz Bhutto, Bhutto's cousin: 'Your cousin is a madman', Ayub was reported to have said, 'Don't follow him! He'll lead you astray, get you into trouble' (Wolpert, *Bhutto*, 91–2). On the morning of 6 September Pakistan was indeed in trouble, and although Ayub may have been justified in his reaction to Bhutto's most recent analysis, he had chosen to believe that India would not react in the way that it did despite all the evidence to the contrary, and was prepared to risk going to war semi-prepared as a result.

Confirmation that Pakistan was taken aback came from the US embassy in Karachi which quoted a Pakistani 'Military Briefer' that Riddle had come as a 'complete surprise' (6/9/65, Karachi to State Department, POl 27, India-Pak, NA). Ayub called a cabinet meeting and said he would announce that Pakistan was now at war with India, a declaration he did make that day on national television; the sombre but defiant tone in his speech raised morale in the country.

The British reacted quickly on the news of the Indian offensive, with Wilson sending telegrams to both Ayub and Shastri on that day, the tone and content of which caused huge resentment in India. Wilson said that he was 'horrified at the rapid escalation of fighting' and that the situation was extremely dangerous not only for India and Pakistan but also for the whole world. Wilson said that he would not apportion blame as he felt that 'both seem to me to be responsible for the steady escalation which has occurred', but did criticise India for having escalated the war by launching an attack in Punjab and thereby across an undisputed international border. Wilson ended by asking for an unconditional and immediate ceasefire (CRO to Rawalpindi, 6/9/65 DO 196/384 PRO).

The second message sent to Shastri that day caused even more offence in India as Wilson also requested an assurance that British weapons supplied without charge to India should not be used against Pakistan and those that were at the front line should be withdrawn (James, 137). The criticism of Operation Riddle and the equation of both sides as being equally to blame was received badly in Delhi, and is thought to have damaged much of the goodwill Britain had built up with military aid following the war with China and also in helping to negotiate a settlement over Kutch. In addition, the second telegram caused resentment as the US had made no such request to Pakistan. Wilson later appeared to regret the tone of the telegrams by saying that he was misadvised by a 'pro-Pakistani faction in CRO' (James, 138). The Indian impression that Britain was pro-Pakistan on the subject of Kashmir was not assisted by an interview with Clement Attlee, who had been prime minister of the UK at the time of independence; he described Nehru's approach to Kashmir as 'a particular obsession' and said that after Nehru's death he had hoped that 'reason might prevail' in India, and was heartbroken by news of the war (*Dawn*, 8 September 1965).

6 September was therefore a day of high tension in Pakistan as Ayub and GHQ had to absorb the reality of a war which they had done much to provoke and little to prepare for. The former head of the PAF, former Air Chief Marshal Asghar Khan, says that he met Ayub on 6 September and that Ayub 'appeared worried and it was obvious that he was surprised by the Indian action'. Asghar Khan recalls that as he left the meeting with Ayub, McConaughy arrived for his meeting with Ayub (Asghar Khan, *The First Round*, 18–19). Ayub later told Gauhar that the US ambassador was reported as saying to Ayub during the meeting, 'Mr President, the Indians have you by the throat'. Ayub said that his reply was that 'Any hands on Pakistan's throat will be cut off' (Gauhar, 336–7). Whatever the brave talk, there is no doubt that Ayub was facing a major crisis and was deeply concerned about what he had unleashed.

McConaughy also met Musa on the morning of 6 September and asked him if he felt that the capture of Lahore was one of

India's objectives in crossing the Punjab boundary. Musa said that it did not matter much to him whether it was or was not, the fact was that there were Indian troops inside Pakistan which needed to be pushed back. McConaughy was asked for his assessment of what he felt the Indian objectives were and replied that they were more limited than the capture of Lahore and he believed that the Pakistan Foreign Ministry agreed with him. Musa felt that McConaughy would not have been able to make this statement 'so confidently' if he had not some agreement from that source, and thought the only reason he had visited GHQ was to try and gauge Pakistani counter measures (Musa, 84–5). However calm Ayub managed to be outwardly, Musa was described by the US embassy as 'almost hysterical' in his anger that US weapons provided to India were now being used against Pakistan. Musa was said to have claimed that 'Pakistan had burnt her bridges' and was now 'paying the price' in Pakistan's alliance with the US (Roedad Khan, *The American Papers*, Oxford University Press, 1999, 30).

In what was to be a tense and lengthy meeting, McConaughy was received by both Ayub and Bhutto. McConaughy reported that during the meeting he had been given an official *aide mémoire* informing the US of the Indian attack and formally requesting it to act 'immediately under 1959 Agreement to suppress and vacate Indian aggression'. The *aide mémoire* quoted from the 1959 Agreement in which it was stated that the US declared that any threat to the security, independence and territorial integrity of Pakistan would be viewed with the utmost gravity by the United States and the US would take effective action to assist Pakistan to suppress 'the aggression'. McConaughy also reported that Ayub 'showed signs of strain'; the meeting lasted over an hour but was delayed slightly owing to a telephone call from Musa to Ayub. Ayub was seen as determined and articulate and even managed some small talk regarding golf, but appeared to the ambassador to be in a state of 'inner tenseness' which Bhutto was seen as playing on with 'emotional and provocative interjections'. Ayub still appeared to be in charge but McConaughy felt he was leaning on Bhutto for advice at several points during the meeting. The US ambassador pointed out US concern that the Chinese had a particular interest in exploiting subcontinental differences, adding that the Soviet Union was taking a more uncommitted direction as regards the subcontinent without wishing to alienate India. Ayub agreed and said that when two major countries clash in a strategic place, then naturally people take advantage of the situation. McConaughy asked Ayub whether he anticipated that the current crisis would stimulate communal disturbances; Ayub said he did not believe it would, although he could not speak for what happened in India. Ayub then reverted to his main theme and said, 'We want an answer. You have a role to play; you must and can play it. If the subcontinent goes up in flames, as it will, then if you don't play the role, what then? There are a lot of irresponsible men in the Indian cabinet'.

McConaughy repeated his plea for a positive response to the UN Secretary-General's appeal for a ceasefire made on 4 September, and said that if the Pakistan government would publicly declare that as soon as the Indian troops were withdrawn it would commit itself without reservation to a ceasefire, that would put the Pakistan government in a strong diplomatic position in contrast with the vulnerable position it was in regarding the infiltration. Ayub said, 'We will give them the damn good battle. We're not over optimistic, we're not pessimistic. As to a ceasefire where does that get us?' Bhutto interrupted to say the solution to the basic question of Kashmir was more important than the issue of US arms to both sides. McConaughy asked for prompt access to the president when needed, which he said was readily agreed.

The US ambassador stated that a face-to-face meeting between Ayub and Johnson was imperative and this meeting needed to take place at an earlier date rather than in 1966. McConaughy said it was necessary somehow to arrange a meeting in order to achieve an understanding that would enable the US to go ahead with a pledge of aid, and pointed out that Johnson had himself said only the two leaders at a face-to-face meeting could achieve the meeting of minds that was required. The US had no ultimatum, no set of demands, no desire to interfere with a recognised Pakistan government's sovereign right to formulate policies both foreign and domestic. The American ambassador said the US hoped to use the opportunity to narrow the area of divergences, which was a perfectly legitimate aspiration between friends. Ayub repeated his wish to know what the US position would be regarding the 23 September consortium meeting, to which McConaughy replied that if there was a war still going on 'then all bets would be off' as far as that meeting was concerned.

Ayub said that he wished to visit the US in October but would prefer his visit to Washington and the US consortium pledge not to be tied together; 'Bluntly, I cannot go begging'. Bhutto intervened to say the US must understand that it would make Ayub look vulnerable in the eyes of his people if he seemed to go begging for a pledge—he was both commander-in-chief and chief of state. Ayub repeated that he wanted clarification of the US position on the consortium meeting and after that the trip could be discussed, but he did not wish to link the two. The US ambassador reassured Ayub that the US had no wish to embarrass the Pakistani leader but said the aid consortium could hardly meet as scheduled in view of the new circumstances. Bhutto sarcastically commented, 'India commits aggression and the aid to Pakistan consortium is postponed'. McConaughy said the postponement was caused by disruptions inherent in the combat situation and would not amount to a judgement against anybody. Ayub said the US must understand that given the state of Pakistan's relations with India, Pakistan could not oppose China and the Soviet Union also; if the US wished Pakistan to

225

'do anything which concerns the US only, we will go to the limit to respond', but Pakistan had the right to build up relationships with other countries. Ayub went on to say that he could not see serious difficulties arising between the US and Pakistan when he had the opportunity of seeing President Johnson, and that 'I work like hell for this country and get criticised for it. We have a right to complain over your support to India.... we do not complain to the Indians. It would be pointless. You must understand that we are in a difficult situation'. Pakistan, he went on, knew and honoured the large-hearted nature of the Americans and he could see no fundamental reason for the deterioration of relations. Bhutto said it was now necessary to go back to basics and if one thought only of a ceasefire then the fundamental problem would only get worse and more tangled in charges and countercharges and actions and counteractions. Bhutto pressed the point that now was the time for an honourable settlement and this was not the time for the US to use pressure tactics but to see the realities of the situation and press for an honourable settlement, which was precisely what the US was pressing for in Vietnam.

McConaughy asked Ayub whether he might with confidence report back to Washington that his government had no arrangement or understanding with the Chinese communist regime or the Soviet Union in the present situation. Ayub did not answer the question directly but replied, 'How would the Soviet assist us? How can the Chinese communists? They would only do what suits them. If they were assisting us, India could not have withdrawn troops from the northern border and thrown them against us. We have no obligation with the USSR...'. McConaughy asked whether there might be a Chinese diversionary action on the north-east border with India; Ayub replied, 'What the Chinese and the Soviets would do in future, I do not know. Naturally they won't waste any advantage'. McConaughy stated that the clear use of US weapons in the hands of 'insurgents' across the CFL in Kashmir was not going down well in Washington; Ayub did not deny this but instead gave a 'wry smile' and asked rhetorically, 'How could we deny those people arms?' McConaughy said that those weapons were given to Pakistan on a clear understanding that they were to be used only against communist aggression and not in local wars, and he did not know how the US government and people would react once this fact was widely known.

Ayub also went on to say that he expected a 'desperate fight' and that now Pakistan expected its 'friends or so-called friends' to help. He reminded the ambassador that on Eisenhower's trip to Pakistan in 1959, the then US president had promised that in the event of Indian aggression, the US would assist Pakistan. Ayub spoke about the need for a political solution to the Kashmir issue, with the Kutch resolution as a good model of how a solution could be achieved. McConaughy observed that 'in retrospect, Rann of Kutch increasingly takes on aspects of pilot project for Kashmir operation'. James was reported to have stated his opinion that the Ayub government was 'remarkably deficient in policy as opposed to operational planning...and was unduly self-confident of its capabilities and notably obtuse in anticipating reactions of others'. McConaughy said that he agreed that there was 'considerable basis for these generalisations'. The US ambassador felt that the 'curious thirty-hour delay in middle of advance' (a reference to the change of command from Malik to Yahya) might be explained by Pakistan watching the Indian reaction and weighing the risks. He predicted that the Pakistan government hoped to be able to gain a military edge and, with some international support and diplomatic pressure also, to force India to a political solution of Kashmir, which was always its aim. If however 'the fighting prolonged in the absence of support, the weight of greater Indian resources becomes increasingly apparent, GOP will face a new round of fateful decisions including possible further entanglement with Chinese amidst bitter resentment against US'. A refusal of US aid would be portrayed as a betrayal by the US in not only giving weapons to India but refusing to assist Pakistan (6/9/65, Rawalpindi to Washington, POL 32–1 India-Pak NA).

The State Department responded with predictable speed given the seriousness of the situation. A response was wired back the same day with instructions to McConaughy to respond to Ayub's request for assistance by saying that the US also took very serious note of the developments and there was the risk of 'disaster', and it was now the time for 'sober reassessments' for both India and Pakistan. However, the US said that in order to 'meet the situation effectively...Paks and we need to be completely frank with each other'. This is an obvious reference to the fact that Pakistan was seen in Washington as being less than frank about the degree of understanding with China before the war regarding possible Chinese assistance to Pakistan (6/9/65, State to Karachi, POL 31–1 India-Pak NA). As for the US attitude to the Indian invasion and Pakistan's request for help, Rusk told the Pakistan Ambassador Ghulam Ahmed (brother of Aziz) that 'the US was being invited in on the crash landing without being in on the take off' (G. W. Choudhury, *India, Pakistan, Bangladesh and the Major Powers*, London and New York: The Free Press, 1975, 121).

At midnight on 6 September, Bhutto called a press conference in which he said that Pakistan expected all its friends and allies to come to its assistance and recalled how 'certain countries' had rushed to India's aid in 1962. Bhutto asked rhetorically if it was unfair for Pakistan to expect those same countries to come to Pakistan's assistance now that Pakistan was a victim of Indian aggression (James, 140) Bhutto must have known that there was no chance of Pakistan receiving any military assistance whatever from Britain and the US, and it appears the press conference was more for public relations purposes than a serious request for military assistance.

Pakistan under pressure

On 7 September the CIA was informed by 'a source' that Pakistan would be making three thrusts into Indian East Punjab on the night of 7/8 September. When the source was asked if Pakistan would agree to a ceasefire, the reply implied that Pakistan expected to take Akhnur within twenty-four hours and also some territory in East Punjab and would only then 'be ready to agree to a ceasefire' (8/9/65 CIA to White House, Pakistan Cables, Vol IV Box 151 LBJ). The next day, Shoaib met the USAID director in Pakistan and asked for an urgent message to be relayed to McConaughy that he (Shoaib) believed that it was in Pakistan's best interests to keep close ties with the US and the war was now placing the pro-Americans in the cabinet under pressure, giving Bhutto the opportunity to state the US was not going to keep its promises of assistance. Bhutto was reported to have stated, 'Now we will silence once and for all the American party'. Shoaib was concerned as other countries were already committing themselves to assist and the US was not (7/9/65 Karachi to State, POL 27 India-Pak NA).

On 7 September, James was finally able to have a meeting with Ayub at which Bhutto was also present. James reported that Ayub looked a 'deeply strained and troubled man', more so than he had ever seen him. During the meeting, at which James was pressing for an immediate and unconditional ceasefire, Ayub would constantly look at Bhutto who was present, as if weighing up the rival arguments and trying to decide 'which possessed more weight'. Although Ayub eventually sided with Bhutto, James felt that he had made some inroads with Ayub but that recent news of Indian air attacks on East Pakistan might entrench Ayub's 'do-or-die' attitude. James said that given Ayub's state of mind he did not wish to widen the discussion to the direction of Pakistan's foreign policy, and would continue to work with McConaughy in his pleas to Ayub (7/9/65, Rawalpindi to CRO, DO 196/384, PRO). James also said that he had obtained permission from London to remind Ayub that he, James, had been predicting the Indian response for a few days and had been told by Aziz Ahmed that Pakistan's own intelligence reports did not agree that India would attack across the border. Ayub was said to have listened to this 'without any sign of resentment'; neither was James contradicted by Aziz Ahmed who was also present during the meeting. James said that he had decided not to use this opportunity to discuss the tense state of Pakistan-US relations, but to focus instead on trying to persuade Ayub to agree to an immediate ceasefire (James, 141).

On 7 September the CIA reported to the White House that the situation in East Pakistan was very fluid. The Indian army was said to believe that 'the internal situation in East Pakistan is very favourable for a take-over. Some Bengali Muslim leaders are already in touch with Indian representative, according to— (name redacted). Although the Pakistan army was prepared to defend East Pakistan, Pakistani forces in the area cannot seriously oppose an Indian attack for long'. The meeting between Ayub and McConaughy was also reported, with Ayub said to have been determined to 'gain all-out US support' on Kashmir while McConaughy was said to expect the Pakistan forces to give a good account of themselves while 'gaining sufficient diplomatic support to force through a Kashmir situation'. James was more critical of Pakistan in saying that Pakistan was 'notably obtuse in anticipating the reactions of others in the present crisis' (7/9/65, CIA to White House Situation Room, India Cables, Vol V, LBJ).

On 7 September, James met Ayub for a second time with Bhutto also present. Ayub repeated Pakistan's position: if there was to be a ceasefire, it would have to be 'a purposeful ceasefire'. This was now to be Pakistan's diplomatic code for demanding that the US and other powers persuade India to accept either mediation or a plebiscite in Kashmir. Ayub admitted that the

Pakistanis 'had not been angels' but that India was the aggressor and this was in blatant violation of Indian assurances; Pakistan therefore could do little but defend itself. Ayub proposed the withdrawal of both Indian and Pakistani forces from the whole of Kashmir, which would be handed over to an international force. This would then lead to the conditions for a settlement of the Kashmir issue, otherwise there would be years of talking. Ayub complained that the US had it within its power to force India to stop its actions and was committed to defend Pakistan against aggression, but despite being asked to honour its pledges, had not done so.

James stated that in the Kutch dispute Ayub had shown statesmanship by unilaterally withdrawing Pakistani forces from Kutch on 30 April, which had allowed India to follow and had prevented the escalation of the issue. There had then been a cooling off period and a settlement which had not seemed possible earlier. Bhutto then interrupted to say that the situation was now quite different as Pakistan's territory had been 'violated' and 'national honour was at stake', a comment with which Ayub agreed. Bhutto said that Pakistan had not wanted an all-out war with India and still did not want one. James said that as an old friend of Pakistan, he had to point out that Pakistan did share some responsibility for what had happened; he reported that Ayub took this comment well and made no serious attempt to rebut it. James said again that the British government believed that force would not resolve this issue; only peaceful negotiations could do that. He felt it worth pointing out to London that Ayub did not request any assistance under CENTO or SEATO (8/9/65 Rawalpindi to CRO, DO 196/384, PRO).

On the same day, James was summoned to the Pakistan Foreign Ministry and was met by Agha Shahi (later to become the Foreign Secretary of Pakistan) and given Pakistan's official reply to Wilson's messages of 3 and 6 September. James thought that it was a standard text which had been prepared as a reply to all messages urging restraint on Pakistan, referring to India's 'naked war of aggression' and Indian bombing of civilian areas. The specific reference to the UK requested that the UK, as a permanent member of the Security Council of the UN, should take action to assist Pakistan with 'material and moral assistance' to help Pakistan defend itself.

Pakistan's conditions for a ceasefire were:

1. It must be immediate.
2. Withdrawal of forces from each other's undisputed territory.
3. Withdrawal of all Indian forces from Kashmir.
4. A UN force to take over Kashmir.
5. A plebiscite to be held in Jammu and Kashmir within three months under UN auspices.

James said that he was disappointed not to see any agreement for an unconditional ceasefire agreement from Pakistan, but promised to pass on the message in full to London, including a copy to Hilaly (the Pakistan High Commissioner to the UK and Agha Shahi's brother) (8/8/65 Rawalpindi to CRO, DO 196/384 PRO).

On 7 September, U Thant arrived in Pakistan where he was to meet Ayub in the hope of persuading him to accept an immediate ceasefire, and was then to fly to India to see if Shastri would be prepared to do likewise. Despite the lengthy talks with both Bhutto and Ayub for the next two days, Pakistan essentially refused the UN's ceasefire request of 6 September and Bhutto continued the increasingly incredible line that Pakistan had nothing to do with the Gibraltar forces in ICK. Disappointed but undeterred, U Thant left for India on 11 September (Shastri, 256).

Meanwhile in London, Wilson met Hilaly and the High Commissioner said that although he had no specific instructions to ask for aid under CENTO and SEATO, Pakistan did feel that it was entitled to such assistance as Pakistan was resisting forces which were four times the size of their own. Hilaly did however express gratitude for the British condemnation of India's actions, as no other Western power had condemned them. Wilson said Pakistan should be under no illusion that the sole objective of the Chinese in this conflict was to 'fish in troubled waters', and it was very serious to imagine how China could exploit the Kashmir situation. He said that the British government's position on SEATO and CENTO was clear (namely that the provisions of those agreements were irrelevant) and although the British government condemned Pakistan's infiltration across the CFL, India's actions were even more serious in the escalation of the conflict.

Wilson said that his government supported the UN wholeheartedly and wanted a four-stage end to the conflict:

1. A stop to the fighting.
2. Both sides to return to previous positions.
3. Measures to quieten situation in Kashmir.
4. Future settlement of Kashmir issue.

Hilaly said that if Pakistan agreed to (1) and (2), then the next two stages would never come about, and the Pakistan government would only agree to the previous CFL if assurances were given on (3) and (4) (8/9/65, CRO to Karachi, DO 196/384 PRO).

Cornered and deserted

Almost as soon as news of India's launching of Riddle broke, calls began within the US for an immediate cessation of US military supplies to both countries. Influential figures, such as the former vice-president and future president Richard Nixon and the future president Gerald Ford, called on Johnson to cut off aid to both India and Pakistan. Komer argued for an immediate cessation too 'on the simple ground that in the light of the UN appeals we cannot be in the position of adding fuel to the flames'. Komer also argued that given the rising anger in Congress with both countries, a military aid cut-off could help the administration in trying to provide aid in the future. 'It will certainly be resented in India and Pakistan and risks pushing both off the deep end. On the other hand it may well help bring home to both the consequences of their folly' (Cohen and Tucker (eds), 161).

On 8 September Johnson took the inevitable step of applying a total embargo on military aid and sales to India and Pakistan until further notice. The State Department instructed both Bowles and McConaughy to emphasise that the US decision was not a 'punishment' nor a 'threat' but was 'simply what US opinion requires in a situation of de facto war where (the) US cannot be in the position on one hand of supporting UN appeal for ceasefire and on the other of providing equipment that might be used in further conflict'. The administration faced 'a volcanic reaction in Congress to events in the subcontinent' that made the decision inevitable in any event (Ibid).

The State Department sent a further message to the US embassies to Pakistan and India to officially inform them that 'no, repeat no' further licences for export of munitions to India and Pakistan would be issued with immediate effect and all shipments which had been licensed but had not left the US would also be stopped. The Pakistan embassy in Washington had called to ask why shipments were stopped and had then requested that they be permitted to purchase munitions which had been refused. They had also complained that termination of arms sales would only benefit India (10/9/65, State to Rawalpindi, POL 27 India-Pak NA).

In Washington, Rusk was able to meet the Senate Foreign Relations Committee for a breakfast meeting and inform it that the administration had cut off military supplies for both India and Pakistan. Rusk was asked what the US government assessment was of the likely outcome given the relative strengths of the two sides, to which Rusk replied that although Pakistan was seen as having better fighting men and morale, the Indian numbers would more than counterbalance the greater effectiveness of the Pakistan army. Rusk also made clear that while both sides wished to involve the US, as the US had not been consulted by either side before the escalation of the conflict, therefore the US was not taking sides (8/9/65 State Dept Memo POL 27 India-Pak NA).

The cut-off in military aid, while it applied to both India and Pakistan, inevitably hit the latter much harder as the US had virtually supplied all of Pakistan's aircraft, armour and artillery, and since 1954 this military aid had an estimated worth of $1.5 billion. US military aid to India was estimated to be worth around $75 million, but that only represented 10 per cent of India's weaponry (Choudhury, *India, Pakistan, Bangladesh*, 122).

On 8 September the US Under-Secretary of State, George Ball, met the British Foreign Secretary, Michael Stewart, in London. The British delegation included the Minister of State for Commonwealth Relations, Cledwyn Hughes. Hughes opened the talks by saying that the British had at first viewed the Indian attack on Lahore purely as relieving the pressure on Kashmir, but the recent Indian bombing of Pakistani cities and the opening of the Rajasthan front had made the British feel that India had wider objectives, and it appeared as if the Indian Defence ministry rather than Shastri was directing policy. The British were sure that Ayub was a 'very worried man'. The Indian policy was, however, only strengthening Bhutto's position and making it harder for Ayub to adopt a more conciliatory line and U Thant's mission was therefore even less likely to succeed than a few days earlier, and Britain had decided to withhold all military aid to India as a result; it had in fact done so on 6 September. The British government had decided not to pursue a Commonwealth line and supported the UN mission wholeheartedly.

Ball said that the US had stopped arms shipments to both sides and the US had made it clear to Ayub that it was not possible to give military aid to Pakistan if it took aggressive action, and a similar position had been spelt out to India. This fact was not publicly known but was due to be announced by Rusk. The US had also made no firm decision regarding economic aid to either country for the following year, and still had an open mind on the issue, but was prepared to use this leverage in support of the UN mission if necessary; however, this could be complicated by Congressional moves. Ball asked whether the British thought that the Soviets could be persuaded to play a useful role; Stewart said they planned to sound the Soviets out soon. Ball said this would be useful as the Soviets certainly had an interest in trying to prevent the Chinese from exploiting the situation.

Hughes pointed out that the stopping of US aid to Pakistan was bound to have a major impact as the Pakistanis only had supplies for three weeks' fighting but the Indians had arms factories which meant they could continue for longer. If the war went on for more than three weeks, the Indians would win, but if Pakistan won a major battle in Punjab this would alter the situation and probably lead the Indians to agree to a ceasefire. Ball said the US was keeping a very close eye on the situation and was concerned that by its action or inaction it could assist one side unwittingly. Stewart said Britain had made it clear that CENTO did not apply within the Commonwealth, while Ball stated that the US position was also that there was no commitment to interfere in a conflict between India and Pakistan (Record of Conversation, Foreign Office, 8/8/65 DO/196/384 PRO). The comment that Pakistan could only fight for three weeks is significant as it indicates that the US and British were aware of exactly how long Pakistan could sustain this war and had factored in the third or fourth week of September as the likely end to Pakistan's fighting capabilities.

As instructed by the State Department, McConaughy arranged a meeting with Bhutto to inform him of the US decision to suspend military supplies to both India and Pakistan. The ambassador gave the official line that the decision was 'not punitive, not threatening' as it was based on the desire to persuade both sides to stop fighting and to support the effort of the UN Secretary-General. McConaughy also said that the mood in the US House of Representatives and Senate was 'volcanic'; the US felt a sense of 'outrage' at its weapons being used by both sides for such destructive purposes. Bhutto was reported to have paused theatrically and said, 'We have discussed many serious problems in the past but never more serious than this', and referred to the 1959 Agreement saying that the decision was both disappointing and unexpected; Pakistan was engaged in a battle of survival and that the US had failed to honour its promises and did not appear to appreciate the implications of the present conflict. Bhutto said that Pakistan had feared and known about the prospect of Indian aggression but had not anticipated that the US would cut off military supplies. He also said that no action would frustrate the UN Secretary-General's visit more than this US decision and that Pakistan would fight with its hands if necessary but never surrender, adding emotionally that this was no way to treat an ally in its hour of need. India had managed to obtain arms through a variety of means but as Pakistan was almost exclusively reliant on US arms, this action actually constituted aid to India; Pakistan was now 'cornered and deserted'.

McConaughy said that Bhutto had used some 'very hard words' and while he understood his great concern, Pakistan should recognise that US action applied to both sides. Bhutto said that this action 'would irreparably damage US/Pakistan relations'. The least the US should do, he said, was to allow

Pakistan to buy US arms; it was naive to treat both sides alike as that implied that India had not committed aggression. McConaughy repeated the public feeling in Washington and said that would not be possible, to which Bhutto countered by saying that the least the US could do was to not only to stop arms supplies to both countries but to cut off India's economic aid as well. The US ambassador said that the US did not wish to see Pakistan 'liquidated' by India. He pointed out that it was unrealistic to expect the Indian government to agree to Pakistan's demands, and Shastri's government could easily fall as a result. Bhutto retorted that 'Pakistan did not come into existence to keep Shastri in power' (10/9/65 Karachi to Washington, POL 27, India-Pak NA).

On 10 September, James met McConaughy and was briefed by the US ambassador on Bhutto's reaction to being informed of the US decision to suspend all military shipments to both India and Pakistan. Bhutto had said that although this would only be a pinprick to India, it would be a fatal blow, 'indeed a stab in the back' for Pakistan. Bhutto claimed that the US was mistaken if it thought this action would strengthen the hands of the UN— it would only drive Pakistan towards 'more desperate risks'. Bhutto had requested that the US should reconsider its decision and at the very least allow Pakistan to purchase arms from the US. McConaughy said that it was not a matter of money, as the US did not wish to add any fuel to the fire, and that Pakistan could not lose by accepting a ceasefire call; if India accepted that was for the good of all and if it did not, then Pakistan would have the high moral ground and the US would seriously consider other measures against India. Bhutto had said that even if India accepted, Pakistan could not as it had sacrificed too much to be told that it was to go back to the same position as before the war. McConaughy had replied that it would not be the same situation as Pakistan would have to take it on faith that there would be a new impetus towards a negotiated settlement on

Kashmir following the war (11/9/65 Rawalpindi to London, DO 196/385 PRO).

The China factor

Of all the major powers, the only one that Pakistan knew would be supportive in its war with India was China. However, obtaining practical support from China was fraught with difficulties for Ayub. First, since the Chinese revolution and the creation of the People's Republic of China on 1 October 1949, it had not been recognised as the legitimate government of China by the USA, and China's membership of the UN Security Council was given to the government of Taiwan, which was to hold it until 25 October 1971. Therefore, for all its diplomatic support for Pakistan, China had no voice in the UN Security Council in 1965 and could only support Pakistan on a bilateral basis rather than assisting in the Security Council. Secondly, it was obvious to Ayub through some increasingly blunt messages coming from Washington that any military aid or mutual assistance pact between China and Pakistan would mean the change of status for Pakistan from the category of a US ally to that of a semi-hostile state and all military and economic US aid would be immediately and permanently cut off. Thirdly, any Chinese military activity against India to support Pakistan had the real risk of bringing the US and the USSR into the war on India's side as neither superpower wished to see India defeated by China and the 1962 war had shown the military disparity between the two large Asian states.

Despite these reservations, Ayub was also acutely conscious that Pakistan, although generally having a more sympathetic international reaction on the Kashmir issue than India, had little option but to ask for some military and diplomatic Chinese assistance, as no other major power was willing to assist Pakistan, but the dilemma facing Ayub was how to ask

239

for Chinese assistance without it resulting in either a permanent rupture with the US or another world war. Despite this, Ayub was also conscious that the Chinese threat would be an additional factor for India to consider in prolonging the war and that other than an outright military victory for Pakistan, the only hope of applying pressure on India to compromise on Kashmir was the Chinese threat of entering the war to assist to Pakistan.

On 7 September, China assisted Ayub by declaring that the Indian attack on Lahore was 'naked aggression', and on the same day Chou had a long meeting with the Pakistan ambassador to China, General Raza, and said that China had two conditions for outright support for Pakistan: first, Pakistan should not submit to any Kashmir solution which was on Indian terms, and secondly, it should not submit to US, Soviet or UN pressure to agree to a Kashmir solution. Ayub was said to have cabled these assurances to Beijing by return, and on 8 September President Liu wrote to Ayub stating that if India attacked East Pakistan, then China would attack India not only in Bengal but also along their northern border. Beijing Radio on 8 September also announced that Chinese troops along the Sikkim border had been placed on high alert and an official Note was sent to India stating that India should remove its military structures from their border and end its 'provocative activities' (Choudhury, *India, Pakistan, Bangladesh*, 189).

In an effort to obtain practical assistance for the PAF which had virtually no spare parts or reserves, Asghar Khan set off for China, Indonesia, Turkey and Iran to request military supplies. His first stop was Beijing on 10 September and he and General Raza were invited to lunch by Zhou Enlai, who seemed to be well informed as to the progress of the war. Asghar Khan made a specific request for aircraft, ammunition and anti-aircraft guns and also requested that these weapons be routed via Indonesia—a request which the Chinese leader was said to have found puzzling as it would be much easier to supply these weapons over the Karakoram Mountains on the border between West Pakistan and China. Zhou did however have a precise number of aircraft and other weaponry in mind which China was prepared to give to Pakistan, and also a date by which they could be supplied. Zhou asked Asghar Khan to explain his understanding of what China was required to do in order to assist Pakistan militarily. Asghar Khan said that a concentration of Chinese forces on the border with India would be helpful but the exact degree of assistance was something that China had to determine itself. Zhou replied that although Chinese military interventions would have 'serious international implications', China was 'vitally interested' in Pakistan's security and could not stand by idly while a war was going on.

Asghar Khan was forced into pressing for an immediate answer to his request as he was due to continue his journey to Indonesia, and so Zhou left the table to telephone President Liu. On his return, Zhou said that as the request for military aid by Ayub had such serious implications, it was one that needed to be made by Ayub personally. Zhou said that he was willing to have that meeting with Ayub in Beijing, Rawalpindi or anywhere Ayub wished, but that it was vitally important for China to know whether Pakistan really intended to fight until its objectives had been achieved or not. Asghar Khan assured him that Pakistan did intend to do so and that he would pass on the message to Ayub. After three days and on his return from Indonesia, where Pakistan was promised whatever limited military assistance Indonesia could provide, Asghar Khan was back in Beijing on the return leg of his journey and met Zhou, who was concerned about Pakistan being pressured into accepting the latest UN proposals. Zhou urged Pakistan to continue fighting and said that if Pakistan persevered, India would have to succumb eventually.

The meetings demonstrate that while the Chinese leadership was friendly and willing to assist in principle, it had residual doubts as to Ayub's willingness to stand up to Indian and American pressure for long and needed to know from him personally whether the British-trained and American-equipped Field Marshal was really prepared to fight to the end. The Chinese request to meet Ayub in person was the second recent demand laid down as a condition for any assistance, as it followed the demand from Johnson on 5 September. On his return to Pakistan, Asghar Khan recounts that Ayub was not keen on meeting Zhou and asked why the face-to-face meeting was necessary. Asghar Khan recounts that he replied, 'They want to be reassured that we intend to fight before they make an important commitment on India's northern borders. They want to look into your eyes to see whether you will see this thing through' (Asghar Khan, *The First Round*, 39–41, 49).

China's ultimatum to India on 8 September and its open support for Pakistan had even Komer seriously concerned, and for the first time he wondered if the US would be forced to intervene if China and Indonesia were involved in the dispute. Kashmir was now seen for the first time as becoming a secondary issue if the whole Asian continent was to be dragged into the war on one side or another. Komer felt that the 'whole western power position may be at stake' and that only the US had the clout to stop the war from getting out of control and bringing both sides to the negotiating table; perhaps the US needed to put pressure on India to show 'an honest willingness to negotiate a decent compromise on Kashmir'. This would have been music to Ayub's ears had he been aware of this thought, as it was exactly what he had hoped to achieve. Komer did say that this analysis was the 'worst case' scenario and the US would need to see how things unfolded in the next few days (8/9/65, Komer to President, Pakistan Memos Vol V LBJ). The State Department was also deeply concerned by China's public stance and Rusk updated Johnson on the situation in the subcontinent, which was dominated by the 'very serious' situation in the light of the

Chinese demands and Shoaib's warning that Bhutto would play the Chinese card if needed. Rusk said that although the US was obviously still the only country that could force a solution, the Kashmir dispute was threatening the whole Asian balance of power, and if India were to lose badly, then the ramifications would be felt in Iran, Indonesia, Japan, Turkey and China; although Congress was seen as wanting to leave South Asia alone, that was seen by the administration as dangerous. Rusk felt that Ayub was 'fearful of all out war with India, as he has reason to be' but that India was also wary of China. Rusk said that the only chance the US had of forcing a stop to the fighting was by committing the US to resolving the Kashmir dispute amongst other things. Rusk said that given the state of relations between the two countries, it was 'extraordinarily difficult to keep good relations with both. However, if forced to choose, given India's population, industrial base, rudimentary democracy... it would be a better bet' (9/9/65 Memo to President, 14259 NA).

Proof that Asghar Khan's mission had gone undetected came from the British embassy in Beijing, which reported that in its view Pakistan had not formally asked for any Chinese assistance and might even be embarrassed by it. The embassy felt that the Chinese might, however, decide themselves that the opportunity to embarrass India again was too good to miss. The Pakistan embassy in Beijing was described as having 'gone to ground', and therefore there was no report of any discussions which might have been going on (9/9/65 Peking to London, DO 196 384 PRO).

The Chinese threat also led to a meeting in London on 9 September when Hilaly met British Foreign Office officials concerned by the latest pronouncements from China. The British view was that China would only exploit the war for its own interest and not Pakistan's; a point which Hilaly accepted by saying that China was going to act in its own national interest. Hilaly was recorded as being 'subdued, strained and pessimistic' and concluded by saying that Pakistan hoped that Britain would not 'let her down' (9/9/65. CRO to Rawalpindi, DO 196/384 PRO).

Evidence that, after the initial shock of the Chinese ultimatum had worn off, Johnson was still convinced that Pakistan would not welcome open Chinese assistance and a permanent rupture with the US came when the State Department sent a message to Bowles on 10 September saying that although it would like to be kept informed of Chinese moves and the US was watching the situation closely, it was 'not, repeat not, prepared to initiate contingency planning of any kind' (10/9/65 State to Delhi, POL 27 India Pak NA).

Johnson had obviously decided to call Ayub's bluff on China and was not prepared to intervene diplomatically by placing any pressure on India, believing that Pakistan would lose more than it would gain from Chinese assistance. The USSR was also reported to be unconcerned by the Chinese threats, as the US ambassador to Moscow reported on a meeting between the Pakistan ambassador and Prime Minister Kosygin on 7 September in which the Soviets appeared to be taking a more neutral stance towards Kashmir than previously. However, ominously for Pakistan, although the Soviets expressed their displeasure at the recent visit of Chen Yi to Pakistan, they were said to be unconcerned about Chinese threats to India as they viewed China as a 'paper tiger' (10/9/65 Moscow to State, POL 27 India-Pak NA).

Stalemate

Pakistan's desperate and belated search for alternative sources of weapons following the US arms embargo meant that it now requested Iran and Turkey, friendly countries with Western arms, to send what military equipment they could to assist.

244

However, as these weapons were mostly US aid equipment, American permission was needed before they could be passed on. In Iran the Shah met British and US diplomats and informed them of a telephone conversation with Ayub that day in which Ayub asked for both political and military assistance. Ayub had warned the Shah that Pakistan would have to reconsider its alliances in the light of any assistance received and he was now concerned that a refusal of help was because of a US desire to see Pakistan 'destroyed'. The Shah said that his main concern was that Pakistan might join hands with the Chinese and he was sending his prime minister to Turkey to ensure that the CENTO allies maintained a consistent line (8/9/65 Tehran to Washington, POL 27 India-Pak NA).

More bad news for Pakistan was to follow on 9 September with the expected but still bitterly disappointing US official refusal to the Pakistan's government's request of 6 September for US aid under the mutual defence agreements. McConaughy met Bhutto on that day and delivered the formal negative response to Pakistan's request, and said the US would be supporting the UN and its Secretary-General in trying to secure a peaceful outcome. The US was noncommittal on what the next step would be if the UN was unable to secure a ceasefire but did not 'want to envisage the possibility of it not working'. Bhutto replied that if the US was only going to refer Pakistan to the UN, then Pakistan need not have bothered to sign any bilateral agreements with the US. Bhutto said it would be seen by Pakistan as the US not 'fulfilling its obligations', and the UN was not seen as an effective body by Pakistan as it had done nothing for eighteen years over Kashmir and the US/Pakistan relationship was not dependent on 'UN blessing'.

McConaughy said that he had not said that the UN would be the only US approach but that there had to be a ceasefire and a withdrawal of troops by both sides. Bhutto said that 'time is of essence'. After giving a familiar run-down of India's actions and

245

behaviour, Bhutto said that Pakistan this time could not just accept a ceasefire and troop withdrawal as now sacrifices had been made and Pakistan had no assurance that India would not carry on as before. Bhutto proposed a mechanism for troop withdrawal followed by a UN administration and then by a plebiscite, and said that without this 'there can be no solution'. The ambassador pointed out that India would never accept such conditions; Bhutto replied emotionally, 'Then let them destroy Pakistan. This is a battle of survival for Pakistan. We must either be degraded as nation or prevail. We [are] prepared to fight to finish'.

McConaughy pointed out that Bhutto's approach meant that Pakistan would continue to fight even if India withdrew. Bhutto said that besides the hostilities stopping, India had to withdraw from Jammu and Kashmir, and the US had 'special moral and contractual obligations' as the former Secretary of State Dulles had promised US intervention in the event of Indian aggression. Not so long ago, recalled Bhutto, George Ball at the State Department had become irritated when Bhutto had suggested that the US might not intervene fast enough, and Kennedy had also promised that the US would break relations with India in the event of Indian aggression. Pakistan had attempted to reach a peaceful solution to the Kashmir issue in the UN but had been treated patronisingly there and had been in effect told to be 'realistic'. McConaughy asked Bhutto to keep an open mind when U Thant visited; to which Bhutto said that they would have an open mind but it would be 'on a positive ceasefire, ceasefire which means settlement, plebiscite', and ended by repeating that there would be no ceasefire without a settlement and the US had its obligations (9/9/65, Karachi to Washington, FRUS 1964–68, Volume XXV South Asia, Document 198).

Bowles sent from Delhi on 9 September a summary of the war from 1 September to date, in which he reported that both sides had made vague and unconfirmed reports of their military success which were 'highly emotional and in cases contradictory'. Although requests by the US staff to visit the front had been denied by the Indians, there was frequent telephone contact and all good news from the Indian side was reported quickly. The initial Pakistan attack across the Chhamb sector using tanks did 'enjoy an element of surprise' and the capture of Akhnur would have meant the severance of the single Indian supply line to over 50 per cent of their CFL and the possible loss of Jammu. The Indians believed that a combination of problems—the Pakistan army's difficulties in crossing the Tawi and Indian air attacks— halted the Pakistan assault for around forty-eight hours during which time the Indians tried to rebuild their defences. However, when Pakistan resumed the offensive it was able to advance another 10 to 12 miles towards Akhnur, which meant that the Indians were facing a critical situation, and it was therefore decided that rather than try and reinforce Akhnur, pressure had to be relieved by an attack across the Punjab border which would not only draw away Pakistani troops from Akhnur, but also show Indian determination and resolve.

India's urgent need to relieve the pressure on Akhnur meant that the 6 September attack was not as well co-ordinated as it might have been, and this seemed to be the main reason why India was not able to reach Lahore quickly. The absence of Pakistan's armour to date also indicated that Pakistan had committed it to Akhnur, and the Indians appeared to have made a decision to hold their tanks in reserve or deployed them elsewhere; there had been rumours of a major armoured build-up around Pathankot. The major Indian armoured attack would then be either along the Narawal/Sialkot front or in the Jammu/Sialkot region, which would give the Indians the opportunity of capturing Sialkot and securing the Chenab crossing. The Americans still felt that the Indians would not commit the majority of their armour in the north as they had to protect Delhi, and it appeared to the US embassy that the majority of the armoured forces had yet to meet each other and in the absence of a ceasefire, the next stage of the war would be a major armoured clash (9/9/65, New Delhi to State, POL 27 India-Pak NA).

Bowles followed this message up with one the following day saying that although the Indian cabinet was split between the usual doves and hawks, there was a growing realisation that all-out war had very serious long-term consequences. Bowles repeated his view that an all-out clash of the two armies had not yet happened and so, although both sides wanted a ceasefire, they wanted this on their own terms. The prevailing Indian view was that Pakistan's behaviour was designed to force India to accept a Kashmir settlement, and if the US was to join in that pressure, then it would lose influence. Bowles felt it was as well that Sheikh Abdullah was in prison as he would have been forced to take sides, but he could be used to assist in finding a solution later. The ambassador urged the US to stay out of trying to find a solution as the issue was close to intractable and there was little point in expending good will on it (10/9/65, Delhi to State, POL 27 India-Pak NA).

In Washington the Indian ambassador to the US, B. K. Nehru, met Johnson with a letter from Shastri explaining the Indian reasons for crossing the Punjab border on 6 September. Nehru went on to say that the use of US weapons by Pakistan against India greatly worried India as its defence policy was based on US assurances that these weapons would not be used against India, and complained that the US spokesmen repeatedly stated that both sides were using US weapons, which was not true. Johnson was non-committal in his response and said that the war had to be stopped quickly and the US supported the UN call for a ceasefire and had made representations to Pakistan regarding the use of US weapons (9/9/65, Memo, Nehru meeting with Johnson, NA).

On the same day, Rusk met Sir Patrick Dean, the British ambassador in Washington. Rusk said that if U Thant failed it would be a good idea to launch a Commonwealth initiative to keep the diplomatic talks going. Dean said that the British position was that they felt the Indians were going to try and wear Pakistan down and Britain had told Pakistan that it would not be blackmailed by the Chinese threats and Pakistan should not assume that India would be paralysed by China. Rusk said that there was a strong feeling within the US that all aid should be cut off to the subcontinent, but the administration had managed to restrict this so far to a cut-off of military aid. The US position as far as economic aid was concerned was that if new aid talks could not be held because of the war, then it was the fault of the two sides fighting and there was no prospect of aid for either side while the war continued (10/9/65, Memo of Conversation, POL 27 India-Pak, NA). The diplomatic situation was now at a stalemate as neither India nor Pakistan was willing at this stage to make any concessions on their principles regarding Kashmir, and so now all attention shifted to the battlefield which had to decide if the stalemate could be broken.

9

OPERATION NEPAL AND OTHER FRONTS

India's Second Front—Sialkot

From the outset of all-out war with India, one of the fears of the Pakistani GHQ was the whereabouts and planned strike of the Indian 1 Armoured Division. This was India's main armoured strike force and, like Pakistan's 1 Armoured Division, was believed to have the capability of influencing the outcome of the war. Again, just as Indian intelligence failed to locate and predict the direction of Pakistan's armoured attack in Mailed Fist, Pakistan was in the dark as to the Indian armoured division's location or likely deployment. Given the terrain of West Punjab, however, the most likely attack for an Indian heavy armoured attack was almost certain to be Sialkot as the approach to that city did not have the water obstacles of the Lahore front, and just as Mailed Fist aimed to reach and then cut the GT Road behind Indian lines, the Indians planned an armoured thrust in Sialkot aimed at reaching critical roads and communication points.

The detailed Indian plans for an invasion into the district of Sialkot (with the city of the same name being its district capital) were codenamed Operation Nepal. The exact objective of Nepal appears to have been slightly modified on a number of occasions before its launch whose timing was intended to coincide with

Riddle to produce a simultaneous attack on both Lahore and Sialkot in the early hours of 6 September. That would have undoubtedly stretched the Pakistani defences to breaking point and might well have had the 'paralysing effect' intended, but fortunately for Pakistan, India's I Corps was simply not ready to move on 6 September (H. Singh, 129).

The first occasion when General Dunn unveiled his plans for the push into Sialkot to Generals Rajinder Singh and Thapan was on 2 September. The vagueness of the plan coupled with its inherent lack of aggressive intent led both the generals to object to the corps commander's plans and it was modified on 3 September, but it was still only marginally more ambitious. The plan was for the three Indian infantry divisions of I Corps to advance along a broad front into Sialkot district and establish a bridgehead from which 1 Armoured Division was to break out. The plan was again slightly modified when Pakistan did not, as had been expected, launch its main armoured attack towards Jammu but instead did so in the direction of Amritsar in Mailed Fist. Nepal was designed for an Indian advance towards the Dhallweali-Wuhilam-Daska-Mandhali line. That point has no particular strategic importance, and although it is quite deep in Pakistani territory, it is unknown what the next move of 1 Corps would have been or whether the thrust was considered deep enough to make Pakistan agree to an unconditional ceasefire.

The Indian 1 Corps was headed by Lt General P. O. Dunn (who was in fact junior to General Rajinder Singh, GOC 1 Armoured Division) and there appears to have been some tension between Rajinder Singh and Dunn as the former was reputed to have been promised operational independence by Chaudhri in the event of a war and was senior in command to Dunn. The Indian 1 Corps comprised:

The 1 Armoured Division under Major General Rajinder Singh 'Sparrow'.

1 Armoured Brigade—Brigadier K. K. Singh.

43 Lorried Brigade—Brigadier H. S. Dhillon.

Division Reserve—2 Lancers, 4 Hodson's Horse, 62 Cavalry.

Division Artillery.

6 *Mountain Division* under Major General S. K. Korla.

69 Mountain Brigade—Brigadier Eric Vas.

99 Mountain Brigade.

Division Artillery.

14 *Infantry Division* under Major General Ranjeet Singh.

35 Infantry Brigade.

58 Infantry Brigade.

116 Infantry Brigade.

Division Artillery.

26 *Infantry Division* under Major General Thapan.

19 Infantry Brigade—Brigadier Aban Naidu.

162 Infantry Brigade—Brigadier R. S. Sheoran.

168 Infantry Brigade—Brigadier A. K. Luthera.

On the Pakistani side, Sialkot was defended by Pakistan's I Corps commanded by Lt General Bakhtiar Rana. The Pakistani forces at his disposal in this sector were:.

6 *Armoured Division—under Major General Abrar Hussain.*

Three armoured regiments:

11 Cavalry (from 8 September).

6 Lancers.

4 Cavalry (replaced by 13 Lancers in July 1964).

2 Armoured Infantry battalions.

9 Frontier Force.

14 Frontier Force.

One Field Artillery Regiment—3 (SP) Field Regiment.

Artillery IV Corps—Brigadier Amjad Ali Khan Chaudhry (affiliated to 6 Armoured Division following relocation from Chhamb sector).

15 *Infantry Division—under Brigadier Sardar Muhammad Ismail* (previously under the command of Major General Yahya Khan).

4 Infantry Brigades.
24 Infantry Brigade—Brigadier Abdul Ali Malik.
101 Infantry Brigade—Brigadier Syed Mahmud Hussian.
104 Infantry Brigade—Brigadier Syed Hyder Abbas Rizvi.
115 Infantry Brigade—Brigadier Muzaffar-ud-Din.
4 armoured regiments.
20 Lancers.
25 Cavalry.
31 Tank Delivery Unit (TDU).
33 TDU.

The Pakistan 15 Infantry Division was therefore composed of an armoured regiment, 25 Cavalry, and four brigades with a tank regiment allocated to each brigade. Of these, 115 Infantry Brigade was composed of two battalions which were concentrated around Jassar-Dera Baba Nanak. 101 Infantry Brigade with two battalions, 19 Punjab and 13 FF, was on the Sialkot-Jammu Road. 24 Infantry Brigade under Brigadier Abdul Ali Khan, with two battalions, was located between the border and Chawinda. 104 Infantry Brigade had 9 Baluch and 31 TDU in reserve at Uggoke, approximately 6 miles west of Sialkot. 6 Armoured Division (which in reality was no more than an armoured brigade) had under its command two armoured regiments, the Guides Cavalry and the 22nd Cavalry and one Infantry battalion, the 4th FF. This was located at Kot Daska, 16 miles south-west of Sialkot and 20 miles west of Chawinda.

Nepal's Aims

As in the case of the Lahore offensive, the ultimate territorial objectives of India's offensive in Sialkot are strongly disputed between the two sides. Some Pakistani writers believe that India's objective was to reach the GT Road between Wazirabad and Gujranwala and thereby cut a major highway, while India claims that Nepal's objectives were simply to relieve pressure on

Chhamb and to draw into battle and destroy Pakistani armour. Chaudhri, the head of the Indian army, said on 23 September that 'On 8 September, India put in a diversionary attack, a fairly strong one, in the Sialkot sector with the intention of containing troops there' (B. Singh, 175). The implication is therefore that India had to mount an offensive which credibly threatened Sialkot with either capture or isolation and to threaten Lahore's links with the north-west, and the location of Sialkot was emphasised in order to show its importance. The ancient city of Sialkot is in the north-east corner of Pakistan, 12 miles from the river Chenab, and there are three main routes which link the city of Sialkot with Lahore, which is 68 miles to the south. The shortest of these routes is from the south-west of the city via Daska, Gujranwala and Kamoke to Lahore, a distance of 73 miles. Both a railway and a road follow the other two routes which are about the same length (88 miles) and one passes through Wazirabad and Gujranwala. The other divides at Pasrur, with one branch passing through Narawal and the other through Raya Khas.

To isolate Sialkot completely from the rest of Pakistan would involve Indian forces surrounding it from the east, south and west, and in addition a thrust aimed at blocking the shortest routes would also have to block the town of Wazirabad from the Chenab because there are routes to it from Lahore other than the direct Gujranwala route. Once it had moved beyond the Sialkot-Pasrur line, a thrust would have to be pushed across more than one line of advance, with three large canals needing to be crossed before reaching the Lahore-Gujranwala-Wazirabad Road. These three canals, the Marala-Ravi Link (MRL), the Upper Chenab Canal (UCC), and the BRBD Canal, could be turned into formidable obstacles if the bridges over them were demolished and a defence mechanism established. Even if Wazirabad was taken or surrounded, Lahore would still be linked by road and rail with other towns such as Gujrat and Kharian.

The city of Sialkot was close enough to Srinagar to have been the winter home of the British Resident to Jammu and Kashmir and is only 26 miles south-west of Jammu, Kashmir's traditional winter capital, while the cities of Sialkot and Jammu were linked by a road which crosses the border 6 miles from Sialkot. Jammu in turn is linked to Madhopur, 54 miles away in Indian Punjab. Madhopur was the most direct route for an Indian advance to Wazirabad (in Pakistani Punjab) and on the strategically vital Grand Trunk Road that links Lahore to the new capital of Islamabad. Although the Pakistani city of Sialkot was on the way to Wazirabad from Madhopur, it could be bypassed by a successful Indian advance on the GT Road. However, this border area was fortified by Pakistan with bunkers and pill boxes on the approaches to the city, and more important, there was little room between Jammu, the Chenab and its tributaries and Sialkot for the deployment of a powerful armoured striking force.

Fighting in the Jassar Enclave

A little to the west of the Indian town of Dera Baba Nanak there is a road and rail bridge capable of carrying trains and vehicles across the river Ravi. At its eastern end there is a Pakistan salient on the left bank of the river with a bridge which is situated wholly within Pakistani territory, while there is an Indian salient on the right bank of the bridge. The Lahore-Narawal-Sialkot railway passes near the bridge where it runs through the western outskirts of Narawal, eight miles from the Ravi, before turning north-westwards to Pasrur and Sialkot. The town of Jassar stands three miles from the bridge on the Narawal Road.

Pakistan's 115 Infantry Brigade, comprising two battalions of 3 Punjab and 4 FF, accompanied by an unknown number of tanks including Shermans, was located east of Jassar and was given the responsibility of defending this enclave. This brigade was relatively new, having been formed only in May 1965, with Brigadier Muzaffaruddin as its first commander. On the night of 5/6 September, troops from 3 Punjab were guarding the bridge while others were on the Pakistani side of the east bank. The Indian 29 Infantry Brigade was given the task of capturing the bridge from the Dera Baba Nanak side and then pushing on towards Narawal and Pasrur. Although Nepal was not ready to be launched fully, it was decided by Indian commanders that the Jassar enclave was too risky to leave in Pakistani hands once Nepal was launched, and an Indian attack was therefore launched on the enclave and the bridge to coincide with the launch of Riddle.

The attack on Jassar commenced at 0330 hours, 6 September, and it is agreed by both sides that it took the defending soldiers completely by surprise. The initial Indian attack almost succeeded in capturing the bridge intact within a few hours, but by noon 6 September the Pakistani forces had regrouped and counter-attacked, and the bridge was back in Pakistani hands by that afternoon. The Indian attack caused real concern at 15 Division HQ as it was assumed that this was the launch of India's main assault in this area, and so once the bridge was back in Pakistani hands by the afternoon of 6 September, the decision was made to counter-attack and take the attack to India to clear its enclave opposite Narawal.

However, before any serious assault could be launched and despite the reinforcement of Pakistani troops across the bridge in the enclave, the Indian 2 Rajputana Rifles were ordered to retake the bridge at 0200 hours, 7 September. This time the attack was eventually successful and by the morning of 7 September the bridge was in Indian hands. It was now decided by HQ 15 Division that if the bridge could not be safely held by Pakistan then it should be demolished to deny Indian armour and infantry use of it, and the bridge was blown at 0800 hours, 7 September. However, in the confusion and panic in the

Pakistani ranks, 15 Division HQ and even the local commanders seemed unaware that two companies of 3 Punjab Regiment were still on the east side of the bridge. During the rest of the day, these companies had to discard all non-essential equipment and most were evacuated with surprisingly few casualties by swimming back across the river.

As the fear within 15 Division was still that this was the beginning of the major Indian assault through this enclave, GHQ ordered 15 Division to assist 115 Brigade, not realising that the Indians simply wanted to ensure the enclave did not threaten their position and that it was a limited action. Brigadier Abdul Ali Malik of 24 Brigade tried to persuade Brigadier Ismail not to weaken the defence of Sialkot by moving troops to Jassar, but on being ordered to do so, Brigadier Malik left the majority of his brigade near Chawinda and only moved a small operations team to Narawal. The large-scale movement of reinforcements to this area would have been a real problem for Pakistan as Nepal was about to be launched in a different direction, and whether by accident or design, the Indian attack on Jassar and the bridge had succeeded in causing panic and disruption to 15 Division plans and deployment (Shuja Nawaz, *Crossed Swords*, Oxford University Press Pakistan, 2008, 225). The Indians were themselves seemingly unaware of the confusion caused within Pakistani ranks by this relatively small-scale attack, and had Nepal been launched on 7 September, it would have caused very real problems for Pakistan. The short but intense fighting in the Jassar enclave did not reflect well on the defending Pakistan 15 Division, which was fortunate not to have been made to pay a heavier price for miscalculating both Indian intentions and the strength of the attack. General Ahmed criticises the orders given by General Rana for trying to hold the enclave and missing the strategic importance of the bridge, and also for directing artillery fire in the wrong direction and allowing the Indians an easier ride into Sialkot than they would otherwise have had. The commander of 115 Brigade also comes in for criticism for sending panicked reports back from Jassar, live and uncorroborated, which were said to have concerned troops as far away as Rawalpindi and caused the commander of 24 Brigade and some guns from Artillery 4 Corps to be rushed there when they were not needed. This enclave was now to remain relatively quiet for the duration of the war as India had achieved its objective of eliminating the salient and felt safe from this direction (Ahmed, 351–3).

The launch of Nepal

Despite the reservations of I Corps senior officers regarding the rather vague objectives of Nepal as laid down by Dunn, the operation was ordered to commence on the night of 7/8 September and was to be launched along two axes; one force was to advance along the Aik Nala canal on the Bajragarhi-Sialkot axis and the other was ordered to advance down the Jammu-Sialkot axis, with the latter route containing the major force of the attack. Despite some clear warning signs such as an artillery bombardment on the night of 7/8 September and even an intercepted message from an Indian despatch rider inside ICK, 15 Division still seemed taken by surprise by the launch and direction of Nepal which began promptly with 6 Mountain Division and 26 Infantry Division moving into Sialkot preceded by artillery fire at 2300 hours, 7 September. Operation Nepal was under way.

The initial offensive went well for the Indian forces and 162 Infantry Brigade moved on the Jammu-Sialkot axis with the village of Salia in Indian hands by early morning 8 September. On the Bajragarhi-Sialkot route, 168 Brigade moved quickly up to Ura bridge where it met the first organised defence. On the other axis, 6 Mountain Division led by 99 Mountain Brigade moved on to the border town of Charwa, and although the town was in Indian hands by the morning of 8 September, the Indians conceded that the defenders 'fought with courage and determination' and sporadic fighting in and around the area was to continue for another two days (H. Singh, 137). The other brigade of 6 Mountain Division, 69 Mountain Brigade, was tasked with the capture of Maharjke which it managed to carry out by the morning of 8 September.

26 Infantry was tasked with the attack on Sialkot, although whether this was simply the 'containment of enemy forces' as claimed later or a serious attempt to take the city is still unclear. Two brigades were launched towards Sialkot, 162 and 168 Infantry Brigades, and the move was along the Bajragarhi axis. By 0600 hours, 8 September both the main targets of 26 Infantry, Unche Wains and Niwe Wains, were in the hands of 162 Infantry Brigade. 168 Infantry Brigade, comprising three battalions and two more in support, captured its target of Bajragarhi. The capture of these strategic targets left the city of Sialkot vulnerable and the Indians were now within 5 miles of the city. General Ahmed believes that the Indians' intention could not have been to capture the city as they did not make any serious move at this time towards it, and it was just as well that the Indians did not have that intention as they did not appear to realise how lightly the city was defended, particularly if approached from Bajragarhi. The incompetent handling of the defences on the Pakistan side meant that Brigadier Ismail, GOC 15 Division, was relieved of his command at 0660 hours, 8 September and replaced by Major General Tikka Khan, who had earned plaudits from his command in Kutch earlier in the year; this was almost precisely eight hours after the commencement of Nepal. Brigadier Ismail, however, was retained magnanimously by Tikka Khan as second in command.

1 Armoured Division enters the scene

From Chawra, 16 miles east of Sialkot, the road runs southwards through Phillora and on to Chawinda, and the Indian infantry division had managed to secure bridgeheads on these two roads, which had cleared the way for 1 Armoured Division to swing into action. At 0600 hours, 8 September, advancing 10 miles along the Charwa-Phillora road, the lead elements of 1 Armoured Brigade were close to the strategic village of Phillora which General Rajinder Singh 'Sparrow' had been ordered to capture. Unfortunately for Nepal, the 43rd Lorried Infantry Brigade which should have covered the right flank of the thrust was stuck in the border area and had hardly moved at all. There have been differing explanations of this, from a heavy downpour to the fact that the brigade had been attacked by the Pakistan Air Force, but whatever the reason the Indian armoured attack now ground to a halt, and it appears that regimental commanders lost control of their units (Johri, 144).

Not only was the 43rd Lorried Brigade unable to progress very far, 16 Cavalry and 17 Horse seemed unable to move either and 1 Armoured Division was, according to an Indian general, 'fumbling around ineffectively in a chaotic situation of our own creation, the enemy had that vital breathing space so essential for a quick rally round from the stunning impact of surprise'. It had to be conceded that '1 Armoured Division, staked to turn the tide of war, had made a bad beginning' (H. Singh, 143). It is interesting to note that almost exactly the same errors that Pakistan's 1 Armoured Division was making that day in Khem Karan—lack of co-ordination between infantry and armour, dissipation of force and breakdown of communication between the brigade commanders—appeared in the assault on Phillora by the Indian 1 Armoured Division. It was not an auspicious beginning and by the end of the day, hardly any progress had been made by India's main armoured assault force.

The confusion within the Indian troops near Phillora gave the Pakistani defenders invaluable time to regroup, and they were now determined to turn the Indian attack from a speedy advance into a slogging match with every mile being hard fought. Given the strength of the defence put up by the smaller and outnumbered Pakistani units in the area of Phillora, there was now a mood of caution within the Indian commanders which led to the Nepal offensive being effectively halted for two days, 9 and 10 September, when a relative lull fell on the battlefield while the Indians regrouped and tried to regain the initiative. This breathing space was undoubtedly welcomed by the Pakistanis as they were in no position to launch a strong counter-offensive at that time and the overall initiative still rested firmly with India given the relatively small forces available to the Pakistanis on this front. During this respite, the defenders were strengthened by the arrival of the 11th Cavalry and the 10th Infantry Brigade with two battalions, the 6th FF and the 14th Punjab (G. Ahmed, 140). The Indian inaction may have been induced by considerations other than the setback received by the armoured division on 8 September, as there was an element of regrouping and reinforcement being carried out and also a degree of apprehension within the Indian ranks about the outcome of the fierce battle taking place near Asal Uttar at the time. A decisive Pakistani breakthrough on 9 September at Asal Uttar might well have altered the whole plan for Nepal and conceivably could have led to orders for the troops to withdraw to defend Amritsar.

By 10 September it was clear that Mailed Fist had been decided in India's favour, and so at first light 11 September 1 Armoured Division was ordered to advance again on two fronts, Charwa-Chawinda and Kaloi-Pagowal towards Phillora. This was a clear change of tactics and now the plan was to bypass areas of strong resistance and encircle the strategically important targets before attacking them. For the whole of 11 September, Indian armour locked horns with Pakistani tanks and artillery as a determined and co-ordinated attempt was made by India to secure Phillora. Despite fierce Pakistani resistance, the Indians managed to capture the town at 1530 IST on 11 September and it was left to 99 Mountain Brigade to hold the Phillora while the Gurkha Rifles were ordered to take Zafarwal.

The capture of Phillora was the first major success of 1 Armoured Division since its rather unimpressive beginning on 8 September. The Pakistanis later claimed that had the Indians pushed on to Pasrur without resting it would have caused real problems for the Pakistani defences which were still recovering their balance from the fighting in Jassar and in a state of general confusion, as Pakistan's GHQ sent direct orders to units rather than via the corps commander. There was pressure from the corps commander, Rana, to order 6 Armoured Division to attack and retake Phillora that night, but Major General Abrar managed to persuade both Rana and Musa that this was not possible at that time and his troops needed to regroup and plan such an attack carefully. Fortunately for the Pakistanis, Rajinder Singh of 1 Armoured Division, now gave his forces a forty-eight-hour rest period; time which was invaluable to the Pakistanis to prepare their defences for Chawinda and Zafarwal which were the obvious next targets.

Zafarwal was the new focus of India's 14 Infantry Division. This town had been almost completely undefended by the Pakistan Army until 11 September and also relatively ignored by the Indians. 5/5 Gurkha Rifles were sent on the night of 11/12 September to probe the defences of Zafarwal and to occupy it if it was undefended. It is rumoured that the Gurkha regiment, on reaching Zafarwal, managed to successfully persuade the locals that they were Chinese soldiers come to fight with Pakistan, and some locals provided food and shelter. Whatever the truth of that story, by early morning 12 September the Gurkhas were digging in at the southern end of the town and 13 FF was despatched to try and dislodge them, which they were able to do by mid-morning of 12 September with just machine guns and recoilless rifles. By the night of 12/13 September the Pakistanis had managed to get both armour and infantry into Zafarwal to prepare for its defence; on 13 September the Indians made a more serious attempt to capture Zafarwal, sending tanks and artillery in to try and seize the town, but by now Pakistani defences were well prepared. A fierce battle was fought all day but by the evening it was apparent that the defences would hold and Indian troops pulled back to Mirzapur. Harbakhsh Singh visited the front on 12 September and said that he made his dissatisfaction known 'not only with the Zafarwal operations but also on the apathy or lack of enterprise on the part of 1 Armoured Division' (H. Singh, 149). Apart from some serious clashes on 21/22 September, the area around Zafarwal remained relatively calm and the Indians did not make another serious attempt to seize the town again. On 13 September the Indian 69 Mountain Division was ordered to capture the town of Bhagowal, which it managed to do without encountering much opposition as the town was almost undefended; by 0600 hours, 13 September, it was in Indian hands. Despite Pakistani attempts during the day to retake the town, it remained in Indian hands for the duration of the war.

The battles for Chawinda

The next target for the Indian 1 Armoured Division was now the town of Chawinda. By 12 September, Pakistan had managed to reinforce the defence of Chawinda with the despatch of various brigades of its own 1 Armoured Division which it had managed to send over from the unsuccessful battles at the Khem Karan sector during Mailed Fist. On 13 September, Dunn drew up detailed battle plans for the capture of Chawinda. The idea was again for the first phase to be a large-scale encirclement of the town using 43 Lorried Brigade, 99 Mountain Brigade and 1 Armoured Brigade, and this was to be executed at first light the next morning. The second phase was for the breaching of the town's defences and then its capture.

At first light on 14 September, the Indians again moved towards the town of Chawinda from Phillora in a number of directions in an attempt to surround the city in a large pincer movement. An earlier tank battle had meant that the Pakistanis had managed to capture orders from an Indian tank regarding the battle plans, and the orders specified that 1 Armoured Division had not only to secure the capture of Chawinda but also 'in the process destroy remainder of enemy's 6 Armed Div' (Major General Abrar Hussain, *Men of Steel*, Rawalpindi: Army Education Publishing House, 2005, 96).

By the afternoon of 14 September, the full force of 1 Armoured Division was engaged in a furious battle around the town using armour, artillery and infantry. Between 1200 and 1800 the Indians tried repeatedly to break through but were unable to do so, and by early evening they withdrew to consolidate the few gains made that day in the shape of a few villages. Yet again 1 Armoured Division had 'thrown away a cheap success and added another failure to its spate of lost opportunities' (H. Singh, 152). The Indians claimed to have knocked out 18 Pakistani tanks in this battle but admit that the assault was unsuccessful owing to 'the armour having failed to create the tactical precondition for an infantry assault on Chawinda'; in other words, the failure to penetrate the defences of the town (Chakravorty, 213). The successful defence of Chawinda was not purely due to Indian errors; the defensive fighting was brave and although outnumbered, the defenders always appeared to be in control of the town. Despite the disparity in numbers the first battle of Chawinda (as it has become known) showed again that neither side was totally comfortable with attacking manoeuvres and both were better at defence. One of the factors helping Pakistan defend Chawinda on 14 September was the PAF which played a close and decisive role in breaking up Indian positions and was even able to knock out some heavy Indian artillery guns with repeated low-level bombing (Ahmed, 459). The GOC of 6 Armoured Division tasked with the defence of Chawinda admits that by nightfall on that day: 'Both sides appeared exhausted and were licking their wounds' (Hussain, 40).

On 16 September, Dunn had a meeting at Maharajke with the senior officers involved in Nepal to plan the next phase, whose objective was reiterated to be the capture of Chawinda, Badiana and Zafarwal. 6 Mountain Division was tasked with the capture of Chawinda and Badiana, Zafarwal being now the responsibility of 1 Armoured Division. At this stage it appeared to the Pakistani defenders that the next Indian attack was now likely to try to bypass Chawinda and move instead towards Badiana, in an area which was relatively undefended. Plans were formulated by Pakistan's I Corps on 15 September that 1 Armoured Division should now plan a counter-attack rather than defend, but eventually it was decided to err on the side of caution, which allowed the Indians the initiative in this sector for the remainder of the war.

After a heavy artillery bombardment in the early morning of 15 September and some fierce skirmishes, the Indian troops of 43 Lorried Brigade began their attempt to encircle Chawinda using similar outflanking tactics in the morning of 16 September. 6 Mountain Division, with 35 and 58 Infantry Brigades together with 1 Armoured Division, was to capture and hold Chawinda by the night of 16 September, and so three co-ordinated attacks were launched on Badiana and Chawinda. The first commenced at 0730 hours, the second at 1230 hours and the third from 1630 hours. As 1 Armoured Division had now developed a reputation for timidity, the heavy artillery was deployed well ahead of the other positions, which enabled the guns to fire down quickly on any area which looked vulnerable to Indian armour (Hussain, 44).

The first attack in the early morning was fierce and the western defences of Chawinda gave way, and by 1000 hours the village of Jassoran was in Indian hands. The assault was led by 9 Dogra operating under the command of 17 Poona Horse. It was from Jassoran that 8 Garhwal Rifles supported by 17 Poona Horse now moved to the capture the village of Buttar Dograndi. The Indians' advance was slow as they were under sustained shelling from Pakistan's artillery and the commanding officer of 8 Garhwal Rifles was killed by a shell. There was now fierce fighting between tanks and infantry for the village of Buttar Dograndi and by late afternoon, the Indian troops had entered the centre of the village. 3FF who were the main Pakistani infantry unit inside the village fell back in some confusion and according to 6 Armoured Division's own record, some of the men left their trenches and had to be ordered back by the gunners (Ahmed, 469). The withdrawal of 3FF left the western approach to Chawinda almost undefended and the guns of the Artillery IV Corps exposed.

Despite Buttar Doagrandi being temporarily evacuated by Indian troops, a fresh push ensured the village was in Indian hands, and the Pakistani defensive position was under such severe pressure that the commander of 24 Brigade began to express his doubts as to whether he would be able to hold his position and asked for permission to withdraw. This was refused and he was told to hold the city at all costs as 'There was no question of withdrawal...but the situation was now critical' (Hussain, 45). There was then an hour of fierce fighting between tanks and heavy guns on both sides and there were unfounded rumours among 3FF troops that the railway station at Chawinda had fallen into Indian hands. It was not until an hour or so later, at approximately 1800 hours, that it became apparent that the worst of the assault was over as far as Pakistani forces were concerned. The Indian 1 Armoured Division had failed to capture Chawinda but had cut the road between Badiana and Chawinda; however, critically, it had not cut the Chawinda-Pasrur road at Sarangpur, an action which would have caused real problems for the future defence of Chawinda and would have allowed 1 Armoured Division to then move towards Pasrur.

17 September was a relatively quiet day with limited counter-attacks being launched by Pakistan's 4 Armoured Brigade, and that evening it was decided that a larger counter-attack would be launched by 4 Armoured Brigade and 24 Brigade to try to clear Indian positions in the Badiana-Chawinda area. The counter-attack was launched at 0800 hours, 17 September and by the afternoon Pakistani forces managed to retake a number of strategic villages including Butur Dograndi after a gallant defence by the Indian Garhwali regiment which had to fight two days without food rations or reinforcements.

On 18/19 September 6 Mountain Division attempted yet again to capture Chawinda, but this time the attack began at night rather than at first light. The GOC 6 Mountain Division had requested a postponement of the assault by 24 hours in order to give him time to prepare properly, but this was overruled. To assist 6 Mountain Division, 35 and 58 Infantry Brigades as well as 99 Mountain Brigade were placed under its command in addition to all the artillery available to I Corps. Prior to the attack, 1 Armoured Division was permitted to withdraw from certain villages and positions held for the last few days in order to consolidate its line and to prepare for the next offensive. One of the villages evacuated was Jassoran, a decision which was later described as 'an inexplicable misunderstanding' (H. Singh, 114).

The attack began at 0100 with heavy artillery shelling and was led by 35 and 58 Infantry Brigades which were ordered to capture Chawinda by first light. The other units of 1 Armoured Division remained in place facing 6 Armoured Division and were ordered to prevent any Pakistani reinforcement of Chawinda and to maintain pressure. The Indian assault on Chawinda again fell on 3FF, but unfortunately for the Indians, Pakistani defences were well prepared and the attack attracted heavy and sustained fire from Pakistani artillery. It is suspected that because of poor Indian security measures, the Pakistanis knew exactly where the Indian forces were poised to attack from and the troops preparing for attack were shelled even before the offensive started; 'The operation was, in consequence, dislocated from the very beginning' (H. Singh, 155).

The official Indian history describes the shelling as 'so intense that it unnerved the troops' and led to such confusion within the Indian forces that some of them began shooting at each other, and 500 Jammu and Kashmir riflemen were reported to have deserted (Chakravorty, 217–18). 35 Infantry Brigade had been beaten back but 58 Infantry performed even worse, a fact acknowledged by both sides. 58 Infantry Brigade 'ceased to be a cohesive force... and we came out of the battle badly battered and bruised' (H. Singh, 155). As nightfall came, the situation for 6 Armoured Division holding Chawinda, particularly on its right flank which had been under severe pressure, now began to ease. By dawn of 19 September, a final Indian move near the Chawinda railway line ran into the tanks and heavy guns of 25 Cavalry and 24 Brigade. It became obvious that the Indian attack had been a disaster for the latest move of Nepal. Pakistani claims that in the early morning of 19 September Pakistani forces killed hundreds of Indians and inflicted thousands of casualties may not be an exaggeration. Harbakhsh Singh was scathing about the attack and the manner in which it was carried out, but credit must be given to the Pakistani defences which managed to hold the town while being badly outnumbered. By the afternoon of 19 September, the Pakistani troops were confident enough to counter-attack and managed to retake Jassoran and Janewal.

The Indian assault on Chawinda had now failed for a second time and it became obvious that Nepal was now running out of steam; just as Mailed Fist was unable to break past Asal Uttar earlier in September, Indian GHQ had to absorb the reality that India's 1 Armoured Division was unable to break past Chawinda and with the losses it had suffered in trying to do so, it was unlikely to be able to have any other major impact on the war. If

Nepal had now ground to halt, albeit deep into Pakistani territory, it at least gave India some territory to use as a bargaining counter, and the Indian government was now markedly more interested in the war ending sooner rather than later. By the morning of 20 September, 6 Armoured Division held the same line it had held on 12 September; in the intervening eight days of heavy and brutal fighting, Nepal had little additional territory to show and heavy losses inflicted on 1 Armoured Division. It was doubtless a severe disappointment for the Indians that their much vaunted 1 Armoured Division was unable to make much headway against weaker Pakistani forces in Sialkot. India claimed to have lost only six tanks in the area while destroying 67 Pakistani tanks—figures which seem highly unlikely. Pakistan claimed to have knocked out 160 to 180 Indian tanks in Sialkot sector and lost 61, figures that are also probably exaggerated but appear more plausible (Ahmed, 484).

By the evening of 20 September, Pakistani GHQ now began to seriously consider a counter-offensive in Sialkot and ordered I Corps to prepare a plan urgently. This was delivered to GHQ on 21 September with the codename 'Operation Wind Up', and was quickly approved by GHQ. Wind Up was envisaged to carry out an assault on numerous Indian positions and 6 Armoured Division was to recapture Bhagowal if possible, with support from Artillery IV Corps and the PAF, H-Hour being fixed at 0430 hours, 22 September. As the orders were being given and confirmed, it was obvious that there was serious talk of a ceasefire and the UN resolution demanding one had been passed. Wind Up was never therefore executed, and was in any event a limited counter-offensive which was unlikely to have made any major difference to the outcome of the war.

Review of Nepal

It hardly need be pointed out that not many of the objectives and plans laid down by Dunn for Operation Nepal materialised.

First, it was to be launched simultaneously with Riddle, which proved to be impossible, and so it was launched almost forty-eight hours late. Secondly, the relatively flat and open terrain of the Sialkot area was seen as ideal for India's main offensive force, 1 Armoured Division, to operate and sweep all before it, which turned out not to be the case. Thirdly, the relatively stretched Pakistani forces in the area were not expected to put up such a strong fight, and it appeared that Indian troops were not being resupplied or reequipped as smoothly or quickly as they would have liked. The small force holding Sialkot managed to hold on despite the odds.

The results were therefore mixed. On the positive side for India, Nepal did achieve some good results:

(i) Redeployment of Pakistan's 1 Armoured Division from Khem Karan to Sialkot to help defend the area. Although it is unlikely that after 11 September, Pakistan's armoured division and brigades were in any shape to undertake more offensive activity, this still relieved pressure on Indian Punjab and put Pakistan firmly back on the defensive. The move away from Khem Karan meant that India did not need to worry about that front any longer as it knew Pakistan was now on the defensive.

(ii) The capture of a large chunk of Pakistani territory was a boost for the Indian army after the relatively poor showing of Kutch and more recently Riddle, where the Indian offensive forces had been pushed back with relative ease by a much smaller defensive force. Although the exact area captured by Nepal is disputed, there is no doubt that India did manage to capture a large amount of land in Sialkot and was able to hold it with relative ease.

On the negative side, India failed either to destroy 6 Armoured Brigade or to deliver a knockout blow to Pakistan. In fact it was the Pakistani forces in Sialkot that by 20 September had their tails up with their successful defence of Chawinda, and the Indians' inability to take the town must have been demoralising for the troops. The casualties inflicted on Indian troops in the last assault on early 19 September effectively meant that 1 Armoured Division was also no longer able to carry out major offensive operations from that date. It appears that tensions amongst the senior commanders of this operation did not assist and it seems that there was also a failure to command from the front, from brigade commanders down. The Indian commander on the whole western front was highly critical of his own forces: 'an indifferent leadership made disaster inevitable' (H. Singh, 157). The reasons why Nepal failed to achieve its objectives are similar to those of Pakistan's failure in Mailed Fist. Poor leadership and co-ordination amongst such large forces meant that elementary mistakes were made in the deployment of troops and tactics. The constant assaults on Chawinda made little military sense as it would have been militarily more advantageous to India to bypass the town and move to cut off strategic roads and railway lines. It proved yet again that both India and Pakistan lacked senior officers with the experience and ability to handle large-scale manoeuvres, and both sides proved that their defensive rather than offensive abilities were superior.

Some Indian politicians and writers later claimed that the Indian forces of Nepal were still well poised after the latest failure at Chawinda to win the battle of attrition and thereafter push on to the original objectives of Nepal. However, as the British review was to phrase it succinctly, 'neither the objective nor the aim was fully realised' by the Indians (British military review, 16). Once the dust of war settled and an objective eye was cast over the performance of India's 1 Armoured Division, it was clear that 'the formations record of operational performance was virtually a catalogue of lost victories...we must concede the fact that it fell far short of a decisive defeat when it was within our capacity to do so and for which the circumstances were so favourable...The meagre gains we made were due to a fluke of a chance' (H. Singh, 159–62). Some Pakistanis also claimed later that Wind Up was poised to recapture Sialkot from Indian troops and to inflict a crippling blow on Indian troops. That is also implausible given not only the limited objectives of the operation but also the relatively limited troops and ammunition available to the offensive forces.

Other military fronts

The Rajasthan front was a relative sideshow compared to the large-scale clashes in Kashmir and Punjab. Since the Kutch clashes earlier in the year, the Indians now had more troops on the Rajasthan/Sindh border which was over 1,000 miles long, and their military planning had decided on 4 September to use 30 Infantry Brigade based in Rajasthan for offensive operations should the need arise. The immediate objective for the brigade in the event of hostilities was to capture and hold the town of Gadr, a large village a few miles across the border in Pakistan. Indian troops managed to achieve this objective without heavy fighting on 8 September, but Pakistan retaliated by capturing the Indian town of Munabao and other territory in Rajasthan, including Rohera and Panchla by 13 September. Considering that Pakistan had only one brigade in the region compared to the Indian 11 Infantry Division, it was a credible effort by the Pakistani brigade. In the final analysis, however, the only real benefit of the sector's fighting for Pakistan was the capture of some Indian territory which was a useful bargaining chip in the later peace talks, and the intensity of fighting and casualties on this front were far less than on the Punjab front.

There was also a clash along the southern part of the Punjab border, which occurred in the Sulaimanke-Fazilika area. Fazilika is about 100 miles from Amritsar in the south-west corner of Indian Punjab and about 6 miles east of the river Sutlej. The

Pakistan border lies eight miles away to the south and the fighting in this area took place between the town and the border. On the evening of 6 September two battalions, the 4th and 10th Punjab from Pakistan's 105 Infantry Brigade, crossed the border and occupied three villages, and Pakistan claimed to have occupied a further twenty-seven Indian villages over the next two weeks. India does admit that Pakistan was in occupation of some territory in this area and there was some fierce fighting in the run-up to the ceasefire as both sides wished to be in an advantageous position by occupying as much territory as possible. Again the number of troops involved and the strategic gains were limited and although it was another arena of the war, it was not to have a major impact on the outcome for either side.

One front which was potentially important, however, and which was relatively ignored, was that of East Pakistan/West Bengal. In the light of heavy fighting on the western front of the war, one of the more surprising facts of the 1965 war was the almost complete lack of action on this front, and this is all the more surprising given the massive Indian invasion in 1971 which resulted in East Pakistan becoming the independent state of Bangladesh. For a number of reasons, however, just six years earlier neither India nor Pakistan opened up this front, which saw virtually no ground fighting. From Pakistan's point of view the reason is not hard to see; Pakistan only had one division of the army based in East Pakistan, 14 Infantry Division under Major General Fazal Muqeem Khan, which was facing eleven Indian divisions of the Eastern Command of General Sam Manekshaw, the man who led the Indian forces into East Pakistan in 1971. Any aggressive action taken by Pakistan in the sector would therefore have been foolhardy given the disparity of forces and the difficult defensive terrain.

India's reasons for not opening up this front can only be understood as reluctance to open a front without a clear objective and international pressure. Given that India was always likely to be able to defeat the much smaller Pakistani force based in East Pakistan, India would have found itself with issues of refugees and communal unrest to deal with, as well as strong international pressure from the US and the threat from China which all combined to persuade the Indian government not to open this front. What fighting there was on this East Pakistan/West Bengal front was mostly confined to the air. The PAF's main air base in East Pakistan was at Tezgaon near Dhaka, the capital of East Pakistan; No 14 Squadron comprising 12 F-86Fs was the total air strength. The IAF base in Bengal was at Kalaikunda, some 60 miles from Calcutta and on 7 September, the PAF was ordered to raid Kalaikunda. The attack appears to have taken the Indian base by surprise as a number of IAF planes were damaged on the ground. Despite this attack, the British believed that Chaudhri, the Indian Commander-in-Chief, was 'given a direct order' not to make 'retaliatory attacks' (British military review, 21). There are references to Indian assurances given to the US that India would not open up the eastern front, in order to keep China out of the war. Other than that solitary incident, the rest of the war was spent with occasional air raids by both sides on each other's targets, but by and large an uneasy calm remained on this front.

Air and naval war

There was virtually no war at sea as neither navy come under direct fire from its opponent. India had by far the larger naval force with a light fleet carrier (INS *Vikrant*), two light cruisers (*Mysore* and *Delhi*) and seventeen escort vessels of various types. Pakistan had a single light cruiser (PNS *Babur*), seven escort vessels and a submarine which had been transferred on loan from the US Navy in June 1964. However, in September 1965 it appears that neither *Babur* nor *Delhi* was battleworthy, and when Operation Riddle was launched, the Indian carrier was in dock while *Mysore* was also reported to be undergoing repairs, and both were in the Bombay naval dockyard; but despite that India still had an advantage of seventeen to seven escort vessels. Despite its greater strength, however, the Indian fleet did not take the offensive and instead, on the night of 7/8 September, two Pakistani destroyers bombarded the Indian post of Dwarka, around 220 miles south-east of Karachi. This town is sacred to Hindus; later Indian historians admitted that the Indian Navy was caught napping, but insist that the town was of no military significance (Manekar, 142). India does not appear to have retaliated against the bombardment and neither navy appears to have intercepted the other's merchant shipping. However, both sides did seize each other's ships which were in port on 6 September; but as most bilateral trade was carried out using foreign registered ships, any attempt at blockade would have been highly unlikely as it would almost certainly been ruled out by the diplomatic repercussions.

In 1947 Pakistan had no real air force and had to start one from scratch. By 1965, its strength was estimated at 17 squadrons which included 12 F-104 Starfighters, the most advanced aircraft on either side of the war. This was a US plane capable of flying at Mach 2 (twice the speed of sound) which could be used in both defensive and offensive roles and had advanced radar and missile equipment; it had been supplied in 1961, to much Indian concern. Galbraith had written to Kennedy in July 1961 objecting to their transfer as he felt 'they will contribute nothing to our security in the area...and another source of suspicion so far as we are concerned' (Galbraith, 175).

In terms of numbers of aircraft, India had the greater numbers in the air by some distance, with eighty Canberras capable of night bombing while the PAF possessed twenty-four of these aircraft and had no all-weather interceptors, while India had at least ten supersonic MiG-21 aircraft and was in the process of installing in Punjab batteries of Soviet SA-2 surface-to-air missiles, then capable of shooting down aircraft flying at between 3,000 and 80,000 feet. The IAF also had 100 Mystere IVAs, 100 Gnats, 150 Hawker Hunters and several other aircraft with a total of 775 aircraft in twenty-nine squadrons. These combined heavily outnumbered the PAF 100 F-86F Sabres, twelve F-104As and twenty-five B-57 jet bombers and twelve T-33 training planes, giving a total of 141 combat aircraft in nine squadrons (John Fricker, *Battle for Pakistan—The Air War of 1965*, Ian Allan, 11).

Asghar Khan says that the PAF Air Marshal Nur Khan debated for most of 6 September whether to carry out the air offensive which had been previously planned by him, involving pre-emptive strikes on IAF bases to destroy as many planes on the ground as possible and try to neutralise the numerical disadvantage. Asghar Khan describes this day of debate as 'the most frustrating moments of my life'. The go-ahead for this plan was given at 3 pm on 6 September, and it was to be carried out at dusk that day. Since the sun was to set at 6 pm, only two hours were left for planning, whereas Asghar Khan felt that a minimum of eight hours was desirable (Asghar Khan, *The First Round*, 20–21). The British believed that the IAF was under 'political orders to confine its activities to the battlefield areas' and that this resulted in the IAF 'losing a golden opportunity' to launch pre-emptive strikes against PAF bases (British military review, 19).

In the event the PAF was bolder and took the initiative with its aircraft flying from Sargodha and Peshawar air bases and launching attacks on IAF bases at Pathankot, Adampur and Halwara. It seemed to the British that the Indians did 'not appear to have given serious thought to the protection of aircraft on the ground against air attack', and if rumours that financial considerations had hampered the defence of the IAF bases were true, it 'was inexcusable in the circumstances to allow this to override operational requirements' (British military review, 20).

The PAF strikes were successful, particularly the raid on Pathankot where it appears that the IAF was caught so unaware of the raid that its planes were refuelling in a line which had presented an ideal target for the PAF. The success of the initial raid persuaded Nur Khan to follow up these initial attacks with nightly bombing raids. After the PAF raids, it appears that the political restrictions were lifted and the IAF retaliated with raids on PAF bases and radar installations on 7 September, but the Pakistani defences were better prepared and not only were the planes better dispersed, they were also well camouflaged so that they presented a difficult target. In addition, the IAF tended to attack from high altitude which meant there was a greater risk of missing the targets altogether, which according to the British meant 'very unimpressive results'. The first IAF strike was intercepted by the combat air patrols of F-104As which downed two Indian Mysteres. The Pakistanis claimed to have shot down three Mysteres and five Hunters in aerial combat as well as four Mysteres shot down by anti-aircraft artillery fire, for the loss of a single Sabre. Perhaps because of India's alleged losses and lack of success, the Indians do not mention the raids, but they do not deny that they took place. After this raid it appears that the IAF confined itself to night bombing (Manekar, 133).

After 10 September there was a marked falling off in air activity by both sides and although bombing raids continued on air bases, it appears that both air forces now prioritised support of military operations on the ground rather than risking loss of aircraft in aerial combat. The air war therefore, although dramatic, did not alter the strategic balance to any large degree, although the actions of the PAF in inflicting losses on India do appear to have given the Pakistan Army more freedom to operate, and the air war appears to have gone in Pakistan's favour, if only by continuing to operate against larger numbers and without great restrictions. Ultimately, however, the reliance on US spare parts hurt the PAF far more than the IAF, and in a long conflict the PAF would have struggled to maintain its level of effectiveness. With Nepal having failed in its objectives and failure also in the air war, the Indian government was by 20 September ready to accept the UN call for an immediate ceasefire. As Pakistan was running short of military supplies and had seen its major armoured offensive fail, as well as being under sustained Western pressure, the question now was whether it too would agree to the call for a ceasefire or hold out to fight an attritional and long drawn out conflict, which might bring other countries into the war, in the hope of persuading India that major concessions on Kashmir were needed. All eyes were now on Ayub and Pakistan.

10

PRESSURE FOR A CEASEFIRE

Diplomatic and political moves, 11 September 1965

By 11 September Pakistan's main offensive, Mailed Fist, had failed and although the fact was obviously hidden from the Pakistani population, Ayub and his senior generals were well aware that that there was little or no chance of winning the war militarily after that day. However, Ayub was equally well aware that having initiated the war with both Gibraltar and Grand Slam, he could not simply agree to a ceasefire with the Pakistani population having been told that Pakistan was not only winning the war but also determined to fight until the Kashmir issue had been resolved once and for all. Although there was more international sympathy for Pakistan than for India on the subject of Kashmir, most countries, particularly the members of the UN Security Council, urged an immediate end to the fighting with only vague promises of talks on Kashmir after the fighting had stopped. India was determined that no concessions on Kashmir would be given under pressure, and so the pressure was on Pakistan to continue the war in the faint hope that pressure on India might result in some diplomatic gain for Pakistan. However, the real problem for Pakistan by 11 September was that not only had Mailed Fist failed, but also the US arms embargo was in force, both superpowers wanted an end to the war and were both opposed to any Chinese involvement in the conflict.

In Washington on 11 September British ambassador Dean met Rusk as the British wished to gauge the American reaction to the Chinese threats to India and their views on the situation on the ground. Rusk said that he felt that neither side appeared to be making a real military push for victory and they had allowed themselves the opportunity to pull back without the need for much face-saving in the event of a ceasefire. Rusk went on to say that he supported the idea of a Commonwealth initiative if the UN mission failed, and that the US was quietly exploring with India that East Pakistan should be kept out of the conflict. Rusk appeared unwilling to discuss US options in the event of Chinese involvement but said that Congress was in no mood to sanction aid to either country and it would be better for Pakistan to request a postponement of the aid meeting scheduled for 23 September (11/9/65, Washington to London, DO 196/385). This conversation confirms the impression that the US was discouraging India from opening up the eastern Bengal front for fear of Chinese intervention and did not appear to have any firm plans in place should China intervene militarily.

In Pakistan on the same day, James met Bhutto and had a long discussion with him about Pakistan's response to the UN cease-fire call following on from U Thant's unsuccessful visit to Pakistan from 8 to 10 September to try to persuade Ayub to accept an immediate and unconditional ceasefire. Bhutto said that the current UN Security Council resolution favoured India as it contained no reference to a resolution of the Kashmir issue, and as the last 18 years at the UN had led nowhere, Bhutto felt there was little point in Pakistan agreeing to this latest proposal. As far as the future was concerned, Bhutto said that Pakistan would determine future relations with nations on how they behaved now, which led on to the complaint that the US had not only failed to honour its treaty obligations with Pakistan but imposed an arms embargo which was inevitably harming Pakistan more; the US actions were carried out regardless of Pakistani loyalty over the years, membership of military pacts and their reliance on US weapons.

James defended the US action by pointing out that the US was simply trying to stop the fighting and that although US bilateral responsibilities to Pakistan went beyond the UN, the US would see how countries responded to the UN calls. James went on to say that Pakistan's conditions for a ceasefire were unacceptable to India, and so to expect India to agree to them before any talks could begin was simply unrealistic and there had to be some mutual concessions. Bhutto said that Pakistan's terms would be judged on the success or otherwise of the Pakistan Army, following which the terms offered by Pakistan could look reasonable. James said that to date neither side had been able to deliver a knock-out blow and if the fighting did not stop soon, there would not be a 'tolerable outcome' for either party. James added in his comments following the meeting that he felt Pakistan was still hoping that Britain would step in to mediate in the same way as it had in the Kutch dispute, which might explain why Pakistan had not embarrassed Britain by appealing for assistance under the terms of either SEATO or CENTO. The other clue James had was that the Pakistanis had not cut off the British teleprinter link from Rawalpindi to Peshawar as they had done with the US embassy (11/9/65 Rawalpindi to London, DO 196 384 PRO).

On 11 September Bowles met the Indian president Radhakrishnan at the latter's request, described as 'urgent'. The Indian president indicated that India was prepared to accept the UN ceasefire call provided Pakistan moved its troops back to where they were before 5 August and removed all the infiltrators. Bowles felt that India was prepared to be reasonable as regards the CFL but was not going to be flexible on Kashmir.

Radhakrishnan said that India had tried to keep the fighting to a minimum during U Thant's visit but Pakistan had initiated an armoured attack and 12 Patton tanks had been captured that day when their crews had deserted. Bowles' question regarding the president's estimate of Indian casualties elicited the response of around 8,000, which surprised Bowles as this figure seemed higher than all other estimates available to date. As far as China was concerned, Radhakrishnan said that the Indian government was 'deeply worried' about the possibility of a Chinese attack on India as the language used by China in its recent ultimatum was reminiscent of that of 1962, and he wanted to know what the US position would be in the event of a Chinese attack. Bowles replied that the US position was that it wished to see China contained and did not want to see a situation where India or part of India was overrun by China; however, the US would not underwrite India's war effort and a large part of the US response 'would depend on genuineness of India's efforts to reach agreement with Pakistan so that bulk of her resources could be used against China'. Bowles emphasised that he was giving his personal view and this was not necessarily that of the US president. This cool response from Bowles must have disappointed the Indian president who said he thought this was a fair analysis but then turned to Indian concerns about Indonesia, Turkey and Iran providing aid to Pakistan; he also asked if it was true that the US had loaned a submarine to Pakistan and if so, wanted assurances that this would not be used against India. Bowles said that this request would place the US in a dilemma as Pakistan could just as reasonably ask for assurances that the US radar system given to India should also not be used; the US position was therefore to steer clear of the whole subject. The Indian president then said there were rumours that Ayub had been overthrown by Bhutto and Musa and he 'earnestly hoped that this rumour was false' (11/9/65, Delhi to State, POL 27 India-Pak NA).

McConaughy on 11 September sent the State Department an outline of the situation as of that day and the events leading up to it. He felt that for Pakistan to send guerrillas into ICK on 5 August and believe that this would not provoke a severe Indian reaction had been its 'greatest mistake'. The Indian government had in fact reacted by responding along the CFL and at the Uri-Poonch sector appeared to give Pakistan the impression that it was threatening Muzuffarabad, the capital of Azad Kashmir. Pakistan had then moved in the Chhamb sector to Akhnur, and when its forces appeared to be a few hours away from taking the town, they stopped for almost two days. McConaughy said that while the reason for the delay was 'not completely clear', it was possible that Pakistan was trying to avoid an all-out war and wanted to limit the area of conflict to along the CFL. The first Indian air strike on 1 September had marked a serious escalation of the unofficial rules of engagement as Ayub had twice refused Pakistani air support in the Chhamb sector. The 6 September invasion of West Pakistan had escalated the conflict to all-out war but with East Pakistan largely kept out of it. McConaughy ended by recognising that the arms embargo would affect Pakistan hugely as India had a varied supply of arms and that pressure on Delhi to date had been purely diplomatic, and he considered that it was a 'legalistic formality' to say it was an even-handed move as it was far more onerous to Pakistan. The US was also dissuading Pakistan's allies Turkey and Iran from providing military assistance to Pakistan, and he said that it was only a matter of time before Pakistan became aware of this (11/9/65 Karachi to State, POL 27 India Pak NA).

On precisely that point, on 11 September, the Shah of Iran met British and American diplomats to inform them that his prime minister had returned from Turkey and that both Iran and Turkey were distressed by India's actions and wanted to assist Pakistan. The Shah asked specifically if the British would allow him to purchase military equipment outright and then loan it to Pakistan, and also if the US would turn a blind eye to Iran providing practical assistance to Pakistan such as use of airfields in Iran. Hoveyda, the Iranian prime minister, later elaborated on these requests by saying that Iran wished to provide 'token aid' which would maintain influence with Ayub and prevent Pakistan from joining the Chinese communist alliance. The US response was to maintain the position of refusing this, to the obvious disappointment of the Iranian prime minister. The Iranians were told in no uncertain terms that any transfer of military equipment would have 'serious repercussions' (11/9/65 Tehran to State, POL 27 India-Pak NA).

A change of tone: 12–15 September

On 13 September, the CIA reported to the White House that by the evening of 11 September, there was a 'subtle change in tone' from Pakistani officials as there now appeared to be a shift from justifying the war to a position where they were discussing how peace might be achieved. This was consistent with the view given to the CIA by a presumably well-connected Pakistani informant (name redacted) that the Pakistani use of arms was 'to escalate political concern and not to engage the Indian army or capture territory'. The CIA felt that this new tone was used because the bulk of the Pakistan Army was now engaged in defending Lahore and Sialkot and Pakistan might not be able to resist another large-scale Indian attack. The predicted shortages of fuel, ammunition and spare parts were being felt and therefore the CIA felt that Pakistan might want an end to the war while the effectiveness of the army was intact. The US Defence Attaché estimated that Pakistan would have another ten days' supplies left for 'effective action'. The CIA did warn however that the 'temptation to call on CHICOMS [Chinese Communists] for diversion will rise as Pak Military fortunes wane' (13/9/65, CIA to White House, Pakistan Cables Vol IV Box 151 LBJ).

During the course of the war, the Indian foreign service was becoming increasingly concerned by the appearance of what it dubbed the emerging 'Muslim League' against India. An official from the Indian Foreign Ministry informed Bowles that since the outbreak of war, Indian ambassadors had noticed hostility in Turkey, Iran and Indonesia, not to mention Saudi Arabia, Jordan and Iraq. India was concerned that if help was to reach Pakistan from these Muslim countries it would not only encourage Pakistan to continue fighting, but also have 'explosive religious overtones' (13/9/65 Delhi to State, POL 27 India-Pak NA). This feeling was also expressed on 15 September when the Defence Minister Chavan told a US embassy official that India was feeling 'isolated diplomatically', and was reported to have said with some bitterness that it was US arms supplies to Pakistan that made a Pakistani attack possible (16/9/65, Delhi to State, POL 27 India-Pak NA).

On 13 September the State Department sent a telegram to the US ambassadors in Tehran and Ankara. The US estimate was that even with the US arms embargo India could continue to fight for another thirty days, and that India's main problem was not ammunition but transport issues as its rail and road infrastructure was in poor condition. The IAF was seen as having equipment to fight for another seventy days, but in contrast the Pakistan Army could keep 70 per cent operational ability for another sixty days; however, with some losses this would soon plummet to thirty to forty-five days. The PAF was seen as having even fewer spare parts than the army and its estimated effectiveness was estimated at fewer than thirty days (13/9/65, State to Tehran/Ankara, POL 27 India-Pak NA).

In Pakistan McConaughy met the Iranian ambassador to Pakistan, Hoshang Ansary, who had come from a meeting with Ayub and Bhutto. Ansary said that the meeting was very friendly as Ayub had expressed a 'disproportionate measure of gratitude' for Iranian gestures, which indicated to McConaughy how 'desperately Paks are grasping for every straw of support, tangible or intangible'. Ayub was reported to have been aware of how strained relations with the US had become and repeated to the Iranian ambassador that there was no understanding between Pakistan and China regarding military assistance from China, and the fact that India had been confident enough to move troops away from the border with China showed how confident India was of not being attacked there. Ayub told Ansary that he was willing to make a short trip to Washington to meet Johnson in October as he recognised that this visit had become vital to restore relations, but he just wanted a signal from Johnson that the US would support the aid consortium in October as that would prevent him from 'looking like a beggar' (13/9/65 Karachi to Washington, POL 27 India-Pak NA).

In Washington, a week into the outbreak of full-scale war, the consensus within military circles was that India now felt itself in a winning position and the chances of persuading India for an immediate ceasefire were diminishing. Pakistan was seen as likely to stop only when it saw the military writing on the wall and had some strong diplomatic support. The US State Department suggested that a strong plea from Johnson to both Ayub and Shastri should be made in order to bring about a ceasefire and it was now desirable for more direct pressure to be brought (14/9/65, Memo, Talbot to Under Secretary POL 27 India-Pak NA).

On 14 September James reported from Pakistan the contents of his recent conversation with McConaughy in which the US ambassador felt that Pakistan's position was now more flexible than officially stated. Bhutto had been reported as being non-committal regarding the US request for East Pakistan to be kept out of the fighting, and McConaughy also reported that U Thant was unhappy about the timing of the US announcement of an arms embargo as he felt it made his mission more difficult (14/9/65, Rawalpindi to London, DO 196/385 PRO). Further evidence of a softening of the Pakistani position came at a breakfast meeting between the Iranian ambassador Ansary with Bhutto. Bhutto had been asked in the 'greatest confidence' whether Pakistan would be prepared to accept the idea of an independent Kashmir, and agreed that Pakistan could accept such an outcome if it had to, but this was not to be publicised. Ansary asked if he could pass on this message to McConaughy and Bhutto agreed to this request but asked for this to be kept secret until 17 September, a date which meant nothing to Ansary (15/9/65, Rawalpindi to State, POL 27 India-Pak NA).

On 15 September, Agha Shahi stopped in London en route to New York for the UN debate on the war and was met by Cyril Pickard of the CRO at Heathrow airport. Agha Shahi said that his instructions were to reject the two Security Council resolutions of 4 and 6 September and to declare Pakistan's intention to continue the fight until India accepted Pakistan's proposals. Pickard said he thought that these instructions were disastrous as he believed that world opinion would not tolerate the continuation of fighting, as it was unacceptable that this fight should be allowed to 'endanger world peace', and the British view was that in these circumstances the diplomatic advantage would lie with whoever accepted the ceasefire call first. Shahi said that Pakistan was ready to fight to the last man and that the Pakistan government could not survive a ceasefire call given the sacrifices that had been made, and also hinted strongly that Pakistan would take assistance from whoever was prepared to give it. Pickard said that the British had already discounted the Chinese and that although the military situation seemed in the balance, Pakistan could not impose conditions. Shahi said Pakistan had been abandoned by its allies, especially the US, owing to the US policy of bolstering India against China. Pickard said that was 'nonsense' and Pakistan's entire policy was based on misconceptions; the US and Britain had tried their best to date to resolve the issues between India and Pakistan, and the latest advice was again in Pakistan's best interest. Shahi was described by Pickard as being 'sobered' by this analysis but said that he could not alter his instructions (15/9/65, CRO to Rawalpindi, DO 196/385 PRO).

Later on the same day, 15 September, Hilaly (Shahi's brother) also met Pickard and said that while he 'welcomed the plain speaking' to Shahi, the basic problem now was that India would not accept a ceasefire call with reference to Kashmir within it and Pakistan could not accept one without this. Hilaly said that India could survive the fall of Shastri but that Pakistan could not survive without Ayub, and he felt that the best way to get Pakistan to agree to an immediate ceasefire would be to suggest that it would put Pakistan in a better position to dictate terms in the UN. Pickard thought it was 'rather thin' but said the leadership in Pakistan might wish to clutch at such straws as means of ending the fighting (15/9/65 CRO to Rawalpindi, DO 196 385 PRO).

By mid September, the State Department had sent a message to its ambassador in India and Pakistan saying it had the impression that both sides were becoming more amenable to the idea of a ceasefire, and although Rusk had praised the Soviets for their helpful attitude, there was no evidence of any Soviet arms embargo on India. The US position was to remain in support of the UN position and urge an immediate ceasefire on both sides (15/9/65, State to Karachi, POL 27 India-Pak NA).

McConaughy sent his analysis of the situation to Washington on 15 September. He said that although the Pakistanis recognised that they could not defeat India without US military aid, they might decide to fight on as long as they were under attack from India. He said that Pakistan recognised the limits to the assistance that China could give and that the Chinese threats were more to inhibit India than to offer any prospect of real assistance. The only way Pakistan would abandon the idea of US aid and throw in its lot with China would be if it faced total military defeat at the hands of India, and although it was seen as exploiting China's threat to India, Pakistan was not seen as tempted to join an anti-Western alliance led by China.

McConaughy saw Pakistan as being more flexible on Kashmir than previously thought and felt that some options on this topic could be explored. As far as Ayub was concerned, he was still viewed by the US Embassy as in firm control, but having committed himself and his army to a military solution in Kashmir, he could not back down now without a serious erosion of his authority unless there was a reasonable prospect of a successful conclusion. Acceptance of a ceasefire without any reference to Kashmir solution would 'represent a complete defeat of its Kashmir policy' (15/9/65, Karachi to State POL 27 India-Pak, NA).

Ayub's press conference on 15 September best summed up the change of tone in Pakistan. Addressing the national and international press on Pakistan's position, Ayub was coming to the press conference fresh from a meeting with Musa and Nur Khan. They had impressed on him the rapidly diminishing armaments stocks available for the army and air force and the press conference, instead of showing a defiant and resolute stance, degenerated into Ayub appealing for Johnson and the US government to intervene in the dispute. This appeal showed clearly to the world that Pakistan was now desperate to end the war despite all its official statements to date, and it was seen as so potentially demoralising that Bhutto attempted to have all transmissions of the conference blocked. Only after a meeting between Gauhar and Ayub later that day was it decided that it was less harmful now to allow the press to file their reports uncensored. This was an obvious change of tone and one which could hardly fail to be picked up by India (Gauhar, 349–50).

China's shadow

On 16 September China followed up its previous note of 7 September by saying that so long as India continued in its aggression against Pakistan, China would not stop supporting Pakistan. In addition, the note went on to say that India had built a large number of military installations on the India/China border either on the Chinese side of the border or on the boundary itself, and had sent troops into China for reconnaissance missions and kidnapped Chinese citizens living near the border and their livestock. India was given an ultimatum of three days (until 19 September) in which to dismantle the border installations, stop the intrusions and undertake not to carry out any more raids across the border. Shastri replied by suggesting a joint Indian/Chinese commission to examine the truth of these allegations and declared in the Lok Sabha that any Chinese attack would be met with determination by India. Shastri said that if any structures were found to be inside China, they would be removed (James, 143–4).

The US, concerned about the ambiguous stance taken by China and the latest threats to carry out some military action in support of Pakistan, kept a close eye on possible Chinese/Pakistani co-operation. On 16 September the US Intelligence Board approved a memo from the Special National Intelligence Estimate on the likelihood of Chinese action in the war. The summary was that China would avoid direct major intervention and would restrict itself to propaganda, political support and military gestures. China was not seen as being able to offer anything more than 'token support' to Pakistan in terms of military aid; the odds were seen as even that it might launch token raids on the Indian border, but even if these were carried out, they should be viewed as likely to have 'political and psychological effects greater than the military importance' (16/9/65, State to Karachi POL 27 India-Pak NA).

On 17 September a report was sent from the US embassy in Moscow which stated that the recent Chinese ultimatum worried the Soviets more that it did the West. The reason was the Soviets believed that long-term Chinese intentions in Asia were to 'make India a satellite and conquer the hegemony of the Asian continent', and it was against this background that the Soviets were determined to support India and had decided to continue to supply weapons to India during the war. If China did take military action then 'Moscow will react with some response'. This confirmed that the two superpowers were united in their desire to keep China out of the conflict, and also implied that the US might not need to intervene in the event of a Chinese attack if the Soviets were determined to do so (17/9/65, Moscow to Bundy India Memo and Misc Vol VI LBJ). Johnson seemed to remain relaxed about the Chinese threats and felt he knew Ayub well enough to know that he would not abandon the US alliance for one with China, and he was sticking to his conditions laid down on 5 September—that Ayub had to visit Johnson in Washington for a resumption of US military and economic aid. The main effect of the ultimatum appeared to be concerted superpower pressure on both India and Pakistan to agree to an immediate ceasefire.

India, as confirmed by its president in his meeting with Bowles on 11 September, was already nervous about possible Chinese action, and in the light of the latest ultimatum of 16 September, the Indian embassy in Washington approached the State Department to inquire what the US position would be regarding military aid to India in the event of a Chinese attack on India: whether the US was prepared to commit to assist India to meet 'this new situation' (Rusk to Delhi/Karachi, 16/9/65 DEF 19 US-India, NA). The Indian embassy also provided the State Department with a list of what it claimed was Turkish military assistance to Pakistan, which included mortar shells, guns, ammunition, anti-tank guided missiles and F-86 fighter jets which had been repainted in Pakistan Air Force colours (17/9/65, State to Karachi, POL 27 India-Pak NA).

A meeting in the White House chaired by Johnson and attended by Rusk, McNamara, Bundy and other relevant persons was held on 17 September to review the situation. Johnson directed that the US position concerning the ongoing war was:

1. Continue to use the UN as the best means of a ceasefire and support the current resolution
2. No direct message to be sent from him to either Ayub or Shastri for the time being
3. The State and Defence Departments to develop contingency plans for 'possible next steps'
4. No preparatory military moves to be made in the area
5. Ball to prepare a memo on the advantages and disadvantages of cutting off food supplies
6. A U2 reconnaissance flight from Thailand over the India-China border to be deferred until the Chinese reply to the UN.

As far as the Indian questions were concerned, Johnson was non-committal on the Indian request for clarity in the event of a Chinese attack, and was only prepared to say that the US was watching developments closely and had taken note of the Indian request (6pm 17/9/65, White House Note, POL 27 India-Pak NA).

On 18 September, McConaughy was asked by Shoaib to meet him urgently, a request that McConaughy took seriously enough to fly to Rawalpindi specifically for the meeting. Shoaib said that as the Pakistan government's new rules dictated that an official note taker had to be present at every meeting with a foreign diplomat, there were only four minutes available for Shoaib before the note taker was to arrive in which to speak frankly to McConaughy. Shoaib said that Ayub wanted to remain in the US camp but needed some gesture from the US in order to do so as all US actions during the outbreak of the war had been unhelpful; Ayub was quoted as having said, 'Why do US actions seem designed to push me toward the Chinese? I don't want to sit in Chinese lap and I won't do so if it can be avoided. But if US can't give me any help, I'll have no choice'. McConaughy replied that he was unsure what sort of gesture would suffice for Ayub. Shoaib said that even a condemnation of India's attack on 6 September would be very helpful, and, if possible, a strong statement that the US would use its influence to reach a solution to the Kashmir issue in the event of a ceasefire. McConaughy felt that the next thirty-six hours were critical and sought State Department instructions on what he was permitted to say to Ayub in this regard, adding that he felt that 'it was doubtful that Pakistan can be held in line without some assurance' (18/9/65, Rawalpindi to State POL 27 India-Pak NA).

The State Department replied immediately with instructions to McConaughy not to seek a meeting with Ayub but to convey via Shoaib and Bhutto the following points:

1. The Chinese ultimatum put Ayub firmly in the spotlight and he had to make a decision on whether to encourage the Chinese intervention and if he did so, 'he will have alienated himself from the West. This is not a threat but a reality'. If the Chinese were to intervene, then again Ayub would be blamed as he had not agreed to a ceasefire;
2. The Chinese ultimatum gave Ayub the opportunity to move from his present position of rejecting the ceasefire and such a move at this stage would not lead to any loss of face for him and would be 'viewed as statesmanlike';
3. The US recognised the underlying causes of the war (the diplomatic code in this context for Kashmir) could not be ignored and the US was helping to formulate a UN resolution for the use of peaceful means to resolve the issue;
4. While these talks were ongoing, it was of 'utmost importance' that Pakistan should put itself in a position of political advantage as India had agreed to an unconditional ceasefire and Pakistan had not (18/9/65, State to Karachi, POL 27 India-Pak NA).

US frustration with India's refusal to move on the Kashmir issue had now reached the state where George Ball felt that there might be some advantage if China 'were to give some degree of substance to their threats' in becoming involved militarily, if that was what it took for India to feel the pressure in order to agree to a ceasefire. The US government view to date was that even if China was to get involved it would be limited military intervention in terms of aggressive patrolling along the Indian border; skirmishes would have 'sobered' the Indians but the US position was still to let 'both sides sweat it out for a bit' and support the UN effort (18/9/65 Dean to FO, DO 196/385 PRO).

UN pressure

U Thant had to report his failure to obtain agreement between India and Pakistan on the previous two UN Resolutions calling for a ceasefire (Resolutions 209 and 210) and now urged the UN Security Council to exercise its powers under Article 40. This was the power under Article 39 of the UN Charter to request/ order both governments to heed the UN Resolution or be in breach of the peace under the terms of the Article. These were:

Article 39

The Security Council shall determine the existence of any threat to the peace, breach of the peace, or act of aggression and shall make recommendations, or decide what measures shall be taken in accordance with Articles 41 and 42, to maintain or restore international peace and security.

Article 40

In order to prevent an aggravation of the situation, the Security Council may, before making the recommendations or deciding upon the measures provided for in Article 39, call upon the parties concerned to comply with such provisional measures as it deems necessary or desirable. Such provisional measures shall be without prejudice to the rights, claims, or position of the parties concerned. The Security

Council shall duly take account of failure to comply with such provisional measures (Charter of the United Nations).

A draft resolution was circulated on 18 September. Agha Shahi had been sent to New York on 15 September with clear instructions to push for the inclusion of reference to previous UN resolutions to Kashmir and to resist the call for the removal of fighters from Kashmir, but the wording of the latest draft resolution proposed by the Netherlands fell short of what Pakistan was prepared to accept, at least officially and on the record. Aziz Ahmed was reported to have told James when given a copy of it, 'If you force this resolution down our throat, you will be starting a world war' (Gauhar, p. 351).

In the face of the latest UN draft resolution which 'demanded' a ceasefire, Ayub had to consider his options. On 19 September China extended its ultimatum to India by another three days; the immediate threat of Chinese military action against India had been lifted, even if temporarily. It was now approaching decision time for Ayub; time was against Pakistan as it was running out of options, both military and diplomatic. James met Ayub in the late afternoon of 19 September after a Pakistan cabinet meeting to discuss the latest UN resolution. Bhutto and Aziz Ahmed were present at the meeting but James reported that they hardly spoke during this meeting, which in itself was significant given their normal tendency to interject with sarcastic comments. Ayub was reported by James as being 'worried and chastened' and he felt that Ayub had 'belatedly returned to his old self'.

Ayub repeated the mantra of the need for a meaningful ceasefire but asked James if he thought the Indians would compromise on their stance on agreeing to talks about Kashmir if a ceasefire was agreed. James said that information on what the Indian leadership was thinking was too sketchy to reach a decision on that, but India had compromised on Kutch and other issues. James said that time was fast running out and Chinese involvement would take the war to the nuclear level. The fact was that India had accepted the ceasefire call and Pakistan had not, and as India had not got all it wanted in the UN ceasefire resolution, it was unrealistic for Pakistan to hold out for all it wanted. Pakistan had shown the world the depth of its commitment to Kashmir and a big gesture from Ayub at this juncture would help tilt world opinion his way. James repeated his impression that Bhutto's 'malign influence over Ayub' had weakened and Ayub was now returning to 'his senses' (19/9/65, James to CRO DO 196/385 PRO) James added some detail to this telegram by stating in his memoirs that he had asked Ayub at this meeting for permission to talk frankly 'discarding all diplomatic flannel'. James said that to push for more on Kashmir now would not only risk a nuclear war but also endanger Pakistan itself. Ayub was said to have remained 'cold and formal' and James wondered if he had gone too far (James, 149–50).

McConaughy met Bhutto and Aziz Ahmed formally at the Foreign Ministry on that day and relayed the points contained in the State Department telegram of 18 September. McConaughy said that he wanted to convince them of the absolute necessity of a ceasefire and that his points were carefully taken down by the official note taker. Bhutto was reported, with Aziz Ahmed's support, 'to have taken a hard-nosed and disquieting position' by repeating the line that there was no chance of Pakistan accepting a simple ceasefire call without any undertaking for the resolution of the dispute. The UN draft resolution fell short for Pakistan as it did not appear to mention the possible withdrawal of Indian forces or the need for settlement of the Kashmir issue (19/9/65 Karachi to State, POL 27 India-Pak NA).

James was briefed in some detail by McConaughy regarding the latter's meeting with Bhutto and Shoaib. The US ambassador confirmed that he deliberately chose not to meet Ayub but to meet the two senior ministers and explain the US position to them, as it was well known that Bhutto and Shoaib were the two ministers who had opposing views on the war. McConaughy had said that the latest Chinese ultimatum placed a grave responsibility on Ayub and if he encouraged China in this approach or failed to agree to a ceasefire he risked 'alienating Pakistan from the west'. The US recognised that talks would have to take place after the ceasefire, but if Pakistan wanted US assistance in pressuring India into meaningful talks, then Pakistan would have to provide 'definitive assurances that Ayub was not going over to the Chinese. There would not (repeat not) be one thin dime for any country supporting Red China'. Bhutto was said to have repeated the hard line that China or no China, Pakistan would not agree to a ceasefire 'without strings' and went on to say that that he was prepared to make a 'secret offer' to McConaughy on his own initiative but with the conviction that it would be approved by Ayub. This offer was that Pakistan would agree to the immediate ceasefire called for by the UN if the US promoted the withdrawal of all armed forces from Kashmir, an obvious reference to Indian forces. Bhutto said that Ayub had no knowledge of Chinese intentions and Pakistan would not endorse a Chinese attack on India; however, given India's behaviour, Pakistan could hardly be expected to make a pro-Indian statement in the event of a Chinese attack. In his talks with Shoaib there was, as expected, more encouragement for McConaughy as Shoaib said that in his view Ayub was increasingly worried by events and was now wanting a face-saving way of agreeing to the UN ceasefire call. Shoaib did not feel that Ayub could survive without some form of face-saving, but he went on to say that there was a good deal of resentment against Bhutto for having got Pakistan 'into this mess'. Shoaib also made an ethnic point of a Sindhi having got Pakistan into a situation where 'so many Punjabis and Pathans were dying on the battlefield' (20/9/65, James to CRO DO 06 385 PRO).

McConaughy sent a message to the State Department on 19 September in which he outlined the struggle going on within the Pakistan cabinet. The ambassador felt that Ayub now 'wants a respectable way out' and 'the fact that he can blame Bhutto is helpful to Ayub'. The conclusion was that although Ayub wanted Kashmir dearly and was willing to take high risks for it, at the end of the day he would not want to be 'on a collision course with the US and aligned on the wrong side of a major US-Chinese conflict' (19/9/65, Rawalpindi to State, POL 27 India-Pak. NA) Giving McConaughy confidence on this point was a private meeting that he was able to have with Shoaib at the home of a mutual friend, and as it was a private meeting, there were no official note takers present and Shoaib was able to speak freely. Shoaib said that he was greatly encouraged by Ayub's increasingly 'moderate attitude' as Ayub was reported to be 'disenchanted' with Bhutto's 'reckless adventurism' and strongly averse to entering into any agreement with the Chinese. Shoaib felt that Bhutto's job was now in jeopardy and he had not been permitted to attend the Security Council meeting as he was seen as too biased. Ayub was said to be looking for a face-saving means of agreeing to a ceasefire by having the Security Council specify that it called for a fair resolution to the Kashmir issue. McConaughy felt that this was a modest and sensible proposal and promised to recommend it as he felt that it gave Pakistan a modicum of encouragement in order to pull back from the brink (19/9/65, Rawalpindi to State, POL 27 India-Pak NA).

Ayub's China card

With pressure building in the UN and Johnson having studiously ignored Ayub's appeal of 15 September, there was only one final option left to Ayub to explore—China. Despite his earlier reluctance to do so, Ayub now decided to fly to China and meet Zhou Enlai directly as requested during the visit of Asghar Khan. Ayub had been reluctant to meet Zhou, presumably for fear that news of the meeting during the war might stretch US patience too far, but by 19 September Ayub had little to lose as he was now conscious that an unconditional ceasefire would cause outrage in Pakistan and threaten his regime. There are two accounts of this meeting, recounted by Ayub to two close advisers, Altaf Gauhar and G. W. Choudhury. According to the account given by Gauhar, Ayub flew to China on the night of 19/20 September from Peshawar in complete secrecy with even his security guards unaware of Ayub's departure. Ayub was accompanied by a small team which included Bhutto, and had two long meetings with Zhou Enlai and Marshal Chen Yi. Ayub outlined the military situation and said that Pakistan was in a very difficult position given India's superior numbers. Zhou said that numbers would not assist India in a long war and 'numerical superiority cannot prevail on the will of the people'. Marshal Chen Yi stated that China would maintain pressure on India the whole time and would support Pakistan for as long as Pakistan fought, and advised that even if Pakistan lost some large cities, it should continue to fight and not give up. Ayub was warned against succumbing to American pressure and also against trusting the 'unreliable' Russians.

During the meeting, the reason for the Chinese leadership wanting to meet Ayub personally became clear, as did its advice for Pakistan about winning the war. In order to obtain full Chinese support, Pakistan would have to prepare itself for a long and drawn out war in which the loss of cities would have to be accommodated, and fight on with full Chinese support and a people's army. Ayub was unprepared for this kind of long, grinding war and obviously highly reluctant to heed this advice. The whole strategy of the war had been a quick and relatively pain-free war with international (especially US) intervention forcing India to hold a plebiscite or agree to binding international arbitration on the future of Kashmir. With neither now remotely possible, Ayub was now looking to China to rescue him from a situation of his own creation (Gauhar, 252–3).

The account given by Choudhury is different in perspective and far less detailed. He says that some Pakistani 'military chiefs' (without naming them) wanted to see a joint Pakistani/Chinese assault on India by 20 September. This was envisaged as a Chinese attack on the north-east Indian border so that Pakistan could recapture territory lost while, India defended its border with China. 'With this contingency plan in mind, some Pakistani generals urged Ayub to opt for a prolonged and expanded war', according to interviews Choudhury had carried out. Choudhury believes that Ayub was opposed to such an escalation and a prolonged war and had already decided to accept the ceasefire by the time he flew to China to meet Chairman Mao (whose name does not appear in the account given by Gauhar), and that the purpose of the trip was to take the Chinese leadership into 'full confidence' to explain his reasons for doing so. Chinese leaders were said to have respected the decision to accept the UN cease-fire but said they were ready to support Pakistan if Pakistan decided it wanted to continue to fight and needed China's help to do so. Mao was said to have told Ayub that 'if there is nuclear war, it is Peking and not Rawalpindi that will be the target'. Ayub was said to have returned from his trip satisfied that the decision to accept the ceasefire would not damage relations with China (Choudhury, *India, Pakistan, Bangladesh*, 190–1).

In the absence of Chinese documents to show which of the two accounts is more accurate, and with only second-hand accounts available of the dramatic trip, it seems the general conclusion was that China was prepared to stand by Pakistan in whatever decision it took but recommended Pakistan to continue the fight and not to accept the UN resolution. China was aware that it did not have the military and economic clout of the USA but had learned the value of self-reliance since 1949 and was recommending the same course to Ayub.

The last push for a ceasefire

On 20 September, the UN Security Council passed Resolution 211 on the situation in Kashmir under the terms of Article 40. It is short enough to be reproduced in full:

Adopted by the Security Council at its 1242nd meeting, by ten votes to none, with one abstention (Jordan), on 20 September 1965.

The Security Council

Having considered the reports of the Secretary-General on his consultations with the Governments of India and Pakistan.

Commending the Secretary-General for his unrelenting efforts in furtherance of the objectives of Security Council resolutions 209 (1965) AND 210 (1965) of 4 and 6 September 1965.

Having heard the statements of the representatives of India and Pakistan.

Noting the differing replies by the parties to an appeal for ceasefire as set out in the report of the Secretary-General, but noting further with concern that no ceasefire has yet come into being.

Convinced that an early cessation of hostilities is essential as a first step towards a peaceful settlement of the outstanding differences between the two countries on Kashmir and other related matters.

1. *Demands* that a ceasefire should take effect on Wednesday, 22 September 1965, at 0700 hours GMT, and calls upon both Governments to issue orders for a ceasefire at that moment and a subsequent withdrawal of all armed personnel to the positions held by them before 5 August 1965;
2. *Requests* the Secretary-General to provide the necessary assistance to ensure supervision of the ceasefire and the withdrawal of all armed personnel;

3. *Calls on* all States to refrain from any action which might aggravate the situation in the area;
4. *Decides* to consider, as soon as paragraph 1 of Council resolution 210 (1965) has been implemented, what steps could be taken to assist towards a settlement of the political problem underlying the present conflict, and in the meantime calls on the two Governments to utilize all peaceful means, including those listed in Article 33 of the Charter of the United Nations, to this end;
5. *Requests* the Secretary-General to exert very possible effort to give effect to the present resolution, to seek a peaceful solution, and to report to the Security Council thereon.

There was now a deadline for Pakistan, 0700 hours GMT, 22 September, to either accept or reject this resolution, barely 48 hours for Ayub to decide what to do, and the most he had managed to extract from the UN Security Council was the wording to consider 'the political problem underlying the present conflict'. There were no assurances of any binding arbitration and even the mention of Kashmir was made obliquely.

Despite the official Pakistani reaction to Resolution 211, on 20 September McConaughy was beginning to feel cautiously optimistic that Ayub was inclined to accept the UN ceasefire resolution, and recommended that it might be time for a final push with Johnson sending a direct appeal to Ayub urging him to accept and assuring him that there was no irreparable damage to US-Pakistan relations. McConaughy said that the Iranians were also being very helpful as they were strongly recommending Pakistan heed the UN call. James was also described as working hard to this end and in tandem with McConaughy to secure this decision (20/9/65, Rawalpindi to State, POL 27 India-Pak NA).

McConaughy managed to meet Ayub on that day and said that although Ayub seemed to be 'deeply disturbed' he was reported to be 'leaning in the direction of a ceasefire' but finding himself unable to make that bitter decision. Ayub hinted at the acceptance of a ceasefire by complaining that that he was being expected to agree to it 'just to help the Indians', and that too with 'justice for Kashmiris almost within our grasp'. Although this was not at all the way McConaughy viewed the situation, diplomatically he did not contradict Ayub on this and Ayub was said by the ambassador to recognise that although US actions had hurt Pakistan, they were not intended that way. Ayub now began to complain that the Indians had exploited the Chinese card by opening up the threat of a wide-ranging international war, which was 'trickery'.

Ayub said he regretted that it had not been made clear to all sides that fighting within the disputed area of Kashmir and fighting across the international border were very different things and this had allowed the Chinese an opening to interfere, which India had exploited. McConaughy said that without arguing about the background, the fact was that the Chinese ultimatum to India had made it necessary for Pakistan to publicly declare its hand one way or the other. The fact was the Pakistanis had not disassociated themselves from China throughout the war, and this was something the US found hard to understand. McConaughy said that 22 September was therefore a critical day for both the UN and the Chinese ultimatum, and any failure by Pakistan to completely disassociate itself from an attack by a communist country on a free one would 'put Pakistan beyond reach of US help'.

Ayub said that there was no collusion or consultation with the Chinese and all he knew of their moves, he would read in the press. Ayub said that he had sent a message to the Chinese asking them, 'For God's sake, do not come in'. McConaughy said that this was significant and asked if he could report this fact back to Washington, a request to which Ayub agreed. Ayub went on to say that the great obstacle now was Pakistan public opinion, as it would appear to them that their government was agreeing to a ceasefire to assist India. McConaughy said that if he knew anything of the Pakistani people it was that they inherently disliked communism as it was 'inherently incompatible with Islam'. Ayub agreed with this sentiment but said that Pakistanis still saw China as less of a threat than India. McConaughy said that he was sure that Ayub could carry his people with him and that the US would do everything it could to assist him in this. If Kashmir had not been treated as a serious issue before, it would now, given what had happened. On bidding each other goodbye, Ayub was said to have put his hand on McConaughy's shoulder and said, 'God bless you'. McConaughy said that he repeated these words back to Ayub.

McConaughy said that it was significant that Ayub did 'not seem to see that the situation in which he found himself is at least in part of his own making', nor did Ayub show full comprehension of the dangers of a world war. Ayub was simply feeling that he had to choose between the alliance of a superpower and the Kashmir settlement which he thought was within reach, blaming this on 'Hindu trickery'. McConaughy believed that Ayub was ultimately a practical man who had winced when informed by Shoaib that the war had set back Pakistan's economic development by at least two to four years. McConaughy said that this was 'an agonising dilemma' for Ayub as it was 'hard reason pitted against emotional sense of losing honour and justice', and this might lead Ayub to hold on for a little longer. The decision whether to accept the UN resolution appeared too close to call for McConaughy, given that Ayub's advisers had misled him before (20/9/65, Rawalpindi to State, POL 27 India-Pak NA).

Asghar Khan said that after 18 September he, Bhutto and Nazir Ahmed, the Defence Secretary, would meet Ayub in the evenings to try and bolster his morale but 'it was clear it could not go on much longer'. Asghar Khan says that Ayub had begun to meet James alone as he could express views to him that he did not want his own advisers to hear and James was said to be warning Ayub of the consequences of rejecting the UN resolution. Musa had always been cautiously against Gibraltar and Grand Slam and now had an opportunity to say that Pakistan had achieved what it could, blaming Ayub's civilian advisers for having talked him into this situation. Asghar said that he made a final plea with Ayub after the UN resolution not to accept it; he 'entertained little hope of being able to swing him round' but wanted to try. According to Asghar Khan, Ayub said that the army was fighting against heavy odds and was under pressure. Asghar Khan said he wanted to advise against acceptance of the ceasefire call as national morale was very high, the Air Force had control of the sky and China was both willing and able to help, an offer that might not be repeated. He went on to say that India was also stretched and a ceasefire might well benefit India more than Pakistan. Ayub seemed to be unconvinced but welcomed the discussion as 'these views were so different from what he had heard from his advisers during the last few days'. However patiently Ayub listened, it appeared to Asghar Khan that his mind was made up, and he left the meeting 'disappointed but not surprised', and 'as if to put a seal' on Ayub's decision, Asghar Khan saw James was waiting to meet Ayub on his departure (Asghar Khan, *The First Round*, 102–5).

The meeting with Ayub on 21 September is described by the High Commissioner who said that although Ayub listened attentively, he was reported to have shown signs of 'restiveness' and gave no indication of whether he would accept the ceasefire call or not. Ayub said that he had made a call to China to ask it not to aggravate the situation, and agreed that James could inform London of this fact, but Ayub refused to make the request public. James said that his US counterpart was confident that Ayub would accept the ceasefire, but James felt the chances were no better than even (22/9/65, James to CRO DO 196/385 PRO). It appears from the meeting that although Ayub's mind was made up, he was determined to keep up the bluff of being unsure in the hope that India might make more concessions at the last minute.

Fire-bandi

Although Ayub knew by 21 September that he was going to have to accept the UN resolution, given the diplomatic and military position, he wanted it to appear to be a cabinet decision. A meeting of the Pakistan cabinet was therefore held on 21 September and Bhutto was said to have recommended accepting the cease-fire by saying that the best deal possible had been achieved diplomatically. At the meeting, Ayub said that he wanted Bhutto to travel to New York to see if he could achieve some guarantee of a mechanism to try to force India to accept mediation or arbitration on Kashmir. It was said that even during the cabinet meeting, Ayub received messages from the leaders of Turkey and Iran urging him to accept the resolution (Gauhar, 355–7).

With less than twenty-four hours to go and the Pakistani decision still awaited, American and British diplomats met to agree a future plan of action following either acceptance or rejection by Pakistan of the ceasefire call. If Pakistan did agree to a ceasefire, the practical difficulty would be in trying to persuade India to enter into meaningful negotiations over Kashmir. If Pakistan did not agree, then the prospects would be 'most serious'. That would almost certainly mean not only a complete cut-off in aid but also censure and sanctions (21/9/65, State to Rawalpindi, 27 India-Pak NA).

Bowles reported from Delhi that Jha had called on him that evening (21 September) and described the Indian position to him as regards that UN ceasefire call. India was worried about China and wanted nothing from Pakistan, and would agree to an immediate ceasefire if Pakistan agreed to stop shooting at the same time. Jha was said to be flexible on other issues such as a return to the 5 August boundary, and asked for the US reaction to the Soviet offer of a peace conference at Tashkent following a ceasefire. Bowles said that it was ultimately a matter for the Indians to decide but was appreciative that they had sought the US view on this. Bowles thought the US should support the Soviet invitation but expected Pakistan to refuse it (21/9/65, Delhi to State, India Cables, Vol V Tel 177 LBJ).

On 21 September McConaughy met Ayub, who was accompanied by Aziz Ahmed in the garden of Ayub's residence. Ayub was reported to be 'outwardly calm' but determined to do the right thing; however, according to McConaughy he 'was not sure what that was'. The ambassador said that the conversation was polite but slightly formal owing to the presence of Aziz Ahmed. Ayub said that if there had been any collusion with China, China would have attacked earlier, and he blamed the Indians for exaggerating the Chinese threat. Ayub also said he wanted to let the US know that India had launched a fresh attack that morning on all three battle fronts (22/9/65, Rawalpindi to State, POL 27 India-Pak) NA.

The US State Department and the White House were informed that Bhutto was expected in New York that day, and the official line from Pakistan was that Ayub would decide on whether to accept or reject the ceasefire after Bhutto had reported on US and British 'seriousness' in taking a new look at the Kashmir situation. Ball felt that this line 'might be window dressing' as it would give Ayub the opportunity to say that he had received assurances on this point and therefore could justify the ceasefire (21/9/65, Memo of Conversation, State Department, POL 27 India Pak NA).

The US delegation at the UN described the last-minute flurry of diplomatic activity by Bhutto on his arrival at the UN. It appeared to the US delegation that Bhutto had arrived with instructions to accept the ceasefire but was seen as determined to make it as dramatic as possible to try and improve the terms of the ceasefire, and also to appear to have dissociated himself from the decision (22/9/65, New York to Rawalpindi, 27 POL India Pak NA). On 21 September the State Department sent a message to the US ambassador to the UN, Arthur Goldberg, with instructions to inform the Pakistan delegation there that although Pakistan was frantically engaged in a last-minute push for better terms, the time for positioning was over and now it was decision time for them. If Pakistan had decided to accept or reject the ceasefire, it would have to accept the consequences of the decision.

Rusk said that McConaughy would not want to commit himself to any Kashmir solution brokered by the US as India would not agree to that, and the net result would be that the US would be able to satisfy neither side and would allow the Chinese to assist Pakistan and the Soviets to assist India at US expense. Goldberg was instructed to inform Bhutto that the US was committed to UN-sponsored peace talks on Kashmir but could go no further than that (21/9/65, State to US UN Delegation, POL 27 India-Oak NA). Rusk also sent a message to both Goldberg and McConaughy saying that if Pakistan wanted a face-saving means of accepting the ceasefire, the UN Security Council Resolution had undergone a slight last minute amendment to now read: 'Convinced that an early cessation of hostilities is essential as a first step toward a peaceful solution on the outstanding differences between the two countries *on Kashmir* and other related matters'. Rusk pointed out that the new wording provided the addition of the word Kashmir, and said, 'if Ayub wants to get off the hook, the SC resolution provides rationale' (21/9/65, State to Rawalpindi, POL 27 India-Pak NA). Later that day, Goldberg at the United Nations reported that Gromyko had expressed gratification at the excellent co-operation between the Soviet and US teams at the UN throughout the war and said that although he had no knowledge, he had heard that both India and Pakistan had agreed to accept the ceasefire call the next day. If that was indeed the case, then the Soviet ambassadors to those countries were probably better informed than their American counterparts (21/9/65 New York to State, POL 27 India-Pak NA).

On the morning of 22 September, James received a call from Ayub's office asking for an urgent meeting. India had accepted the UN resolution and the ball was now firmly in Pakistan's court. James said that on arrival in Ayub's office he found that Ayub's 'tone and mood had changed dramatically...with the relief and good humour of a man who has at last shed an intolerable burden'. James said that he was addressed by his first name and informed that Bhutto had been instructed to accept the UN ceasefire resolution. James said that both his government and he were happy with the news and Ayub and James then shared 'a large drink' to celebrate the decision (James, 151).

Bhutto now had the opportunity to speak to an international audience for the first time since the beginning of the war and, fully aware that the speech was being carefully followed not only in Pakistan and India but in many world capitals, he used the speech to full effect. In a dramatic and emotional speech, Bhutto declared that Pakistan was bound to prevail as justice was with it, but concluded the speech by confirming that Pakistan would give the UN a final chance to resolve the Kashmir issue and would observe the ceasefire call and would 'stop firing' on 0300 hours, 23 September (the new time arranged for the ceasefire to take place by the Security Council). Bhutto went on to warn the UN that this was its final chance to act; failure to resolve the issue this time would mean that Pakistan would leave the UN—a threat that was quickly and firmly denied by the Pakistan government (Wolpert, *Bhutto*, 94–5). In Pakistan, once Bhutto had formally conveyed the decision of the government to the UN, Ayub went on national television to announce the decision to stop fighting using a new

Urdu phrase of '*Fire-bandi*' which translates as an order to hold fire, rather than using the expected phrase of '*Jang-bandi*' which would have meant a ceasefire. This implied to the nation that Pakistan had only agreed to hold fire rather than agreeing to a ceasefire, but few were fooled. The reaction to the speech in Pakistan was that 'millions of people heard him (Ayub) with surprise and anger. Many in the Armed Forces...wept as Ayub Khan spoke' (Asghar Khan, 106). Whatever the fiery rhetoric in New York or the linguistic evasiveness in Rawalpindi, the fact was that Pakistan had accepted UN Security Council Resolution 211 and at 0300 PST, 23 September the war was over.

11

RUN-UP TO TASHKENT

An uneasy ceasefire

Now that the main fighting had stopped, an uneasy and tense ceasefire descended on the battlefield, punctuated by occasional violent skirmishes. Both sides still remained in occupation of the territory they had managed to take during the war and neither was prepared to step back; in fact both sides made the occasional attempt to improve their battlefield positions, leading to fears that localised battles would lead to breakdown of the ceasefire. On the diplomatic front, the superpowers were in full agreement on the need for a ceasefire and very anxious for it to hold and for formal talks to take place between India and Pakistan to ensure that war did not break out again. Both the superpowers were nervous about China's potential role in South Asia and the combined pressure from the US on Pakistan and from the Soviet Union on India was immense. The fact that neither India nor Pakistan was in any real position militarily to continue the war despite their respective rhetoric meant that both sides were now primarily interested in a peace agreement on their terms.

The desired scenarios for the two sides were not difficult to gauge. Pakistan was keen for either the UN or the West—the USA and/or Britain—to host the post-war talks in order to apply some pressure on India over Kashmir. The Soviets were seen by Pakistan as being too pro-Indian and therefore any summit hosted by the USSR was unlikely to mean any diplomatic pressure on India. The obvious flaw to this Pakistani desire was the glaringly obvious reluctance of the US to waste any more diplomatic energy on Kashmir and its willingness to hand over this issue to the Soviets. The tense US-Pakistan relations in the run-up to and during the war meant that in any event, a pro-Pakistan stance on Kashmir had all but disappeared and the only reason that the US was even prepared to advise India to adopt a conciliatory stance on Kashmir was fear of China, not any pro-Pakistan sentiment. India was keen on a peace conference being hosted by the Soviets with whom it had built a close relationship during the 1950s, and was equally determined not to concede an inch of land to Pakistan, nor to have the status quo in Kashmir changed in any way whatsoever.

Britain was viewed by India as having been a little too neutral during the war, a stance which offended India as it wanted clear condemnation of Pakistan's plan to send thousands of armed infiltrators into Kashmir; Indians were still offended by Wilson's harsh criticism of India's attack on Lahore on 6 September. In any event, the reality was that however skilled British diplomacy was, Britain was now a second rate power in South Asia as compared to the USA and the USSR, and British pressure would not have had the same clout as either of the superpowers on either India or Pakistan. British military and financial aid to Pakistan was now dwarfed by even China, and so Britain was not even in a position to pressure Pakistan, and certainly not to pressure India.

The Soviet offer at the end of the war to host a summit between India and Pakistan at the Soviet city of Tashkent therefore came as huge relief to the US administration and India, but as bad news to Pakistan. The Soviet offer to mediate was first accepted by Shastri on 22 September, while he announced the ceasefire to the Lok Sabha, but initially resisted by Pakistan.

Ayub tries to elicit US support

After making the ceasefire announcement on Pakistan Television and taking advantage of the time difference between Pakistan and the US, on the morning of 22 September Ayub telephoned Johnson to speak to him personally for the first time since hostilities had begun. It must have been a tense call to make and the drama was heightened by the poor line quality; Ayub had to re-dial several times before the conversation with Johnson could be completed. Ayub informed Johnson of the Pakistani decision to accept the ceasefire and said, 'We believe that you are a man of honour and a gentleman and will see that an honourable settlement is reached to prevent such unfortunate happenings occurring again'. Given the studied and deeply irritated silence from Johnson during the whole war and the fact that the US was annoyed with Pakistan for having started a major war in Asia using US weapons, Johnson's tone was friendly in reply. However, the US president was strictly non-committal about any request to try to take the lead in resolving the Kashmir issue; he said that the US supported the idea of a settlement of the Kashmir dispute as it was 'needed and is essential', but added meaningfully and clearly, 'I cannot give you any assurance of any particular form of settlement'. Johnson ended the conversation by inviting Ayub to Washington, which Ayub accepted 'as soon as he could arrange it'. It was soon to be increasingly obvious that Johnson had decided that Ayub had to present himself in Washington to explain himself and reassure the US that Pakistan was not going to be a secret Chinese Trojan horse in Asia. Ayub was equally aware of Johnson's real intention and so pleaded domestic issues for his reason not to go to the US (22.9/65, 10.55am Tape F65.05 Side A, PNO 2 FRUS 1964–68 Volume XXV, South Asia, Doc 158)).

The British embassy in Washington was able to receive a summary of the Ayub/Johnson conversation from Komer as there were no US officials present during the conversation between the two presidents. Komer was quoted as saying Ayub had said that Pakistan had accepted the UN resolution 'in the knowledge that the US was a friend of Pakistan'. However, Komer felt it was significant that Johnson avoided any US commitment on Kashmir and Ayub seemed to have accepted that fact; Ayub was reported to have sounded relaxed, 'even jocular', which confirmed James' impression that Ayub was relieved that the war was over. Komer said that speaking for himself he did not see any prospect of 'making any real progress in the foreseeable future on the Kashmir question in the sense desired by Pakistan. Ayub had played his last card'. Komer felt that any attempt now by the Americans to try and tilt the balance towards Pakistan would not only be unsuccessful, it would lead to serious resentment in India; the Indian ambassador in Washington had apparently received assurances from the Soviets that they would not pressure India on Kashmir. The most the US would do in this regard would be to support the UN position on Kashmir, and Komer felt that Ayub did not appear to be aware of how badly Pakistan's standing had been damaged as a result of the war and the West needed to try and protect him from this reality (23/9/65 Washington to London, DO 196/385 PRO).

On 23 September Ayub also spoke with Wilson by telephone and stated that the reason Pakistan had agreed to the ceasefire was that it hoped the US and Britain would 'put their full weight behind a purposeful settlement of the Kashmir problem'. Ayub said that the two issues still to resolve were military disengagement and the political mechanism for a resolution, and he would leave this for the Americans and British to work out. Wilson said that Ayub had been absolutely right to accept the ceasefire call and although he knew it was not an easy decision, it was the right one. On the issue of moving forward, Wilson said that it was important to let the UN take the lead in this and asked Ayub how he viewed the Soviet offer of mediation. Ayub said he viewed this as a 'propaganda stunt' and if he and Shastri were to meet face to face, they would merely restate their views and no solution could be reached. Ayub said that he favoured a Rann of Kutch style mechanism of intermediaries and this could be best performed by the UN. This was to be a forlorn hope; Pakistan continued to push for it in the immediate aftermath of the cease-fire, but both the US and Britain politely declined to support or encourage it. It was agreed by Ayub and Wilson to keep the fact and content of the phone call secret (Record of Telephone Conversation, 1pm 23/9/65 DO 196/385 PRO).

On 24 September the CIA prepared a special memorandum on the war for the president and the relevant departments. The paper recognised that Ayub had only agreed to the ceasefire for two reasons, (i) that he was aware that if fighting continued his forces would be worn down and defeated, and (ii) that only a Chinese attack would militarily threaten India, but that would mean Pakistan breaking ties with the West and aligning with China. Ayub was said to have tried to limit his loss of face by agreeing to a ceasefire but not pulling troops back, and although India also had reservations regarding the ceasefire, neither side was seen as wanting to resume hostilities.

India was viewed both during and after the war as being in no mood to negotiate on Kashmir, but the prevailing mood in Pakistan was described as dangerous as the propaganda line of the government was that 'perseverance in the military struggle would have forced India to give up Kashmir'. The internal danger in Pakistan after the war had ended was that popular expectations had been aroused by the war and while Ayub was aware of Pakistan's deteriorating military position, he could not admit to this without 'raising the question why Pakistan embarked on the course it did'. The survival of the Ayub regime was now seen as in jeopardy but the CIA felt on balance that he probably would survive and return to 'giving a high priority to patching relations with the US'. Chinese aid was now seen as less useful to Pakistan as India had not backed down in the face of Chinese threats and a Chinese attack would in fact have created serious problems for Pakistan.

Ayub was also aware that 'his bargaining power with the US has declined', but he would press for economic and military assistance from the US in time. Ayub's possible future removal was seen as an event that would considerably alter US relations with Pakistan and might lead to a break with the US and the UN. India was seen as having emerged more confident from the war but in poor shape economically, with food shortages (24/9/65 CIA, Office of National Estimates, India Memos and Misc Col V, LBJ).

The CIA then produced another report soon afterwards with more emphasis on the military aspects of the war. The US view of the recent war was that in 'finite terms India won the September war with Pakistan', but despite having taken more territory and suffered fewer proportionate losses, India's performance against a much smaller opponent was seen as 'quite uninspiring' as losses in real terms were higher and the strategic objectives of Lahore and Sialkot were not reached. It was estimated that Pakistan lost 250 tanks out of a total of 900 while India lost 300 out of 1,500. Air losses were seen as difficult to quantify, but it appeared that the PAF had performed better though it had suffered more from shortages of fuel and spare parts (1/10/65, CIA Office of Current Intelligence, India Memos and Misc, Vol VI LBJ).

Pakistan reluctantly accepts Soviet mediation

Ayub became increasingly aware that a visit to the US at this time would be domestically very unpopular, and with tension still high after the ceasefire call, he decided to delay his proposed visit to see Johnson. At a meeting on 29 September Ayub told McConaughy that although he had wanted to visit the UN and Johnson in Washington, he was now unable to leave Pakistan for the immediate future. Ayub said he had already informed the British that the long-planned state visit there would have to be cancelled and he hoped that Johnson would understand the reason for his postponement. Ayub said that with popular feeling in Pakistan running high despite his attempts to 'damp down those feelings', he needed another six to eight weeks before he could leave Pakistan; he was not reluctant to visit the US, in fact he would be flattered, but it could not be now. McConaughy tried to persuade Ayub to make the trip soon by saying he understood that Ayub's visit to the US only needed to be short, but, he felt, a visit as soon as possible was vital for a negotiating session. Ayub said that in any event his visit would not be for economic issues (that is, aid) but political issues (that is, Kashmir and future relations). McConaughy said that while he understood that it would be hard for Ayub to leave Pakistan while the ceasefire was not fully effective, in order for US-Pakistan relations to be fully restored there had to be a meeting of the two presidents. Ayub, probably anticipating some blunt talking from Johnson, said that Johnson 'can say what he likes in our discussions...all we want is that you do not add to our problems' (29/9/65, Rawalpindi to State, POL 7 Pak NA).

On 2 October Bhutto made clear his dislike of the idea of a Soviet-mediated conference during a visit to London, and said he would much prefer a Four Power committee and had 'begged' Goldberg, the American ambassador to the UN, not to give the Soviets the impression that the US supported the Soviet idea (2/10/65, CRO to Rawalpindi, DO 196/387 PRO). It is not known whether Bhutto was aware that privately the US was delighted by the Soviet offer and wanted nothing more than for Pakistan to accept it. Further evidence of Pakistan's reluctance to take up the Soviet offer came on 6 October when James was informed by Shahi that Gromyko had told the Pakistan delegation at the UN that the USSR did not support the idea of a Four Power Commission, although Shahi felt the Soviets might

319

be open to persuasion on this point. The Pakistan government had no other idea for the implementation of the 20 September UN Resolution and Shahi said that he was very dubious about the idea of a Soviet-sponsored summit achieving anything (6/10/65, James to CRO, DO 196/388 PRO).

By mid October Pakistan had realised that the Soviet offer was the only one on the diplomatic table, and on 16 November India learned that Ayub had accepted the Soviet offer to meet Shastri in Tashkent. Shastri announced that he was willing to meet Ayub there and was prepared to discuss anything but Kashmir (Dev Sharma, *Tashkent: The Fight for Peace*, Varanasi: Gandhian Institute of Studies, 1966, p. 146). Komer noted that the Soviets were resisting any move by U Thant to set up any commission on Kashmir and was concerned that Ayub's attitude to the US 'appeared to have hardened ... we're not quite sure why'. Ayub had declared himself unavailable to visit the US for at least six to eight weeks and was allowing the Pakistani media to be highly critical of the US. The worry again for the White House was that 'we are simply not in effective communication with Ayub at this critical moment so if he's unable to come here it may now be important to send someone there' (1/10/65, Komer Memos Vol 2 (1) LBJ).

A good clue as to why Ayub was delaying his visit to the US comes from an account from Asghar Khan, who says that after the end of hostilities and when Pakistan's participation at the Tashkent summit had been agreed, Ayub took a small team of Nur Khan, Bhutto, Asghar Khan and Ghulam Faruque (the Commerce Minister) with him to Beijing to have yet another secret visit to China to meet the president of China, Liu Shao-chi, Zhou Enlai and Marshal Chen Yi. President Liu was said to have been so openly critical of Pakistan's military tactics that the diplomatic and sophisticated Zhou was 'obviously embarrassed'. Asghar Khan says that the detailed talks that Ayub had with the Chinese leadership were not conducted in his presence but he

RUN-UP TO TASHKENT

had been made aware later of the content. The Chinese 'gave their blessings' to the Tashkent meeting but warned Ayub of the Soviet desire to take advantage of the situation (Asghar Khan, *The First Round*, 111–13).

Behind the scenes preparation for Tashkent

On 19 October the British attempted to see if Shastri was willing to be flexible on Kashmir. Freeman was able to meet Shastri alone, who agreed to the meeting 'at great personal inconvenience to himself at 22.45 to 23.45pm'. Shastri was immovable as far as a political solution to Kashmir was concerned and said that there was simply 'no question of concessions over underlying political causes if these meant Kashmir'. Freeman said he pressed Shastri hard on whether India could make any concessions at all on Kashmir, but Shastri repeated his refusal and, ominously for Ayub, went on to say that any ideas in the past about concessions to Pakistan 'were now out of the question' as they would not be tolerable to either India's public or its parliament. Freeman asked what Shastri's position would be if the USSR and the West agreed to India's position but Pakistan, aided by China, did not. Shastri said there was no way to avoid that and he hoped that all the other countries could 'persuade Pakistan of the hopelessness of her cause' (20/10/65, Delhi to CRO, DO 196/388 PRO).

The State Department also tried behind the scenes to persuade India to be more flexible now on the subject of Kashmir by providing India with a summary of its own views regarding the strategic position in the subcontinent on 20 October. The US government believed that although India had proved its military capabilities in a bilateral conflict with China, there was a real danger of a Pakistan/China 'close military axis' which would leave India with a potential war on a number of fronts, and the US believed that it was in India's best interest to seek a *modus vivendi* with Pakistan; which was clear reference for Kashmir (20/10/65, State to Delhi, POL 27 India-Pak NA).

Pakistani allegations of Indian brutality inside ICK were often dismissed as exaggerated or hyperbolic, but British diplomats were informed by Nimmo and Colonel Achton of the UNMIOP in November 1965 that the Indians had behaved in Kashmir in the war the way the 'Germans had behaved in the Balkans during World War II'. This was a very serious allegation but one that remained classified (3/11/65, Fortnightly Summary, DO 196/389 PRO).

In a separate message James regretted that 'the rather special relationship' which used to exist between the British and Pakistani armed forces 'was disappearing'. During the war the British were unable to visit any Pakistani military officer, establishment or unit and this had left the British High Commission in Pakistan 'frustrated' as almost all the news they received was either from the press or 'third hand'. James went on to say that before the war the British were 'constantly being lectured by Pakistanis and told that we do not understand the Hindu mentality'. But, he went on, 'At least we understood it sufficiently to be certain that the attack on Akhnur would bring the Indians into Punjab' (Report for the month of September, DO 196/395 PRO)).

On 4 October, the British embassy in Beijing produced a report entitled 'China and the Indo-Pakistan Conflict'. The summary was that China 'had afforded full moral support to Pakistan...as it could not miss such a good opportunity of embarrassing India'. It was felt that the Chinese position was at odds with all the other major powers which wanted to see an end to the war as soon as possible, and the embassy believed that Pakistan had not wanted Chinese intervention. On 7 September China had unleashed its full propaganda machine against India, which had culminated in the Chinese ultimatum of 17 September for India to remove its fortifications on the Sikkim border. After issuing the ultimatum, China then declared that India had removed the fortifications, which removed the tension, and the Chinese were seen to have backed down in the face of the US position and confined themselves to diplomacy.

General Raza, the Pakistan ambassador to China, was reported as having told a senior British diplomat after the cease-fire that Pakistan's interests lay with the West but 'beggars can't be choosers', and Raza claimed that he had told Zhou Enlai of this on 21 September. The first Chinese threat of 7 September was in response to alleged Indian aggression and border violations, and then, on 14 September, the Chinese brought up the old issue of the Indian seizure of Bank of China assets in 1962. On 17 September, there were the allegations of Indian border violations in the Sikkim area, an area close to the East Pakistan border. The British embassy felt that China had overstepped the mark and had 'lost face' as a result of its threats and language, a policy described as 'maximum noise and minimum risk', the recent India-Pakistan war being a 'heaven sent opportunity' for China as it involved all its enemies: the USA, the Indians, the USSR, the British and the UN (4/10/65, China and the India-Pakistan Conflict, DO 196/387 PRO).

'No place else to go'

On 28 October, McConaughy met Shoaib who said that the war had led to 'sober reappraisal' of the army's capabilities and there was now recognition that without major rearmament, it would be impossible to have another war with India. Although this was still secret, it meant that Bhutto did not 'have the influence or the good access' he used to enjoy with Ayub. Shoaib said that offers of Chinese military assistance had been received but these were general rather than offering any specific help. McConaughy said that for the Pakistanis to accept Chinese military aid would 'put them beyond the pale' for any US aid and he wanted Ayub and all concerned to be fully aware of this fact. The ambassador also said that this would drive the US 'to the wall', which was known to be a favourite expression of Ayub's (29/10/65, Rawalpindi to State, POL 27 India-Pak NA).

On 10 November, Komer felt that both countries were now 'increasingly nervous over our intentions' and both their heads of government were eager to visit the US; Komer preferred Shastri to visit first as Ayub would then 'be easier to deal with', as Ayub 'has no place else to go—will be more malleable if we let him sweat awhile'. Ayub had been given first refusal by Johnson but he had delayed his arrival, while Shastri had accepted quickly, and so Komer recommended 'the longer we let him worry, the more he'll listen instead of argue (and the less we'll have to talk about Kashmir)'. Komer's view was that the recent war had effectively settled the issue of Kashmir and Johnson might wish to consider some tough-minded emissaries to South Asia to keep matters quiet (10/11/65, Memo—Komer to McBundy, India Memos and Misc Vol VI LBJ).

On 11 November Freeman met his Soviet counterpart, Mr Benediktov, the Soviet ambassador to India, who made some important comments. The Soviets felt it was essential that the ceasefire be maintained but did not want to assist India in holding on to any territory across the CFL. The Indians were seen by the Soviets as being in no mood to concede anything on Kashmir and it would need patient diplomacy to persuade Pakistan and India to negotiate face to face, but Benediktov felt that the Indians were not looking for another war and Pakistan was in no shape to have another war for some time. Ayub was reported to have made a good impression in Moscow and the Soviets would 'like to believe what he said about wanting to live in peace with India'. Freeman said the discussion showed that the Soviets would support peace but remain committed to their Indian allies (11/11/65, Delhi to FCO, DO196/389 PRO).

On 13 November Bhutto met James at the former's suggestion; the meeting took place at Bhutto's residence for around one and a quarter hours. Bhutto said he was still sceptical about Tashkent producing anything useful and sarcastically commented that Shastri was 'quite the little Napoleon these days'. Bhutto spoke about the war and emphasised that he was speaking 'academically and without bitterness'. Had the war lasted a few more days, Pakistan was about to 'gain a decisive military advantage' as the Pakistan Army had been about to launch a counter-attack, whereas India could not advance any further and Indian morale was cracking. This was doubtless a reference to Operation Wind Up and possible Chinese involvement. James said he had expressed 'firm disagreement' with this thesis and said neither side had any prospect of a clear military victory, nor was there any evidence of Indian morale 'cracking'. Bhutto had listened but 'gave no sign that he was convinced'. Bhutto then said the fact that China had backed down before US threats had shown it was a 'paper tiger'; it is unclear whether this comment was for James' benefit or if Bhutto was genuinely disappointed that China had not launched an attack on India in the final week of the war. Bhutto ended by saying that world opinion was overwhelmingly sympathetic to Pakistan and no country apart from Yugoslavia and Ethiopia had supported India. James said that Bhutto was 'more subdued than I have ever known him' and 'employed none of his customary posturing and histrionics'. To James the most significant fact of the conversation was that Bhutto obviously still disagreed with Ayub's decision to agree to the ceasefire on 23 September (18/11/65, Rawalpindi to CRO, DO 196/390 PRO).

On 23 November Bhutto was sent to Moscow by Ayub to discuss the agenda and timing of the Soviet-hosted summit at Tashkent. Bhutto's visit was reported by the US embassy in Moscow which felt that the main purpose of this trip was to gauge Soviet sincerity in hosting a summit at Tashkent; Bhutto was reported as puzzled by the Soviet desire to be the mediator for the 'thankless task' of talks on Kashmir, and while he was convinced that Soviets were pressuring India to attend, the fact was that India was not going to be pressured at the UN (27/11/65, Moscow to State, POL 7 PAK NA).

On 3 December the CIA prepared an intelligence memorandum on the India-Pakistan situation, with Pakistan seen as being preoccupied with rebuilding its military and attempting to pressure India on Kashmir. The US suspension of arms aid was seen as causing severe damage to Pakistan's military effectiveness, which would only become more serious with time. India was seen as less concerned than Pakistan regarding the US military aid suspension but more concerned about economic aid.

Ayub's decision to stir up the Kashmir issue had succeeded in bringing Kashmir to world attention, but the 'costs were unexpectedly high and rewards uncertain'. The extensive loss of equipment badly damaged Pakistan's ability to fight and left it weaker than before the war. The leadership in Pakistan was said to be 'deeply frustrated' but pro-Western elements had been strengthened by the realisation in Pakistan that only the US could supply the economic and military assistance that Pakistan needed. The US military aid cut-off was seen as widely unpopular as it affected Pakistan far more than India, and there was believed to be a major policy review going on within Pakistan following the war, with Ayub considering stepping back from China and towards the US, but a final decision was said to rest on 'diplomatic, economic and military advantages relative to other courses of action'. Pakistan was seen as overestimating the Chinese capacity for offsetting Western aid, and despite reports that China was willing to supply MiG aircraft, tanks and a tank assembly plant, China was seen as too involved with Vietnam to part with many weapons to Pakistan.

Despite an improvement in relations between Pakistan and the USSR of late, Moscow was seen as 'unlikely' to abandon India and was expected only to seek to widen a rift between the US and Pakistan and try and counter Chinese influence. India was now seen as more confident and proud of its ability to stand up to China and Pakistan at the same time, and so any concession by an Indian leader now on Kashmir was seen as 'political suicide'. Although there had been some anti-US feeling caused by the suspension of economic aid, the military aid suspension was recognised as having hurt Pakistan more. Indian relations with Moscow were said to have improved during the war and Moscow was promising generous terms for arms sales.

On the economic front, Pakistan was seen as in much better shape than India thanks to the previous Five Year Plan and large US aid. The total military aid programme to Pakistan from 1954 to June 1965 was valued at $676.6 million and the economic aid programme from 1948 to 1965 at $3,315.6 million. US aid to India had also been generous with a total from 1948 to 1965 of $6,040 million, the Pl-480 aid being seen as particularly useful to India, where it alone fed thirty-eight million people. US military aid to India was valued from June 1962 to June 1965 at $92 million delivered out of an aid package of $160 million (3/12/65 CIA Intelligence Memorandum, India Memos and Misc Vol VI LBJ).

Wiping the slate clean

By November, Ayub realised that he could not delay his long awaited visit to the US any longer. In April 1965, Ayub had been due to visit the US but had found his invitation withdrawn by Johnson with weeks to go and then, from 5 September, Johnson had insisted that for any US aid to Pakistan to resume, Ayub would have to visit Washington and have 'a full and frank discussion' on future relations between the US and Pakistan. Ayub had been reluctant to do this as he felt that he would be made to 'look like a beggar', but with over a month having passed since the ceasefire, Ayub now bowed to the inevitable and informed the US government that he would be in the US to address the UN and would like to meet Johnson.

The State Department felt that the visit provided an opportunity for 'wiping the slate clean' and having a more realistic Pakistan policy as Pakistan had 'amply demonstrated its own desire to reduce its previous dependence on us' and now US interests and Pakistan's requirements could not sustain the previous close relationship. The war and Ayub's visit gave the US a 'rare opportunity' to develop a policy that was 'more responsive' to US needs and interests, but the State Department recognised that it was not possible to base a US policy purely on India as Pakistan had 'sufficient resources' to upset the balance of power and there were also US interests in Pakistan to consider. US interests in Pakistan were defined as (i) political stability and economic growth with a pro-Western government in place, (ii) trying to moderate Indian terms to allow a Kashmir settlement to take place, (iii) limiting Pakistan's relationship with China, (iv) the US base in Peshawar (0/11/65, State Department Memo, POL 27 India-Pakistan NA).

On 29 November the State Department recommended to Johnson that Ayub be told that the US could not force a Kashmir settlement on India and that Ayub should be pressed for support on Vietnam and in restraining the Pakistan press. The summary was that although the US was prepared to work with Ayub, it could only do so to the extent that Ayub was prepared to 'co-operate on all the outstanding issues', and Ayub should be in no doubt that all further aid to Pakistan would 'depend on performance; i.e. that before we can consider resumption of long-term aid we will need to be assured that it will not be wasted in a resumption of hostilities or diverted to greatly increased defence spending' (29/11/65 State Department Memo, POL 7 Pak NA).

Komer reminded Johnson on 29 November that now the visit was finally fixed for December the Pakistanis were 'losing no time in setting out their position', and this opportunity should not be wasted by Ayub complaining about US betrayals and aid to India; instead there should be a focus on how to improve future relations. The best way of achieving this was to 'soften up Ayub first', which would mean that Ayub would come 'in a mood to listen rather than rant'. Komer went on that both he and Rusk had little faith that McConaughy was capable of delivering such a message to Ayub (29/11/65, Komer to Johnson, George Bundy, Vol 17 Box 5 LBJ).

On 1 December Hoops of the US State Department met Pickard of the CRO at the CRO in London to discuss the Kashmir situation and the British desire to resume arms sales to India. Pickard said the UK wanted to resume some arms exports to India as they were parts that India would otherwise manufacture itself and Britain had refrained to date in doing so out of deference to US policy. He also said the British government was disappointed by the lack of progress at the UN and was worried about the prospect of Tashkent representing a Soviet victory if India agreed to a withdrawal of troops after those talks. Pickard said that while Britain recognised that the US and the USSR had the best chances of influencing the Indians, the British still had some influence in Pakistan and Ayub was due to stop off in London en route to Washington and could assist. Hoops said the US view was that Ayub had recognised he was at a crossroads and had been sobered by the war, and Johnson was going to take a 'very firm line' with Ayub and tell him that the US could not buy or force a Kashmir solution and Pakistan had to choose between good relations with either the US or China. While the US recognised that Pakistan needed good relations with China, it could not be at the cost of 'vital American interests'. The US was now prepared for a more 'detached' relationship with Pakistan, and Ayub was going to be told to adjust to the reality of India as the major subcontinental power. If this was accepted by Ayub, then US aid would resume but it would depend on Pakistan's performance. Food aid could resume quickly, economic and military aid could also resume but not for some time (1/12/65, Record of Meeting, CRO DO 196/390 PRO).

On 4 December McConaughy had a meeting with Aziz Ahmed to discuss the forthcoming talks in Tashkent, Ahmed asked McConaughy what the US position was in relation to the talks. McConaughy replied that if the Soviets were prepared to treat Kashmir as a dispute then that was a change in their current position and it was for the Pakistan government to decide whether to attend. Whatever they decided, the US would remain committed to working through the UN; to this Aziz replied that the UN would not lead to any resolution of the Kashmir dispute as the USSR had a veto there. Aziz went on that the Pakistan government saw no possibility of the Soviets changing their position in relation to Kashmir, and without serious US pressure, India would not change its position. McConaughy said that such pressure could easily backfire on the US. Aziz ended by saying that Pakistan could not understand why India was prepared to wreck its economy rather than seek a 'reasonable settlement' (4/12/65, Rawalpindi to Washington, DO 196/390 PRO).

On 8 December 1965 a simultaneous announcement was made in Moscow, Delhi and Rawalpindi that a summit between Shastri and Ayub was to be hosted by the Soviets at Tashkent on 4 January 1966. On 10 December, Ayub stopped in London for a meeting with Wilson en route to the US. Ayub gave Wilson a long and apparently impassioned account of the war and how difficult the ceasefire decision had been. Wilson asked Ayub if he felt the Soviets would be mediators or facilitators at Tashkent, to which Ayub said he felt it would be the latter. Wilson then tried to probe Ayub as to Chinese intentions and said that China was expansionist and a real threat to Asian peace, but Ayub replied blandly that the Chinese position was one for them to take. Wilson warned Ayub that the forthcoming meeting with Johnson was going to be tough as the Americans do 'not like being kicked in the teeth or belly' and returned to his main topic of Chinese influence, saying that Pakistan 'had let the animal into your house, perhaps as a good watch dog'. Wilson asked his Foreign Secretary, Michael Stewart, for an assessment of the Soviet position as he had just returned from Moscow. Stewart said that the Soviets were as concerned about Chinese intentions as the West and Pakistan would have to convince them of its desire to keep China out. Ayub said rather regretfully that he was going to Tashkent because the West had left him with little option. Wilson said that Ayub was right to go 'but obviously you are not going with excessive hopes', which was a clear hint that Pakistan could expect little from the talks. Ayub suggested hopefully that the Commonwealth could hold talks on Kashmir if Tashkent was to fail, but Wilson was quick to provide reasons why that was not feasible, and Wilson made it clear 'that it is the Americans who hold the key' (10/12/65 Note of Meeting, DO 196/390 PRO).

Ayub in the US, December 1965

Ayub flew to the US on 13 December and went first to New York to address the UN General Assembly before flying to Washington to meet Johnson. In his UN speech, Ayub criticised India's position on Kashmir, which led to the by now almost customary Indian walkout. However, the serious talking was to take place in Washington with Johnson in what was sure to be a tense and far-reaching encounter.

Before Ayub's first meeting with Johnson, Komer prepared a memorandum for the president in which he reiterated his advice on how to handle the talks. China was described as Ayub's 'most vulnerable point' and Ayub was expected to say that he would not deal with the Chinese if the US assisted on Kashmir. Komer said that such a proposition was simply not feasible and it had to be made clear to Ayub that he could not expect to have 'a Chinese ally against India and massive US aid'. The US had information that Ayub was not going to ask for anything specific, and in case he did, Johnson was advised to say that no commitment could be made until Johnson's meeting with Shastri. Johnson was told that the more he talked about Vietnam 'the more Ayub will realise that we're serious about China'. Johnson was told to tell Ayub that the future was more important than the past and there was still seen to be plenty of common ground 'on which the two countries can build if they can reason together'. Ayub was to be reminded that the US could not allow Pakistan to 'dictate our India policy' or to become 'tacit allies of China'. If Ayub was in US shoes, he would have been sure to feel the same way, and as the US was investing heavily to ensure that communism did not spread in Asia, US aid was unlikely to be given to a country which 'played ball' with China. The US simply did not share Pakistan's view that India wished to destroy it, but the US was prepared to 'do our best to see that India doesn't swallow up Pakistan so long as Pakistan itself takes the road of peace and alignment with its real friends'. On Kashmir, Ayub 'must realise that we cannot force India out of Kashmir. Nor can the Paks. To be brutally frank, we think that only out of a process of reconciliation with India is any compromise likely to emerge'. The most that Johnson could offer Ayub was that although the US could not help Pakistan in Kashmir, it could do something which no other state could: that is, 'help assure Pakistan's future viability and security—which we see as its ultimate insurance against any Indian threat'. Before that was to happen, Ayub had to reassure the US that he would not:

a) and b) (redacted)
c) waste money on an arms race
d) let anti-US public abuse continue (13/12/65 Memo for President Pakistan Memos Vol V LBJ).

Ayub visited Washington for two days, 14 and 15 December. The content of the first meeting, which was doubtless the most frank and interesting, was alluded to later by Johnson and Ayub, and so some clues are available as to the agenda and conversation. As Ayub and Johnson went off alone (without any advisers present) to meet at 10am on 14 December, the Acting Secretary of State, George Ball, suggested to the Pakistan delegation that as the meeting could easily take a couple of hours, the two teams could examine the draft communiqué. In the event, Ayub and Johnson did not appear until a little after 1 pm for a slightly delayed lunch. The official US notes of the meeting are so heavily redacted that it is almost impossible to know precisely what was discussed, but they do indicate the serious nature of the conversation. One point of the conversation was later confirmed by Johnson himself in a later conversation with former president Eisenhower; he said that he had warned Ayub about Bhutto: 'I just said to him—now Mr President, I know that you rely on Bhutto just like I rely on Dean Rusk and like Eisenhower relied on Dulles but you can't rely on him that way and I am not entering your internal affairs but this man is damn dangerous as far as you are concerned and you are my friend and I am going to give you this warning and I know whereof I speak' (Johnson Library 4/11/67 10.05 am Tape 67.14 Side B LBJ).

Once the presidents had emerged, Johnson was said to have taken Bhutto by the arm and said, 'Young man, you're doing extremely well! I've got my eye on you. You're going to go very far'. Bhutto was reported to have known at that moment that his imminent dismissal had been part of the presidential conversation (Wolpert, *Bhutto*, 99).

Johnson said over lunch how much he admired and liked Ayub and concluded by giving his view of world trouble spots. Ayub in reply spoke about the UN needing to be involved; on Kashmir, there could be either a plebiscite or arbitration and there was a precedent for this in the Radcliffe Commission on the Kutch border dispute. Ayub said the US was the greatest power in the world and should apply itself to bringing about a settlement between India and Pakistan. As far as China was concerned, Pakistan was in a difficult location 'with three major powers breathing down our necks' and so relations with China were a 'compulsion of circumstances' (Gauhar, 375–7).

After the first meeting with Ayub, Komer said that Ayub 'had used all his charm to convince us that if only we get Kashmir arbitration and cut back Indian arms all would be rosy'. Johnson was said to have replied that much as he admired Ayub, the US could not 'get into bed with China'. Komer recommended that Johnson should disabuse Ayub firmly of the idea that the US backed a plebiscite in Kashmir as otherwise Ayub would go to Tashkent with that idea in mind and 'would not even begin to compromise', and the US would be back where it started (14/12/65, Komer to President, George Bundy, Vol 17 Box 5 LBJ). Ball was deputed in his forthcoming meeting on the evening of 14 December with Ayub to spell out in explicit detail the US position on the following:

i) the US was in no position or mood to try and get involved with the Kashmir issue and was happy for the Soviets to take the lead in this (from their point of view) thankless matter
ii) the US viewed Pakistan's growing links with China with suspicion and hostility and the Pakistan government's position put all future aid in jeopardy
iii) the US would not allow Pakistan to dictate the US government's relations with India.

Before the meeting took place, Ball telephoned Johnson to check if there was anything in particular that Johnson wanted Ball to stress, and to discuss Johnson's earlier meeting. Ball said Ayub had mentioned to him over lunch that day his desire to meet Goldberg. Johnson said that he had informed Ayub that Goldberg would be at the dinner in the evening of the 14th, and Johnson intended to have a private chat with Ayub after the dinner but had not intended Goldberg to be present. Ball said that both Ayub and Bhutto had questioned him over lunch as to what would happen if the Tashkent talks failed, which Ball took as a clear question about what the US position would then be if they were prepared to become directly involved. Ball said he thought the US should be very careful on this point as it did not want to give Ayub the impression that it would be prepared to get involved if Tashkent did not succeed. Johnson said that Ayub had not raised this question with him and all Ayub had said to him was that he favoured a plebiscite in Kashmir but failing that, would accept arbitration.

Johnson had told Ayub that the US had no more influence over India than it had over Pakistan, and that although the Americans desired peace in that part of the world they 'were not able to achieve it'. Johnson said rather sarcastically to Ayub that 'when he needed Ayub he was in Peking or Moscow', to which Ayub replied that he had no use for China but had to protect himself. Johnson said that he offered Ayub 'no hope, no promises, no commitment except that he hated for us (Pakistan) to go along as we were now'. Johnson said that those who had been friends of Pakistan did not understand Pakistan using China against the US and India. Johnson's only glimmer of hope to Ayub was to say that the 'Indians were disappointing us as much as the Pakistanis'. Ayub said that he was not offended by this and said he 'sympathised with the Pres and his problems'.

Johnson had told Ayub that he was 'glad to see him go to Tashkent' and if he could achieve a satisfactory solution, that was fine but if not, Johnson could not see what he could do in view of Pakistan's 'peculiar relationship with Chinese communists'. Ball said that this was a point he was anxious to emphasise that evening; that the US should be clear that it was 'not prepared to pick up the pieces if Tashkent fails'. Ball said that the US could inject a little hope in Ayub on 15 December after having 'softened him up', as Ayub appeared over lunch to be 'subdued and 'verging on despair'; an assessment Johnson agreed with, saying his own impression was that Ayub appeared 'pathetic' and 'spoke with an inferiority complex'. Johnson had gone on to tell Ayub that he was 'deeply disappointed' in the position that Ayub now found himself in as the US position was that it was not sympathetic to any allies of the communist Chinese. Johnson said that at this 'Ayub jumped out of his chair and said he wants nothing to do with the Chinese' but was trying to protect Pakistan from India. Johnson had then reassured Ayub that he should not be worried in talking to the US government 'anymore than Lady Bird does—that we feel very close to them'. Johnson went on to say that Ayub was free to choose his own cabinet ministers—mentioning Bhutto. This was a reference to the warning which Johnson had later mentioned to Eisenhower. Ayub was said to have 'defended Bhutto saying that it was Bhutto who had encouraged him to come to the US and reaffirm their friendship'. Ball said he would continue 'a pretty tough line tonight' and that any hope should come from Johnson himself (14/12/65 6.40pm, Memo of Conversation Ball and Johnson, Ball Papers Presidential Telecons *FRUS 1964–68*, Volume XXV Document 264).

In the evening of 14 December, as scheduled, Ball led an American delegation to meet Ayub and his team. Included on the US side were Ball and McConaughy, while the Pakistan delegation was led by Ayub and included Bhutto, Aziz Ahmed, Gauhar and others. Ball said that he had spoken to Johnson regarding the meeting he had with Ayub earlier that day, and that Johnson hoped to speak to Ayub again that night. Ball said that Pakistan should understand the critical importance the US gave to Vietnam, and although the US understood the geographical position Pakistan was in vis-à-vis India, China and the USSR, the fact remained that 'Pakistan's policies have created anxieties'. Both sides now needed to 'realistically face the differences' between them and try and identify areas of common interest. When Ball began to talk of a possible military alliance Pakistan had with China, Ayub began to say 'No Sir No Sir No Sir'. Ayub said that there was absolutely no military alliance between Pakistan and China and he had told Johnson so earlier that day. Ayub went on to say that Pakistan could only survive with the help of a larger army and Pakistan 'was in alliance with the United States'. Even the alliance with the US was not meant as threat to anyone but a 'deterrent to possible aggression'. Ayub claimed that Pakistan had never given any thought to a military alliance with China and in any event it knew that China 'couldn't bring much against India'.

Ball moved on to Tashkent and said that he had discussed this with Johnson, and the United States' position was that it hoped that 'something productive' could come from the meeting. The Soviets had good ties with India and were trying to improve their ties with Pakistan, and so the US 'welcomed an initiative of this kind and wished it well'. The US support for Tashkent had been relayed to the Soviets via the US ambassador in Moscow. In a separate discussion, the Soviets had asked the US if there was any particular Kashmir formula that the US favoured before the summit, and the US had replied that there was not. The Soviet reply was that they did not have such a formula either and did not propose to suggest one at Tashkent. Ayub said that this point was one that had already been relayed to Bhutto from Goldberg at the UN. Ayub said that despite this he hoped that the US and Britain would also take an initiative; Pakistan was not 'irrevocably attached to the plebiscite' and was open to arbitration. Ayub said that another war would shatter both countries' economies and open the door to communism, and that there was nothing to stop the USA taking the initiative in Kashmir as the US had more of a stake in the subcontinent than the USSR.

Ball said that if there was progress at Tashkent the US might be able to help in improving relations and future steps might be best taken through the UN, but he repeated that Pakistan 'should approach Tashkent with the hope of achieving something'. The US said that the USSR had in the past taken a very pro-Indian approach and the US was 'pleased that they were now taking the initiative' as the US was not concerned about winning the Nobel Peace Prize on Kashmir. Ayub said laughingly, 'But you should want the Nobel Peace Prize'. Ball said the US was also very concerned about the military expenditure on the subcontinent and hoped this would be curtailed (14/12/65, Blair House, 7.15 pm. *FRUS 1964–58*, Vol XXV South Asia 265).

On 15 December, after the main discussion, Johnson was due to meet Ayub again. Komer said that Johnson was the best judge of 'whether all the essentials have been covered'; the US president's statement to Ayub that he should be under no illusions that the US could settle Kashmir, since 'if this were possible we would have settled it already', showed that Johnson needed no coaching. Ayub should now be satisfied that the US was not his enemy but was not going to be taken for granted and now he had to judge himself whether to choose the Chinese or the Americans. Ayub was to be reminded that the anti-US rhetoric had to stop, especially as Johnson had never 'uttered an unkind word about Pakistan'. Komer said that Johnson's attention to Aziz Ahmed had obviously 'worried Bhutto, who is his direct superior' (15/12/65, George Bundy Vol 17 Box 5 LBJ).

In a final meeting of the delegations at 5.20pm on 15 December at the White House, Johnson, Ball, McConaughy and others met Ayub, Bhutto, Aziz Ahmed, Gauhar and others. Johnson said that Ayub and he had 'rehearsed and reviewed' the problems of both countries. He wished that the trip had taken place a year or two before and said of Ayub that there was 'no leader with whom he had more rapport, understanding or friendship'. Johnson said that he was 'praying' that Tashkent would be a success and was sure that nothing Pakistan did was against US interests. Johnson said that Ayub had come asking for nothing but had taken away friendship, trust and confidence, 'Indeed everything that we have got'. Johnson recalled his visit to Pakistan and said that 'he had never visited any country where he was treated better or that he loved more'. He said to Ayub directly that if 'your life (Pakistan) is threatened, ours will also be threatened'.

Ayub said that 'he wished the US had felt the same way a few months ago when Pakistan's life was being threatened'; the talk with Johnson had done 'his soul a lot of good' and although he knew Pakistan had no right to dictate terms to the US, he hoped that the US would take Pakistan's opinion into account when making decisions. Ayub mentioned Vietnam and how Pakistan hoped to be a force for moderation, and ended by hoping that Johnson would visit Pakistan soon (15/12/65, Memorandum of Conversation, *FRUS 1964–68*, Volume XXV Doc 266).

Once Ayub and his delegation had left the White House, Johnson discussed the visit with some of his advisers and said the US should realise that 'Ayub felt himself threatened by India and was deeply afraid that Pakistan would be "gobbled up"'. Johnson said that Ayub had been advised to do his best at Tashkent and if it failed something else should be tried, but Ayub had been told by Johnson that he should 'not be under illusions that we can force a settlement as if we were able to, we would have done so already'. Johnson said he had told Ayub that if Pakistan wanted close relations with the US there could be no serious relationship with the Chinese as 'we could not live with that'. At the same time the US 'understood certain relationships just as a wife could understand a Saturday night fling by her husband so long as she was the wife'. Ayub was said to have got the point. Johnson concluded by saying that he was 'impressed that Ayub had asked for nothing specific and felt that good groundwork had been laid by Prime Minister Wilson and by our people in the field' (15/12/65 Memo of Conversation, India/Pakistan Military Assistance 8/66–4/67 LBJ). The slate had indeed been wiped clean and Ayub had been told in no uncertain terms that the special relationship was over and he should expect no US assistance over Kashmir. The bitter truth that the war was not going to result in any movement on Kashmir from India was now clear, and all that was needed was for Ayub to accept the ground reality at Tashkent.

12

TASHKENT

'They know it, as do we'

The Tashkent Summit has entered the pantheon of great conspiracy theories in both India and Pakistan, but particularly in the latter as the highly successful (possibly too effective) Ministry of Information campaign in Pakistan had convinced most of the population that the Pakistan Army was winning the military war and now only had to seal the diplomatic win. This was of course far removed from reality, and the fact was that unless Pakistan was prepared to ditch the alliance with the US which had been a cornerstone of its military strategy since the early 1950s, and fight a guerrilla war with India with the possible (but by no means certain) assistance of China, it was in no position to fight on. This was something that India was aware of, but because of the failure of Mailed Fist, India was no longer in a position to force an early military victory and was concerned that a protracted dispute might well drag China into the conflict—a prospect which India viewed with some dread.

The visit of Ayub to Washington had been designed not only to try to repair some of the damage done to bilateral relations, which had been sliding since 1962, but also—more urgently from Pakistan's point of view—to try and gain some assurance that the US would back Pakistan in holding out for Indian assurances of genuine movement on Kashmir before signing a peace treaty. Given the level of anger in Washington with Ayub since the outbreak of the war and Pakistan's use of China as a possible ally against India, there was no realistic chance of such an approach working. The mission to Washington was therefore a complete failure and Ayub had not only failed to win any such assurance, he was told in no uncertain terms that if Pakistan wished to continue to be a recipient of US aid, he would have to be far more careful in his foreign and defence policy. The special relationship, such as it ever was, was over.

Ayub left Washington 'deeply disappointed' and in no doubt what the American and British positions were. Wilson had told Ayub clearly that the Commonwealth had no role to play in the Kashmir dispute and had passed the buck to the US. Johnson had told Ayub that the US was 'praying for success' of the talks at Tashkent, but he made it very clear that he had absolutely no intention of either hosting an India-Pakistan summit on the subject of Kashmir or even sponsoring the UN as a forum to discuss Kashmir any longer. Ayub had also been warned about his future relations with China and left in no doubt that if it was Pakistan and China versus India and the USSR, then the US would choose India over Pakistan. Ayub now knew that he was going to Tashkent with a very poor hand and there would be no pressure on India at all to be accommodating towards Pakistan on the question of Kashmir, from either of the two superpowers (Gauhar, 377).

Following Ayub's departure, Johnson sent a personal message to Ayub to be delivered by the US ambassador to Turkey during his stopover on his journey back. Johnson obviously felt that having been blunt and unyielding with Ayub in Washington, it was now time to give Ayub some good news. Johnson said that he had decided to resume aid on some specific programmes and that he regarded 'our talks as a major step toward re-establishment of mutual confidence and am very glad you came' (17/12/65, State to Ankara, DEF 19–8 US-Pak. NA) Shoaib told McConaughy on 22 December that he was delighted at the way in which Ayub's meeting with Johnson had gone and Ayub was 'profoundly impressed' with Johnson's wisdom. That comment appears to have been for US ears and it appears to confirm that Ayub continued to use Shoaib as a conduit for sending unofficial messages to the US. Shoaib also informed Johnson that Ayub had received an offer of Chinese military aid. This was to assist Pakistan to rearm, and the offer as described by Ayub to Shoaib was of arms from China purely as a grant; Ayub had said Pakistan could have 'whatever equipment they wanted'. This report appears to be either exaggerated or untrue, but was designed to send a message to Johnson that Pakistan was seriously considering the Chinese offer of weaponry. Like other similar threats, it did not have the desired effect, and it appears that there was no reaction from the US to this 'news' (22/12/65, Karachi to State, POL 7 PAK NA).

A review of Ayub's meeting was recorded by the State Department on 29 December 1965, which stated that one of the outcomes of the visit was that the 1954–62 alliance was 'dead. They know it, as do we'. Pakistani expectations of US help on Kashmir finally 'conform to reality' and the limitations of Pakistani relations with China were discussed although 'not explicitly spelt out', which meant that there was a possibility of a new beginning. Ayub was said to have reduced the need for US pressure by agreeing to go to Tashkent and the US was glad that someone else was willing to take on this issue after 'the frustrations we have experienced over the past eighteen years' (29/12/65, POL 7 PAK NA).

On Christmas Eve, Bowles was also assured by Benediktov, the Soviet ambassador to India, that the only Soviet interest in Tashkent was to prevent a joint Pakistan/Chinese attack on India. The Soviet plan was going to be to let Ayub and Shastri meet each other and attempt to resolve things themselves. The Soviets only intended to intervene if that did not work and they felt they had to step in. The Soviet ambassador said Moscow understood that on Ayub's recent trip to Washington, Ayub had agreed to let the US keep its bases in Pakistan. This is yet another clue to a point in the secret agenda of the 14 December discussion between Ayub and Johnson, and also demonstrates that the Soviets were well informed by top level sources within Pakistan (27/12/65, Delhi to State, POL 27 India-Pak. NA). The Soviet reasons for getting involved in an attempted peace summit were consistently portrayed as a genuine desire for peace by the USSR and it appears that the US did believe the reason to be genuine as there was little to gain otherwise for the USSR.

In preparation for the Tashkent Summit, Ayub met his ministers and advisers on 31 December 1965, a few days before his departure. Ayub was reported by Gauhar to have stated to the gathering that he was unsure of the precise agenda at Tashkent as none had been agreed; however, Ayub said, he was conscious of India's likely intransigence on the subject of Kashmir. More tellingly, Ayub had ended the discussion by saying, 'I know of people who want to risk Pakistan for the sake of Kashmir'; which appears to be a barbed comment directed at Bhutto and those who strongly objected to acceptance of the UN ceasefire (Gauhar, 378–9). This appears to show the shift in Ayub's thinking, as he had now seemingly been persuaded by the line that Pakistan was not worth sacrificing for the sake of Kashmir and was using this justification for not continuing the war. This is an indication of the recriminations which had broken out within the Pakistan establishment—with particular finger pointing at Bhutto. Bhutto was being blamed not only for having 'risked Pakistan for Kashmir' but also, behind the scenes, for spoiling the close relationship with the US and confidently assuring Ayub that India would not cross the international border at Lahore.

Bhutto, however, was hardly the sort of personality to take criticism lying down, and he retaliated by accusing his critics of lacking the stomach for a long war and the military commanders of bungling both Gibraltar and Mailed Fist. The harsh fact was that Pakistan had not won the war, and tension within the Pakistan camp was now becoming obvious. Before his departure for Tashkent, Ayub was called upon by Averell Harriman, a senior US diplomat with a message from Johnson, the contents of which are unknown but were very likely to have been a reminder not to rely on the US to rescue Pakistan out of a situation of its own creation.

The Indian delegation was also preparing for the summit, and on 3 January 1966 the CIA reported that Shastri had met Indian editors at his residence a day before he was to attend the Tashkent talks. Shastri had told the editors that the main sticking point was likely to be pressure on India to return to the CFL as the border in Kashmir prior to 5 August without Pakistan being willing to recognise the CFL as the international boundary. Shastri felt that as Pakistan was almost certain to refuse this it would lead to the breakdown of the talks, and that the deadlock would cause problems for India as both the US and the USSR considered that a withdrawal of Indian forces from Haji Pir Pass, Kargil and Tithwal was necessary. Shastri said the US would be content with the status quo in Kashmir provided that India could establish a popular government there (3/1/66 CIA Cable, India Cables, Box 130 LBJ).

The opening of the Tashkent summit

On 3 January Ayub and his delegation landed in Tashkent, two hours before Shastri and his delegation arrived. The Soviets had made great efforts to give both India and Pakistan equal treatment and provided identical high quality accommodation for the delegations. Kosygin himself had taken personal charge of the arrangements and had been based in Tashkent for some days prior to the summit to ensure that accommodation and other conference facilities were of the highest standard. All three sides had arrived with large and formidable delegations. The Soviet team, headed by the Prime Minister Alexei Kosygin, included the Foreign Minister, Andrei Gromyko, the Defence Minister, Marshal Rodion Malinovsky, the former Chief of Staff of the Red Army, and South Asian experts from the Soviet Foreign Ministry.

The Indian delegation was headed by the Prime Minister, Lal Bahadur Shastri, and amongst others it included the Defence Minister Y. B. Chavan, the Foreign Minister Swaran Singh, the Foreign Secretary C. S. Jha, the Home Secretary L. P. Singh, and the Vice-Chief of Army Staff, P. P. Kumaramangalam. The Pakistani delegation was naturally headed by Ayub and comprised amongst others the Foreign Minister Bhutto, the Foreign Secretary Aziz Ahmed, Altaf Gauhar (designated as official spokesman for Pakistan), Asghar Khan and various senior cabinet ministers. It was soon apparent to all that the Pakistani delegation was split between those who seemed resigned to ending the war with as much good grace as could be mustered and those who preferred to leave without an agreement if no tangible movement from India was forthcoming.

Kosygin met both Shastri and Ayub separately in the evening of 3 January and the opening positions of both sides were now explained to the Soviets, who were at this stage simply willing to act as conduits of messages between the two sides. India's main priorities in Tashkent were summarised by Shastri to the Soviet delegation as (i) an assurance that Pakistan would not launch another pre-emptive strike against India, (ii) a Pakistani assurance not to carry out any future repeat of Gibraltar, (iii) the acceptance by Pakistan of a no-war pact with India, (iv) agreement by Pakistan to accept the CFL as the international border in Kashmir, on which India was unwilling to make any concession. The main point, however, was that the Indian delegation did not view the Tashkent summit as an opportunity to resolve the Kashmir issue but as the mechanism to end the war and return to the pre-war situation.

Pakistan's priorities were of course very different and were laid out to Kosygin as follows: a resolution to the Kashmir dispute (either by agreement or plebiscite) was the main objective of the summit, and Pakistan wanted Soviet assistance in pressuring/persuading India to agree to make some concessions on Kashmir which would help resolve the Kashmir problem; Pakistan hoped that the possible Chinese threat might help persuade the Soviets to apply some pressure on India to make some concessions in order to avoid a war on two fronts. Pakistan would then be willing to agree to a no-war pact with India if the Kashmir issue was honourably resolved

The personal relationship between Ayub and Kosygin was not helped when during the meeting with Kosygin on 3 January, Ayub informed Kosygin that he did not want to shake hands with Shastri the next day when they were due to meet. This was almost certainly to avoid photographs of the image being sent around the world and particularly to Pakistan; Ayub was conscious of how badly such a photograph would go down there. Kosygin was said to have reacted with anger at this comment, saying that Shastri was entitled to respect as the head of government of a large and neighbouring state; at which point Ayub had backed down, no doubt realising the pettiness of such an approach and the inevitability of such a photograph. It was yet another example of Pakistan's haphazard and ad hoc approach to the summit (C. P. Srivastava, *Lal Bahadur Shastri*, Oxford University Press India, 1995, 351).

The opening meeting between Ayub and Shastri had been organised in a neutral villa with Kosygin as the host on the morning of 4 January, as a means of breaking the ice and allowing the two leaders to talk face to face. The formal summit itself opened after lunch with speeches from Shastri, Ayub and

Kosygin in the main conference centre. Shastri's speech was said to have been received with applause from all present except Bhutto, who had to be nudged by Ayub in order to join in (Srivastava, 354). This was to be the beginning of Bhutto's public hard line display and the barely concealed splits within the Pakistan camp.

Shastri spoke of the need for a lasting peace and a no-war pact, issues which were very much India's objectives for the summit. Ayub responded by saying that a no-war pact was acceptable to Pakistan once 'outstanding issues' had been resolved: that is, Kashmir. The lines were now drawn publicly by the two sides and Kosygin had the task of trying to bridge that gap in order to reach some form of an agreement. That same evening (4 January) Kosygin met Shastri at the latter's villa and tried to persuade him that if the UN Security Council resolution was to be implemented in full, this would not only involve Pakistan removing Gibraltar forces from ICK but also India giving up its gains in Azad Kashmir, especially Haji Pir Pass and others. Shastri refused this request politely, saying that it was impossible to trust that future infiltrators would not be sent by Pakistan so India wanted to keep those passes for its future security. Kosygin was too skilled a diplomat to push the issue any further that night, but the logic of what he said must have registered with Shastri; however, at this stage India did not want to be giving Pakistan an easy concession of the Haji Pir Pass, and neither did the USSR want to push India too far without any Pakistani movement (Srivastava, 355–9).

In the morning of 5 August, despite his position the night before, Shastri discussed the issue of withdrawal from the Haji Pir Pass and other Indian gains with India's Foreign and Defence ministers, who both informed him that in their view these territories could in fact be given up for the sake of peace without endangering Indian security. Behind this decision there was also, inevitably, the political factor that Kosygin had pointed out the evening before, that Indian failure to do so would lay it open to the charge that it was defying UN Resolution 211 and would place India in the role of the obstructive party. The Indians were also prepared to give in to the Pakistani request for an agenda with the strict provision that there was no mention of the future of Kashmir on the agenda as a specific item. At 11am that morning Shastri and Ayub met for the first time for substantive talks face to face. There was a detailed exposition by both leaders of their respective positions on Kashmir, the origin of the war and its possible solutions. By all accounts, it was a polite and courteous discourse but with neither leader conceding an inch diplomatically, which meant that no headway was made other than the leaders familiarising themselves with each other and understanding each other's perspectives.

There was also no agreement on even the formal agenda at Tashkent when the Foreign Ministers Swaran Singh and Bhutto had met that afternoon. They were well-known to each other through previous negotiations on Kashmir, but Swaran Singh had flatly refused to have Kashmir on the agenda. Much to Bhutto's frustration, there was nothing he could do to persuade the Indians otherwise. In the middle of tension and frustration within the Pakistan camp, it was discovered that 5 January was Bhutto's birthday and a small impromptu birthday party was held for him, organised by Gauhar that evening, but from his demeanour and mood, there is little doubt that Bhutto would rather have been anywhere but Tashkent that day.

That evening the first concession came from the Indian side, which gave in to the inevitable and informed Kosygin that India would be prepared to move back to the 5 August 1965 border, with the obvious implication that the Indian troops would give up the territorial gains they had made along the LOC during the war. The capture of Haji Pir Pass had been both a strategic and morale boosting move by India and so its return was not without opposition within India. The Soviets were obviously delighted and grateful for this Indian move as it meant the UN Security Council Resolution for which they had voted would be implemented and now Kosygin could focus his attention on Ayub, with whom he had not had substantive talks since his arrival in Tashkent.

6 January was spent with Kosygin shuttling between the villas of Ayub and Shastri, there was no face-to-face meeting between Ayub and Shastri that day. The Soviet team of Kosygin and Gromyko spent most of 6 January with Ayub and Bhutto trying to secure some concessions from the Pakistan delegation on their insistence on trying to resolve the Kashmir issue at the summit. The Soviets became aware that Ayub was in fact more conciliatory on this issue than Bhutto, and so they needed to try to focus on Ayub individually. The Soviets described Ayub as 'gentlemanly' but Bhutto as 'obstructive' as the Foreign Minister took a harder line on many issues than Ayub. However, the Soviet team was a formidable one and anyone who had risen to power (as Kosygin and Gromyko had) surviving the Stalinist purges and negotiated with their great rival superpower, the USA, would not have found Bhutto too hard to handle (Srivastava, 365).

On 6 January Ayub briefed the Pakistan delegation about his talks with Shastri. Shastri had been modest and had told Ayub that he was a little man who had stepped into the shoes of a giant (Nehru). Ayub had said it was an opportunity for Shastri to go down in history as the person who resolved the Kashmir issue. Shastri had made it clear that public opinion in India would not allow any change to the basic situation inside Kashmir. Bhutto was alleged to have commented publicly that Ayub should have pointed out that he too was answerable to public opinion and did not have a 'heavenly mandate'. Ayub was now facing the harsh reality which he knew even before arriving in Tashkent: that India was not going to compromise or make any concessions on Kashmir, other than a return to the pre-war border, and Ayub would have either to walk away from the talks and risk the wrath of both superpowers by refusing a deal or sign a rather meaningless agreement with India, with no deal on Kashmir, and risk the wrath of the Pakistan population and some factions of his own government.

The remote Pakistani hope of some Soviet assistance which might come in the shape of some pressure on the Indian delegation to persuade Shastri to make some movement on Kashmir was fading fast. Ayub must have known deep down even before arriving that this hope was unrealistic. Bhutto had been depressed following his own daily meetings with Swaran Singh, who if anything was even more emphatic than Shastri was to Ayub that Kashmir was non-negotiable, and Bhutto felt that Soviets were not going to pressure India on this point.

That evening (6 January) there was a meeting at Ayub's villa between Ayub and Kosygin and their respective teams. Kosygin had brought a delegation with him, including Gromyko, and said that now he had had the opportunity to speak to both Ayub and Shastri at length and so wanted to present the Soviet perspective. The Soviets emphasised that Tashkent was a historic opportunity for the two nations which should not be missed. If no settlement was reached, said the Soviet team, then it would send a message to the world that solutions to political problems were only military. Kosygin was said to have looked at Bhutto and said, 'I can see from the Foreign Minister's face that his meeting with the Indian Foreign Minister has not been encouraging'. Bhutto's face was indeed often described as expressive and Kosygin was not contradicted by any of the Pakistan delegation.

Kosygin then handed over a draft declaration of points which they hoped could form the basis of an agreed text. He said that he did not want the delegations to see it as a Soviet document but as one that both delegations could use as a basis of discussions and amend accordingly while trying to reach eventual agreement. Kosygin went to say that Shastri had, after some persuasion, agreed to the inclusion of a reference to Kashmir, but had been adamant that there should be no reference to any mechanism for trying to resolve the Kashmir issue. This document was therefore the maximum that the Soviets had been able to extract from the Indian delegation with reference to Kashmir.

When the Soviet team had departed the Pakistani delegation examined the document in detail. Bhutto felt that it was an achievement for the Soviets to persuade the Indians to have some reference to Kashmir in the document, but recognised that it would be extremely difficult to sell the document back home. The document in its current form was therefore one that Pakistan could not accept.

The Soviet account of this meeting was recounted some years later by one of the Soviet delegates to Shastri's adviser. The Soviets found Ayub to be 'decent and gentlemanly', but the problem was that he only spoke in general terms and left the specific details to Bhutto. The Soviets therefore felt that there were 'two simultaneous channels from the Pakistan side speaking with different voices'. This made the Soviet job 'complicated and difficult'. However, whatever their opinion of Ayub, Bhutto was described as 'really obstructive' and a 'destroyer of all ideas'. As Bhutto had an excellent command of English he would suggest a comma to be inserted in a draft or removed which could have changed the entire meaning of a sentence. Therefore the Soviets felt that one had to be on full guard with Bhutto (Srivastava, 365).

The following day (7 January) there were two relatively brief meetings between Ayub and Shastri. Again no headway was made on the issue of Kashmir as Shastri refused to have the issue even discussed formally at the summit, let alone any attempt made to find a means of resolving the dispute. It was at this meeting that Ayub was said to have practically begged Shastri for some assistance by saying in Urdu, '*Kashmir ke mamle men kuchh aisa kar deejiye ki main bhi apne mulk men munh dikhanay ke kabil rahoon*' ('Please give me some assistance on the issue of Kashmir so that I may be able to show my face in my own country'). Shastri was reported to have politely but firmly replied, '*Sadar Sahib, main bahut maafi chaheta hoon ki main is mamle main koi apki khidmat nahin kar sakta*' ('Mr President, I am very sorry but in this matter I cannot be of any assistance to you') (Srivastava, 367). Although this is for obvious reasons a story recounted from the Indian side, it has the ring of truth about it and shows the level of desperation that Ayub had reached in his dealings with Shastri and the new tone he was now forced to adopt, different from the contempt with which he had referred to Shastri in the previous year.

Later that day the Pakistan delegation formally rejected the Soviet draft, a decision which reportedly left Swaran Singh speechless. However, that short-lived and pyrrhic diplomatic point scoring aside, there was increased tension within the Pakistan delegation as the Foreign Ministry team of Bhutto and Aziz Ahmed was maintaining its hard line but Ayub appeared to realise the diplomatic end game was approaching and was noticeably softening his line. This was to be almost a repeat of the ceasefire announcement positions, but Ayub was reportedly feeling that he could not realistically leave Tashkent without some form of an agreement, even an imperfect one.

By 8 January Shastri and the Indian delegation had handed the Soviets their own minor amendments of the Soviet text, and ominously for Ayub, Shastri also let it be publicly known that he was fully intending to stick to his original schedule of leaving to return to India on 11 January. As if on cue—and to both Soviet and American diplomats the timing was no coincidence—China chose 8 January as the day to deliver another threatening Diplomatic Note to India complaining of continuing aggressive Indian behaviour and warning India that 'China will strike back resolutely' against it, without detailing what Indian behaviour it was that it was complaining of. It seemed obvious to all observers that the message was intended to remind all parties that China had an interest in the outcome of the summit and to remind Pakistan that China was prepared to stand with Pakistan even if no agreement was reached at Tashkent. By 8 January, there were widespread rumours and press reports that the talks had broken down and the summit would end in failure as the two sides' positions were simply too far apart. All communication between the Indian and Pakistani delegations had ceased and it was difficult to maintain the pretence that talks were continuing when in fact they had all but ceased.

Behind the scenes, however, Kosygin was tirelessly meeting both delegations throughout the day without a break. Newspaper reports from the collected world press were mainly predicting a breakdown in the talks as no final text could be agreed on, a prediction further encouraged by a witty remark of Gauhar's in which he said, 'A communiqué is not a ticket home, you can leave a place without a communiqué' (Srivastava, 377). That evening, as a means of trying to lighten the atmosphere, a musical evening was laid on by the Soviet hosts which included some local Uzbek artists. Kosygin sat between Ayub and Shastri and persuaded them to continue to talk and not to give up hope of reaching a settlement (Gauhar, 386). Kosygin even allowed briefing by his delegation to a senior US journalist that the Soviets were 'very hopeful' of a breakthrough and permitted the journalist to say that this was from a 'reliable and authoritative source' (Srivastava, 374).

On the following morning, 9 January, Kosygin decided to concentrate his energy and focus on Ayub alone. Ayub was taken outside the city of Tashkent by Kosygin and shown around a Soviet aircraft factory. Kosygin said that despite all the tanks and aircraft being produced, new weapons such as long-range rockets and nuclear warheads had made all the impressive looking weaponry being produced redundant. Ayub was reported to have been deeply impressed by Kosygin's arguments that trying to resolve territorial disputes by armed force was madness. He was reported to have returned to Tashkent later that morning convinced that Kosygin was right, but his big worry now was how he could sell a perceived climbdown to the Pakistan public without a major backlash, and whether he could survive the backlash. Gauhar said that he warned Ayub that there would be a backlash in Pakistan if there was no apparent concession from India. Gauhar was no doubt conscious that Ayub was now convinced that he would have to sign a document that was less than ideal from a Pakistani point of view. Gauhar and Bhutto were obviously conscious that the ceasefire was tolerated by the Pakistani public as there was the expectation that there would be some major diplomatic movement on Kashmir following the war; failure on that front too would leave Ayub and his regime very unpopular (Gauhar, 386). However, it seemed that the international diplomatic pressure on Ayub had convinced him that no agreement in Tashkent would be more damaging to his own position in the world than concern about public opinion in Pakistan.

Breakthrough in Tashkent

In the evening of 9 January, before Kosygin was due to meet Ayub, he made a final attempt to persuade Shastri to make some concession to Pakistan on Kashmir. There was a dramatic moment when Shastri said politely that he would rather resign and give up politics than compromise India's position. Kosygin then immediately backtracked and realised that Shastri would not be pushed further on this point (Srivastava, 376–7). After Kosygin left to meet Ayub, Shastri was asked by a close adviser what prospects he believed there were of Ayub giving way now. Shastri was quietly confident that Ayub would agree as 'President Johnson…made it clear to President Ayub that he wants compliance with the Security Council resolutions…on Kashmir, President Ayub probably realises by now that he cannot force open the issue at this conference...Ayub realises the ground realities and very possibly will opt for peace'. Ayub was also seen as not wishing to offend the UN, the USSR and the US by resuming a war with Indian troops close to Lahore and Sialkot (Srivastava, 379).

At the meeting that evening over dinner between Ayub and Kosygin the Soviet draft was discussed clause by clause, word by word. There was heated discussion within the Pakistan delegation over the issue of agreeing not to use force, and when Ayub tried to insist on a mechanism to resolve the Kashmir dispute, Kosygin is reported to have said, 'It is too late to insist on that. Your Foreign Minister gave us an assurance in Moscow that Kashmir will not be made the decisive point in these negotiations'. This was a reference to Bhutto's visit to Moscow on 23 November, and Kosygin turned to Bhutto who did not reply (Gauhar, 388). A source relates that an exhausted Kosygin then directed his remarks to Ayub and asked him, 'If you leave without an agreement, what will be your prestige? What will be the future? Real war? What will be the reaction of world public opinion?' The no-war clause was dealt with indirectly as Kosygin said that all member states of the UN had already agreed to use peaceful means to resolve disputes and so Pakistan could hardly state its position as being one of wanting to use force. The mention of the fact that Kashmir was discussed was the diplomatic straw to which Ayub had to clutch. Faced with what he saw as little choice, Ayub then agreed to the text with the request that all armed personnel should withdraw to their pre-war position by 25 February 1966. The Soviets knew Shastri would agree to that as an early withdrawal of troops was in both sides' interest, and effectively the negotiations were over. Kosygin had managed to produce an agreed text which was now acceptable to both sides and the Pakistani delegation had been forced to accept the reality of its weak position. The bluff and the wishful thinking had met with Soviet persistence and Indian intransigence; neither of which should have been unexpected to the Pakistanis.

At close to midnight, 9 January, the Soviet team returned to Shastri's villa to give him the good news. Both the Indian and Soviet teams were delighted and there was an atmosphere of mutual congratulation. However, there was one final attempted spanner in the works while both delegations were still celebrating. A message came for Gromyko that Bhutto wished to speak to him on the telephone urgently; this was described as a 'chilling moment'. Gromyko took the call and listened with growing anger and surprise to Bhutto; it appeared that Bhutto wished to have the clause relating to agreement not to use force to be deleted from the text. Gromyko pointed out that the entire text had just been agreed by Ayub and Bhutto and it was too late to pull out now as it would be 'very bad, very bad'. After a few tense moments, Bhutto then backed down (after apparent discussion with Ayub) and the last-minute moment of tension was over (Srivastava, 380).

The Soviets could now prepare to host the signing ceremony of what was to become known as the Tashkent Declaration, which they arranged for the next day—doubtless aware of the potential of something or someone else in the Pakistan delegation threatening the signing ceremony.

Signature of the Tashkent Agreement

The Tashkent Declaration was signed in the afternoon of 10 January 1966. The text agreed and signed was:

The Prime Minister of India and the President of Pakistan, having met at Tashkent and having discussed the existing relations between India and Pakistan, hereby declare their firm resolve to restore normal and peaceful relations between their countries and to promote understanding and friendly relations between their peoples. They consider the attainment of these objectives of vital importance for the welfare of the 600 million people of India and Pakistan.

I. The Prime Minister of India and the President of Pakistan agree that both sides will exert all efforts to create good neighbourly relations between India and Pakistan in accordance with the United Nations Charter. They reaffirm their obligation under the Charter not to have recourse to force and to settle their disputes through peaceful means. They considered that the interests of peace in their region and particularly in the Indo-Pakistan Sub Continent and, indeed, the interests of the people so India and Pakistan were not served by the continuance of tension between the two countries. It was against this background that Jammu and Kashmir was discussed, and each of the sides set forth its respective position.

II. The Prime Minister of India and the President of Pakistan have agreed that all armed personnel of the two countries shall be withdrawn not later than 24 February, 1966, to the positions they held prior to 5 August, 1965, and both sides shall observe the ceasefire terms on the ceasefire line.

III. The Prime Minister of India and the President of Pakistan have agreed that relations between India and Pakistan shall be based on the principle of non-interference in the internal affairs of each other.

IV. The Prime Minister of India and the President of Pakistan have agreed that both sides will discourage any propaganda directed against the other country, and will encourage propaganda which promotes the development of friendly relations between the two countries.

V. The Prime Minister of India and the President of Pakistan have agreed that the High Commissioner of India to Pakistan and the High Commissioner of Pakistan to India will return to their posts and that the normal functioning of diplomatic missions of both countries will be restored. Both Governments shall observe the Vienna Convention of 1961 on Diplomatic Intercourse.

VI. The Prime Minister of India and the President of Pakistan have agreed to consider measures towards the restoration of economic and trade relations, communications, as well as cultural exchanges between India and Pakistan, and to take measures to implement the existing agreements between India and Pakistan.

VII. The Prime Minister of India and the President of Pakistan have agreed that they will give instructions to their respective authorities to carry out the repatriation of the prisoners of war.

VIII. The Prime Minister of India and the President of Pakistan have agreed that the two sides will continue the discussion of questions relating to the problems of refugees and eviction/illegal immigrations. They also agreed that both sides will create conditions which will prevent the exodus of people. They further agreed to discuss the return of the property and assets taken over by either side in connection with the conflict.

IX. The Prime Minister of India and the President of Pakistan have agreed that the two sides will continue meetings both at the highest and at other levels on matters of direct concern to both countries. Both sides have recognized the need to set up joint Indian-Pakistani bodies which will report to their Governments in order to decide what further steps should be taken.

The Prime Minister of India and the President of Pakistan recorded their feelings of deep appreciation and gratitude to the leaders of the Soviet Union, the Soviet Government and personally to the Chairman of the Council of Ministers of the U.S.S.R. for their constructive, friendly and noble part in bringing about the present meeting which has resulted in mutually satisfactory results. They also express to the Government and friendly people of Uzbekistan their sincere thankfulness for their overwhelming reception and generous hospitality.

They invite the Chairman of the Council of Ministers of the U.S.S.R. to witness this declaration.

There is little doubt that the declaration was a diplomatic triumph for India and a defeat for Pakistan. Whatever the ambiguity of the result on the battlefield, the only reference to Kashmir—for which the whole war had been fought—was a passing reference in Clause I which merely recorded that the issue of Kashmir 'was discussed'. The reality was that even on the most generous reading of the account of the Tashkent Declaration, in fact quite the opposite had happened in reality—

the issue of Kashmir was simply not discussed by the Indian delegation at all. The Indians had steadfastly refused even to have Kashmir as an agenda item and had maintained this position throughout their time in Tashkent. The reference to the issue of Kashmir having been 'discussed' was obviously to placate the Soviets and to give Ayub a diplomatic fig-leaf to cover up for the fact that he had signed a declaration that formally ended the war without any territorial or political gain whatsoever for Pakistan. Even Ayub's colleagues and advisers knew that the Declaration was a diplomatic defeat for Pakistan, but Ayub had gone to Tashkent with very few cards to play and he had ultimately calculated that he could not afford to upset both superpowers by leaving Tashkent without an agreement. For a general who had been largely shielded from democracy and public opinion, what the people of Pakistan thought seemed not to have figured in Ayub's thinking. It was left to the more politically savvy Bhutto to make his distaste of the agreement known by refusing to applaud the signing ceremony and shaking his head regularly and pointedly—even when Ayub was speaking. Whether in fact Bhutto would have refused to sign or not is another matter, but he visibly and obviously distanced himself from the Declaration (as much as he dared, as he was still keen to remain in his post as Foreign Minister).

The immediate reaction

To celebrate this victory of Indian and Soviet diplomacy, there was a formal farewell banquet on 10 January at which the two leaders, Ayub and Shastri, were billed as joint hosts. There was barely disguised Indian and Soviet satisfaction mingled with Pakistani disappointment and despair. Ayub was forced to put on a brave face during the evening and act as if Pakistan had signed the declaration through choice and, by putting Kashmir back on the world centre stage, had achieved its objective. The Indian delegation was now charm itself as it had won the diplomatic tussles, and actively sought out the Pakistani delegates to chat to and try and befriend them.

There was to be yet another dramatic and tragic twist to the conference to mark the end of a tragic and dramatic war. During the night of 10/11 January, after the banquet which had been such a major triumph for the quiet but firm diplomacy for which he was now known, the Prime Minister of India, Lal Bahadur Shastri, died in his sleep of a heart attack. He had survived two heart attacks before but this time it proved fatal at the conclusion of his greatest moment of triumph. The Indian prime minister was short in physical stature but had stood up to the much larger size of Ayub and had not moved on any principle with which he had set off for Tashkent. After many of the conspiracy theories surrounding the war, theories about the sudden death of Shastri were inevitably added to the list, but like many of the theories surrounding the war they were unfounded; it appears to have been a natural event without any sinister undertones.

Early the next morning, 11 January, news that Shastri had died was flashed around the world. The Soviets capped their excellent arrangements throughout the conference by ensuring that all the three national flags on the route from the city of Tashkent to the airport were flying at half-mast by the early morning. At the airport, after a gentle gesture from Kosygin, Ayub assisted Kosygin in lifting Shastri's coffin onto the aeroplane to return his body to India. The photograph of Ayub, looking sombre and moved, acting as a pall bearer for Shastri added to the sense of shock and outrage in Pakistan as the text of the Tashkent Declaration made clear that it was obviously a diplomatic defeat for Pakistan, since no solution to Kashmir had even been attempted, and the realisation that the war may have been in vain was dawning on the Pakistani people. This impression was only highlighted when Ayub returned to Pakistan and made no speech or public declaration on Tashkent, further raising suspicions that Ayub had come away with nothing and was embarrassed even to defend the outcome publicly.

FROM KUTCH TO TASHKENT

Review of Tashkent

The practical effect of the Tashkent Declaration was that Pakistan had agreed to effectively place the Kashmir issue on hold and deal with India on a host of practical outstanding issues which had to be resolved because of the war and in some cases in spite of it. The mutual exchange of prisoners and evacuation of territory were the immediate priorities, but the wider issues of mutual hostile propaganda were also to be dealt with, as well as an improvement of bilateral relations between India and Pakistan.

Many historians and commentators were puzzled by Ayub's last minute acceptance of the Soviet draft which had been largely unchanged since it was shown to Ayub on 6 January and rejected. Was Ayub merely bluffing at the time, hoping that the Soviets would then pressure the Indians into some concession on Kashmir but always intending to sign regardless, or did Ayub have a genuine change of heart when Kosygin was able to talk to him alone? It is of course very hard to say definitively as only Ayub himself could answer that question and he chose not to for obvious reasons. The indications are however that the former explanation is more likely, as Johnson had made it clear during Ayub's visit to Washington that the US fully supported the Soviet initiative and was not willing to expend any American diplomatic effort or goodwill on trying to change India's mind on Kashmir. Knowing this, Ayub knew that US aid would soon dry up if Pakistan remained on a collision course with India and was forced to use the Chinese threat in order to do so.

For Shastri, the equation was much simpler and successful. He had not been willing even to discuss any changes to the way ICK was run, and was willing to return to the pre-war borders but nothing else. That is precisely what he achieved, and his tragic death at the moment of his greatest triumph ensured that reaction to the decision to return Haji Pir Pass to Pakistan was now muted. There were some medium-sized demonstrations in

India to protest the handing back of certain territory to Pakistan, particularly the Haji Pir Pass, but these soon fizzled out as the realisation that India had managed to maintain its position in Kashmir, despite the war and some limited international pressure, caused the agreement to be viewed in India as a satisfactory result.

An immediate verdict on the Tashkent Declaration (as it was now known as the Pakistani delegation had refused to call it an agreement) was made by the US State Department on 11 January. It felt that the Declaration was 'more productive than had been expected'. Kosygin had played the role of the middleman and had managed to get the Indian and Pakistani delegations to (i) resolve to normalise relations, (ii) reaffirm obligations under the UN Charter to preserve peace, (iii) agree to withdraw all forces by 25 February. The important gain for Pakistan was perhaps a better relationship with the USSR, and although India had only had to concede a direct mention of the Kashmir issue, the biggest winner was seen as the USSR which would make 'much of its success'. The Soviets were seen as keen on limiting Chinese influence on Pakistan. The State Department noted that the Declaration did not reflect the full story as the reporters on the ground had thought the summit was sure to end in failure and there must have been strong Soviet pressure on both sides. It remained to be seen what inducements had been offered, but on the whole Western interests were seen as having been served by a more durable peace (11/1/66, State to Paris, POL 32–1 India-Pak NA).

However much Western interests may have been served by the Declaration, it did not appear to the population of Pakistan to have served their country's interests. On 13 January two students were killed in large and angry demonstrations in Lahore, and the chant 'Hume khoon ka jawab do' ('Give us an answer for the blood we have spilt') was a devastating new slogan on the streets of Pakistan. On 14 January the Ayub government was desperate enough to order the closure of all educational centres. Bhutto kept up a half-hearted public defence of the Tashkent Declaration, but the impression to the population at large was that Bhutto had not wanted to agree to the Declaration but Ayub had succumbed to international pressure and had surrendered on the negotiating table the hard fought victories of the battlefield.

Ayub tried to explain the reasoning behind the Tashkent Declaration at a cabinet meeting on 12 January to which the three heads of the armed forces were also invited. At the meeting Ayub said the Soviets had offered their good offices to try and resolve disputes between India and Pakistan, and although he 'had gone to Tashkent without any hope that the problem of Kashmir would be resolved' he had hoped that it would at least provide a framework in which India and Pakistan could live together. Ayub admitted that leaving Tashkent without any agreement would have meant 'rebuffing' the USSR, the USA and all the other countries who had supported the Tashkent initiative. This rebuff, according to Ayub, would have lead to greater Soviet intransigence in the UN, and a refusal by Pakistan to compromise would have led the world to blame Pakistan and 'encouraged extremist elements' inside the country—which may have been a reference to Bhutto and others who were seen as willing to walk away from Tashkent without an agreement. Pakistan had, according to Ayub, refused to sign a no-war pact, refused to give assurances on its dealings with China, managed to lower the tension in South Asia and built up a better Soviet understanding on Kashmir. Ayub also claimed that he had managed to persuade Kosygin of the necessity of trying to find a long-term resolution to the Kashmir issue. Bhutto was said to have remained silent throughout the meeting, and began to be viewed in time as the person who was keen to distance himself from the decision to agree to the ceasefire and the Tashkent Declaration (Gauhar, 394–6).

In fairness to Ayub, the superpowers had indeed decided both during and after the war that they had certain joint interests in

South Asia. Both were anxious to end the war as quickly as they could, both wanted to see India and Pakistan not to have another war any time soon, and crucially, both saw China as a destabilising factor in the region 'ranking the containment of Chinese influence as an overriding policy objective' (Cohen and Tucker (eds), 165).

Ayub had been left in no doubt after the visit to London and Washington in December 1965 that the West had washed its collective hands of Kashmir and the only option available to Ayub was to refuse the invitation to Tashkent or to walk away from there without an agreement, which would have resulted in diplomatic isolation, no military support from the US, and tacit US encouragement of Soviet support for India. Pakistan would have been left with the sole option of support from China, a country which in 1966 was still relatively poor, with no ability to provide economic or military aid to Pakistan on the scale of the US aid in the period from 1954 to 1965 and with none of the sophisticated military hardware that the US had supplied to Pakistan.

Faced with a military stalemate in which Pakistani tanks and aircraft had no spare parts and ammunition supplies were running low, Ayub was reminded many times after the ceasefire that he could not achieve on the diplomatic field what the army had failed to achieve on the battlefield. India held territory in Sialkot and near Lahore while Pakistan had few reserves and only a small portion of land on Indian territory at Khem Karan and some land in Chhamb since Grand Slam. In order to continue to fight with India in 1965, the Pakistan Army would have had to transform itself into a Chinese-style 'Red Army', a concept which the predominantly Sandhurst- or US-trained Pakistani senior military officers were simply not able or willing to contemplate. Tashkent was therefore the natural acceptance of the inevitable result of a war which had begun on a wing and a prayer, had been conducted with an all too successful propaganda campaign persuading Pakistanis that they were winning, and had ended with a declaration that neither resolved the Kashmir problem nor reduced tension between India and Pakistan.

More than anything, however, Tashkent demonstrated what few cards Ayub had left once the ceasefire was agreed without any Indian concession. As seen earlier, there was in fact little choice open to Ayub at that stage and continuing to fight would only have turned the war decisively in India's favour. However, once that principle was conceded, the resumption of war was not an even remotely serious option available to the Pakistan Army. Neither the Soviets nor the Americans were worried about China actually declaring war on India for Kashmir's sake. Pakistan's failure to win any major military victory or end the war with a strategic advantage meant it was simply not realistic to expect any Indian concession at Tashkent. That was the simple fact that Ayub grasped, but his own Information Ministry had misled much of the Pakistani public during the war to convince them that war would have been won had the fighting continued but in fact, inexplicably, Pakistan agreed to a ceasefire. That decision in itself was viewed with some patience as the feeling was still that India would have to concede some major points of principle during the peace talks. Once details of the Tashkent Declaration came out, it became obvious that nothing had changed. Slowly but surely the truth began to dawn: Pakistan had not won the war, and Tashkent merely reaffirmed that fact.

13

REFLECTIONS ON THE WAR

The American position reviewed

As the guns fell silent, the world began to take stock of the war and almost all the main players carried out reviews or commissioned accounts of the war in order to see what lessons could be learnt. A notable exception to this analytical process appears to have been Pakistan, whose government was less than enthusiastic about providing an account of the war. Given the background to and progress of the war, this was not too surprising, but it has been left to some senior Pakistani participants, both civilian and military to write their own accounts with, it has to be said, varying degrees of reliability. The reviews and insights provided by many of the Western observers at the time offer an invaluable glimpse into the motivations of the major players at the time.

One of the best insights into the mood within the White House during hostilities, was the account of Robert Komer, the National Security Adviser to Johnson and someone very much in the centre of the diplomatic action. In a detailed interview some years later Komer explained how at the outset of his relationship with Johnson—the then vice-president to Kennedy— he had been summoned by Johnson while on Air Force One to explain Kennedy's pro-India stance. Johnson had asked Komer:

'You know, I like Ayub. Ayub is a very good guy and those Indians are the worst people to deal with I've ever seen in my life. Why is Kennedy switching around to a more pro-Indian and less pro-Pakistani?' Komer had replied,

I like Ayub too and I think that any American who has ever had much to do with the Indians and the Pakistani ends up liking the Pakistani a hell of a lot more than the Indians. In the first place the Pakistani is the—their forbearers were the Aryan invaders of India so they're more western like us. And in the second place the Indian-Hindo philosophy is quite antithetical to our way of thinking whereas Mohammedism is much closer...you don't make foreign policy on the basis of who you like and who you don't like. Pakistan has a hundred million people. India has five hundred million people and if we're going to try and do something with South Asia as a counterweight to China, we had better look at India as first priority and not Pakistan which has one fifth the size'.

Komer said that the fact was that Pakistanis were 'much more presentable and, that they talked much more our lingo...the Pathans and Punjabis are tall upstanding guys and little Shastri come over dressed in his white habit, little high pitched voice. He doesn't look much...but sure the Paks are terribly likeable'. Komer went on to explain that the US had realised that Pakistan is 'interested in one thing—India and Kashmir, the whole Pakistani policy is centred around trying to find friends and big brothers as counter wedge to India. Well, we have no interest in helping Pakistan against India and we have a hell of a strategic interest in building up India against China as a counterweight'.

Johnson and Komer were said to have carried on this discussion for half an hour and eventually Johnson said, 'Well then I'm not sure I agree with you and I still think we've maybe gone overboard and we're not giving Ayub a fair deal but I want to tell you that that's a pretty doggone convincing explanation that you gave me'.

Komer went on to praise Johnson's cool response to the outbreak of war in 1965. He said that while the State

Department had been very worried about the possible outbreak of a general Asian war, Johnson's approach was that 'our policy will be a plague on both your houses' and the White House refused to be too drawn in to the war. Komer also said that by the end of the war it had been apparent to Johnson that 'my Indians beat his Paks, which I suspected surprised him more than it did me'. Komer said that he enjoyed telling Johnson every time they managed to catch Ayub out and in retaliation Johnson would often refer to Komer as 'that God-damn India lover Komer', which, Komer said, Johnson knew would hurt him.

Komer felt, even years later, that Ayub 'was the victim of bum advice' and conceded that he could see why Pakistan was upset with the US during the war, as the US had suddenly pulled the military plug. Komer said Johnson was uncomfortable with the decision as he felt that 'it was sort of two-timing a friend for reasons of national policy'. Komer went on to say that in his view Pakistan 'was conning' the US and although Johnson was 'very nice to Ayub and although he would repeat frequently his view on the Paks and how we were mistreating the Paks on policy and decisions he was down the line in what he thought was sensible...and his decisions were very cool, calm and collected...In fact he finally hung Ayub on several aid affairs'.

As far as Tashkent was concerned, Komer said 'We strongly encouraged the Paks and the Indians to settle this thing by compromise. Our cutting off military aid to both sides was a major reason for compromise. Ayub could see that if the war continued much longer that he was up the creek. He would run out of military resources. That was why he had to go to Tashkent'. Komer conceded that the cutting off of military aid turned out to be a 'pro-Indian gesture because it hurt the Paks much more than the Indians'.

On the subject of Tashkent, Komer was asked if Johnson minded that the Soviets claimed credit for the settlement. Komer said,

Quite the contrary. That was a deliberate policy of ours, approved by the President, that for once we would try and get the Soviets hooked into being in the middle and taking the onus for failure, taking heat— if possible—and if they got the thing settled, getting the bulk of the credit for it. I thought that was a very shrewd and astute move on our part. Not only did the President approve but I do not recall offhand any unhappiness on his part. It turned out quite a relief that getting the Soviets in there in the middle had managed to solve the thing. Now when the inside story of the Three Week War is written, I think people will find that the Americans had at least as much to do with pressuring or persuading both sides to lay off as the Russians. But our role was quiet and their role was the overt one, with whats-his-name (Kosygin) calling them to Tashkent etc...and patching up a compromise between Ayub and Shastri.

Komer recounted that the Johnson administration decided that it was not in the US interest to 'advance Pak interests vis-à-via India...even though many people were quite sympathetic with the Pakistani position on the thorny issue of Kashmir'. Despite this underlying sympathy, Komer said that the US had decided that 'we were going to disengage from the Kashmir issue too and not back the Pakistanis in their constant attempts to raise it again in the UN or in other forum or to get the Americans in the middle to force a compromise' (Robert W. Komer, AC 94–3 Oral History LBJ).

Dean Rusk, Secretary of State at that time, was also interviewed for the Johnson Presidential Library, and although Rusk had not played an overtly major role during the war—as Johnson decided that the US was not going to directly intervene in the war—he was inevitably a close observer. Rusk confirmed Komer's quoted comment that the US attitude in the war was one of 'plague on both your houses'. Rusk said that both India and Pakistan had 'allowed the matter to escalate very fast, on both sides, contrary to the advice that was being given to them by the United States so we in effect shrugged our shoulders and as good as said "Well, if you're going to fight, go ahead and fight but we're not going to pay for it". So we suspended our aid to both countries during that period and tried to express our disapproval of the struggle'. On Tashkent, Rusk again confirms Komer's view that the US was happy for the USSR to take the lead on this issue after the ceasefire:

We encouraged the Russians to go ahead with the Tashkent idea because we felt we had nothing to lose. If they succeeded in bringing about any detente at Tashkent then there would be more peace in the subcontinent between India and Pakistan and we would gain from that fact. If the Russians failed at Tashkent at least the Russians would have the experience of some of the frustration that we had had for twenty years in trying to sort out things between India and Pakistan.

Rusk said that prior to Tashkent he had even offered the Soviets, 'in a semi-joking way', all the paperwork the US had built up over twenty years in trying to resolve the issues (Dean Rusk III and IV, AC 74–425 Oral History LBJ).

Review of the High Commissioners to India and Pakistan

Substantive reviews of the war were written by the British High Commissioners to India and Pakistan, Freeman and James, and are well written and sufficiently interesting to deserve to be quoted at length. On 19 October 1965 Freeman's report on the war headed 'India and Pakistan: The Three Weeks War' was despatched to London. The summary of his report was that the British response to the Indian attack on Lahore had caused the British to be viewed by India as a 'semi-hostile nation'. India had sought British and US help in pressuring Pakistan to call off the infiltrators from Kashmir, but although few Kashmiris joined the infiltration, India was disappointed by the lack of international support and even the USSR did not condemn Pakistan for the infiltration in August 1965. Communal relations within India had remained good despite the war. The lack of open British support in the face of Chinese threats had not gone down well in India; the Indian view was that the mere fact that Britain believed there was a Kashmir dispute to be resolved made it pro-Pakistan. The Pakistan government's technique of the 'Big Lie' contrasted with India's poor public relations presentation, which allowed 'the calculated decision on the part of Pakistan to use force to resolve a political dispute to pass uncondemned and unchallenged by the world and in particular by Britain'.

It seemed 'ironical' to Freeman that 'the professional soldier' Ayub had received a major military setback from 'that most unmilitary of leaders', Shastri. Nimmo had confirmed the basic Indian charge of the infiltration and documents captured from some of the infiltrators showed that the plan was hatched in May 1965. India's actions in Kashmir in August were designed to stop the infiltrators and safeguard Indian communication lines, but the Pakistan Army had responded with an armoured thrust against ICK in Kargil, Tithwal and Uri-Poonch. Freeman pointed out that if Pakistan had captured Akhnur, which was very close to Jammu, and in turn had the only road from India to the Valley, 'it would have been a strategic disaster for India'. The Indians had hoped that a Labour prime minister would be pro-Indian but Wilson's tone had shocked the Indian establishment, and the additional British request that its arms should not be used against Pakistan had not gone down well, particularly as the US had made no request to Pakistan regarding its arms and the suspension of export licences also raised questions regarding Britain's reliability as a supplier.

Pakistan was seen as having a 'superior publicity machine' and British criticism of civilian bombing seemed to have no foundation in fact as both sides avoided cities as targets. India had adhered to its pledge not to attack East Pakistan, in response to Washington's request on 10 September. The Chinese threat on 16 September had led to both Soviet and US warnings to China but the British had remained muted and the Indians were seriously concerned by the Chinese threat; the real fear was of a Chinese move in Ladakh with a large Pathan infiltration into Skardu. British generosity in 1962 had led to close British/Indian relations which the recent war had now badly damaged, and the fact that the British argued for a Kashmir solution made it look as if Britain was taking Pakistan's side. India had not been pleased by British references to 'the underlying political problem' but was satisfied by the reference to the 5 August infiltration. The war had changed India's perception of Kashmir by revealing that Pakistan was not only prepared to use force, it was also now in collaboration with China. Freeman said that the British approach to the conflict had been based on three factors:

a) 'Disgust at the squalid method of the Maharaja's original accession to India' and the feeling that the majority of Kashmiris wanted to be part of Pakistan.
b) Belief in the principle of self determination.
c) Pakistan's pro-West foreign policy compared with India's non-alignment.

Freeman said that the British had never openly challenged the Maharaja's accession and 'it is late in the day to do so now', and that the reality was that Britain could not afford to take a neutral position in the subcontinent as it had vital interests there. He said that if Britain had to choose sides in the subcontinent, then it would have to be India, which possessed 'four-fifths of the population and resources of the subcontinent'. Freeman said that in the past the British assumption had been that Pakistan was not only morally but also militarily stronger, but that the military assumption was now invalid and the moral one was now more 'open to argument than we have usually admitted'. The new reality was that India would never give up the Valley and Pakistan did not have the military power to force this to happen. The peace settlement would have to be in India's favour as Pakistan had tried to resolve the issue by force and had 'demonstrably failed'. Freeman said that he was aware that such a policy might tilt Pakistan even further towards China, but it was obvious that China could not offer the same level of development aid as the West to Pakistan. Freeman ended by recognising that this assessment and these recommendations were 'controversial' and amounted to a recommendation for a major shift in British policy (19/10/65, Freeman to CRO, Memo DO 196/387 PRO).

The next day James delivered his report on the war, entitled 'Pakistan and Kashmir: A Tragic Misadventure'. The summary was that Pakistan had been in a 'truculent and self-confident mood' in the summer of 1965, with the Indian government under Shastri being viewed with 'increasing contempt'. Bhutto was singled out by James as having led a group of 'adventurists' into persuading Ayub that military action in Kashmir was necessary and the plan for an armed insurrection had 'great appeal' amongst military and civil officers. Pakistani success in the Kutch skirmishes had finally convinced Ayub of the chance of success. Although the war had succeeded in focusing world attention on Kashmir with many more countries openly sympathetic to Pakistan's position than to India's, by the end of the war it was India's position which was stronger diplomatically and militarily. Pakistan had managed to miscalculate 'the effects of their actions on all other parties involved without exception' and Ayub's government was now in a 'blind alley' as its actions had made a Kashmir resolution harder. The Pakistani public had been misled in the run-up to and during the war and believed it had won. James believed that Ayub's position would become very difficult once the people realised this was not so and Ayub would therefore be forced either to make the West 'the scapegoat or resume the war', and so James recommended that Britain should continue to support Ayub as 'despite his deficiencies, he is still the West's best bet'. His recommendation was that Britain should assist in the Security Council, to ensure that diplomacy was given a chance, provide economic aid to Pakistan and try to ensure that the US did not decide 'to shut up shop in Pakistan'.

James believed that if the West was to move from a vaguely sympathetic position towards Pakistan and to begin instead to support India's position on Kashmir, it would lose all influence in Pakistan as Pakistan would never accept 'overwhelming inferiority to India' and would be forced to look to other patrons—which would be either the USSR or China. The High Commissioner recalled that Ayub had first met Shastri in October 1964 and ever since then had 'spoken of him in terms of the greatest disrespect'. As far as the Kashmir plan was concerned, James felt this to be the 'brainchild' of Bhutto and Aziz Ahmed and these two men were seen as 'different in character and ambition but united in their reckless resolve that Pakistan should acquire Kashmir'. James said it was a measure of both these men's shortcomings that even after the war was over, they did not appear to appreciate 'how appalling the risks were' into which their 'bad advice' had led the country. The two men's thought processes were seen by James as 'visceral rather than cerebral'. The rationale of the Pakistan foreign ministry seemed in James' opinion to be: (i) the chances of India giving up Kashmir peacefully were almost zero, (ii) the Security Council members were not interested in forcing a resolution to the issue, (iii) if a military solution was to be sought, then it had to be quickly as US military aid to Pakistan was tapering off, India's military strength was increasing and India had even talked of a nuclear weapon, (iv) with Chinese help, Pakistan could use a guerrilla force in Kashmir and at the same time, Chinese threats would ensure a large part of the Indian Army would be tied down, (v) Pakistan's recent attempts at reaching out to the non-aligned movement had ensured a more sympathetic response from Afro-Asian countries.

James felt that the plan had 'enormous intrinsic attraction' for Pakistanis as it 'appealed to their impulsive, unreflecting, pugnacious temperament', and although Ayub was seen by James as having a good grasp of dealing with people like himself, where he was 'confident and decisive', when faced with unfamiliar situations, he tended to 'flounder and fumble'. James felt the situation had resembled Shakespeare's play *Othello* with Ayub as the Moor and Aziz Ahmed as Iago. The fighting and subsequent ceasefire in Kutch, ending with India's willingness to accept outside mediation, had persuaded Ayub that his army could 'thrash the Indians'. The threat of an all-out war in the subcontinent (possibly involving China) would mean the Indians would be leant upon by the Western powers to abandon their hard line on Kashmir and this, coupled with Pakistan's predicted military edge, would force a settlement on Pakistan's terms.

The aims of the war seemed vague to James; indeed, a precise aim would, according to James, need 'calculation and forethought', which would itself have been uncharacteristic of the Pakistan government. However, as long as the fighting was confined to Kashmir, Pakistan had nothing to lose as if things went according to plan; there would be a large-scale uprising inside ICK, China would neutralise India's overall strength and Pakistan could dictate terms. Even if it went badly, the 'revolt' would at least focus world attention on Kashmir and persuade the world powers to try and seek a long-term solution. What the Pakistan government had not grasped was that nationalism and chauvinism in India had reached a level where no government there could hope to survive if a large portion of Kashmir was given away or lost. The US was the only power with sufficient strength and leverage to bring about a change in India's attitude and its failure to do so had strained US/Pakistan relations even before the war had begun and they had deteriorated even further during the war. US goodwill to Pakistan now seemed 'all but exhausted'. In purely military terms Pakistan was far worse off than before the war and although India's losses might well be larger, the fact was that Pakistan was almost exclusively dependent on US weapons meant its badly depleted supplies were going to be difficult to replace. Indian Army morale was also raised as it was no 'longer disturbed by the prospect of fighting Pakistanis'.

James blamed Pakistan's ultimate failure on the fact that it 'totally miscalculated' the effects of its actions. The Kashmiris did not revolt when they had been expected to do so, the Indians had reacted toughly by attacking Lahore, and the West had stayed out of the conflict. The Chinese were seen as offering a 'Faustian pact' to Pakistan as a price for their support, a pact which Bhutto was seen as willing to make, but a formal alliance with China and a break with the US was a step too far for Ayub. James felt that no-one could believe that China's actions had benefited Pakistan, but had instead raised the possibility of a nuclear war in Asia, which meant that 'any trace of especial favour towards Pakistan in Washington (and especially the White House) had by now entirely disappeared'. James described the mood in Pakistan during the war itself as 'jingoistic euphoria', and that feeling was strengthened by the hardship of the war. That prevailing mood left Ayub in an 'unenviable predicament' when the Security Council demanded a ceasefire on 20 September. The UN Resolution gave only the smallest comfort to Pakistan and did not mention the possibility of a plebiscite, much less guarantee one. Ayub wondered whether he could survive in Pakistan if he accepted the terms offered and indeed had informed the Iranian ambassador that he 'would be lynched' if he agreed.

However, Ayub was forced to face up to the fact that by 20 September India was in an overwhelmingly stronger military position, and the US had let it been known clearly that if Pakistan was seen as having encouraged China to intervene, there would be a total cut-off of US aid. Ayub had therefore managed to sell the ceasefire 'with difficulty' to the public by presenting it as a 'magnanimous but strictly temporary concession to the United

Nations' with the expectation that India would now finally be forced to make some real concessions on Kashmir. James felt that Ayub's position would deteriorate as 'the truth becomes apparent' and Ayub gave the impression of a deeply worried man. Ayub had disappeared from the public view and in private 'appeared a shadow of his former robust and confident self'. James hoped that Ayub would realise the 'full bankruptcy' of Bhutto's advice, but Bhutto's obvious opposition to the ceasefire had made him popular amongst students and the intelligentsia who opposed Ayub. James said Bhutto's 'charm and forensic brilliance' meant that even Ayub recognised he was Pakistan's 'best public relations officer', and so Bhutto might survive as he was needed by Ayub.

In the immediate term, James felt that Pakistan would simply have to hope against hope that a diplomatic solution would transpire for Kashmir, and apart from the UN, the Soviet offer of a summit of the two leaders under their auspices was open. A cut-off of US aid would assist in persuading Pakistan to start 'sane thinking' but as Bhutto and Aziz Ahmed were still in charge and even 'well-educated Pakistanis in responsible positions now talk in the most wild and irrational terms', the West should not abandon Pakistan or Ayub. The high Commissioner believed that the West had to help Ayub survice the crisis as the result would be that the West would be made a scapegoat for ending the war and/or there would be a resumption of the war. James said there was no alternative to the Ayub regime for the 'turbulent and boneheaded people' of Pakistan. He said Britain had to reassure Pakistan that it still supported a solution to the Kashmir issue and it also needed to work closely with the US to maintain this as a Western position. James and McConaughy had worked very closely together in the run-up to the ceasefire and were in 'absolute harmony' diplomatically despite US patience having been tested by a campaign of 'vitriolic nastiness' towards McConaughy and his staff within.

James said that he had read Freeman's recommendations, and although he accepted that a reappraisal of the British position on Kashmir might be needed, it should not be rushed and the UK should be under no illusions about the results of the adoption of the proposed new policy. The Freeman recommendations would lead to the end of British influence in Pakistan, as Pakistan would view its relations with Britain as 'having no further value', and James believed that it would cause 'our material assets to be harried out of existence'. This can only be an allusion to Western/British military/intelligence bases inside Pakistan. If the US cut off aid, Pakistan was so determined to keep some parity with India that it would be prepared to look to either the USSR or China in order to obtain the weapons it needed. James strongly recommended that the best policy was therefore to keep aid, both military and economic, flowing, with military aid limited to just enough to provide self-defence to both nations. James said that although Pakistan realised it could not defeat India alone, a war with China involved with Pakistan remained a 'grim possibility', and it was this threat that should persuade India to negotiate seriously on Kashmir. It was on that point alone, James was hopeful there might still be a chance of diplomatic settlement (25/1065, James to CRO, Memo of War, DO 196/388 PRO).

Reflections from Pakistan

As the decision to go to war over Kashmir was taken in Pakistan and Pakistan had the advantage of surprise as well as the luxury of being able to plan ahead, the failure of the Pakistani plans to succeed needs to be examined.

Although the war was relatively short, its impact (as with all wars) was far-reaching, but before the impact is assessed, it is necessary to review the crucial decisions from planning to execution from a Pakistani perspective.

The decision to use force to resolve the Kashmir issue in Pakistan's favour was one that was gathering momentum in Pakistan since early 1965. The official decision to use force can be dated from 13 May 1965 when Ayub approved the plans for Gibraltar and Grand Slam. From that day, Pakistan had, in effect, committed itself to send thousands of armed men into ICK in order to both create and direct trouble for the Indian forces based there. Grand Slam was directed at the capture of the strategic town of Akhnur and the approval was given by Ayub personally with the conviction that neither of these actions would lead to all-out war with India. This was to prove the first fundamentally flawed premise, and was so shockingly poor a decision as to merit further discussion. Once the war was over, many generals and senior government figures blamed Bhutto and his Foreign Ministry for the repeated assurances that Indian troops would not cross the international border. Bhutto defended himself by pointing out that even if that was his assurance, many in the Pakistani military establishment had agreed with this assessment at the time and the ultimate decision was one for Ayub to take. The point is fair and Ayub cannot, as both effective head of the armed forces and president, shirk his responsibility for taking the decision based on this premise.

The second fundamental error Ayub made in the execution of the war was to commit only to a limited military action. This in many ways is related to the first error; as an intrinsic and critical part of the planning for Gibraltar and Grand Slam was based on Ayub's fervent and genuine desire to avoid all-out war with India, which meant that military planning was restricted and cautious. If Malik had been allowed to take Akhnur and had then been been permitted to continue to lead the armoured thrust towards Jammu or indeed lead an armoured attack straight on Jammu from Sialkot on 25 August, there is a very real chance that Malik would have succeeded and India would then, as Freeman later said, have been facing a 'strategic disaster'. Despite India's larger number of troops inside ICK and Punjab, the strategically vital route from Sialkot to Jammu would have been very difficult for India to defend, Pakistan would have been in a strong military position and as a result would have been able to force India to contemplate some form of compromise on Kashmir.

Thirdly, even if Ayub and the Pakistani establishment were convinced that India would not launch a counter-attack across the international border following Grand Slam, any responsible plan should have contained at least some preparation for such an eventuality. Pakistan needed to warn its front line commanders on the Punjab front to prepare for a possible Indian military response to such an offensive. Any prudent and sensible plan should have allowed for that possibility and made it an intrinsic element of Grand Slam that the Pakistani units on the Punjab border should have been on full alert from the moment Gibraltar was under way or, at the very latest, when Grand Slam was commenced.

As noted by many close observers, Ayub was crudely dismissive of both the Indian Army and its prime minister, and while it is true that Indian forces had not distinguished themselves in either the war with China in 1962 or the fighting in Kutch in early 1965, the conclusions drawn by Pakistan were misleading. Those had been limited campaigns in which India was fighting at a strategic disadvantage and was caught off guard. India had much larger military resources and reserves than Pakistan and an ability to fight for much longer and on more fronts. Ayub's contemptuous attitude towards both Shastri and the Indian Army meant that he seriously misjudged and underestimated the Indian Army's ability and capacity to fight. Although it may have been true that Pakistan inflicted larger casualties on India than vice versa, it is also true that when it mattered, as with the battles around Asal Uttar, Indian troops fought well and bravely and proved to be a match for the better equipped Pakistani forces. Responding with irritation on being lectured by Pakistan, before the war, that the British did not understand the 'Hindu mentality', James was able to respond by pointing out that 'we understood it sufficiently to be certain that the attack on Akhnur would bring the Indians into Punjab'. This miscalculation was to prove almost fatal as Lahore was poorly defended and unprepared until the Indian troops had almost reached the outskirts of the city. Ayub and the Pakistani military have to shoulder the responsibility for this lack of preparation and planning due to his and GHQ's directions. For the Pakistani troops to have been caught napping (literally in some cases) was a collective and inexcusable failure of Pakistani military planning.

The fourth fundamental error was lack of military planning for a sustained military conflict. Even if Ayub was deluded enough to imagine that India would not respond to Grand Slam, given the history of tension between the two countries since independence in 1947, an all-out and sustained war was always a possibility, especially with Pakistani artillery and armour sent on their way to Akhnur on 1 September. The lack of planning for a war of more than a few weeks meant that when India did counter-attack by launching Riddle and Nepal, Pakistan had only between three and four weeks' supply of spare parts and ammunition to fight an all-out war. Ayub had been Commander-in-Chief of the Pakistan Army from 1951 and was still the effective head in 1965 as well as being one of the architects of Pakistan's military pacts with the USA. He therefore should and must have known better than anyone that the level of military aid from the US was only designed to provide Pakistan with a few weeks of ammunition as a holding position until international military aid arrived. In addition, Ayub must have been fully aware that Pakistan was wholly dependent on the US for military supplies and spare parts. There was very little indigenous military production or readily available arms purchases from other countries, which meant that a possible US decision to cut off the supply of arms and spare parts would mean Pakistan fighting a war with ammunition and supplies being irreplaceably depleted on a daily basis. Every day of the war meant depleted ammunition supplies, every tank or aircraft damage meant a depletion of spare parts and therefore a reduced capacity to fight. This was soon to take a far heavier toll on Pakistan's ability to fight than on India's.

The fifth error made by Pakistan was to completely miscalculate the international reaction. The predictability of the Indian response has already been discussed, but in addition Ayub had either not thought through the likely reaction of other countries and the implications of a negative reaction or he had completely misjudged them. Although Ayub was persuaded of the need to build up a good relationship with China by 1964 and also to improve the almost previously non-existent relations with the USSR, this was done mainly at the cost of losing American goodwill—and in 1965 the US was Pakistan's only military supplier. Whilst few would argue with the principle of Pakistan seeking new alliances and lessening its over-dependence on the US, for Ayub to have been able to stand up to American anger at his friendship with China, Pakistan should have first been absolutely sure that China would in fact be willing and able to replace the US as a source of military aid. As China was Pakistan's northern neighbour, Pakistan should have taken China into its confidence before any military planning was finalised and asked for Chinese assurances on assistance before any steps were taken rather than after. The failure to do so not only irritated the normally diplomatic Chinese, it also tied Chinese hands and limited what aid they could provide at short notice. Asghar Khan was despatched by Ayub to the Far East on a mission to request military aid only after fighting had broken out. He was politely informed by the Chinese that such a request had to come from Ayub himself. Given the far greater Chinese military expertise after holding the Americans to a draw in Korea and more recently having defeated India, Pakistan should, at the very least have had the benefit of Chinese advice before the war.

Instead, Ayub's decision again ensured the worst of both worlds for Pakistan during the war: American irritation to the point where all arms supplies to Pakistan were cut off, but with no Chinese weapons which could have replaced American arms and enabled Pakistan to fight on. Although China was publicly supportive of Pakistan's aims during the war and provided it with valuable diplomatic and strategic breathing space in threatening India, the Chinese threat was effectively neutralised by the two superpowers warning China not to enter the war. India may have felt uncomfortable at the Chinese threat but it was assured by both the USA and the USSR that any Chinese entry into the war was adamantly opposed and would be contained. The China factor was therefore probably more a tactical weapon for Pakistan than a serious threat to India.

Perhaps most seriously, the US response was also completely miscalculated. Not only was Johnson furious with Ayub for starting a war in Asia when the military conflict in Vietnam was preoccupying America, it also meant that China, the American enemy in both Korea and Vietnam, was now threatening India, the new American bulwark against communist expansion. Ayub was sorely mistaken if he imagined that the US would allow a Chinese attack on India to happen without American support for India. With the possiblility of China opening up hostilities with India there was even a theoretical risk of Pakistan indirectly fighting a war against the USA. That was a scenario that Ayub did not even wish to contemplate, and during his secret visit to China on 19/20 September, Ayub does not appear to have asked the Chinese to take any military action in support of Pakistan. Not only were the Chinese highly unlikely to enter the war directly, but, it would have meant an irreparable rupture to relations with the US and would have put Pakistan on a collision course with the USSR as well.

The above list of critical errors meant that Pakistan's only chance in this war was, despite these mistakes, either to capture a strategically vital point such as Jammu or to inflict a heavy military defeat on the Indian Army. In the event, neither was possible during the war, owing to a combination of poor leadership and lack of ambition. Although Pakistan came close to capturing Akhnur, there is serious doubt, once Malik was replaced, whether Yahya intended to capture or simply to threaten the town. In the event the hesitation proved fatal and the final ignominy for Pakistan was the failure of Mailed Fist by 10 September. After that date, India was on the offensive and Pakistan was fast running out of supplies and options despite some local counter-attacks and talk of a long war with Chinese help. Although Pakistan initially resisted the UN ceasefire call and later held out against the Tashkent Declaration, the USA and USSR both knew that Pakistan had no other option. The myth that Pakistan was somehow in a winning position on 22 September does not stand up to scrutiny and Ayub knew it. The simple fact is that Pakistan was fast running out of military spare parts and ammunition and by the end of September would have been unable to put up any meaningful resistance which would have put India in a position to force Pakistan to surrender. After the war, owing to its inconclusive end, with neither side able to claim an obvious outright victory, the Pakistani public reaction was incredulity that its army had stopped short of pressing home its allegedly strong position. The Pakistani people had been roused by the government but now they needed placating. Having initiated the war and having claimed victory after victory on the battlefield, Ayub could, never admit how close Pakistan had come to losing outright and how Pakistan had little choice but to agree to a ceasefire and to the wording of the Tashkent Declaration. The deception was dangerous and ultimately self-defeating, but entirely one of Ayub's own creation.

Reflections from India

Although India had come out of the war relatively unscathed and with its rather battered military reputation enhanced, there were some important lessons that thoughtful observers felt that India should heed.

First, the fact that there was a military conflict in Kashmir in 1965 at all was at least partly India's fault. It was India that imposed a military solution in 1947 by sending its troops to Srinagar and forcing the Maharaja to accede to India in a manner which even the British described as 'squalid'. India's indignation at Pakistan using force in 1965 smacked of hypocrisy given that India had used superior arms to ensure that a large portion of the state of Jammu and Kashmir was under Indian control by the end of 1947. Pakistan could therefore argue with some justification that Indian outrage in 1965 was simply a display of double standards as not only had India acquired Srinagar and surrounding areas by force, it had also held on to them using force from 1947 to 1965.

Most neutral observers had believed in 1965 that India had no moral high ground on the Kashmir question and it was only the simple reason of not wanting to offend India that prevented many governments from saying so publicly. The UN observers inside ICK in 1965 described the Indian troops' behaviour during the war as similar to that of the Germans in the Balkans during World War II. While that appears to be an exaggeration, it was still sobering for India to realise that during the war it was viewed by an overwhelming majority of countries in the UN as effectively an occupying power in Kashmir. The official Indian line that Kashmir had willingly acceded to India was not given widespread international credibility, and it was mainly thanks to its close relationship with the USSR that it was given diplomatic cover in the UN Security Council, while it was a large enough country to escape serious international pressure. Indian diplomats were shocked to discover at the UN how unpopular India's stance on Kashmir was in the world community, when the majority of countries either sided with Pakistan or maintained a diplomatic silence during the war.

India had not improved its standing in Kashmir by the attitude it displayed towards the wishes of the local population and its obvious reluctance to hold a plebiscite, despite early explicit promises to do so. Sheikh Abdullah was initially described by Nehru as the authentic voice of the Kashmiris and then arrested and detained without trial for many years. It was generally accepted that popular sentiment inside Kashmir was either pro-Pakistan or pro-independence and whatever the lack of Kashmiri response to Gibraltar, the fact remains that India was only able to maintain its hold on Kashmir because of its military strength rather than the wishes of the Kashmiri people. Whatever Indian diplomats and politicians maintained publicly, the pledge to hold a plebiscite was also dropped by India for the simple reason that the Indian government was aware that it was almost certain to lose on the simple question of whether the Kashmiris wished to join India or Pakistan.

From a military point of view, there is also little doubt that India was also caught off guard by Grand Slam, which is surprising given Pakistan's military build-up in the decade from 1954 to 1964 with the aid of some sophisticated US weapons. The disturbances inside Kashmir in 1964 were serious and most observers could see that Pakistan might have a military crack at ICK given the seemingly opportune political and military situation. Later Indian generals and politicians have admitted this failing, and had Pakistan been bolder and better prepared, India would have found itself in real difficulty through a lack of military intelligence and political alienation within ICK. It was due to the ineptness of the enemy rather than any good planning that India was able to hold off Pakistani offensives.

Thirdly, although India's army had given a far better account of itself during the 1965 war as opposed to the 1962 war, there were some embarrassing incidents such as field guns being abandoned during Grand Slam and even senior commanders losing their nerve at critical times. However, it is to the credit of the Indian Army that despite being wrong-footed on a number of occasions, there were enough checks and balances within the Indian establishment to ensure that heads did roll when necessary and that politicians of all hues were able to work together during the war.

The old adage of the worst democracy being a better system of government than the best dictatorship was shown during the war to have more than an element of truth to it. Ayub had developed a relatively benign autocracy and built up a powerful fighting force; however, the lack of accountability and serious debate meant that some incompetent and unsuitable Pakistani generals not only kept their jobs during and after the war, but some were even promoted. By contrast, the Indian Prime Minister and Defence Minister never lost control of the army high command and the lively Indian parliament in turn kept its ministers vigilant and relatively open.

In the final analysis of India's performance during the war, the Indians did enough not to lose the war. Indian generals were later criticised in some quarters for their inability to defeat a smaller enemy and their lack of a killer instinct. The results of Indian offensives were less than impressive and notably unsuccessful given that India had the numbers and advantages of plentiful supplies to have pushed for military victory. The fact that they did not do so was due to poor leadership and tactics, but it should not be forgotten that the Indian army did manage to blunt Pakistan's armoured attack with some brave and imaginative defensive work. The bogey of US-made Pakistani armour and artillery now rapidly receded from Indian military minds, to the extent that they recognised that Pakistan was now only going to fall further and further behind India in the future military balance.

Pakistani and Indian leadership during the war

Despite Ayub's large, not to say critical role in planning, approving and directing the war from the outset, he was very fortunate not to be blamed by his Western allies and friends either for the outbreak of the war or for the unofficial alliance with China, as much as one might expect. Even Komer, one of Ayub's main critics, felt that Ayub had been led astray by extreme factions within Pakistan such as Bhutto and other hawks. Ayub was seen as the victim rather than the lead role, and hence it was Bhutto's removal that Johnson appeared to demand during Ayub's visit to Washington following the war as a sign that Ayub was serious about maintaining a pro-Western line. Ayub, however, appeared to have been personally affected by the miscalculations and errors and was a shadow of himself following the ceasefire. Many years after the war, a former Pakistani cabinet member asked Ayub if he had not debated the advantages and disadvantages of war with his inner circle, if only to see what potential weaknesses existed in the 1965 war plans; Ayub was reported to have groaned and asked not to be repeatedly pressed on his 'weakest spot' (Choudhury, *The Last Days*, 20).

Being a more adroit politician than Ayub, Bhutto used rhetoric and the language of defiance, however unrealistic it increasingly became and seemingly oblivious of his own role in placing Pakistan in what rapidly became a precarious position. Bhutto's speech in the UN accepting the ceasefire resolution should have been a humiliation for him; Pakistan was accepting a ceasefire without any Indian concession on Kashmir and no promise from the Western powers to apply any meaningful pressure. These were the terms that Bhutto had scornfully rejected many times in the last three weeks, and yet he was sent to the UN to accept those precise terms and did so. Yet his speech, which may have gone down badly in the UN assembly and amongst neutrals, thrilled the Pakistan public with its tone of defiance and pride. Bhutto was then to endure the American cold shoulder during Ayub's visit to Washington and was sidelined in Tashkent. His public demeanour, his obvious disagreement with Ayub and deliberate snubs of his Indian counterparts went down well with his domestic audience and he was able in the final event not only to distance himself from his own incorrect assurances regarding the war but in fact to become the leader of the nationalist mood sweeping Pakistan. In the post-war phase Bhutto's rhetoric was far more popular than Ayub's pragmatism. Within a few years it was Bhutto who was prime minister of Pakistan and Ayub was forced into a quiet but ignominious retirement.

Unsurprisingly, Shastri's stock rose as a result of the war, an outcome that few could have predicted as he had inherited a nation still coming to terms with the death of Nehru and was viewed by many even within his own party as a stopgap prime minister who would merely tide things along until a suitable replacement could be found. With his short stature and high pitched voice, Shastri was viewed with a mixture of contempt and ridicule by Ayub, who often judged people on physical appearances rather than character. Shastri proved to be not only firm under extreme pressure but also an adroit politician who ensured that he kept even the opposition parties on board during the war and even in the Tashkent negotiations. Although there was some criticism of Shastri's decision to return the Haji Pir Pass to Pakistan after the war, most Indians recognised that it was the price of peace and probably a small price for not conceding an inch on the issue of ICK. Shastri's death at the moment of his greatest triumph robbed him of the opportunity to explain his reasons in person and to bask in the glory of a successful war and a very satisfactory peace conference. The only major failing to be laid at the door of Shastri was the degree of official complacency as regards the situation inside Kashmir in 1965. Not only were thousands of Pakistani infiltrators able to enter ICK without any alarm from the border guards, there were regular public statements from Indian ministers that there was no need for any concern regarding the internal situation within ICK. However ill prepared the Pakistani guerrilla force may have been, the fact that many thousands of them were able to last so long behind enemy lines must have been due, at least in part, to a large degree of co-operation from the local population. That in turn indicates a high level of disenchantment with Indian rule from within ICK and the ultimate responsibility for this state of affairs lies squarely with Nehru and the Indian governments since 1947.

The other members of the Indian government came out with varying degrees of credibility. The key portfolios of Defence and Foreign Affairs were handled competently if not with any degree of flair. The Indian Foreign Ministry in particular came in for criticism from opposition politicians and sections of the Indian media when it was discovered how few countries in the world were prepared to support India's position on the war when it was in full swing. Although this was blamed by the Indian government on a failure of communication rather than lack of sympathy, it was being either disingenuous or delusional.

Military ebbs and flows

The war had an unusual beginning if one is to include Grand Slam as the opening salvo, as Pakistan was acting with caution and restraint rather than launching an all-out assault designed to deliver a knockout blow and win the war. 1 September saw Pakistan move quickly in the Chhamb region, but barely 24 hours later the general who had planned and executed the first phase of the operation was removed from his command and the next commander moved at a pace which indicated he had been ordered not to capture Akhnur, but merely to threaten it. The change of command by Ayub on the afternoon of 2 September was effectively ignored by the Indians and they were unimpressed with the fact that Pakistani forces were still inside ICK. The Indian army therefore launched Riddle on 6 September and although it took Pakistan by surprise (for almost inexplicable reasons discussed above), it was a military failure in terms of its wider objectives. It was soon stopped in its tracks by a smaller and initially off-balance Pakistani force. Pakistan in turn launched a major counter-attack with Mailed Fist by 8 September, but its failure, which was apparent by the evening of 10 September, meant that all attention was on the Indian offensive in the Sialkot area. That too did not go according to plan for India as although some territory was captured, the offensive did not inflict any serious damage on the Pakistan Army, so when the repeated attempts to capture Chawinda failed, India was ready to accept the call for a ceasefire.

Air power, although used during the war, was not a critical factor and there was poor use of it by both sides, but the PAF provided useful cover to its army and ensured that the Indians did not have air superiority. The relatively small size of the PAF and the lack of spare parts meant that it had to be used sparingly and with caution by Pakistan, and the IAF suffered losses through poor planning, older aircraft and occasionally through a lack of basic defences. The PAF is very proud of its role during the war and the service ended the war with its reputation in Pakistan much enhanced, but its role was essentially defensive and in support of the army. The PAF was never designed for nor capable of delivering any fearsome blows to the IAF, and the US arms embargo meant that the PAF had to be even more cautious than its smaller size dictated, for fear of damaged aircraft being unusable. The IAF performed poorly and even failed in its support role to Indian front line soldiers, and allowed itself to be over cautious to the extent of being ineffectual.

The fighting was in many ways limited both in territory and in scope and was not an all-out war to the finish as many had initially feared. The most obvious restraint was that shown by India by not attacking East Pakistan, where India would have almost certainly enjoyed an easy victory given the disparity of forces in that region. It appears that this restraint was not purely charitable but due to an assurance sought by the US on 10 September, as America feared that an Indian attack on East Pakistan could well result in China entering the war. It was therefore more the fear of China entering the war, if India moved into East Pakistan, and US pressure that ensured that the Bengal front was relatively quiet during the war.

The second restraint was the lack of civilian casualties on both sides and a lack of urban bombing. Both countries restricted their air forces to military targets and it goes to the credit of both governments that civilian casualties were low during the war. Given the recent horrors of civilian bombing in Europe during World War II, this was a commendable decision as such bombing would have served no military purpose and could well have inflamed communal violence in India.

Thirdly, both sides observed the Geneva Convention and the bodies of solders were returned to opposing armies with full military honours; and prisoners of war were generally treated well and in accordance with international law. Given the breakdown of communal relations in 1947, this again was a relief and both sides deserve credit for maintaining a disciplined and honourable record of military conduct during the war.

In summary, therefore, the war quickly became attritional with neither side able to deliver a knockout blow and a military stalemate ensuing after a few weeks of fierce fighting. One British magazine said after the second week of fighting that 'it is not much of a war. Whether this is a result of political intent or military inefficiency is not clear' (*The Economist*, 18 September 1965).

Although India was the eventual victor by the fact that it had a large number of troops inside substantial Pakistani territory, the US saw it as an 'uninspiring' victory as India, despite its much larger numbers and supplies, was unable to defeat Pakistan in any battle, except for holding the line in the crucial battle of Asal Uttar. Other than that, India's offensives generally failed and a combination of inexperience in large-scale battle manoeuvres and poor application meant that India's forces tended to resemble a large elephant—of an impressive size, but slow in responding and less effective on the battlefield than previously thought. Pakistan's armoured division was similarly unable to have the effect Ayub and GHQ in Rawalpindi had hoped for, again through poor leadership, and the tank losses were heavy enough to leave a real defensive weakness in that area for years to come.

When the fog and noise of war cleared, medals were awarded, bodies buried and Tashkent signed, India and Pakistan were exactly in the same positions geographically as before the war. That appears to imply that nothing changed because of the war—which would be a highly misleading conclusion to draw. The war badly damaged Pakistan's close relationship with the US, which was not to be rekindled until 1979 when the Soviet Union invaded Afghanistan. This meant that Pakistan was no longer the recipient of large-scale US military and financial aid, and in the absence of any other donor being able to fill that gap, both the economy and—from a military point of view, even worse—the army were for years unable to make up the losses from the war. This in turn damaged the Pakistan Army's ability to fight, to the extent that India was now confident enough to start planning its own war. In 1971 the Indian Army swept into East Pakistan to help create the state of Bangladesh and faced no serious Pakistani threat even on the Kashmir/Punjab border. Ayub's unpopularity and Bhutto's corresponding popularity meant that in 1969 Ayub was forced out and Bhutto was the prime minister of Pakistan by December 1971. From the battlefields of Kutch to negotiations at Tashkent, Pakistan had tried hard but unsuccessfully to do what it could to force ICK from India's grasp. It failed in that attempt as Indian Controlled Kashmir remained firmly within Indian hands.

Finally, it must be remembered that the real price paid for this war was not in political or military careers but in the soldiers and civilians on both sides who lost their lives during the conflict and the people of Kashmir—on both sides. It is a tragic fact that even at the time of writing, the people of Kashmir are still divided by a wholly artificial border, created from a conflict in which they were never given a say and they have been denied the right to exercise their right of self-determination to this day. It may well be, as India has argued repeatedly, that Pakistan joined US military pacts and refused certain conditions, which India could use as a pretext for never holding a referendum it feared it would lose. However, the people of Kashmir did not break any promises and cannot rightfully be held responsible for the shortcomings and decisions of the Pakistan government of the time. Tens of thousands of Kashmiris have died in the last two decades at the hands of Indian security forces and it is hoped that one day all the killing will stop and the Kashmiri people will be given an opportunity to decide their own fate—whatever that may be.

BIBLIOGRAPHY

Primary sources

National Archives UK

Commonwealth Office:
CO 1036/1403
CO 1045/1414
CO 1045/1168

No 10 Downing Street Files:

PREM 13/390–396
PREM 13/462
PREM 13/463

Cabinet Office files:

CAB 164/123
CAB 130/200
CAB 148/18/20
CAB 148/18/38
CAB 148/18/49
CAB 148/20/31
CAB 148/23/24

Ministry of Defence:

DEFE 25/167

US National Archives

59.3.5 State Department Files: National Archives, Maryland, USA

Records of offices responsible for Near Eastern, South Asian, and African affairs

BIBLIOGRAPHY

Johnson Presidential Library

1. National Security File (NSF).
   "Eisenhower, Dwight D., General" [India, Pakistan struggle for Kashmir].
   "Hamilton Memos" [India, Pakistan].
   "Vice President, Vol. 1" [India, Pakistan].
   "Spurgeon Keeny Memos" [India].
   "Komer, Volume 1" [India, Pakistan].
   "Komer, Volume 2" [India, Pakistan].
   "Saunders Memos" [India, Pakistan].
   "Wriggins Memos, 1966" [Pakistan, India, Ceylon].
   "Wriggins Memos, 1967" [Pakistan, India, Ceylon, Nepal].
2. White House Central Files—Confidential File (C.F).
3. Robert W. Komer: Material on South Asia.
4. Central Intelligence Agency.
5. Oral History Collection.

Foreign Relations of the United States, 1961–1963, Volume XIX: South Asia

Indian official publications

Chakravorty, B. C. (1992), *History of the Indo-Pak War, 1965*, History Division, Ministry of Defence, New Delhi, (Chief Editor S. N. Prasad).
Indian Information, Ministry of Information, New Delhi, 8:17, 1 October 1965

Secondary sources

Abid, Ali (ed.) (1986), *The Secret Documents Recovered from the US Embassy Tehran*, Karachi: Forerunners Publications.
Ahmed, G. (1967), *Pakistan Meets Indian Challenge*, Rawalpindi, Al Mukhtar Publishers.
Ahmed, Lt Gen. Mahmud (2006), *History of Indo-Pak War—1965*, Karachi, Services Book Club.
Ahmed, S. (1973), *The Indo-Pak Clash in the Rann of Kutch*, Rawalpindi: Army Education Press.
Arif, K. M. (1995), Working *with Zia; Pakistan's Power Politics 1977–1988*, Karachi: Oxford University Press.
Asghar Khan, M., *see under* Khan.
Ayub Khan, M., *see under* Khan.
Azhar, K. M. Khan, Major General, SQA, 'Battle Lore: Offensive in the Desert', published in *Soldiers Speak—Selected Articles from Pakistan Army Journal 1956–81*, Army Education Press, GHQ Rawalpindi, 1981.
Bhagat, Lt Gen. P. S. (1974), *The Sword and the Shield—India 1965*, New Delhi: Vikas Publishers

BIBLIOGRAPHY

Bhutto, Z. A. (1971), *The Great Tragedy*, Karachi: Pakistan People's Party.

Brecher, M. (1959), *Nehru: A Political Biography*, London: Oxford University Press.

Brines, R. (1968), *The Indo-Pakistani Conflict*, London: Pall Mall Press.

Brown, W. N. (1963), *The United States and India and Pakistan*, Cambridge, Mass: Harvard University Press.

Burke, S. M. and L. Ziring (1990), *Pakistan's Foreign Policy, An Historical Analysis*, Minneapolis: University of Minnesota Press.

Chari, P. R., P. I. Cheema and Iftekharuzzaman (eds) (1996), *Nuclear Non-proliferation in India and Pakistan: South Asian Perspectives*, Lahore: Vanguard Books.

Chand, Maj. Gen. N. Das, (1995) *The Rajputana Rifles—Brief History*, New Delhi: Reliance Publishing House.

Chaudhry, Brig. A. A. K. (1977), *September 1965*, Lahore: Ferozsons.

Chenevix-Trench, Charles (1988), *The Indian Army and the King's Enemies*, London: Thames and Hudson.

Chishti, F. A. (1996), *Betrayals of Another Kind: Islam, Democracy and the Army in Pakistan*, Lahore: Jang Publishers.

Choudhury, G. W. (1975), *India, Pakistan, Bangladesh, and the Major Powers*, London and New York: The Free Press (Macmillan).

—— (1993), *The Last Days of United Pakistan*, Karachi: Oxford University Press.

Cloughley, B. (1999), *A History of the Pakistan Army*, Karachi: Oxford University Press.

Cohen, Stephen (1984), *The Pakistan Army*, Berkeley: University of California Press.

Cohen, Warren and Nancy Bernkopf Tucker (eds) (1994), *Lyndon Johnson Confronts the World: American Foreign Policy, 1963–1968*, Cambridge University Press

Cunningham, Sir G., *Diaries, Unpublished*: Oriental and India Office Collection, London.

Durch, W. J. (ed.) (1997), *UN Peacekeeping, American Policy and the Uncivil Wars of the 1990s*, London: Macmillan Press.

Farwell, B. (1989), *Armies of the Raj*, New York: W. W. Norton.

Feldman, H. (1976), *The End and the Beginning: Pakistan 1969–1972*, London: Oxford University Press.

Fricker, J. (1979), *Battle for Pakistan: The Air War of 1965*, London: Ian Allan.

Galbraith, J. K. (1969), *Ambassador's Journal*, London: Hamish Hamilton.

Gauhar, A. (1993), *Ayub Khan: Pakistan's First Military Ruler*, Lahore: Sang-e-Meel Publications.

Gaylor, J. (1992), *Sons of John Company: The Indian & Pakistan Armies 1903–1991*, Tunbridge Wells: Spellmount.

BIBLIOGRAPHY

Hassan, General Gul (1993), *Memoirs*, Oxford University Press.

Gurcharan Singh Sandhu, Major General (1987), *History of the Indian Armoured Corps (1941–1971)*, New Delhi: Vision Books.

Hasan, K. S. (ed.) and Z. Hasan (1966), *Documents of the Foreign Relations of Pakistan: the Kashmir Question*, Karachi: Pakistan Institute of International Affairs.

Hersh, S. H. (1983), *Kissinger, The Prince of Power*, London: Faber and Faber.

Hussain, Maj. Gen. Abrar (2005), *Men of Steel: 6 Armoured Division*, Rawalpindi: Army Educational Publishing House.

Islam, R. (1974), *A Tale of Millions: Bangladesh Liberation War 1971*, Dhaka: Ananna.

Jackson, R. (1975), *South Asian Crisis*, New York: Praeger.

James, Sir M.,(1993), *Pakistan Chronicle*, Karachi: Oxford University Press.

Johri, Sita Ram, Major (1967), *The Indo-Pak Conflict of 1965*, New Delhi: Himalaya Publications.

Kathpalia, P. N. (1986), *Mission with a Difference: The Exploits of 71 Mountain Brigade*, New Delhi: Lancer International.

Kaul, B. M., Lieutenant General (1971), *Confrontation with Pakistan*, Delhi: Vikas Publications.

Kavic, Lorne (1967), *India's Quest for Security: Defence Policies*, Berkeley and Los Angeles: University of California Press.

Kennedy, Paul (1988), *The Rise and Fall of the Great Powers*, London: Fontana Press.

Khan, G. H. (1993), *Memoirs of Lt.-Gen. Gul Hassan Khan*, Karachi: Oxford University Press.

Khan, M. Asghar (1979), *The First Round: Indo-Pakistan War, 1965*, Islamic Information Services.

——— (1983), *Generals in Politics: Pakistan 1958–1982*, New Delhi: Vikas Publishing House.

Khan, M. Ayub (1966), *Speeches and Statements*, Lahore; Mohammad Ali Academy.

——— (1967), *Friends Not Masters, A Political Biography*, London: Oxford University Press.

Khan, Roedad (1998), *Pakistan—A Dream Gone Sour*, Karachi: Oxford University Press.

——— (1999), *The American Papers*, Karachi: Oxford University Press.

Khan, Z. A. (1988), *The Way it Was*, Karachi: Defence Journal.

Kissinger, H. (1979), *The White House Years*, London: Weidenfeld & Nicolson and Michael Joseph.

Lakhanpal, P. N. (1965), *Essential Documents and Notes on Kashmir Dispute*, Delhi: International Books.

Lamb, A. (1991), *Incomplete Partition*, Oxford: Oxford University Press.

BIBLIOGRAPHY

—— (1992), *Kashmir: A Disputed Legacy, 1846–1990*, Karachi: Oxford University Press.

Manekar, D. R. (1967), *Twenty-two Fateful Days: Pakistan Cut to Size*, Bombay: Manaktalas.

Maxwell, N. (1970), *India's China War*, London: Jonathan Cape.

Mudie, Sir F., 'The Mudie Papers', Unpublished: Oriental and India Office Collection, London.

Musa, M. (1983), *My Version: India-Pakistan War 1965*, Lahore: Wajidalis.

—— (1987), *Jawan to General: Recollections of a Pakistani Soldier*, Karachi: East & West Publishing Company.

Nawaz, Shuja (2008), *Crossed Swords*, Karachi: Oxford University Press.

NCID, 'Neutral Country Intelligence Document', Unpublished.

Niazi, A. A. K. (1998), *The Betrayal of East Pakistan*, Karachi: Oxford University Press.

Noor-ul-Haq (1993*)*, *Making of Pakistan: The Military Perspective*, Islamabad: National Institute of Historical and Cultural Research.

Norman, Omar (1990), *Pakistan: A Political and Economic History since 1947*, London: Kegan Paul International.

Pakistan Air Force (1988), *The Story of the Pakistan Air Force*, Islamabad: Shaheen Foundation.

Pradhan, R. D. (2007), *1965 War, The Inside Story* New Delhi: Atlantic Publishers and Printers.

Praval, K. C. (1974) *India's Paratroopers—History of the Parachute Regiment of India*, Delhi: Thomson Press (India).

—— (1976) *Valour Triumphs—A History of the Kumaon Regiment*, Delhi: Thomson Press (India).

—— (1982) *The Red Eagles—A History of the Fourth Division of India*, New Delhi: Vision Books.

—— (1993), *Indian Army After Independence*, New Delhi: Lancer International.

Qayyum, A. (1997), *Zia-ul-Haq and I*, Islamabad: International Consortium of Consultants and Technical Services.

Riza, Major-General S. (1980), *Izzat-O-Iqbal: History of Pakistan Artillery (1947–1971)*, Nowshera: School of Artillery.

—— (1984), *The Pakistan Army War 1965*, Lahore: Services Book Club.

Rizvi, H. A. (ed.) (1976), *The Military and Politics in Pakistan 1947–1986*, Lahore: Progressive Publishers.

Salik, S. (1978), *Witness to Surrender*, Karachi: Oxford University Press.

Schofield, Victoria (2000), *Kashmir in Conflict: India, Pakistan and the Unending War*, London: I. B. Tauris.

Sen, L. P. (1969), *Slender was the Thread*, New Delhi: Orient Longman.

Sethna, Lt Gen. A. M. and Lt Col Valmiki Katju (1983), *Traditions of a*

BIBLIOGRAPHY

Regiment—The Story of the Rajputana Rifles, New Delhi: Lancers Publishers.

Sharma, Dev (1966), *Tashkent: The Fight for Peace*, Varanasi: Gandhian Institute of Studies

Shastri, Lal Bahadur (1965), *When Freedom is Menaced*, Ministry of Information and Broadcasting, Government of India.

Singh, Lt Gen. Harbakhsh (1991), *War Despatches: Indo-Pak Conflict 1965*, New Delhi: Lancer International.

Singh, Lt Col Bhupindher (1982), *1965 War—Role of Tanks in India-Pakistan War*, Patiala: BC Publishers.

Singh, Sarbans (1993), *Battle Honours of the Indian Army*, New Delhi: Vision Books.

Singh Lachhman, Maj. Gen. (1997), *Missed Opportunities—Indo-Pak War 1965*, Dehra Dun: Natraj Publishers.

Singh, Sukhwant (1981), *The Liberation of Bangladesh*, Vol. 1, New Delhi: Vikas Publishing House.

Sisson, R. and L. E. Rose (1992), *War and Secession: Pakistan, India and the Creation of Bangladesh*, Karachi: Oxford University Press.

Smith, C. (1994), *India's Ad Hoc Arsenal: Direction or Drift in Defence Policy?*, New York: Oxford University Press.

Srivastava, C. P. (1995), *Lal Bahadur Shastri: A Life of Truth in Politics*, New Delhi: Oxford University Press India.

Stephens, Ian (1955), *Horned Moon*, Indiana University Press, 1955.

Syed, A. M. (1992), *The Twin Era of Pakistan: Democracy and Dictatorship*, New York: Vantage Press.

Tahir-Kheli, S. R. (1998), *India, Pakistan and the United States: Breaking with the Past*, Lahore: Vanguard Books.

Taseer, S. (1979), *Bhutto, a Political Biography*, London: Ithaca Press.

Verghese, B. G. (1965), *India Answers Pakistan*, Bombay: *Times of India*.

Viceroy's Personal Reports. In the series *India, the Transfer of Power*, HMSO, London, 1980, 1981, 183.

Vorys, K. V. (1965), *Political Development in Pakistan*, Princeton University Press.

Wirsing, R. G. (1991), *Pakistan's Security Under Zia, 1977–1988: The Policy Imperatives of a Peripheral Asian State*, London: Macmillan Academic and Professional.

Wolpert, S. (1993), *Zulfi Bhutto of Pakistan: His Life and Times*, New York: Oxford University Press.

———— (1996), *Nehru: A Tryst with Destiny*, New York: Oxford University Press.

Wright, A. (1972), 'The Indo-Pakistani War 1965', unpublished PhD thesis, Australian National University.

BIBLIOGRAPHY

Ziring, L. (1971), *The Ayub Khan Era: Politics in Pakistan, 1958–1969,* Syracuse, NY: Syracuse University Press.

—— (1997), *Pakistan in the Twentieth Century,* Karachi: Oxford University Press.

INDEX

INDEX

42, 222, 390; family of, 37; foreign policies of, 222, 391; Indian Prime Minister, 6, 22
Netherlands: 297
Nixon, Richard: 233
Non-Aligned Movement: 24

Operation Arrow Head: 83; objectives of, 78–80
Operation Gibraltar: 103, 110–12, 116, 118, 125, 132, 148, 151, 184, 186, 193, 281, 307, 346, 380–1, 387; failures of, 125–6, 151, 345; objectives of, 104, 154; personnel of, 107–9, 113, 115–17, 120, 124, 127, 129, 141, 232, 348; planning for, 106–7, 144
Operation Grand Slam: 103, 105, 125, 127–9, 131, 133–5, 140–1, 148, 151–2, 155, 186, 193, 205, 216, 281, 307, 365, 380–1, 388, 391; briefing for, 134–5; objectives of, 105–6, 132, 134, 136, 154, 159, 162; personnel of, 132, 138, 154, 156, 203; shortcomings of, 137, 151, 159, 213–14
Operation Mailed Fist: 203–4, 207, 209, 212–13, 217, 252, 262, 264, 269; objectives of, 193, 198–9; personnel of, 193–4, 211, 216–17, 251; shortcomings of, 198, 272, 281–2, 341, 345, 385
Operation Nepal: 257–8, 262, 269–71, 382; objectives of, 251–2, 254–5, 266, 279; personnel of, 252–3; shortcomings of, 279
Operation Riddle: 172–3, 175, 179, 182, 188, 193, 195, 216, 219, 221, 233, 251–2, 271, 275–6, 382, 392; objectives of, 171, 182–3, 185–6; personnel of, 168–

72, 181, 191, 197, 272–3; shortcomings of, 178, 181–3, 185, 187–9, 222
Operation Wind Up: 270, 273; objectives of, 270; potential Chinese involvement in, 325

Pakistan: 3, 7–8, 11–12, 17, 19–20, 22, 24, 26–7, 30, 37, 42–4, 46, 49–50, 52, 55, 58–62, 65–6, 70, 73–6, 79–86, 88–9, 91–3, 95, 99–101, 106, 111–12, 115, 121–3, 125, 129, 133, 136–8, 141–3, 145, 147, 154–5, 165, 187, 189, 221, 226, 228, 230, 234, 236–8, 246, 249, 279, 283, 298, 305, 310–11, 314–15, 317, 319, 321, 326–9, 336, 341–2, 347, 354–5, 359, 364, 368–71, 373–6, 379–80, 383–5, 391, 393; agricultural industry of, 11, 27; Air Force (PAF), 76, 101, 103, 117, 139, 144, 167–8, 171, 184–5, 201, 217, 222, 240, 261, 265, 270, 275–6, 278, 293, 307, 318, 365, 392; Awan Sharif, 147; Badin, 66; Bamanwala-Ravi-Bedian-Diplapur (BRBD) Canal, 163–5, 170–2, 174–7, 180–1, 183, 189, 255; Barki, 164, 169, 176–9, 195; Bengal, 2, 4, 67, 393; borders of, 27, 65, 81, 87, 89, 166, 241, 274, 323; Chahiwal, 174; Constitution of (1962), 29–30; Dhaka, 43; Ding, 68, 73; economy of, 306; General Headquarters (GHQ), 73, 75–6, 80, 83, 94, 98, 103, 117, 122, 126, 129–31, 149–50, 152, 176, 178, 182, 191–3, 196, 204, 206, 212, 215–16, 220, 222–3, 251, 258, 263, 270, 382, 394; Gilgit, 39; govern-

411

INDEX